Basic Management Accounting for the Hospitality Industry

Basic Management Accounting for the Hospitality Industry

Michael N. Chibili

First edition

Noordhoff Uitgevers Groningen | Houten

Cover design: G2K Designers
Cover illustration: Photodisc

If you have any comments or queries about this or any other publication,
please contact: Noordhoff Uitgevers bv, Afdeling Hoger Onderwijs,
Antwoordnummer 13, 9700 VB Groningen, e-mail: info@noordhoff.nl

0 1 2 3 4 5 / 14 13 12 11 10

© 2010 Noordhoff Uitgevers bv Groningen/Houten, the Netherlands

ISBN 978-90-01-79635-8
NUR 782

Preface

Welcome to the *Basic Management Accounting for the Hospitality Industry*. This text provides an introduction to the basic management accounting concepts and applications relevant to students in any hospitality or tourism-related education. It examines the basic concepts and shows how they can be used to improve the quality of decisions made by managers in the related fields. Geared towards students who use English as a second language, the language is simple and in case of need, the concepts are illustrated with worked examples to ease their understanding. This book is introductory in nature, and whenever necessary, the student can independently explore some of the topics in other books which could provide more detailed information.

In this text, I have interchangeably made use of company, business entity, concern, organization, operation, and establishment, to mean the same in the sense that they represent the desire for entrepreneurship with the profit motive in mind. It should not be confusing to anyone. The topics have been selected based on the need of the target group and include the introduction to management accounting, the balance sheet, the profit and loss account statement, adjustments to the balance sheet and the profit and loss account statement, the cash flow statement, analyzing financial statements, ratio analysis and types of ratios, management of working capital, cost management, pricing and revenue management, cost-volume-profit analysis, internal control, forecasting, budgeting and variance analysis, and lastly, capital investment decisions. Each chapter ends with a complete glossary of the key words, five multiple choice questions and four practice exercises.

I want to place on record my gratitude to colleagues and friends for the advice and help I received in the course of writing this text. I am particularly grateful to Klaas-Wybo van der Hoek for believing in me. The management and staff of the Mövenpick Hotel, Amsterdam are recognized for their help. To the dean – Hans Zwart, and my colleagues of the financial management team in the Institute of International Hospitality Management – Marcus Hoekstra, Ale Hoekstra, Jurgen Coerts, and Cor Penning, I say once again thanks for the support through all the stages of writing this text. For help with reviewing the manuscript, I would have not been able to complete this text without the gallant assistance of the following colleagues and students – Harry Jippes, Eef Heinhuis, Billy Stelljes, Richard Henricus (Rik) van der Berg, David Dirk de Roest, Stephanie Enninga, Frank Schoenmaker, Harpinder Singh, Sjoerd Gehrels, Koen Bramer, Annika Jochheim, and Osborne Green. Special thanks go to Miss Ramona Nolde who has worked tirelessly to make sure that the content should be as error-free as it is humanly possible.

This book is accompanied by a website www.hospitalitymanagement.noordhoff.nl that contains exercises and other materials for both students and lecturers.

As a new book, comments and suggestions will be very welcome.

Michael N. Chibili
February 2010

For Lebongwo, Njingu and Afiandem
in the hope that their lights shine brightly

Table of contents

1   Introduction to management accounting 13
1.1   Setting the scene 14
1.1.1   Information needs – management and external users 14
1.1.2   Financial accounting and management accounting 15
1.1.3   Basic principles of accounting 16
1.1.4   The management accounting process 18
1.2   Understand the hospitality industry 19
1.2.1   The nature of the hospitality industry 19
1.2.1.1 Goods and services offered 20
1.2.1.2 The distinguishing features 23
1.2.2   Industry organization and recent developments 24
1.2.3   Summary of the key characteristics of the hospitality industry 25
        Glossary 26
        Multiple choice questions 28
        Exercises 28

2   The balance sheet 31
2.1   The components of a balance sheet 32
2.1.1   Assets 32
2.1.2   Liabilities 36
2.1.2.1 Current liabilities 36
2.1.2.2 Long term liabilities 38
2.1.3   Owners' equity 39
2.2   Formats of balance sheets and accounting standards 42
2.3   Establishing simple balance sheets 43
        Glossary 47
        Multiple choice questions 49
        Exercises 49

3   The profit and loss account statement 51
3.1   Definition and categories of activities 52
3.2   Formats and content of the profit and loss account statement 54
        Glossary 60
        Multiple choice questions 61
        Exercises 61

4   Adjustments to the balance sheet and the profit and loss account 65
4.1   Accounting conventions – accruals and recognition 66
4.2   Adjusting the accounts 66
4.2.1   Stock (inventory) 66
4.2.2   Accounts receivable 68
4.2.3   Depreciation and amortization 69
4.2.4   Returns of goods 70
4.2.5   Discounts 71
4.2.6   Delivery charges 71
        Glossary 72
        Multiple choice questions 73
        Exercises 73

5   The cash flow statement (also called the statement of cash flow) 75
5.1   Cash in the business 76
5.1.1   The importance of cash in the business 76
5.1.2   Differentiating profits from cash 77
5.1.3   The need for cash flow statements 77
5.1.4   The categories of activities 78
5.2   Establishing cash flow statements 80
5.2.1   Determine the net cash flow from operating activities 80
5.2.2   Determine the net cash flow from investing activities 82
5.2.3   Determine the net cash flow from financing activities 83
5.2.4   Collate all the previous 3 net cash flows into the definitive SCF 83
5.3   A worked example in the establishment of the SCF using the indirect method 83
         Glossary 89
         Multiple choice questions 90
         Exercises 90

6   Analyzing financial statements 93
6.1   Purposes of analyzing statements 94
6.2   Horizontal analysis 99
6.3   Base-year analysis 101
6.4   Vertical analysis 102
         Glossary 106
         Multiple choice questions 107
         Exercises 107

7   Ratio analysis and types of ratios 111
7.1   Purpose and usefulness of ratio analysis 112
7.2   Classification of ratios 113
7.2.1   Liquidity ratios 114
7.2.2   Solvency ratios 116
7.2.3   Profitability ratios 119
7.2.4   Activity ratios 122
7.2.5   Operating ratios 125
7.3   Performance review process 127
7.4   DuPont analysis 129
         Glossary 133
         Multiple choice questions 138
         Exercises 138

8   Management of working capital 141
8.1   The importance of working capital management 142
8.2   The working capital cycle 142
         Glossary 149
         Multiple choice questions 150
         Exercises 150

9   Cost management 153
9.1   The nature of costs and assumptions 154
9.2   Types of costs 154
9.3   Activity-based costing 157
9.4   Allocating indirect (overhead) costs to the operating departments 160
9.4.1   Responsibility accounting 160

9.4.2	Determining allocation bases	*161*
9.4.3	Common methods of cost allocation	*162*
9.4.4	Illustration of the direct method of cost allocation	*164*
9.4.5	Illustration of the step method of cost allocation	*166*
9.5	Separating mixed-costs between their fixed and variable elements	*169*
9.5.1	High/low two-point method	*170*
9.5.2	Scatter diagram	*173*
9.5.3	Regression analysis	*174*
	Glossary	*177*
	Multiple choice questions	*179*
	Exercises	*179*

10	Pricing and revenue management	*183*
10.1	The importance of pricing and the relationship between price and quantity	*184*
10.2	Approaches to pricing	*185*
10.3	Pricing rooms	*186*
10.3.1	The rule of a thousand approach	*186*
10.3.2	The bottom up approach (Hubbart formula or required rate of return)	*187*
10.3.3	Relative room size approach	*188*
10.3.4	Differential room pricing	*190*
10.3.4.1	Calculating single and double rates	*190*
10.3.4.2	Integrating the effects of seasonality	*192*
10.3.5	Room rate discounting	*193*
10.4	Pricing food and beverage products	*195*
10.4.1	Subjective pricing methods	*196*
10.4.1.1	The reasonable price method	*196*
10.4.1.2	The highest price method	*196*
10.4.1.3	The loss leader method	*196*
10.4.1.4	The intuitive price method	*196*
10.4.2	Objective pricing methods	*196*
10.4.2.1	Using a mark-up multiplier	*197*
10.4.2.2	Contribution margin pricing method	*200*
10.4.2.3	Ratio pricing method	*201*
10.4.2.4	Simple prime costs method	*202*
10.4.2.5	Specific prime costs method	*204*
10.5	Menu engineering	*208*
10.6	Revenue management	*212*
	Glossary	*215*
	Multiple choice questions	*217*
	Exercises	*217*

11	Cost-volume-profit analysis	*219*
11.1	Definition, assumptions and limitations	*220*
11.2	Contribution margin	*220*
11.3	Breakeven analysis	*221*
11.3.1	Establishing the breakeven point	*221*
11.3.2	Single service analysis	*222*
11.3.3	Other considerations in breakeven analysis	*225*
11.3.3.1	First situation – two room types	*225*
11.3.3.2	Second situation – two room types plus additional services	*226*
11.3.3.3	Third situation – integrating desired profit levels	*228*
	Glossary	*230*
	Multiple choice questions	*231*
	Exercises	*231*

12	Internal control 233
12.1	Need for internal control 234
12.2	Special characteristics of the hospitality industry from an internal control perspective 235
12.3	Principles of internal control 236
12.4	Basic internal control proposals 241
12.5	Bank reconciliation 249
	Glossary 252
	Multiple choice questions 253
	Exercises 253

13	Forecasting 255
13.1	Nature and limitations of forecasting 256
13.2	Understanding historical data patterns 257
13.3	Approaches to forecasting 258
13.3.1	Qualitative forecasting methods 259
13.3.2	Quantitative forecasting methods 259
13.3.2.1	Time series forecasting methods 260
13.3.2.2	Causal forecasting methods 263
13.4	Selecting forecasting methods 265
13.5	Forecasting in hospitality industry practice 266
	Glossary 267
	Multiple choice questions 269
	Exercises 269

14	Budgeting and variance analysis 273
14.1	The budget and the budget process 274
14.2	Objectives of budgeting 275
14.3	Approaches to budgeting and types of budgets 276
14.4	Types of budgets 280
14.5	Variance analysis 282
14.5.1	Identifying and attributing variances 282
14.5.2	Variance analysis overview 283
14.5.3	Analyzing variances to ascertain causes 284
	Glossary 290
	Multiple choice questions 292
	Exercises 292

15	Capital investment decisions 295
15.1	Types of capital budgeting decisions 296
15.2	Basic methods for making investment decisions 297
15.3	Simple and compound interest 302
15.4	Process of discounting 304
15.5	Understanding factor tables 305
15.6	Discounted cash flow (DCF) methods 314
15.7	Incidence of taxes on DCF analysis 322
15.8	Choosing between projects 326
	Glossary 328
	Multiple choice questions 330
	Exercises 330

Literature *335*

Answers to end of chapter multiple choice questions *335*

Appendix Factor tables *337*

About the author *350*

Index *351*

Introduction to management accounting

1

1.1   Setting the scene
1.2   Understanding the hospitality industry

Information is very important for the management process and accounting is one of the main information systems that can be found in an organization. It is as such necessary that managers within an organization obtain a basic understanding of accounting for them to be able to effectively and responsibly carry out their management functions. The information needs to come from all the areas of their management activities as well as used in all the related areas. Section 1.1 sets the scene by showing how information is generated and used within an organization; by differentiating management from financial accounting; by introducing the basic principles of accounting; and by introducing the management accounting process. In section 1.2 the hospitality industry is introduced with the aim of highlighting some of its special characteristics as well as how it is organized.

1.1 Setting the scene

Organizations of very different types affect us on a daily basis by providing all the goods and services needed for our existence. All these different types of organizations have two things in common. First, every organization will have its set of goals or objectives. An example is that of the Compass Hotels Ltd. They state their goals and objectives in the following way: *"Our goals and objectives are straightforward and seek to ensure we run a professional, profitable and ethical company, building relationships with suppliers and investors, driving business in the hotels and developing the business as a whole"*. In these goals, they have highlighted some important aspects of their relationship with all their major stakeholders (professional – management and employees; profitable – shareholders; ethical – all stakeholders) as well as mentioning their suppliers and investors. Second, for an organization to be able to meet their established goals, its managers will need information. This section attempts to show why this information is needed, who uses it, as well as establish the general characteristics of the hospitality industry. The structure of the subsections is as follows:

1.1.1   Information needs – management and external users
1.1.2   Financial accounting and management accounting
1.1.3   Basic principles of accounting
1.1.4   The management accounting process

1.1.1 Information needs – management and external users

Before proceeding with the discussion on managements' need for, and use of information, accounting will be defined. Accounting is generally concerned with the reporting, summarizing and recording in monetary terms the transactions of an individual or an organization. A basic definition of accounting as provided by the American Institute of Certified and Public Accountants (AICPA) in 1941 is *"the art of recording, classifying, and summarizing, in a significant manner and in terms of money, transactions and events which are in part at least, of a financial character, and interpreting the results thereof"*. However, this definition of accounting left some issues that could not be fully understood. In this regard, the American Accounting Principles Board in 1970 defined accounting as a service activity: *"Its function is to provide quantitative information primarily financial in nature, about economic entities that is intended to be useful in making economic decisions and in making reasoned choices among alternative courses of actions"*.

To the individual, accounting information can be used in planning future spending levels, planning the acquisition of additional finance, controlling spending levels, and making decisions on how best to spend their money. As such, at this level accounting basically has 3 functions which are; planning, controlling and decision support.

On the contrary, at the level of an organization, accounting is used to control its activities, plan the acquisition of finance, plan future activities, and finally report upon the activities and successes of the organization to other users.

The users of accounting information can be broadly split into two major categories; the internal users and the external users. The internal users would basically be the management of the organization. They will need this information due to the following reasons: planning; controlling; stewardship; and decision making. This type of accounting is by nature mostly managerial and would differ depending on the type of organization. The external users would generally be limited to the other major stakeholders of a company. These will include the employees of a company, the owners, lenders, suppliers, customers, the local community, and the government. Generally, these stakeholders are provided with accounting information through the establishment of annual reports. This type of accounting would on the contrary be mostly financial in nature.

1.1.2   Financial accounting and management accounting

Financial accounting is that area of accounting mostly concerned with the preparation of financial statements destined for decision makers. These decision makers may include shareholders, suppliers, financial institutions, employees, local authorities, and government agencies. The fundamental need of financial accounting is to bring to a minimum any possible conflicts between principals and agents by measuring and monitoring the agent's performance and reporting the results to the interested users on an annual or more frequent basis. There are many similarities between financial and management accounting, because they all collect data from a company's basic accounting system. This basic accounting system is a system of procedures, personnel and computers used to accumulate the financial data from within a company. It should be noted that financial accounting is generally regulated by various standards at the international level. Exhibit 1.1 shows in a table form the basic differences between financial accounting and management accounting arranged around some simple features.

Management accounting is much more concerned with the provision and use of accounting information to managers within an organization. This permits the managers to be able to make informed business decisions and as such become better equipped in their management and control functions. As opposed to financial accounting, management accounting information is usually confidential and used by management alone. Secondly, it is forward looking, historical, and computed using extensive management information systems and internal controls instead of complying with accounting standards, be they national or international.

Management accounting experience and knowledge can be obtained from various fields and functions within a company such as information management, treasury, auditing, marketing, valuation, pricing, logistics, etc. Some of the primary services performed by

Exhibit 1.1 **Comparison between financial accounting and management accounting**

Features	Financial Accounting	Management Accounting
Who	Principally outsiders to the organization (investors, creditors, the state, analysts, and reporters)	Principally insiders of the organization (the management and operators)
What	General information on the whole organization	Internal information on the subunits of the organization
Type	Financial and monetary data	Economic, financial, and physical data such as data related to employees, sales volumes, and customers etc.
Rules	Regulated by the various accounting standards' boards and based on the GAAP	Unregulated but mostly based on cost/benefit analysis
Characteristics	Factual information based on reliability, objectivity, accuracy, and consistency	Estimated information to ensure efficiency, relevance and timeliness
Time	Historically perspective	Historical, current as well as forward looking such as sales budgets and cash flow forecasts
Format	Determined by different regulatory elements such as company law, accounting standards and the stock exchanges	No pre-determined format but aligned to the specific wishes of management
Frequency	Delayed with emphasis on annual reports	Continuous reporting

management accountants can comprise the following: cost allocation; annual budgeting; capital budgeting; product profitability; cost benefit analysis; cost-volume-profit analysis; variance analysis; cost analysis, etc.

1.1.3 Basic principles of accounting

The basic accounting principles form the foundation of the understanding of accounting methods. These are called the generally accepted accounting principles (GAAP) and they provide the basis for the preparation of financial statements. Below are the most important principles:

Cost principle
This principle indicates that a transaction should be recorded at its acquisition price or cash cost and this should represent its accounting value. It is difficult for example to compare income statements for different periods during periods of long-lasting inflation or deflation. There are however some exceptions such as in the case of valuing inventory for resale, which can be done in terms of current currency values instead of the historical value.

Business entity principle
This principle indicates that accounting and financial statements are based on the concept that each business maintains its own set of accounts and that these accounts are separate from those of the owners. By this principle, the separation of the personal transactions of the owners from the company is an accounting or more so legal obligation that must be maintained. It should be this way even in the

cases whereby such owners work in or for the company. The assets, debts and expenditures of the owners form no part of the company.

Time period principle
This principle indicates that a company has to complete its analysis to report the financial condition and profitability of its business operation over a specific operating time period. This could be daily, weekly, monthly, quarterly, semi-annually, or annually. An accounting year is an accounting period of one year. In hospitality businesses, statements are regularly prepared on monthly or even weekly basis

Going concern principle
This principle indicates that at the time the business is preparing its statements, it is expected to live forever and that liquidation should not be a prospect. Generally, the going concern principle assumes that a company will operate indefinitely. This also assumes that the cost of business assets will be recovered over time by way of profits that are generated by successful operations.

Monetary unit principle
This principle indicates that the financial statements should be based on transactions expressed in the primary national (or regional in the case of some European countries with the Euro) monetary unit. This should be used to record the numerical values of business exchanges and operating transactions. The monetary unit also expresses financial information within the financial statements and reports.

Objectivity principle
This principle indicates that all accounting transactions should be justified as much as possible on objective evidence. This evidence is required to support a transaction before it can be entered into the accounting records. Some examples include the receipt for the payment of a guest cheque, or an invoice for the purchase of a new oven. In rare situations where such evidence cannot be obtained, expert estimates can be assumed.

Full disclosure principle
This principle indicates that the financial statement should provide all information necessary for the understanding of the financial statement. Financial statements are primarily concerned with a past period. This principle states that any future event that can have an impact on the financial position of the business should be disclosed to the readers of the statements and these disclosures will normally be found in the footnotes to the statements. These disclosures could be of the following types: changes in accounting practices during the period, any contingent liabilities, and exceptional events.

Consistency principle
This principle indicates that once an accounting method has been chosen by management, this should be used from period to period unless a change is necessary and this change must be disclosed. This principle was established to ensure comparability and consistency of the procedures and techniques used in the preparation of financial statements from one accounting period to the next.

Matching principle

This principle indicates that expenses should be related to their revenues. This principle requires that for each accounting period all sales revenues earned, whether received or not, must be recognized. It goes the same way with operating expenses, in the sense that they should all be recognized during the period, whether paid or not paid. This principle ensures that resulting net incomes or net losses provide the most accurate estimate of profit or loss for the period.

Conservatism principle

This principle indicates that expenses should be recognized as soon as possible whereas revenues should be recognized only when they are verified. A business should not understate its expenses or liabilities. On the other hand it should not overstate its assets or revenues.

Materiality principle

This principle indicates that events or information must be accounted for if they make a difference to the user of the financial information. This means that, items that may affect the decision of a user of financial information which are considered important must be reported in a correct way.

Realization principle

This principle indicates that revenues are only recognized only when it is earned. Generally, realization occurs when goods are sold or a service is rendered.

1.1.4   The management accounting process

The management accounting process revolves around the identification, measurement, accumulation, analysis, preparation, interpretation and communication of information used by management to plan, evaluate and control and to assure appropriate use of, and accountability for resources. The process can be summarized in the following four topics:

Setting business objectives

This is the identification of the objectives of the organization and directing the activities of the business to meet these objectives.

Assessing alternatives and making decisions and plans

The management will need information about alternative actions it can take. With such information it will be able to make decisions and detailed plans for the future.

Monitoring the outcomes

The management will use the information to assess how correctly their plans have succeeded or their objectives met.

Controlling and redefining its objectives and plans

Based on the review of planned and actual outcomes, the management might find it necessary to redefine the general objectives of the organization and as such redefine plans to achieve these new objectives.

1.2 Understand the hospitality industry

One of the fastest growing sectors of the economies of today is the hospitality industry. It is an expanding multi-billion euro business. It is exciting, never boring and offers unlimited opportunities. The hospitality industry is diverse enough for people to work in different areas of interest and still be employed within the hospitality industry. It covers such areas as lodging, restaurant, travel and tourism, institutional management, recreational management and meeting and convention planning industries. All of these separate yet related segments of the hospitality industry are interrelated to deliver kind and generous services to guests. It is one of the oldest businesses in history. People have always gone out to eat sometimes and travelled for work or leisure purposes. The structure of the subsections is as follows:

1.2.1	The nature of the hospitality industry
1.2.2	The organization of the hospitality industry and recent developments
1.2.3	Summary of the key characteristics of the hospitality industry

1.2.1 The nature of the hospitality industry

People all over the world are called on a daily basis to travel for a variety of reasons. These could be for business, tourism or simply to visit friends and relatives. Whatever the reasons behind their travel, many of them will end up staying in hotels or other types of temporary accommodation. Some of these types of accommodation are not only places to stay, but are considered destinations in their own right. In the Arnold Encyclopaedia of Real Estate a destination hotel is defined as a place of lodging not chosen for convenience and not chosen for people in transit to other areas. The following typically are characteristics of a destination hotel:

- Amenities which are quite complete and self-contained
- Upscale nature of the lodging operation
- Distinctive characteristics of the building, gardens or adjacent natural feature
- Activity set which makes leaving the property unnecessary

There are several distinct types of destination hotels that would include geographically remote locations, urban settings, conference centre oriented, specialized activities, unusual construction (e.g. ice hotels, cave hotels or tree-house hotels), as well as boutique hotels. Resort hotels and casino hotels are very good examples of destination hotels and the article in Exhibit 1.2 portrays the unusual story of the world's first ice hotel. The structure of the subsection is as follows: 1.2.1.1 introduces the goods and services offered while 1.2.1.2 illustrates its distinguishing features.

■ Exhibit 1.2 **Jukkasjärvi Icehotel**

What is ICEHOTEL? A hotel built of ice and snow, would be the most common response. The first and the largest in the world, someone might add. But we have more thrilling stories to tell. Lean closer to your computer screen and we'll whisper them in your ear.

Like most companies, we have a history and a business concept. Our ideas originate from the place we stand on; Jukkasjärvi. The river Torne that flows outside our office windows, the cold arctic climate, The Northern Lights and the Midnight Sun.

Every season allow us to get inspired by the river, whether it is crystal clear ice, rapids shooting on a riverboat or a magnificent, recently caught grayling.

This is what we have promised to offer the rest of the world; with Jukkasjärvi and Torne River as a starting point, develop and offer sensuous, inspiring and unique experiences within art, nature, accommodation and gastronomy. That reflects all seasons of the year.

So it is not a only a hotel we build each winter, it is an ephemeral art project. And it is not a menu we create for every season, we cultivate the many flavours of Swedish Lapland.

Each year, we attract visitors from all over the world to a little village in Lapland, 200 km north of the Arctic Circle. Many of them we take further north, explore the high mountains, all the way to the northern Norway to visit the fjords.

Others encounter us and the Torne River ice in world cities such as London and Tokyo, or at a trade fair in Chicago or Barcelona. See, our river is not only the most well-travelled one – it is also famous all over the world.

Source: www.icehotel.com

The nature of the hospitality industry can be summarized under the following topics

1.2.1.1 Goods and services offered

The hotels and other accommodations are as different as the many family and business travellers they accommodate. The industry includes all types of lodging, from luxurious 5-star hotels to youth hostels and RV parks. While many provide simply a place to spend the night, others cater to longer stays by providing food service, recreational activities, and meeting rooms. The total number of hotel and other accommodation rooms in the world is difficult to determine as new rooms are constructed on a daily basis. Exhibits 1.3 and 1.4 present an evaluation carried out by MKG Consulting in 2008 showing the 2008 European Hotel rankings split by both the groups and the brands within the groups.

Exhibit 1.3 **Top 10 Hotel groups in Europe 2008**

2008 European hotel ranking
Top 10 hotel groups (27 countries of the EU)

Rank 2008	Rank 2007	Groups	Hotels 2008	Hotels 2007	Rooms 2008	Rooms 2007	Evol. Ch.07/08
1	1	ACCOR	2 207	2 205	239 507	241 046	−0,6%
2	3	IHG	541	505	82 123	77 721	5,7%
3	2	BEST WESTERN	1 201	1 215	79 205	80 318	−1,4%
4	5	GROUPE DU LOUVRE	844	823	58 411	56 339	3,7%
5	8	SOL MELIA	199	198	42 448	41 771	1,6%
6	7	NH HOTELES	298	270	41 270	38 466	7,3%
7	6	TUI	168	190	41 322	48 843	−15,4%
8	9	CARLSON/REZIDOR	207	195	39 079	37 271	4,9%
9	4	HILTON HOTEL	144	257	37 333	56 675	−34,1%
10	11	CHOICE INTERNATIONAL	369	390	35 411	32 243	3,4%
TOTAL 10 GROUPES			**6 178**	**6 188**	**696 149**	**710 693**	**−2,0%**

Source: Data base MKG Hospitality – official supplier of hotel chains – March 2008

Exhibit 1.4 **Top 20 Hotel brands in Europe 2008**

2008 European hotel ranking
Top 20 hotel brands (27 countries of the EU)

Rank 2008	Rank 2007	Brands	Groups	Hotels 2008	Rooms 2008	Evol. Ch.08/07
1	1	BEST WESTERN	BEST WESTERN	1 201	79 205	−1,4%
2	2	IBIS	ACCOR	641	67 112	1,9%
3	3	MERCURE	ACCOR	536	61 406	0,7%
4	5	HOLIDAY INN	IHG	292	44 893	5,5%
5	4	NOVOTEL	ACCOR	252	40 244	−5,9%
6	6	HILTON	HILTON CORP.	137	36 162	2,8%
7	7	PREMIER INN	WHITBREAD	505	31 000	11,0%
8	8	NH HOTELS	NH	254	34 424	9,0%
9	9	ETAP HOTEL	ACCOR	365	34 090	8,4%
10	11	RADISSON	REZIDOR/CARLSON	118	25 362	2,6%
11	13	CAMPANILE	LOUVRE HOTELS	382	24 220	1,6%
12	12	FORMULE 1	ACCOR	315	23 289	−2,7%
13	16	TRAVELODGE	DUBAI INVEST. CAP.	331	22 375	17,4%
14	14	SCANDIC	SCANDIC	114	20 694	−0,5%
15	15	MARRIOTT	MARRIOTT	84	19 616	0,8%
16	17	HOLIDAY INN EXPRESS	IHG	178	18 818	9,9%
17	19	RAMADA HOTEL	WYNDHAM HOTELS	145	18 056	8,4%
18	10	RIU HOTELS	TUI	58	17 911	−19,1%
19	20	QUALITY INN	CHOICE HOTELS	145	16 998	−2,3%
20	24	PREMIERE CLASSE	LOUVRE HOTELS	219	15 614	3,0%

Source: Data base MKG Hospitality – official supplier of hotel chains – March 2008

MKG Consulting equally announced the following prospects for the global hospitality industry as contained in exhibit 1.5.

■ Exhibit 1.5 **Global hotel rooms horizon 2015**

First 20 hotel groups announce 1.1 million rooms by 2015
For the years to come, the major hotel groups have announced tremendous developments. Their projected pipelines signed or under way, are particularly important:
- The first 20 hotel groups have announced the opening of 8 500 hotels to come with 1.1 million new rooms by the end of 2015, that is a 20% increase of their supply.
- Majority of the projects should concern:
  - Northern America with 1 000 hotels for 400 000 rooms
  - Pacific Asia with 1 100 hotels for 230 000 rooms
  - Europe with 1 000 hotels for 180 000 rooms
  - South America, 780 hotels for 80 000 rooms
  - Africa and Middle East with 250 hotels and 70 000 rooms

As an example, Marriott announces 80 000 rooms, Accor more than 200 000 rooms by 2010, Hilton Hotels forecasts 900 hotels and 120 000 rooms, Choice International goes towards 78 000 rooms and even the Chinese group Jin Jiang has 22 000 new rooms under way.

Source: Data base MKG Hospitality – official supplier of hotel chains – March 2008

Hotels and motels make up the majority of establishments in the hospitality industry and are generally classified as offering either full-service or limited service. Full-service properties offer a variety of services for their guests, but they almost always include at least one or more restaurant and beverage service options – from coffee bars and lunch counters to cocktail lounges and formal restaurants. They also usually provide room service. Larger full-service properties usually have a variety of retail shops on the premises, such as gift boutiques, newsstands, and drug and cosmetics counters, some of which may be geared to an exclusive clientele. Additionally, a number of full-service hotels offer guests access to laundry and valet services, swimming pools, beauty salons, and fitness centres or health spas. A small, but growing, number of luxury hotel chains also manage condominium units in combination with their transient rooms, providing both hotel guests and condominium owners with access to the same services and amenities.

The largest hotels often have banquet rooms, exhibit halls, and spacious ballrooms to accommodate conventions, business meetings, wedding receptions, and other social gatherings. Conventions and business meetings are major sources of revenue for these properties. Some commercial hotels are known as conference hotels – fully self-contained entities specifically designed for large-scale meetings. They provide physical fitness and recreational facilities for meeting attendees, in addition to state-of-the-art audiovisual and technical equipment, a business centre, and banquet services.

Limited-service hotels are free-standing properties that do not have on-site restaurants or most other amenities that must be provided by a staff other than the front desk or housekeeping. They usually offer continental breakfasts, vending machines or small packaged items,

Internet access, and sometimes unattended game rooms or swimming pools in addition to daily housekeeping services. The numbers of limited-service properties have been growing. These properties are not as costly to build and maintain. They appeal to budget-conscious family vacationers and travellers who are willing to sacrifice amenities for lower room prices.

1.2.1.2 The distinguishing features

Hotels can also be categorized based on a distinguishing feature provided by the hotel:

Conference hotels

These provide meeting and banquet rooms, and usually food service, to large groups of people. They are usually designed to meet the business needs of the guests offering all types of services to cater for the needs of the conference delegates.

Airport hotels

These are hotels located on airport properties in major urban markets. These hotels permit guests to walk directly between one's hotel room and the flight boarding area and also save travellers time and money related to ground transportation. If in addition they have conference facilities, this adds to the convenience for meetings involving parties from multiple destinations. They are particularly convenient for guests with flight delays or cancellations.

Resort hotels

These offer luxurious surroundings with a variety of recreational facilities, such as swimming pools, golf courses, tennis courts, game rooms, and health spas, as well as planned social activities and entertainment. Resorts typically are located in vacation destinations or near natural settings, such as mountains, seashores, theme parks, or other attractions. As a result, the business of many resorts fluctuates with the season. Some resort hotels and motels provide additional convention and conference facilities to encourage customers to combine business with pleasure. During the off season, many of these establishments seek for conventions, sales meetings, and incentive tours to fill their otherwise empty rooms; some resorts even close for the off-season.

Extended-stay hotels

These typically provide rooms or suites with fully equipped kitchens, entertainment systems, office space with computer and telephone lines, fitness centres, and other amenities. Typically, guests use these hotels for a minimum of 5 consecutive nights often while on an extended work assignment or lengthy vacation or family visit. *All-suite hotels* offer a living room or sitting room in addition to a bedroom.

Casino hotels

These provide both lodging and legalized gaming on the same premises. Along with the typical services provided by most full-service hotels, casino hotels also contain casinos where patrons can wager at table games, play slot machines, and make other bets. Some casino hotels also contain conference and convention facilities.

Bed-and-breakfast inns

These provide lodging for overnight guests and are included in this industry. *Bed-and-breakfast inns* provide short-term lodging in private homes or small buildings converted for this purpose and are characterized by highly personalized service and inclusion of breakfast in the room rate. Their appeal is charm, with unusual service and decor.

RV parks and campgrounds

These cater to people who enjoy recreational camping at moderate prices. Some parks and campgrounds provide service stations, general stores, shower and toilet facilities, and coin-operated laundries. While some are designed for overnight travellers only, others are for vacationers who stay longer. Some camps provide accommodations, such as cabins and fixed campsites, and other amenities, such as food services, recreational facilities and equipment, and organized recreational activities. Examples of these overnight camps include children's camps, family vacation camps, hunting and fishing camps, and outdoor adventure retreats that offer trail riding, white-water rafting, hiking, fishing, game hunting, and similar activities.

Other short-term lodging facilities in the hospitality industry include *guesthouses*, or small cottages located on the same property as a main residence, and *youth hostels* – dormitory-style hotels with few frills, occupied mainly by students travelling on limited budgets. Also included are *rooming and boarding houses*, such as fraternity houses, sorority houses, off-campus dormitories, and workers' camps. These establishments provide temporary or longer term accommodations that may serve as a principal residence for the period of occupancy. These establishments also may provide services such as housekeeping, meals, and laundry services.

1.2.2   Industry organization and recent developments

In recent years, the hotel industry has become dominated by a few large hotel chains. To the traveller, familiar chain establishments represent dependability and quality at predictable rates. Many chains recognize the importance of brand loyalty to guests, and have expanded the range of lodging options offered under one corporate name, to include a full range of hotels from limited-service, economy-type hotels to luxury inns. While these big corporations own some of the hotels, many properties are independently owned but affiliated with a chain through a franchise agreement or management contract. As part of a chain, individual hotels can participate in the company's national reservations service or incentive program, thereby appearing to belong to a larger enterprise.

For those who prefer more personalized service and a unique experience, *boutique hotels* are becoming more popular. These smaller hotels are generally found in urban locations and provide patrons good service and more distinctive décor and food selection.

While RV parks and campgrounds could be found around any country and managed nationally or internationally, most small lodging establishments are individually owned and operated by a single owner, who may employ a small staff to help operate the business.

The lodging industry is moving towards more limited-service properties mostly in suburban, residential, or commercial neighbourhoods, often establishing hotels near popular restaurants. Many full-service properties are limiting or quitting the food service business altogether, choosing to contract out their food service operations to third party restaurateurs, including long-term arrangements with chain restaurant operators. Urban business and entertainment districts are providing a greater mix of lodging options to appeal to a wider range of travellers.

Increased competition among establishments in this industry has spurred many independently owned and operated hotels and other lodging places to join international reservation systems. This allows travellers to make multiple reservations for lodging, airlines, and car rentals with one telephone call or Internet search. Nearly all hotel chains and many independent lodging facilities operate online reservation systems through the Internet or maintain websites that allow individuals to book rooms. Online marketing of properties is so popular with guests that many hotels promote themselves with elaborate websites and allow people to investigate availability and rates.

1.2.3 Summary of the key characteristics of the hospitality industry

The key characteristics of the hospitality industry are summarily listed below:
- As a service sector industry the production of the service is inseparable from its delivery
- The main product (rooms space) is highly perishable because if not sold on any day, it is lost forever
- The customers are regarded as guests who must always be satisfied
- It is a round the clock (24/7) activity and it is very labour intensive
- There is a lot of ethnic, cultural and religious diversity of both guests and staff
- The industry suffers from a lot of occupational and public health and safety issues
- It is seasonal and results from people making their spending decisions after all other obligatory expenditures have been taken care of (discretionary expenditure)
- The industry has high fixed capital costs
- The industry has highly irregular variable operating costs
- The industry has low barriers to entry for capital and labour
- There is a big inequality of functions within the industry and these functions depend on each other
- There is high sales volatility within the day, week, season, or as defined by the economic cycles

Glossary

Accounting system – is the system of procedures, personnel and data management tools that exist within a company and used to accumulate its financial information. It is made up of the set of manual and computerized procedures and controls that provide for identifying relevant transactions or events; preparing accurate source documents, entering data into the accounting records accurately, processing transactions accurately, updating master files properly, and generating accurate documents and reports.

Business entity principle – is where the business is seen as an entity separate from its owner(s) that keeps and presents financial records and prepares the final accounts and financial statements. The accounting is kept for each entity as a whole.

Conservatism principle – is where the accounting for a business should be fair and reasonable. This principle indicates that expenses should be recognized as soon as possible whereas revenues should be recognized only when they are verified. A business should not understate its expenses or liabilities. On the other hand it should not overstate its assets or revenues.

Consistency principle – is where the accountants are expected to use the same methods from period to period unless a change is necessary and this change must be clearly explained in the financial statements.

Cost principle – is where a company is required to record its transactions (especially those related to fixed assets) at the acquisition price or cash cost and this should represent the accounting value of the transactions.

Financial accounting – is the area of accounting concerned with reporting financial information to external stakeholders.

Full disclosure principle – is the requirement that the financial statement should provide all relevant and material facts necessary for the understanding of the financial statement.

Generally accepted accounting principles – is a recognized common set of accounting principles, standards, and procedures. GAAP is a combination of accepted methods of doing accounting and policy board set authoritative standards.

Going concern principle – is the assumption that the accounting entity will maintain proper accounting records from the date of its establishment to the date of its liquidation.

Hospitality industry – the industry that is most concerned with the cordial reception of guests. It is made up of a wide range of businesses, each of which is dedicated to the service of people away from home.

Management accounting – is the process of identification, measurement, accumulation, analysis, preparation, interpretation, and communication of financial information used by management to plan, evaluate, and control within an organization and to assure appropriate use of, and accountability for its resources.

Matching principle – is the requirement for the recognition of all expenses that are directly related to the realization of the revenues in the income statement of the period.

Materiality principle – is the requirement that events or information must be accounted for if they make a difference to the user of the financial information.

Monetary unit principle – is the requirement that financial statements should be based on transactions expressed in the primary monetary unit of the environment.

Objectivity principle – is the requirement that all accounting transactions should be justified as much as possible on objective evidence. This means that accounting transactions should be based on fact and not on personal opinion or feelings.

Realization principle – is the recognition of revenues only when they are earned.

Time period principle – is the requirement that a company has to complete its analysis to report the financial condition and profitability of its business operation over a specific operating time period.

Multiple choice questions

1.1 Which of the following is one of the key characteristics of the hospitality industry?
a consistent activity level throughout the year
b long distribution channels
c low barriers to entry for capital and labour
d slow transformation of the raw materials into a finished product

1.2 The full disclosure principle of accounting is:
a the assumption that the accounting entity will maintain proper accounting records from the date of its establishment to the date of its liquidation
b the requirement that events or information must be accounted for if they make a difference to the user of the financial information
c is the requirement that events or information must be accounted for if they make a difference to the user of the financial information
d the requirement that the financial statement should provide all relevant and material facts necessary for the understanding of the financial statement

1.3 The generally accepted accounting principle that supports recording the value of a property at the purchase price when the market value is higher is the:
a conservatism principle
b cost principle
c going concern principle
d monetary principle

1.4 Which of the following branches of accounting is often limited to preparing and distributing financial reports?
a auditing
b cost accounting
c financial accounting
d managerial accounting

1.5 One of the basic purposes of managerial accounting is to provide information to various management levels in order to:
a be better equipped for the management and control functions
b determine the business' competitive position
c evaluate the accounting records and procedures of the business
d improve the business's products and services

Exercises

1.1 Fill in the blanks below with the accounting principle that best applies.

Business entity	Matching
Conservatism	Materiality
Consistency	Monetary unit
Cost	Objectivity
Full disclosure	Realization
Going concern	Time period

a A new terrace is recorded at the amount that was paid for its construction instead of the original contract price because of the _____ principle.

b A hotel modifies its inventory values to reflect the market values of its food stocks which are higher than the original cost, because of the _____ principle.

c A restaurant does not reduce the value of its glassware to liquidation value because of the _____ principle

d A hotel records accrued wages at the end of the accounting period because of the _____ principle.

e The cost of beverages taken home for the personal use of the owner is recorded as a withdrawal because of the _____ principle.

1.2 Match the following situations with the accounting principle that best applies. In some cases, more than one principle may apply.

Conservatism	Materiality
Consistency	Monetary unit
Cost	Objectivity
Full disclosure	Realization
Going concern	Time period
Matching	

a A hotel corporation is preparing its end of year financial statements. Management has informed the accountant that in six weeks it will begin to close 12 of its properties. The accountant will provide information related to these future actions on the current end of year financial statements because of the _____ principle and the _____ principle.

b A caterer purchases a delivery van for €7,500 from another caterer having problems. Based on the _____ principle, the delivery van purchase is recorded at €7,500, even though the caterer could sell it again for €10,000.

c A hotel receives advance payments of €2,500 from a conference organizer. This is not a sale due to the _____ principle.

d A restaurant has traditionally used the straight line method to depreciate all its heavy duty kitchen equipment. This year it decides to start using the double declining balance depreciation method on the same equipment. This change must be announced in the financial statements due to the _____ principle.

1.3 Which branch of accounting is best described by each statement below?
- This branch of accounting is unregulated but mostly based on cost/benefit analysis.
- The type of data in this branch is mostly financial and monetary.
- The time perspective of this branch is principally historical.
- This branch of accounting has no pre-determined format but is aligned to the specific wishes of management.
- This branch of accounting provides general information on the whole organization.
- The branch of accounting is based on a continuous reporting frequency.
- The main characteristic of this branch of accounting is the focus on estimated information to ensure efficiency, relevance and timeliness.
- This branch of accounting will provide information to external stakeholders.

1.4   Write brief explanations on the following types of hospitality operations:

- Airport hotels
- Bed-and-breakfast inns
- Casino hotels
- Conference hotels
- Extended-stay hotels
- Guesthouses
- Resort hotels
- Motels
- RV parks and campgrounds
- Youth hostels

The balance sheet

2.1 The components of a balance sheet
2.2 Formats of balance sheets and accounting standards
2.3 Establishing simple balance sheets

The balance sheet also at times called the statement of financial position is a list of all the assets owned by an organization, the debts owed by the organization and also the sum of all the investments brought into the organization by its owners. Despite the fact that the balance sheet is a result of the organization's activities over time, it however is a representation of the worth and obligations of the organization at a very specific date. It is one of the most prominent financial statements of any organization. Section 2.1 introduces the various parts of the balance sheet. In section 2.2 various formats used in establishing balance sheets will be discussed while section 2.3 will illustrate the establishment of a simple balance sheet.

2.1 The components of a balance sheet

The balance sheet shows the balance between the assets of an organization with its liabilities and owners' equity. This balance is symbolized in the fundamental accounting equation as follows:

Assets = liabilities + owners' equity

For this fundamental equation to be respected at all times, an increase in an asset must be accompanied by a corresponding decrease in another asset or an increase in either a liability or owners' equity. The balance sheet is the only one of the four major accounting statements that is established at a given point in time and that shows a balance between its two parts. The major sections of the balance sheet are as defined in the fundamental accounting equation and they define the structure of the subsections as follows:

2.1.1   Assets
2.1.2   Liabilities
2.1.3   Owners' equity

2.1.1 Assets

An asset is everything of value that is owned by a person or a company. In a balance sheet, all things owned are recorded in their monetary values. There are two major classes of assets which are tangible and intangible assets. Tangible assets are those that have a physical substance whereas intangible assets lack a physical substance but have a value to the company. In the hospitality industry, assets are sub-divided into the following categories: current assets, non-current receivables, investments, property and equipment, and other assets. These are all explained below.

Current assets
Current assets are those assets that are expected to be converted into cash in a relatively short time or in the normal operating cycle of the business. These assets are continually turned over in the cause of a business during normal business activity. Current assets are generally listed in their order of liquidity. The primary items in this category of current assets within the hospitality industry are the following:

Cash: it is the most liquid asset and includes cash on hand (house banks), demand deposits, and temporary cash investments (that have to be collected within 3 months). Cash is shown in the balance sheet at its face value.

Restricted cash: relates to cash that has been restricted for a specific purpose. In the current assets section, such purposes could be for example to pay for current debts or other current expenses.

Short term investments (marketable securities): as opposed to temporary cash investments, these are securities bought and held for sale within the year. The near future should generate income on short term price differences. Short term investments are shown in the balance sheet at their market value.

Receivables: these consist of accounts receivable, notes receivable, current maturities of non-current receivables, other receivables, and the allowance for doubtful accounts. Receivables are usually reported as net of the allowance on collectible allowance. Accounts receivable are open accounts carried in the guest and city ledgers by the customers. Notes receivable due within a year are equally listed within this category. An allowance for doubtful accounts should be subtracted from receivables. Other receivables are those that fall under none of the previous categories of receivables such as accrued interest receivable. The allowance for doubtful accounts is the part of receivables that the property, based on experience and account appraisal, will consider very difficult to collect.

Due to/from owner, management company, or related party: these contain the balances due to or from the respected parties such as loans, advances, management fees, other expenses and advances provided to a property.

Inventories: these consist of merchandise that has been purchased for resale such as food, beverage and supplies used in running the property. The inventory value reported on the balance sheet is most of the time the historical cost or fair market value. If the cost of unused supplies to be used in operating the property is significant, then these too should be included in the value of the inventory. The method of valuing the inventory should be disclosed in the footnotes to the financial statements. In cases where, individual inventory categories are significant, these should be listed separately in the financial statement.

Operating equipment: these will include items whose estimated usage is less than one year. At the time of the purchase of the operating equipment, the property should establish the consumption period of the equipment and then expense the purchase over the determined period.

Prepaid expenses: these represent the use of cash to purchase goods, services or benefits to be used by the property with the passage of time. These are generally reduced on a monthly basis and shown in the income statement as expenses. Examples include prepaid insurance, prepaid rents, prepaid advertising, prepaid license fees, and prepaid taxes. Prepaid expenses that would benefit a company beyond the scope of one year should be classified as other assets.

Deferred income taxes (current): these represent the tax effects of temporary differences noticed between the bases of current assets and current liabilities for financial and income tax assessment purposes.

Other: these include items that have not been included in other parts of the current assets and which are expected to be transformed into cash in the coming year.

Non-current receivables

Different from the receivables described under current assets, non-current receivables are those accounts that are not expected to be collected within the year. In this sub-category are included amounts due from owners, officers, employees, and other third parties. As with current receivables, an allowance for doubtful accounts will have to be created for those that are deemed to be very difficult or impossible to collect.

Investments

Investments in other companies or in property or plant not connected with the daily operations of the property are equally considered as a separate asset category. These generally include debt or equity securities as well as ownership interests. Some examples are: shares held in group companies; loans to group companies, shares in related companies; loans to related companies; shares in non-related or group companies; as well as shares in own company in cases where companies can purchase their own shares. The valuation of investments generally poses problems where there is no stock exchange.

Fixed assets (property, plant and equipment – PP & E)

Fixed assets also known as property, plant and equipment (PP & E) refer to those assets and property within a company which cannot easily be converted into cash. Fixed assets are long lived and of a more permanent and physical nature. They primarily exist to be used in the running of the business and not for sale. They include items of value purchased by the organization destined to be used over long periods of time. Fixed assets normally include land and buildings, transportation equipment, office equipment and furniture, computers, fixtures and fittings, construction in progress, and plant and machinery. Fixed assets are usually noted at their acquisition cost. The acquisition cost generally includes their purchase price which might include import duties and other deductible trade discounts and rebates. The acquisition cost will also include all costs attributable to transporting and installing the asset and the initial estimate of dismantling and removing the asset.

With the exception of land, all property and equipment is depreciated over time. Depreciation is simply the expense generated by the use of a fixed asset. It represents the wear and tear of an asset or a reduction in its historical value due to its use. At any point in time, it represents the cost of an asset less any salvage value over its estimated economic useful life. Depreciation is considered to be an expense because it is matched against the revenue generated through the use of the asset.

Depreciation is usually spread over the economic useful life of the asset. Whatever depreciation method is used, it should be disclosed using footnotes at the bottom of the balance sheet and it should be in accordance with the GAAP. The total accumulated depreciation and amortization should appear as a separate item which is deducted from the total plant, property and equipment. This will lead to the net plant, property and equipment line.

Intangible assets

These are defined as non-monetary assets that cannot be seen, touched or physically measured, which are created through time and effort and that are identifiable as a separate asset. There are primarily two forms of intangible assets; the legal intangibles and the competitive intangibles. Legal intangibles generate legal property rights defensible in a court of law. Competitive intangibles directly affect effectiveness, productivity, wastage, and opportunity costs within a company. The legal intangibles include such elements as trade secrets, list of customers, patents, copyrights, trademarks, and goodwill. The competitive intangibles include amongst others, know-how, knowledge, collaboration activities, leverage activities, and structural activities. One very common intangible asset is goodwill which is the excess of the purchase price over the fair market value of a business at the time of its purchase. Rules on amortizing goodwill over time are contained in the GAAP.

Cash surrender value of life insurance

In cases where a company has purchased life insurance on the lives of some of its principal promoters and individuals, the cash surrender values of such life policies can be recorded as an asset. These are adjusted periodically via the insurance expense to reflect any changes in their values.

Deferred charges

A deferred charge is basically a prepaid expense that is recognized on the balance sheet as an asset until it is used. They typically relate to financing activities and represent the direct costs of obtaining such financing. Examples will include loan fees and bond issuance costs. Recording deferred charges in this way ensures that a company respects the principles of the GAAP by matching revenues with expenses. Such costs are usually amortized over the life of the related financing and the amortization method should be disclosed in the notes to the financial statements.

Deferred income taxes (non-current)

These represent the collection of the future tax liabilities of the company that will typically be summed up and shown as one line item on the balance sheet. These are to be paid more than one year in the future. They generally result from income already earned and recognized for accounting, but not tax, purposes. Also, differences between tax laws and accounting methods can result in a temporary difference in the amount of income tax payable by a company. This difference is recorded as deferred income tax.

Operating equipment

As explained above, operating equipment with periods of consumption of less than one year are classified as current assets. In cases where bulk purchases of operating equipment are made for example china, and are expected to be consumed over longer periods, the difference will have to be stated as other assets.

Restricted cash

As is the case with operating equipment, cash that is equally restricted for purposes that go beyond the year should be classified as non-current under other assets.

Other

Items that cannot be grouped into any of the previous categories, such as costs to organize the company, security deposits, initial franchise costs, unamortized franchise costs, and other miscellaneous or individually immaterial assets, are included under this caption. Their nature and amortization policies should be clearly indicated in the notes to the financial statements.

2.1.2 Liabilities

A liability is an amount that an individual or a company is under obligation to pay to other persons or organizations. Liabilities generally have the following characteristics:
- they result from all types of borrowing;
- they represent a duty or responsibility to others that entails settlement by future transfers;
- the duty or responsibility obligates the entity, leaving it little or no discretion to avoid it; and lastly;
- the transaction or event obligating the event has already taken place.

Liabilities are generally divided into the two sub-categories of current liabilities and long term liabilities. In 2.1.2.1 the detailed elements of the current liabilities section of a balance sheet are discussed while in 2.1.2.2, those related to the long term liabilities will be discussed.

2.1.2.1 Current liabilities

These are obligations at the balance sheet date which are reasonably expected to be paid back within the next 12 months. They generally consist of one of the following five types:
- Payables resulting from the acquisition of goods, services, and labour and the applicable payroll taxes.
- Payments received in advance for the delivery of goods or services.
- Obligations to be paid relating to fixed assets purchases.
- Dividends payable.
- Incomes taxes payable.

Exhibit 2.1 illustrates the importance of the prudent management of the liabilities of a hotel, the absence of which might lead to liquidation and bankruptcy.

Exhibit 2.1 **Hotel group yet to repay all its debts**

Hotel group yet to repay all its debts
by Keith Bourke

Breaffy House Hotel has still not paid back cash owed to a number of its creditors but is promising to do so within a matter of weeks. In November last year, an examiner was appointed by the High Court to the hotel's parent company, the Lynch Hotel Group. The examiner met with Breaffy House's creditors at a meeting in the hotel where it was agreed the company would pay back just 10 per cent of its overall debts.

Creditors were supposed to have been paid by December 20, but when contacted last week, several local businesses had yet to receive any payment. "We haven't got a penny from them," said one local business person. "I've been chasing and chasing them." The hotel owed more than €1m to unsecured creditors, the bulk of which are from Co Mayo. The company's accounts revealed that money is owed to a range of local businesses and firms. Mayo County Council is Breaffy House's biggest creditor with €102,784 owed to the local authority, which was listed as a preferential creditor. The debts were across virtually every sector of the local economy – from a florist who was owed €6,000 to a meat supplier owed almost €30,000. Each of the four newspapers in the county was owed money, ranging from almost €7,000 to €1,200.

The Lynch Hotel Group, which employs 530 people in seven hotels in the West of Ireland, gained court protection from its creditors in July. A previous court hearing was told the company had debts of €22.8m, which it was unable to pay. Approximately 125 full and part-time staff are employed at the Breaffy House Resort which was bought by the Lynch Group in 2001. Michael B Lynch, managing director of the Lynch Hotel Group, said the company had decided to go into voluntary examinership to secure the long-term safety of the group. "It is a long-term step to ensure the future of the Lynch Hotel Group. We are professional hoteliers with a fundamentally sound business and, at this time, are planning to restructure our financial position. "We are very confident that our 40 years of experience in the hotel business, our customer and staff loyalty and recognised innovation practices will see the company through this process." Mr Lynch told the Western People yesterday evening (Monday) that the "vast bulk" of creditors had been paid and the remainder will be paid "in the next few weeks". ■

Source: Western People, Wednesday, January 20, 2010

The major classifications of current liabilities are:

Notes payable
Notes payable represent the short term notes due to banks and other creditors that have to be repaid within 12 months.

Due to/from owner, management company, or related party
Due to/from owner, management company, or related party which contain the balances due to or from the owner, a management company, or other related entities for loans, advances for capital improvements, management fees, and other expenses or advances provided to a property. These accounts are classified as current or long term based on their payment terms.

Accounts payable
Accounts payable represents amounts due to suppliers. Amounts due to other parties for guest charges collected by the property may be included with Accounts payable or shown separately.

Accrued expenses
Accrued expenses are expenses incurred before the balance sheet date but are not due till after the balance sheet date. Examples include salaries and wages and related benefits, vacation pay, interest, management fees, rent, taxes other than on income, and utilities.

Advance deposits

Advance deposits represent amounts received that are to be applied as part of the payment for future sales of rooms, food and beverage, or other goods and services.

Income taxes payable

Income taxes payable represents the estimated obligations for income taxes to be honoured within the next 12 months.

Deferred income taxes (current)

Deferred income taxes (current) represent the tax effects of temporary differences between the bases of current assets and current liabilities for financial and income tax reporting purposes. For example, revenue recognized in the financial statements before it is taxable will result in deferred income taxes (current) if it will be taxable in the next year. These can be found in both current assets as well as current liabilities depending on the situation.

Current maturities of long-term debt

Current maturities of long-term debt include the principal payments of mortgage notes, other notes, and similar liabilities, and the instalments on capitalized leases due within the next 12 months.

Other current liabilities

Items that cannot be grouped into any of the previous current liability categories are shown here. The category is normally used to show those small items that cannot be independently classified. Some examples are the unearned portion of amounts received or charged to non-guests for the use of recreational facilities, unredeemed gift certificate sales, unclaimed wages, and the net liability under barter contracts.

Current liabilities are often compared with current assets. The difference between the two is commonly known as working capital (see Chapter 8 for a more profound analysis).

2.1.2.2   Long term liabilities

These are obligations, which on the date of the balance sheet are expected to be paid back beyond the next 12 months. Common hospitality industry-related long term liabilities are:

Mortgage notes, other notes, and similar liabilities

In this caption, information related to the following will have to be disclosed: interest rates, payment of sinking fund requirements, maturity dates, collateralization and assets pledged, financial restrictive covenants, as well as payment and sinking fund payments required for each of the five years following the balance sheet date.

Obligations under capital leases

Just as in the previous caption, disclosure is required with regard to the future minimum lease payments for each of the five years following the balance sheet date and the total future minimum lease obligations.

Other long-term liabilities

Long-term liabilities that do not require satisfaction within a year and are not included under other captions are included here. Examples include deferred compensation, deferred management fees, tenants' lease deposits, and accrued obligations for pension and other post-employment benefits.

Deferred income taxes (non-current)

Deferred income taxes (non-current) represent the tax effects of temporary differences between the bases of non-current assets and non-current liabilities for financial and income tax reporting purposes. They generally result from income already earned and recognized for accounting, but not tax, purposes. Also, differences between tax laws and accounting methods can result in a temporary difference in the amount of income tax payable by a company. This difference is recorded as deferred income tax. For example, the use of accelerated depreciation for tax purposes and straight-line depreciation for financial reporting purposes will result in non-current deferred income taxes.

Commitments and contingencies

These are indicated to draw attention to their existence. Currency amounts are not indicated and adequate disclosure should be made in the notes to the financial statements. Some examples are: employment contracts; management agreements; purchase contracts; long-term leases; pending or threatened lawsuits; as well as third party cautions and guarantees.

2.1.3   Owners' equity

At the start of a business, the owners bring in some funding into the business to finance the acquisition of their assets. Based on the fundamental accounting equation, all acquired assets would have been funded either through debt (liabilities) or by the owners themselves (owners' equity). When all liabilities have been accounted for, the positive difference is considered to be the interest of the owners in the business.

The detail of the owners' equity section in the balance sheet is a function of the type of organization in which the business is operating. There are four major types of business organizations – sole proprietorships, partnerships, limited liability companies and corporations.

Sole proprietorships

The owner's equity section in the balance sheet of a sole proprietorship will simply be denoted using the name of the sole proprietor. Exhibit 2.2 indicates the interest on one owner. Any changes during the period should be indicated in the statement of owner's equity. This section will equally indicate the contributions (invested by the owner) as well as the withdrawals (taken by the owner) during the period.

■ Exhibit 2.2 **Owner's equity section in the balance sheet of a sole proprietorship**

Sole proprietorship
Owner's equity
Accumulated other comprehensive income (loss), net of income tax
     Total owner's equity

Partnerships

Unlike the case of sole-proprietorships with the name of a single individual, in partnerships, the owners' equity section represents the net equity of the partners in the partnership. This can be classified depending on the situation as, general partners' equity or limited partners' equity. Similarly any changes during the period should be indicated in the statement of owners' equity. This section will equally indicate the contributions (invested by the partners) as well as the withdrawals (taken by the partners) during the period. The owners' equity section in the balance sheet of a partnership will as such contain the names and contributions of the partners as shown in exhibit 2.3 in which 3 of the partners are general partners and 2 are limited partners. A general partner manages the partnership and typically holds an economic interest in it. The general partner also receives a percentage of the profits off the top, before the limited partners receive theirs. Limited partners are not involved in the day-to-day management of the partnership and have limited liability.

■ Exhibit 2.3 **Owners' equity section in the balance sheet of a partnership**

Partnership
Partners' equity
     General partners
          Partner A
          Partner B
          Partner C
     Limited partners
          Partner D
          Partner E
     Accumulated other comprehensive income (loss), net of income tax
          Total partners' equity

Limited liability companies

Similar to the partnerships, the owners' equity section in limited liability companies will represent the net equity of the members. This can equally be classified, where appropriate, as general member equity or limited member equity. Similarly any changes during the period should be indicated in the statement of owners' equity. This section will equally indicate the contributions (invested by the members) as well as the withdrawals (taken by the members) during the period. The owners' equity section in the balance sheet of a limited liability company is shown in exhibit 2.4.

Limited liability companies
Members' equity
Accumulated other comprehensive income (loss), net of income tax
                                        Total Members' Equity

Corporations

For corporations, the phrase stockholders' equity (or shareholders' equity) is used to denote owners' equity. The main components of stockholders' equity are the following:

Capital stock

Capital stock represents the common and preferred stock a company is authorized to issue, according to its articles of association. The par or stated value and the number of shares authorized and issued for each class of stock is presented in the balance sheet. As in all cases related to owners' equity, any changes during the period should be indicated in the statement of stockholders' equity.

Additional paid-in capital

A value that is included in the contributed surplus account in the stockholders' equity section of a company's balance sheet. The account represents the excess paid by an investor over the par-value price of a stock issue. Additional paid-in-capital can arise from issuing either preferred or common stock. This includes the cash, property, and other capital contributed to a corporation by its shareholders. As in all cases related to owners' equity, any changes during the period should be indicated in the statement of stockholders' equity.

Retained earnings

Retained earnings represent the portion of net earnings not paid out as dividends, but retained by the company to be reinvested in its core business or to pay debt. It is calculated by adding net income to (or subtracting any net losses from) beginning retained earnings and subtracting any dividends paid to shareholders. Negative retained earnings are called deficits. As in all cases related to owners' equity, any changes during the period should be indicated in the statement of stockholders' equity.

Treasury stock

Treasury stock represents the portion of shares that a company keeps in their own treasury. Treasury stock may have come from a repurchase or buyback from shareholders; or it may have never been issued to the public in the first place. These shares don't pay dividends, have no voting rights, and do not have to be included in the calculation of outstanding shares. As in all cases related to owners' equity, any changes during the period should be indicated in the statement of stockholders' equity.

The stockholders' equity section in the balance sheet of a corporation is shown in Exhibit 2.5 on the next page.

■ Exhibit 2.5 **Stockholders' equity section in the balance sheet of a corporation**

Corporations
Stockholders' equity
     Capital stock
     Additional paid-in capital in excess of par
     Retained earnings
     Treasury stock
     Accumulated other comprehensive income (loss), net of income tax
               Total stockholders' equity

Accumulated other comprehensive income (loss)
The last major element in the owners' equity section of the balance sheet is the accumulated other comprehensive income (loss) and it is relevant to all the types of business organizations seen above. Accumulated other comprehensive income refers to the net income (loss) plus "other comprehensive incomes (losses)." These include certain revenues, expenses, gains, and losses that are reported as separate components of equity instead of net income. The common sources of other comprehensive income (losses) are: foreign currency translation adjustments; gains and losses on foreign currency transactions; unrealized gains and losses on available-for-sale marketable securities; unrealized gains and losses that result from a transfer of a debt security; changes in the fair value of a derivative instrument; gains and losses on inter-company foreign currency transactions of a long-term investment nature following consolidation; and minimum pension liability adjustments.

2.2 Formats of balance sheets and accounting standards

Balance sheets are usually arranged using the account (or horizontal) format or the report (vertical) format. In the account format, the information related to the assets on the one hand, and the liabilities and owners' equity on the other hand, are put side-by-side, with the assets put on the left hand side and the liabilities and owners' equity put on the right hand side. In the report format, the information related to the assets is initially indicated, then the information related to the liabilities and owners' equity is indicated below in a vertical arrangement. The report format is more popular nowadays because it is easier to use it in multi-year spreadsheet analysis with each year's information just occupying one column. Both of these formats are shown in exhibit 2.6 that contains the summary balance sheet headings of the Afilen Hotels.

An accounting standard is a set of rules and regulations containing detailed guidance on the preparation of financial accounts. Since the 1970s the International Accounting Standards Committee (IASC) replaced in 2001 by the International Accounting Standards Board (IASB) has been foreseeing and is responsible for the establishment of international standards known as International Financial Reporting Standards (IFRS). Since 2005, the European Union has decided that all

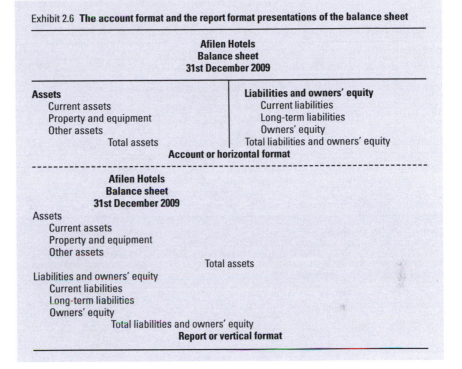

Exhibit 2.6 **The account format and the report format presentations of the balance sheet**

Afilen Hotels
Balance sheet
31st December 2009

Assets	Liabilities and owners' equity
Current assets	Current liabilities
Property and equipment	Long-term liabilities
Other assets	Owners' equity
Total assets	Total liabilities and owners' equity

Account or horizontal format

Afilen Hotels
Balance sheet
31st December 2009

Assets
  Current assets
  Property and equipment
  Other assets
                              Total assets
Liabilities and owners' equity
  Current liabilities
  Long-term liabilities
  Owners' equity
              Total liabilities and owners' equity

Report or vertical format

listed companies should prepare their financial statements in compliance with the international standards.

Most organizations in the hospitality industry (hotels, motels, resorts, restaurants, and clubs) use the Uniform System of Accounts for the Lodging Industry (USALI). This was initiated by the Hotel Association of New York in the original Uniform System of Accounts for Hotels (USAH) in 1925. The system was designed for classifying, organizing, and presenting financial information so that uniformity prevailed and comparison of financial data among hotels was possible. A major advantage of accounting uniformity is that information can be collected and compared between similar organizations within the hospitality industry. In this text, and because of the current absence of any such European-wide system, all of the financial statements will be designed based on the USALI format. To this effect, the previous description of the balance sheet is based on the 10th Revised Edition of the USALI.

2.3   Establishing simple balance sheets

Find below a comprehensive example on how a balance sheet is established based on available information.

The Europa Alliance Hotels Plc. is a corporation and its shareholders have handed over the overall day-to-day management of the hotels in their portfolio to the Alliance Management Company. At the end of operations for the year 2009, the various balance sheet account balances were as follows:

House banks	€	35,400
Demand deposits	€	75,000
Temporary cash investments	€	22,500
Restricted cash	€	92,000
Short-term investments	€	15,000
Accounts receivable	€	135,000
Notes receivable	€	72,000
Current maturities of non-current receivables	€	54,000
Other receivables	€	28,000
Allowance for doubtful accounts	€	32,500
Due from Alliance Management Company	€	84,500
Inventories	€	95,000
Operating equipment	€	123,000
Prepaid expenses	€	46,000
Other current assets	€	12,000
Non-current receivables (net of current maturities)	€	325,000
Investments	€	425,000
Land	€	1,300,000
Building s	€	54,800,000
Leaseholds and leaseholds improvements	€	4,300,000
Furnishings and equipment	€	7,800,000
Construction in progress	€	2,740,000
Accumulated depreciation and amortization	€	13,450,000
Intangible assets	€	158,200
Cash surrender value of life insurance	€	4,200,000
Deferred charges	€	82,000
Operating equipment to be consumed beyond 12 months	€	48,200
Restricted cash above 12 months	€	84,500
Initial franchise costs	€	73,500
Notes payable to banks	€	145,000
Notes payable and to others	€	90,600
Due to Alliance Management Company	€	135,070
Accounts payable	€	154,000
Accrued expenses	€	115,000
Advance deposits	€	41,800
Income taxes payable	€	90,800
Unclaimed wages	€	20,000
Mortgage notes	€	13,568,500
Current maturities of mortgage notes	€	67,000
Other notes and similar liabilities	€	1,120,100
Obligations under capital leases	€	132,000
Other long-term liabilities	€	185,000
Deferred income taxes (non-current)	€	198,130
Commitments and contingencies	€	75,000
Common stock	€	20,000,000
Paid-in capital in excess of par	€	16,500,000
Retained earnings	€	10,062,000
Accumulated other comprehensive income (net of income tax)	€	2,400,000
Treasury stock	€	1,250,000

In conformity with the USALI and using the vertical (report) format of the balance sheet, the balance sheet of the Europa Alliance Hotels Plc. will look as indicated in exhibits 2.7a and 2.7b.

Exhibit 2.7a **Balance sheet of the Europa Alliance Hotels Plc** (assets section)

Europa Alliance Hotel Plc.
Balance Sheet
December 31, 2009

Assets
Current Assets
Cash

House banks	€	35,400
Demand deposits	€	75,000
Temporary cash investments	€	22,500
Total Cash	€	132,900
Restricted Cash	€	92,000
Short-term investments	€	15,000
Receivables		
Accounts Receivable	€	135,000
Notes Receivable	€	72,000
Current maturities of non-current receivables		
Other	€	28,000
Total Receivable	€	289,000
Less Allowance for Doubtful Accounts	€	(32,500)
Net Receivables	€	256,500
Due from Alliance Management Company	€	84,500
Inventories	€	95,000
Operating Equipment	€	123,000
Prepaid Expenses	€	51,200
Other	€	12,000
Total Current Assets	**€**	**862,100**
Non-current Receivables (net of current maturities	€	325,000
Investments	€	425,000
Property and Equipment		
Land	€	1,300,000
Building	€	54,800,000
Leaseholds and leaseholds improvements	€	4,300,000
Furnishings and Equipment	€	7,800,000
Contruction in progress	€	2,740,000
Total property and equipment	€	70,940,000
Less accumulated depreciation and amortization	€	(13,450,000)
Net Property and Equipment	**€**	**57,490,000**
Other Assets		
Intangible assets	€	158,200
Cash surrender value of life insurance	€	4,200,000
Deferred charges	€	82,000
Operating equipment	€	82,700
Restricted cash	€	84,500
Other	€	73,500
Total Other Assets	€	4,680,900
Total Assets	**€**	**63,783,000**

Exhibit 2.7b **Balance sheet of the Europa Alliance Hotels Plc** (liabilities and owners' equity section)

Liabilities and Owners' Equity		
Current Liabilities		
Notes Payable		
Banks	€	145,000
Others	€	90,600
Total Notes Payable	€	235,600
Due to Alliance Management Company	€	135,070
Accounts Payable	€	154,000
Accrued Expenses	€	115,000
Advance Deposits	€	41,800
Income Taxes Payable	€	90,800
Current Maturities of Long Term Debt	€	67,000
Other	€	20,000
Total Current Liabilities	**€**	**859,270**
Long-term Debt (net of current maturities		
Mortgage notes	€	13,501,500
Other notes and similar liabilities	€	1,120,100
Obligations under capital leases	€	132,000
Total Long-term debt	**€**	**14,753,600**
Other Long-Term liabilities	**€**	**185,000**
Deferred Income Taxes (non-current)	**€**	**198,130**
Commitments and Contingencies	**€**	**75,000**
Total Liabilities	**€**	**16,071,000**
Stockholders' Equity		
Common Stock	€	20,000,000
Paid-in capital in excess of par	€	16,500,000
Retained Earnings	€	10,062,000
Accumulated other comprehensive income (net of income tax)	€	2,400,000
Less Treasury stock	€	(1,250,000)
Total Stockholders' Equity	**€**	**47,712,000**
Total Liabilities and Owners' Equity	**€**	**63,783,000**

Glossary

Account format – is an arrangement of balance sheet items that puts the assets accounts on the left side and the liabilities and owners' equity accounts on the right side of the page.

Accounts payable – this account represents amounts due to suppliers.

Accounts receivable – is a current asset representing money due for services performed or goods sold on credit. They are open accounts carrying the guest and city ledgers by the customer.

Accrued expenses – these are expenses incurred before the balance sheet date but are not due till after the balance sheet date.

Additional paid-in capital – this account represents the excess paid by an investor over the par-value price of a stock issue.

Advance deposits – represent amounts received that are to be applied as part of the payment for future sales.

Asset – is anything owned by an individual or a business, which has a commercial or exchange value.

Balance sheet – is list of all the assets owned by an organization, the debts owed by the organization and also the sum of all the investments brought into the organization by its owners.

Capital stock – represents the common and preferred stock a corporation is authorized to issue, according to its articles of association.

Corporation – is a type of business organization chartered by a state and given many of the legal rights as a separate entity.

Current assets – are those assets that are expected to be converted into cash in a relatively short time or in the normal operating cycle of the business.

Current liabilities – these are debts or any other form of claim on the company that are supposed to be honoured within one year.

Fixed assets (property, plant and equipment – PP & E) – refer to those assets and property within a company which cannot be easily converted into cash. Fixed assets are long lived and of a more permanent and physical nature.

Accounting equation – is the mathematical expression used to describe the relationship between the assets, liabilities and owners' equity of the business. The equation states that assets equal liabilities plus owner's equity.

Liabilities – in management accounting, this is a debt, expense, or any other form of claim on the assets of the company that must be paid or otherwise honoured by the company.

Limited liability companies – these are companies in which the separate legal entity that is owned by shareholders for the purpose of carrying on business does not go beyond the shareholders' investment in the business. Assets and liabilities of owners (shareholders) are separate from the company.

Notes payable – this represents the short term notes due to banks and other creditors that have to be repaid within 12 months.

Owners' equity – is total assets minus total liabilities.

Partnership – is an unincorporated business that has more than one owner.

Report format – is an arrangement of balance sheet items that lists the assets accounts first, followed by the liabilities and owners' equity accounts.

Retained earnings – these represent the portion of net earnings not paid out as dividends, but retained by the company to be reinvested in its core business or to pay debt.

Treasury stock – represents the portion of shares that a company keeps in their own treasury. Treasury stock may have come from a repurchase or buyback from shareholders; or it may have never been issued to the public in the first place.

Uniform system of accounts – this is a system of accounts whereby all accounts have the same type of coding and all accounting procedures are done in the same way.

Multiple choice questions

2.1 Which of the following items will not be shown in the balance sheet of a hotel?
a accounts payable
b accrued taxes
c customer loyalty value
d intangible assets

2.2 Which of the following is not a characteristic of a liability?
a liabilities obligate the borrower
b liabilities represent a responsibility still to be honoured
c liabilities result from all types of borrowing
d the obligating transaction event is in the future

2.3 The section of the balance sheet that changes with the type of company is:
a assets
b current liabilities
c long term liabilities
d owners' equity

2.4 Under which category are temporary cash investments reported in the balance sheet?
a current assets
b current liabilities
c investments
d other assets

2.5 Deferred management fees are reported in the balance sheet under:
a current assets
b current liabilities
c other assets
d long term liabilities

Exercises

2.1 The total assets of a hospitality company are €2,150,875.00 and its total liabilities are €1,350,000.00. What amount is the owners' equity?

2.2 Based on the USALI format of the balance sheet, classify the following accounts into the major categories

Accounts payable
Accounts receivable
Accrued expenses
Accumulated depreciation and amortization
Accumulated other comprehensive income (net of income tax)
Advance deposits
Allowance for doubtful accounts
Buildings

Cash surrender value of life insurance
Commitments and contingencies
Common stock
Construction in progress
Current maturities of mortgage notes
Current maturities of non-current receivables
Deferred charges
Deferred income taxes (non-current)
Demand deposits

Furnishings and equipment
House banks
Income taxes payable
Initial franchise costs
Intangible assets
Inventories
Investments
Land
Leaseholds and leaseholds improve-
    ments
Mortgage notes
Non-current receivables (net of cur-
    rent maturities)
Notes payable

Notes receivable
Operating equipment to be consumed
    beyond 12 months
Operating equipment
Other receivables
Paid-in capital in excess of par
Prepaid expenses
Restricted cash above 12 months
Retained earnings
Short-term investments
Temporary cash investments
Treasury stock
Unclaimed wages

2.3 Based on the balance sheet account balances of the newly created Sense of Taste Restaurant at the end of December 2010, prepare its balance sheet according to the USALI format.

Accounts payable	€ 11,500.00
Accrued expenses	€ 30,850.00
Buildings	€ 175.000.00
Cash	€ 31,500.00
Cash surrender value of life insurance	€ 75.000.00
Current maturities of mortgage payable	€ 15.054.00
Current maturities of notes payable	€ 23.676.00
Furnishings and equipment	€ 160,250.00
Income taxes payable	€ 200.00
Intangible assets	€ 7,560.00
Inventories	€ 17,500.00
Land	€ 5.000.00
Mortgage notes	€ 184,946.00
Notes payable	€ 151,324.00
Operating equipment	€ 6.500.00
Owner's equity	€ 107,500.00
Prepaid expenses	€ 23,190.00
Receivables	€ 2,500.00
Restricted cash	€ 1,050.00

2.4 Using its balance sheet as established in 2.3, describe what type of company you think the Sense of Taste Restaurant is. How could you make the difference?

The profit and loss account statement

3

3.1 Definition and categories of activities
3.2 Formats and content of the profit and loss account statements

The measurement of profit is perhaps the most important function of accounting and all the main stakeholders are interested in knowing how well an organization is performing. The profit and loss account statement shows the flow of activities and transactions between the organization's top line (revenues) and its bottom line (net income). Its purpose is to show managers and investors whether the company made or lost money during the period. Charitable organizations that are required to publish financial statements do not produce profit and loss statements but on the contrary produce a statement that reflects funding sources compared against program expenses, administrative costs, and other operating commitments. Section 3.1 defines the profit and loss statement and introduces the various categories of activities, while section 3.2 shows the formats and content of the profit and loss account statement.

3.1 Definition and categories of activities

The profit and loss statement equally known as the income statement, the statement of earnings, and the statement of operations describes a company's financial performance for a period of time and in many cases it is considered as the most important financial statement. The time covered by this statement usually ends at the balance sheet date. Its main purpose is to provide to the users of the financial statements of a company, information relating to the profitability of the organization for a particular period of time. The profit and loss statement can be prepared on a weekly or monthly basis for internal management use and on a quarterly, semi-annual or annual basis for all the external users.

The major elements of a profit and loss account are:

Under operating activities
- Revenues which represent the amount of assets created during business operations from the delivery or production of goods and services. Revenues are usually presented as sales less all sales discounts, returns and allowances.
- Expenses which represent the amount of assets consumed from the performance of business operations during a period while delivering or producing goods and services. Generally, the major expense item is the cost of the items sold to the customers. Other expenses might include salaries, utilities, supplies, transportation, marketing, insurance, research and development, commissions, rents, interests, repairs and maintenance, depreciation and taxes to list a few.
- Net income or net loss represents the difference between revenues and expenses. If revenues are more than the expenses there is a net income. On the contrary, if the expenses are more than the revenues there is a net loss.

Under non-operating activities
- Gains or other revenues represent what the company makes from activities other than its primary business activity. This could include items such as rents and patents.
- Losses or other expenses represent expenses or losses not related to the primary business operation. For example, a loss caused by an act of nature such as a tornado.

Within the hospitality industry, revenues, gains, expenses, and losses are all reported distinctly from each other. Management is generally held responsible in the first instance for their success in operations determined by revenues and expenses. Management is on the other hand only secondarily held responsible for gains and losses. These gains and losses are generally indicated in the profit and loss statement near the bottom of the statement and just before the income taxes.

Exhibit 3.1 is an extract from the hotelsmag.com site illustrating at the beginning of 2009 the broad profitability situation of hotels across Europe based on a TRI Hospitality Consulting survey.

■ Exhibit 3.1 **Profit continues to fall across Europe**

Profit continues to fall across Europe – Hotels, 2/27/2009 10:05:00 a.m.

The trend of falling occupancy, revenue and profit across key European hotel markets continued during January, according to the latest HotStats survey by TRI Hospitality Consulting.

In Vienna the sample of international branded hotels saw daily profit – expressed as income before fixed charges (IBFC) – decline by nearly two thirds to just €9.80 per available room. In Prague profit more than halved and in Amsterdam the decline was 45.2 per cent. The only city in the survey not to report a double-digit decline in profit was Hamburg.

"There has been considerable supply growth in both Vienna and Prague since January 2008. More than 2,000 extra graded bedrooms entered the Vienna market and at least 800 branded hotel rooms opened in Prague. Combined with the decline in overnights from these cities' key source markets (Germany, the UK, and the US) all of which are now firmly in recession, the growing number of bedrooms is diluting performance," said Jonathan Langston, managing director, TRI Hospitality Consulting.

Vienna payroll exceeds 50 per cent. The factor which pushed Vienna's profitability further into the red was its traditionally high labour costs. Payroll increased 8.3 percentage points to 55.5 per cent of total revenue. In Amsterdam, payroll rose from 37.4 to 43.9 per cent of total revenue.

"The fixed payroll component tends to take up a greater percentage of total revenue at the start of the year when sales are generally at their weakest. This January's year-on-year falls in revenue have heightened this trend further, particularly in Austria which has strong labour laws and a high standard of living," said Langston.

Although relatively high, payroll costs were at their most stable year-on-year in Germany. Berlin and Hamburg both reduced the payroll percentage despite falls in revenue and profit.

London drops room rates: Paris and London reported similar falls in occupancy and profit. Occupancy was down 3.3 percentage points to 70 per cent in London and in Paris down by 3.5 points to 69.3 per cent. Profit fell back by 20.6 per cent in Paris and 21.5 per cent in London. There was greater discounting in the London market, however. Average room rate dropped by 8.4 per cent in the UK capital compared to -3.7 per cent in Paris. Relatively high reductions to rack, corporate, conference and leisure rates meant that London slipped from its historical place as the most profitable city in the survey.

In absolute terms, Paris had the highest average room rate and the best room revenue performance making it number one for profit with daily IBFC of €55.13 per available room.

Source: http://www.hotelsmag.com/article/36402

3.2 Formats and content of profit and loss account statements

A uniform system of accounts is used in the hospitality industry, and it contains detailed information about accounts classification and formats that help in standardizing the accounting system. A uniform system of accounts permits easy comparisons between the results of the various entities that make up the hospitality industry. One of such a system of accounts is called the Uniform System of Accounts for the Lodging Industry (USALI) already introduced in the chapter 2. The USALI is designed to be used much more at the property level instead of the corporate level and it can be adapted to single properties or single units.

In general, the basic profit and loss account statement would look as follows:

Revenues
  minus
Cost of goods sold
  equals
Gross profit
  minus
Overhead expenses
  equals
Net income

On the other hand, based on the USALI, the profit and loss account statement will generally look as shown in the table below:

Revenues
  minus
Direct operating expenses
  equals
Departmental operating income
  minus
Overhead expenses
  equals
Net income

This USALI format introduces the notion of the contribution margin profit and loss account statement. The contribution margin profit and loss account statement emphasizes the classification of costs/expenses into their variable and fixed character. In this format, the departmental operating income (in other words the contribution margin of the department) highlights the proportion of the revenue that is taken up by the direct operating expenses made up of the variables costs of sales as well as the variable operating expenses.

For internal management purposes, the summary operating statement in conformity with the USALI will contain the revenue and expenses lines analyzed between operating periods and including forecasts as shown in exhibit 3.2.

Exhibit 3.2 **Basic profit and loss account statement in conformity with the USALI – internal management's use**

Summary Operating Statement

	Current Period						Year-to-date					
	Actual		Forecast		Prior year		Actual		Forecast		Prior year	
	€	%	€	%	€	%	€	%	€	%	€	%
Revenue												
Rooms												
Food and Beverage												
Other Operated Departments												
Rentals and Other Income												
Total Revenue												
Departmental Expenses												
Rooms												
Food and Beverage												
Other Operated Departments												
Total Departmental Expenses												
Total Departmental Income												
Undistributed Operating Expenses												
Administrative and General												
Sales and Marketing												
Property Operations and Maintenance												
Utilities												
Total Undistributed Expenses												
Gross Operating Profit												
Management Fees												
Income before Fixed Charges												
Fixed charges												
Rent												
Property and other taxes												
Insurance												
Total Fixed Charges												
Net Operating Income												
Less: Replacement Reserves												
Adjusted Net Operating Income												

The USALI emphasizes the reporting of profit and loss statement accounting information based on operating centres. These operating centres are generally those areas that have direct contact, and as such, sales to guests and customers. The overhead expenses in most cases result from undistributed operating expenses, management fees and fixed charges. Exhibit 3.3 shows a basic profit and loss account format of a standard hotel in conformity with the USALI and destined for external users.

The main elements of the profit and loss statement are further explained below:

Revenues (also called turnover)
Generally, revenue or as used in many countries nowadays, turnover, is that income that a company receives from its normal business activities. These business activities result from the sale of goods and services to customers. For some types of businesses, most of their

Exhibit 3.3 Basic profit and loss account statement in conformity with the USALI – external users

Profit and loss account

	Period	
	Current year	**Prior year**
	€	€
Revenue		
Rooms		
Food and Beverage		
Other Operated Departments		
Rentals and Other Income		
Total Revenue		
Expenses		
Rooms		
Food and Beverage		
Other Operated Departments		
Administrative and General		
Sales and Marketing		
Property Operation and Maintenance		
Utilities		
Management Fees		
Rent, Property Taxes, and Insurance		
Interest Expense		
Depreciation and Amortization		
Loss or (Gain) on the Disposition of Assets		
Total Expenses		
Income before Income Taxes		
Income Taxes		
Current		
Deferred		
Total Income Taxes		
Net Income	€	€

revenue results from the sale of goods, for example manufacturing companies. On the other hand, service businesses receive their revenues from rendering services such as a bank. There are hybrid cases however in which the primary business of the organization will contain elements of rendering services and selling goods such as a full service hotel. Revenues are usually presented as sales less all sales discounts, returns and allowances from the related revenues.

Some businesses do equally generate revenues that are incidental to their primary business concerns. Such revenues will be considered as revenues but not as sales. For example in a hotel, revenue generated from the exchange of F & B products and room space will be considered as sales, whereas if this hotel disposes of some of its property this will be considered as revenue but not sales.

It is important to note that sales revenue does not include the sales tax and value added tax (VAT) collected on behalf of the taxation authorities by the company. Companies are normally required to disclose in their notes to the accounting statements information related to the analysis of their turnover. This information should include if this organization carried out its business in more than one class of business, if these classes of business are substantially different from each other. Secondly, it should provide information if these revenues were generated in different geographical markets.

Cost of goods sold (cost of sales)
Cost of sales or cost of goods sold is made up of the direct costs/ expenses attributable to the production of the goods sold by the organization. The accounts included in the calculation of the cost of goods sold differ from one type of organization to another. Within the hospitality industry for example, the cost of goods sold is determined as follows:

Beginning inventory
> plus

Inventory purchases
> equals

Goods available for sale
> minus

Ending inventory
> equals

Costs of goods consumed
> minus

Goods used internally
> equals

Cost of goods sold

Beginning inventory represents the value of the inventory existing in the company at the beginning of the accounting period. Inventory purchases represent the acquisition cost of the goods for sale and this will include all shipping and transportation costs. The ending inventory represents the value of the inventory existing in the company at the end of the accounting period. The category of goods used internally will represent those goods that have been given to a certain class of consumers free of charge. This class of consumers might include employees (employee meals), guests for promotional purposes (promotion for food), entertainers (complimentary food), and other departments of the same company (transfers to the department). It should be noted that while these transfers are deducted from the food department they should be accounted for in the other affected departments of the company. For example, cost of employee meals for the Rooms Department employees will have to be shown as an expense in the Rooms Department.

Other expenses
In this section, still respecting the guidelines of the USALI format, the following major expense categories will be looked into:
- Payroll and related expenses
  This category includes the salaries and wages of employees in their respective departments. This category equally includes all the payroll taxes and related benefits.

- Other departmental expenses
  This category includes only the direct departmental expenses.
  Examples could include cleaning supplies, contract services,
  laundry and dry cleaning, uniforms, commissions, reservations,
  etc.

Departmental income or loss
The departmental income or loss will simply represent the net
revenue of each department minus all related cost of sales, payroll and
related expenses, and other expenses. It will be an income if the result
is positive and a loss if it is negative. This will have to be shown on
each departmental income statement in the organization.

Undistributed operating expenses
As not all departments are revenue generating departments in a
company, certain categories of expenses are generated by departments
that are called service departments. A service department generally
supports the profit centres in their revenue generating activities. There
are generally 4 categories in this section of undistributed operating
expenses which are:
1 Administrative and general expenses
  These include such service areas as the general manager's office and
  the accounting office. Items here will include salaries, wages,
  employee benefits and related payroll expenses, information
  services, professional fees, security, training, credit card
  commissions, etc.
2 Sales and marketing expenses
  These include the salaries, wages, employee benefits and related
  payroll expenses of the employees working in the sales and
  marketing department. Additionally they might contain items like
  sales expenses (contract services, trade shows, complimentary
  services and gifts, printing and stationary, etc). Marketing expenses
  will include items such as agency fees, direct mailing costs, media
  costs, photography, etc.
3 Property and operations maintenance expenses
  These include the salaries, wages, employee benefits and related
  payroll expenses of the property and operations maintenance
  personnel as well as the cost of various supplies used in
  maintaining the buildings, grounds, equipment, and all furniture
  and fixtures.
4 Utility expenses
  These represent the cost of electricity, gas, oil, water and other
  fuels. It should be noted that taxes assessed on utilities are included
  in their costs.

Deducting these undistributed operating expenses from the total
operated departmental incomes will lead to the gross operating profit
(GOP). In cases where there are management fees, deducting these
fees from the GOP will lead to the income before fixed charges (IBFC)
also called the earnings before fixed charges (EBFC).

Fixed charges

These represent overhead expenses which are related to the production capacity of a company and not to its actual level of output. Another term for fixed charges is capacity costs as it relates to the organization capacity to provide its goods and services. They generally include expenses such as rent, property taxes, insurance, depreciation and amortization.

Deducting these fixed charges from the GOP or IBFC results in what is called the net operating income (NOI). In deducting the level of interest expenses from the NOI, results in the income before the gains or loss on the sale of property. This category, in the cases where there were no property transactions, will be exactly equal to the income before taxes (IBT). When the level of interest payments are added to the IBT, it becomes known as the IBIT (income before interests and taxes) or as it is more commonly known as the earnings before interests and taxes (EBIT).

Net income (profit) or loss

The net profit or loss equally known as net income or loss represents the bottom line of the income statement. It represents the absolute difference between all the sources of revenue of the company and all its expenses in a given operational period. If this difference is positive it is called the net income or net profit. If the difference is negative, it is called the net loss.

Principally for companies, the net income is used in two ways. It could be distributed as dividends to the owners of the company and/or maintained within the company as reserves. These reserves are normally noted in the balance sheet at the date ending the accounting period as changes in the Retained Earnings.

Glossary

Cost of goods sold (cost of sales) – this is made up of the direct costs of sales, adjusted for closing inventory, plus the overhead expenses attributable to the production of the F & B products sold by the company.

Departmental income (or loss) – this represents the net revenue of each department minus all related cost of sales, payroll and related expenses, and other expenses. This is an income if the result is positive and a loss if it is negative.

Expenses – these represent the amount of assets consumed during the performance of business operations in a period while delivering or producing goods and services.

Fixed charges – these represent overhead expenses which are related to the production capacity of a company and not to its actual level of output. They are operating expenses that are incurred to provide facilities and organization that are kept in readiness to do business without regard to actual volumes of production and sales. Fixed costs remain relatively constant until changed by managerial decision.

Gains – represent what the company makes from activities other than its primary business activity.

Losses – represent expenses or losses not related to the primary business activity.

Net income – represents the difference between revenues and expenses. If revenues are more than the expenses there is a net income. On the contrary, if the expenses are more than the revenues there is a net loss.

Profit and loss account – this is a statement that shows the flow of activities and transactions between the organization's revenues and its net income.

Revenues – represent the amount of assets created during business operations from the delivery or production of goods and services.

Turnover – see Revenue

Uniform system of accounts for the lodging industry (USALI) – this is a standardized system of accounting used by the lodging industry that provides easy comparison with similar business operations and improves decision making.

Multiple choice questions

3.1 What an organization generates from activities, other than its primary business activity, will be shown in its income statement as:
a expenses
b gains
c losses
d revenues

3.2 The amount of assets consumed during the performance of business operations in a period while delivering or producing goods and services will be shown in the income statement as:
a gains
b losses
c expenses
d revenues

3.3 Which of the following questions cannot be answered when analyzing the information presented in an income statement?
a How much was spent to pay salaries during the period?
b What was the cash balance at the end of the period?
c What was the profit for the period?
d What were the sales for the period?

3.4 Which of the following will not be shown as an undistributed operating expense in an income statement destined for internal purposes and based on the USALI?
a administrative and general expenses
b fixed charges
c property operations and maintenance expenses
d utility costs

3.5 Based on the USALI, payroll and related expenses as shown on the income statement include:
a fringe benefits
b payroll taxes
c salaries and wages
d all of the above

Exercises

3.1 Calculate the gain or loss in the transactions that the Caterer's United Services carried out during 2010 when they had to dispose of two of their old delivery vans. The information related to the transactions is as follows:

a The first van that was bought for €12,500.00 and depreciated to the tune of €10,500.00 was sold at €2,500.00

b The second van that was bought for €15,000.00 and depreciated to the tune of €11,500.00 was sold at €3,250.00

3.2 The owners of the Sweet Sauces Restaurant provide you with the following data for the month of November 2010;

	Food	Beverages
Beginning inventory	€ 7,000.00	€ 2,000.00
Ending inventory	€ 11,000.00	€ 4,500.00
Inventory purchases	€ 54,000.00	€ 22,500.00
Goods used internally	€ 2,500.00	€ 500.00

You are requested to determine the following:

- The beverages available for sale
- The food available for sale
- The cost of food consumed
- The cost of beverage consumed
- The cost of food sold
- The cost of beverage sold

3.3   The Falcon Road stop has provided you with the information below related to their operations of the last three months ending at September 30th 2010. The Falcon Road stop has three profit centres – the rooms department, the food department, and lastly the beverage department. The management of the Falcon Road stop desires to have their end of quarter income statement established according to the rules contained in the USALI for external users as shown in exhibit 3.3. You are as well informed that the average tax rate is 32%.

Establish the income statement.

Account	Account Balance
Administration and general expense	€ 780,000.00
Advertising	€ 195,000.00
Amortization	€ 32,500.00
Beverage department salaries and wages	€ 260,000.00
Beverage revenues	€ 1,300,000.00
Cost of beverages sold	€ 390,000.00
Cost of food sold	€ 1,170,000.00
Depreciation	€ 325,000.00
Dividend income	€ 97,500.00
Food department salaries and wages	€ 1,040,000.00
Food revenues	€ 3,510,000.00
Franchise fees	€ 162,500.00
Heating expense	€ 260,000.00
Insurance	€ 130,000.00
Interest expense	€ 552,500.00
POM contact expense	€ 390,000.00
Management fees	€ 325,000.00
Utility cost	€ 195,000.00
Property taxes	€ 325,000.00
Room revenues	€ 6,500,000.00
Rooms department allowances	€ 13,000.00
Rooms department salaries and wages	€ 975,000.00
Supplies rooms department	€ 520,000.00
Supplies beverage department	€ 97,500.00
Supplies food department	€ 260,000.00

3.4 Using the data provided by the Falcon Road stop in 3.3, establish the summary income statement destined for internal management purposes, in conformity with the USALI and as shown in exhibit 3.2. Limit the summary income statement only to the current and actual activity levels.

Adjustments to the balance sheet and the profit and loss account

4

4.1 Accounting conventions – accruals and recognition
4.2 Adjusting the accounts

Quite often, financial statements will be presented using trial balances. These trial balances will be accompanied with a number of adjustments that have to be made in order to arrive at the definitive statements. Although much more relevant within the domain of financial accounting, this chapter will briefly explain some of the underlying principles and conventions related to making such adjustments. Section 4.1 discusses the basic accruals and recognition accounting conventions while section 4.2 shows the major examples of account adjustments. Those interested in furthering their knowledge within the area could consult any financial accounting textbook.

4.1 Accounting conventions – accruals and recognition

Accounting conventions are used when determining the amounts at which items should be stated in the financial statements, or if these items should be stated at all. There are two broad conventions which are:

The accruals convention
This is also called the matching convention, it is very important in the calculation of profit. It simply indicates that the effects of a transaction should be recognized in the accounting period in which this transaction took place. In some cases, this is not necessarily going to be the same period in which the transaction is invoiced or settled.

The recognition convention
This is also called the realization convention comes into play when income and expense items are brought into the accounting statements. Generally, the point at which items are recognized is straight forward in terms of cash sales. However, credit sales are not so straight forward. As a result of this, it should be noted that the total recorded for sales in an accounting period will not necessarily be equal to the cash received. Amounts due at the end of the accounting period will be considered as accounts receivables and as such included in the balance sheet. On the side of expenses for example, goods received till the end of the accounting period are considered as purchases. However, all amounts still to be paid in respect of the acquisition of these goods at the year's end will be considered as accounts payable and included in the balance sheet.

4.2 Adjusting the accounts

For the definitive statements to be made, the trial balances will have to be adjusted. The adjustments will generally impact stock, accounts receivable, depreciation and amortization, return of goods, discounts and delivery charges. The structure of the subsections is as follows:

4.2.1	Stock (inventory)
4.2.2	Accounts receivable
4.2.3	Depreciation and amortization
4.2.4	Return of goods
4.2.5	Discounts
4.2.6	Delivery charges

4.2.1 Stock (inventory)

Generally the value of inventory at the end of the year is equal to the number of items in stock multiplied by the value of these individual items. The number of items in stock is usually assessed by counting these items on the stock taking day which could be the last day of the accounting period. The value of stock is generally affected by certain other factors such as accidental damage or loss in quality.

The basic rule is that inventory should be valued at the lower of costs and net realizable value. The net realizable value is the amount for which the inventory could be sold minus all incidental expenses related to its sale. Comparing the costs and the net realizable value is important to ensure that the balance sheet is not going to contain inventory at overvalued amounts.

Inventory at any time does not constitute a large part of the current assets in most hotels. Using the periodic inventory accounting system, an inventory count is periodically made to determine the level of inventory. Under a periodic inventory system, the purchases of supplies are recorded by debiting the supplies purchases account. Exhibit 4.1 is a worked example of how inventory is determined in a periodic inventory system.

■ Exhibit 4.1 **Worked example of how inventory is determined in a periodic inventory system**

As office manager at the Afilen Hotel that uses the periodic inventory system to evaluate their office supplies, Jan Smits was asked by the accountant on December 31st 2009 to carry out the end-of-year inventory count of office supplies. The count showed that available office supplies were worth €4,000. Jan equally noted that the opening balance of the office supplies account as of January 1st 2009 was €5,600. In the course of the year 2009 Jan had made purchases of office supplies worth €28,000. To determine the cost of office supplies used in 2009 the following schedule can be used to solve for the unknown in it (quantity of supplies used in 2009):

Opening balance (01/01/2009)	€	5,600
add purchases (all of 2009)	€	28,000
equals available supplies (for the year 2009)	€	33,600
less supplies used (to be determined)		unknown
equals ending balance (31/12/2009)	€	4,000

Since it is clear that the available supplies during 2009 was €33,600 and the year ended with only €4,000, then it means that supplies used in 2009 was €33,600 − €4,000 = €29,600

The periodic system of inventory has a major drawback in the sense that the management might not have a complete administrative overview of what is in stock. This drawback can be eliminated by the use of a perpetual inventory system in which the inventory account will be debited immediately every time inventory is purchased, and also immediately crediting the inventory account every time a sale is made or inventory is issued out of the storerooms. The choice between using either a periodic or perpetual inventory system is often hampered by the high costs involved in instituting a perpetual inventory system. Further discussion on this issue is beyond the scope of this chapter.

4.2.2 Accounts receivable

Accounts receivable result from credit sales accorded by the organization to its clients or customers. The recording takes place when the transaction is recognized (matching principle). That is at the time of sale of the product or the rendering of the service. However in real life, there is always a time lag between the sale of the product or delivery of the service, and the reception of the payment for the product or service. Credit sales generally entail a risk. There is a risk that the client or customer might not be able to fully or partially pay for the products or services.

Accounts receivable thus represents the total value of all unpaid sales invoices. An accumulation of unpaid sales invoices generally causes problems to business organizations be they large or small. More large organizations will often have their own credit management departments whereas smaller organizations may have one employee taking care of the management of the credit invoices. Both small and large organizations depend on the size of their accounts receivables and depending on the severity of the impact on their business, might use external consultants and agencies to help them reduce their accounts receivable balances.

To ensure that the balance sheet indicates acceptable figures, the amounts of accounts receivable should be indicated in their recoverable amounts. For this to be done, allowances are normally created. There are basically two types of allowances used to adjust accounts receivable amounts:
- The Allowance for Bad Debts: created in such situations whereby there is a certainty that they will be unable to collect these particular debts.
- The Allowance for Doubtful Accounts: created in such situations whereby they think they might still get back some of their debts whatever part that may be.

To take care of these allowances, provisions are made which are then deducted from the accounts receivable end of year figures. Adjustments to the accounts receivable account is illustrated in exhibit 4.2.

■ Exhibit 4.2 **Steps in adjusting for bad debts and doubtful accounts**

At the end of any accounting period, an adjusting entry needs to be made to account for uncollectible receivables. The following three steps outline a widely adopted approach to accounting for bad and doubtful debts.

Step 1   Create a provision by periodically updating the records to reflect and provide for the problem of potentially non-collectible accounts. If every month credit sales come up to about €40,000 and historically the company has an uncollectible rate of 1.5%, then an amount of €600 should be credited monthly into the allowance for doubtful accounts

Step 2   Adjust for accounts that are definitely bad. If for example one of the debtors becomes bankrupt, the company can no longer expect to receive the payment. In this case the adjustment will be carried out by debiting the allowance for doubtful accounts and crediting the accounts receivable account

Step 3   Carry out an end of year adjustment. If at the end of the year it is realized that the provisions for doubtful accounts made in the course of the year were insufficient to effectively cover for the uncollectible debts, then an appropriate adjustment as in Step 1 above have to be carried out to compensate for the difference. The exact opposite adjustment will have to be made in the instance whereby the provisions turned out to be far more than what the real situation of uncollectible debts were.

4.2.3   Depreciation and amortization

Based on the matching or accruals convention, adjustments for the depreciation and amortization of fixed assets can be made. Fixed assets generally have an economic useful life, at the end of which they will have to be replaced. The cost of using the fixed asset will have to be matched based on the matching convention in the accounting period. There are generally some obvious costs such as insurance and repairs but some are not so obvious. This includes the impact of how much value of the fixed asset is being used in the process within the accounting period. The value attributed to this use of the asset is called the depreciation of the asset.

In exhibit 4.3 two of the commonly used depreciation methods are explained.

■ Exhibit 4.3 **Two common depreciation methods**

To illustrate the commonly used methods of depreciation, assume that the Afilen Hotel has just acquired a new cold storage facility at a cost of €56,000. This new equipment has an assumed economically useful life of 7 years and it is expected that at the end of the 7 years they will be able to dispose of it through a second-hand dealer and receive €12,000 for it. This amount of €12,000 is commonly called the salvage value.

1 **The straight line or linear method of depreciation**
In this most widely used method, the original acquisition cost of the equipment (or other fixed asset) minus any expected salvage value is spread in an equal manner over the life of the asset. The formula is:

Annual Depreciation Charge =

$$\frac{\text{Acquisition value of equipment} - \text{salvage value}}{\text{Estimated life of equipment}}$$

As such, the annual depreciation charge for the new cold storage facility will be €6,285.71 calculated as follows:

$$\text{Annual Depreciation Charge} = \frac{56,000 - 12,000}{7}$$

2 The declining balance method of depreciation

In this method, the company assumes a certain yearly percentage as usage of the equipment and each year, that percentage is applied to the value of the equipment to determine the depreciation charge for the year. In this method, the annual depreciation charge reduces per equipment because the net book value (which is the difference between the acquisition cost of the equipment and all accumulated depreciation on the equipment till that date) reduces as time goes by.

Now, if the Afilen Hotel used the declining balance method of depreciation, then the annual depreciation charges will look as shown in the table below:

Years	Opening Book Value	Depreciation at 25%	Ending Book Value	Accumulated Depreciation
1	€ 56,000.00	€ 14,000.00	€ 42,000.00	€ 14,000.00
2	€ 42,000.00	€ 10,500.00	€ 31,500.00	€ 24,500.00
3	€ 31,500.00	€ 7,875.00	€ 23,625.00	€ 32,375.00
4	€ 23,625.00	€ 5,906.25	€ 17,718,75	€ 38,281.25
5	€ 17,718.75	€ 4,429.69	€ 13,289.06	€ 42,710.94
6	€ 13,289.06	€ 3,322,27	€ 9,966.80	€ 46,033.20
7	€ 9,966.80	€ 2,491.70	€ 7,475,10	€ 48,524.90

Note how the accumulated depreciation on the equipment rises as the years go by and how the salvage value was not taken into consideration in the declining balance method.

Based on the matching convention, the total depreciation for the accounting period should be set off against the sales of the accounting period. This is noted in the income statement as an expense. Since depreciation has an effect on the value of the fixed assets in that it reduces this value as time goes by, it is therefore deducted from the initial values of the fixed assets every year. The accumulation of these deductions is noted in the balance sheet as accumulated depreciation. Amortization, which is accounted for in a similar way like depreciation is applicable only to intangible fixed assets.

4.2.4 Returns of goods

There are cases in business transactions when errors do occur and have to be returned. This could be like a customer buying a pair of shoes for a friend and it turned out that the size was inappropriate or a company ordering some parts for its kitchen equipment which did not fit. In such instances, there are implications for the profit and loss account statement of the parties concerned in the transaction.

In cases where such returns occur frequently, this leads to an accumulation in the course of the accounting period. As such, sales return have to be deducted from the sales of the period as well as purchase returns must be deducted from the purchases of the period before the profit and loss statement is established.

4.2.5   Discounts

Discounts are generally reductions in prices attributed to customers. In normal business these discounts are of two types (trade discounts and financial discounts).

Trade discounts
Trade discounts relate to discounts given to loyal customers or when customers make large purchases. With trade discounts, no special adjustments need to be made to the profit and loss account statement because the prices already indicate the value of either the sales or purchases made by the company or clients.

Financial discounts
Financial discounts result from the fact that businesses provide credit facilities to their customers. One element of providing a credit facility is to determine the possible date of repayment. Whatever the standard used by the company in terms of days, it might, in order to incite the debtors to pay earlier provide them with a financial discount. For example, regular payments are required within 60 days but if this bill is settled within 30 days pay 2% less. However, it should be noted that the costs of such discounts should be carefully weighed against the benefits of receiving the sales revenue earlier. Unlike trade discounts, financial discounts permit that payments will be registered in the balance sheet as accounts receivable pending payment and managed just as indicated in subsection 4.2.2.

4.2.6   Delivery charges

In instances where businesses are called upon to incur the expense of distributing their products to customers, they have to account for these distribution expenses. As such, these expenses will be shown in the expenses section of the profit and loss account statement. These delivery charges might include road costs, handling costs, rail costs, excise duties, and import duties.

Glossary

Accounting conventions – are accounting agreements, principles or statements, either expressed or implied, that are used to solve given types of accounting problems. Placing debits on the right and credits on the left of an account is an example of an accounting convention.

Accruals convention – is the convention that indicates that the effects of a transaction should be recognized in the period in which the transaction took place. This might not necessarily be the same period in which the transaction is invoiced or settled.

Amortization – is the expense charged by the company to compensate for the cost of an intangible asset over its expected life.

Depreciation – is the expense charged by the company to compensate for the cost of a plant or machine over its useful life taking into account wear and tear, obsolescence, and salvage value.

Discounts – these are the reductions in prices commonly attributed to customers by businesses.

Inventory – these are the raw materials and items available for sale or in the process of being made ready for sale.

Matching convention – see accruals convention

Realization convention – see recognition convention

Recognition convention – is the convention that indicates that revenues should be recognized at the time the goods are sold and the services are rendered. Due to the existence of credit sales, the total sales in an accounting period will be different from the cash received. Amounts due at the end of the accounting period will be considered as accounts receivables and included in the balance sheet while amounts still to be paid at the year's end will be considered as accounts payable and included in the balance sheet.

Multiple choice questions

4.1 The accounting convention that indicates that a transaction should be recognized in the period in which it took place is:
a the accruals convention
b the realization convention
c the recognition convention
d none of the above

4.2 The recognition convention is also called the:
a the accruals convention
b the matching convention
c the realization convention
d none of the above

4.3 The allowance for bad debts is created in situations whereby
a the company has cleared the bad debts from their records
b the company thinks they might collect a part of the debt
c there is a certainty that the company will be unable to collect the debt
d none of the above

4.4 Adjustments for depreciation and amortization are made based on the following convention:
a the matching convention
b the realization convention
c the recognition convention
d none of the above

4.5 The salvage value is not taken into consideration in the following common depreciation method:
a declining balance method of depreciation
b linear method of depreciation
c straight line method of depreciation
d none of the above

Exercises

4.1 The management of the Rolling Hills Hotel uses the periodic inventory system to evaluate their guest supplies. On December 31st 2010, the balance showed an amount of €8,000. You are informed that on December 31st 2009, the balance was €10,300. Guest supplies purchases in 2010 came up to a total of €47,250. You are requested to determine the following:

a the available guest supplies for the year 2010
b the guest supplies used in 2010

4.2 New equipment was purchased at a cost of €32,000 and it has an assumed economic life of 7 years. It is expected that at the end of its economically useful life the company can receive €2,800 when disposing of the equipment. You are asked to calculate the annual depreciation charge for the equipment using the straight line method of depreciation.

4.3 Use the information that is contained in 4.2. You are informed that the company applies an annual depreciation proportion for such equipment of 32%. Establish the annual depreciation schedule over the seven years of its economically useful life using the declining balance method of depreciation.

4.4 A motel uses the periodic inventory system to evaluate their office supplies. You are provided with the following information:

Purchases for the year	€ 26,000
Supplies used during the year	€ 34,200
Balance at year's end	€ 2,800

You are requested to determine the following:

a the balance at the beginning of the year for office supplies
b the available office supplies for the year

The cash flow statement (also called the statement of cash flow)

5

5.1   Cash in the business
5.2   Establishing cash flow statements
5.3   A worked example in the establishment of the SCF using the indirect method

Companies can only survive if they have enough cash in hand to be able to take care of all their expenses. Cash is considered as the lifeblood of any business. Users of financial statements who assess only the statement of profit and loss to try and determine the financial health of the company might later on realize that their assessment may have been incorrect. Profitable companies have been known to have suddenly failed because they did not adequately manage their cash flows. An understanding of the importance and management of cash is a must if any company's management would want to avoid sudden liquidity problems. Section 5.1 discusses the place of cash in a business, while at the same time differentiating profits from cash. Section 5.2 provides the rules in the establishment of the cash flow statement, while section 5.3 is a worked example of the cash flow statement using one of the well established methods.

5.1 Cash in the business

Cash is money, in the form of notes and coins, which constitutes payment for goods or services at the time of their purchase or consumption. Cash is not only cash in hand but also deposits and overdrafts which are commonly called cash equivalents. All transactions whether they are settled immediately or settled in the future are ultimately conducted by cash or cash equivalents. Just like all other assets, cash is an asset with the same properties like other assets, and also many more. The structure of the subsections is as follows:

5.1.1	The importance of cash in the business
5.1.2	Differentiating profits from cash
5.1.3	The need for cash flow statements
5.1.4	The categories of activities

5.1.1 The importance of cash in the business

Cash in general represents money in its physical form such as coins and bank notes. Additionally, in businesses it may refer to currency or currency equivalents that can be easily assessed. Cash and cash equivalents generally comprise the most liquid current assets. Cash equivalents are current assets that are readily convertible into cash, for example, money market holdings, treasury bills, short-term government bonds, marketable securities and commercial papers. Cash equivalents are characterized by their short-term existence maturing within 3 months. Cash and cash equivalents form the most basic business resource and without them, transactions would be very difficult to complete. In the absence of cash it would be virtually impossible to pay creditors, to buy inventory and to invest in fixed assets.

Cash is generally generated from the following sources:

- Cash generated from the business itself through its sales
- Cash made available to the business by the owners
- Cash borrowed from third parties, which could include individuals, lending institutions and other businesses

Cash flows (also called net cash flows) represent the net balance between amounts of cash received in the organization (cash inflows) and the cash paid by the organization (cash outflows) during a period of time. Cash inflows represent increases in cash to the organization whereas cash outflows represent decreases in cash to the organization. Net cash flows represent the net effect of cash inflows and outflows.

Profitable businesses are expected to generate enough cash for their day to day operating activities. However, some businesses can be profitable but find themselves short of cash. A better understanding of this paradox would entail an understanding of the principles of working capital management, which is discussed in chapter 8.

5.1.2 Differentiating profits from cash

Over time, profitable businesses are able to generate enough cash. In the short term however, profits are not equal to cash. Based on the matching principle, costs are matched against the revenues they help to generate. As a result of this, income and costs that have not been received or paid in the form of cash can be recognized. An example is annual depreciation and amortization allocations are deducted in the establishment of the net income despite the fact that these do not entail any outward movements in cash.

In situations of the acquisition of fixed assets, cash can be used but this may have no immediate and direct effect on the income statement. For example, purchasing an item of machinery, cash as a current asset item will be used and in the balance sheet this will be replaced by the creation of a fixed asset item. This has no immediate impact on profit, though over time this fixed asset item will be reduced as it is depreciated.

To illustrate this difference between profit and cash, let's use the following example. A company purchases a catering van that will be used for 5 years at a cost of €10,000.00 and the company uses straight line depreciation method. The impact on cash would be a reduction of €10,000.00 and fixed assets will increase by the acquisition value of the van of €10,000.00. There will be no immediate impact on profit. Over the years, there will be an allocation to depreciation of €2,000.00 per year in the income statement but this will have no effect on the cash levels.

5.1.3 The need for cash flow statements

The cash flow statement like the income statement is established over a certain period. The SCF reflects the flow of money in to and out of a business over time. Unlike the balance sheet and income statement which are based on accrual accounting, the SCF is based on actual cash flows. The primary function of the SCF is to provide needed information to concerned stakeholders – especially investors, suppliers, and creditors, about where the money in the business comes from and how it is used. The SCF excludes transactions that do not directly affect the movements in cash.

The importance of the SCF can be summarized as follows:

- Shows the organization's ability to generate positive future cash flows. Despite the fact that the SCF is historical in nature, it at least provides information on how the organization generated its cash in the past which could be used to evaluate the organization's ability to generate cash in the future.
- Shows the organization's ability to honour its obligations to its debtors. By providing information on the organization's liquidity and solvency, concerned stakeholders will be better placed to make decisions on their future transactions with the organization.

- Shows the difference between the organization's profit and its cash movements. The SCF easily shows the sources of cash within a company as it displays such information under the 3 headings of direct operating activities, investing activities and financing activities. Concerned stakeholders will be much more interested in organizations that generated most of their cash from their primary operating activities.
- Shows the effect of both cash and non-cash financing and investing activities during the accounting period.
- Highlights the comparability of different organizations' operating performance in eliminating the effects of different accounting methods. This results from the fact that the SCF is established according to the 3 major categories of activities – operating, investing, and financing activities.

Exhibit 5.1 illustrates how important cash is to businesses without which they will be unable to carry out their day to day activities.

Exhibit 5.1 **The importance of cash**

Topshop billionaire hunts a bargain in Iceland

Robert Booth, The Guardian, Monday 13 October 2008

For retail magnate Sir Philip Green, the rationale for his weekend shopping trip to Iceland to buy debts held by the country's collapsed banks should be obvious.

"If you're on your way home and you go past a house with a sign outside saying 'half price', you're going to knock on the door, aren't you?" he said yesterday.

The Topshop owner jetted to Iceland last Friday to negotiate a deal with the stricken Icelandic retail investor Baugur. It could deliver him, at a big discount, stakes in or control of high-street brands including House of Fraser, Mappin & Webb, Oasis, Warehouse and Whistles. If it comes off, shoppers will be able to throw a stone on London's Oxford Street and be pretty sure it will hit a Green-owned store.

As his advisers tried to untangle Baugur's web of debts and holdings, Green told the Guardian yesterday that the dynamic behind the deal was simple: "There's a buyer and there's a seller and that's how business has always been done. It's just that there are not many buyers now."

Green, 56, is one of the few tycoons with the funds to spare. With a personal fortune estimated at more than £4.3bn by the Sunday Times rich list, he is Britain's ninth wealthiest man. He expects a significant discount on debts that he said yesterday could be worth £1bn to £2bn.

His proposal may appeal to Iceland's authorities because it would inject a substantial amount of foreign currency into the country's monetary system. With most banks and private investors unable to raise funds, Green's move has highlighted the power of cash-rich individuals in the current climate.

Green denied he was preying on a crippled investor, and said that the deal could help prop up confidence on Britain's high street, which is facing a recession.

"It's not my fault they have to sell," said Green. "I don't want to see any of these brands fail. If something happens to shock the high street that may get out of control. We don't want a major retail accident."

He said the deal would take up to 48 hours to complete. ∎

5.1.4 **Categories of activities**

The SCF is split into 3 major categories of activities which are operating activities, investing activities and financing activities as the major areas of activities. However, some non-cash activities are also taken into consideration and must be included in the footnotes to the SCF.

Operating activities

The first sub-heading in the SCF is the net cash from operating activities. Operating activities include the production, sales and delivery of the organization's products and services as well as the collection of payments from its customers or clients. These represent the principal revenue producing activities of the organization and those other activities that do not have an investing or financing character.

Operating activities would include transactions related to revenues (cash inflows) and expenses (cash outflows) linked to the primary activity of the organization. Cash inflows for a hospitality organization might include the following: sale of food, beverages and other goods, receipts on services to guests and interest and dividend income to the organization. Cash outflows on the other hand would include payments for inventory, salaries, wages, taxes, interests, etc.

Investing activities

Investing activities generally relate to the acquisition and disposal of property and equipment as well as short-term investments (marketable securities). Examples of investing activities are the purchase of any asset which will lead to cash outflows, as well as loans made to third parties will also lead to cash outflows. Investing activities are generally much easier to deal with as they affect the balance sheet and the cash flow in the same way. Most investing activities lead to cash outflows only. However there are some exceptions when the company for example disposes of its property and equipment. In such situations cash inflows will be created.

Financing activities

Financing activities include the cash inflows from investors and shareholders, and cash outflows to the shareholders in the form of dividends. These relate to cash flows raised by the issue of shares, debentures, loans, etc., and cash flows used to redeem shares or debentures or pay back long term debt. Summarily, financing activities relate to anything that has an impact on the long term financing of the organization. Examples of financing activities cash flows are:

- proceeds from the issue of shares;
- proceeds from the issue of short term or long term debts;
- payments of dividends;
- repayment of debt principal including capital leases; and
- payments for the repurchase of capital stock

Recognition of non cash activities

These non cash activities are to be included in the footnotes of the SCF. These non cash activities normally have an impact on the financing and investing activities. They should be noted because such non cash activities will have influences on the future cash flows of the organization. Examples of non cash activities are:

- the conversion of liabilities to equity;
- leasing an asset to purchase it eventually;
- exchanging non cash assets or liabilities for other non cash assets or liabilities; and
- issuing shares in exchange for assets

5.2　Establishing cash flow statements

In order to be able to adequately establish a SCF, it is necessary to have the following documents and information:

- The income statement for the period concerned
- The statement of retained earnings for the period concerned
- The balance sheet established at the date beginning the period concerned
- The balance sheet established at the date ending the period concerned
- Details to all transactions that affected all fixed asset elements of the organization in the period between the two balance sheets.

When all of the above documents, statements and information are in place, the SCF is then established through a 4 step approach as shown in the subsections below

5.2.1	Determine the net cash flow from operating activities
5.2.2	Determine the net cash flow from investing activities
5.2.3	Determine the net cash flow from financing activities
5.2.4	Collate the three net cash flows into the SCF

5.2.1　Determine the net cash flow from operating activities

To determine the net cash flow from operating activities, two methods are used, which are the direct method and the indirect method.

The direct method
The direct method requires bringing together the beginning cash level to the ending cash level. This is done by reporting the major categories of cash inflows and cash outflows. Under the direct method, cash and bank accounts are analyzed to identify cash flows during the period. The cash flows can equally be determined using a worksheet for each major account and by eliminating the effects of accrual basis accounting. This will permit the establishment of the net cash effect of that account during the period.

Examples of items that will be included are:

Cash received from customers:

Action	Item	Where found
Start with	Net sales (revenues)	Income statement
Add	Accounts receivable	Initial balance sheet
Deduct	Accounts receivable	Ending balance sheet
Equals	Cash received from customers	

Cash paid to employees:

Action	Item	Where found
Start with	Salaries and wages	Income statement
Add	Salaries and wages payable	Initial balance sheet
Deduct	Salaries and wages payable	Ending balance sheet
Equals	Cash paid to employees	

Cash used to pay for inventory:

Action	Item	Where found
Start with	Inventory	Ending balance sheet
Deduct	Inventory	Initial balance sheet
Add	Accounts payable	Initial balance sheet
Deduct	Accounts payable	Ending balance sheet
Equals	Cash used to pay for inventory	

Cash used to pay interest:

Action	Item	Where found
Start with	Interest expense	Income statement
Add	Interest payable	Initial balance sheet
Deduct	Interest payable	Ending balance sheet
Equals	Cash used to pay interest	

Cash used to pay taxes:

Action	Item	Where found
Start with	Tax expense	Income statement
Add	Taxes payable	Initial balance sheet
Deduct	Taxes payable	Ending balance sheet
Equals	Cash used to pay taxes	

Cash used to pay for operating expenses:

Action	Item	Where found
Start with	Operating expenses	Income statement
Deduct	Depreciation	Income statement
Add or deduct	Increase or decrease in prepaid expenses	Both balance sheets
Add or deduct	Decrease or increase in accrued expenses	Both balance sheets
Equals	Cash used to pay for operating expenses	

Using the direct method the sums of all the totals are reported as cash flows from operating activities in its section of the SCF. Similar types of calculations are used to determine the cash flows to be reported in the investing activities section and the financing activities section of the SCF.

The indirect method

The indirect method of establishing the net cash flow from operating activities requires bringing together the beginning cash level to the ending cash level but starts with the net income for the period concerned. The net income is then adjusted for non cash movements found in the income statement. The most common non cash item that is deducted to determine net income is depreciation.

Depreciation is thus added to net income in calculating the net cash flow from operating activities. The general principle in establishing the operating activities cash flow using the indirect method is to reverse out entries to income and expense accounts that have no cash movement implications, and show the relevant changes to the net working capital. Such movements that affect net income but do not represent cash flows could be for example incomes earned but not yet received, accrued expenses, amortization of prepaid expenses, and depreciation and amortization.

The basic rule of thumb in assessing the changes in working capital is shown in exhibit 5.2:

Exhibit 5.2 Rule of thumb in assessing changes in working capital for SCF establishment using the indirect method

	Changes in the account balance during the accounting period	
	If the account balance increases	If the account balance decreases
Current assets	Deduct the change from the net income	Add the change to the net income.
Current liabilities	Add the change to the net income.	Deduct the change from the net income

Using the indirect method, the operating activities section of the SCF will be determined as such:
- Net income as derived from the income statement
- Plus all entries to expense accounts that do not represent cash flows
- Less all entries to income accounts that do not represent cash flows
- Equals cash flow before the changes in working capital
- Plus or minus the changes in working capital as shown in the rule of thumb above

This will then result in the establishment of cash provided or used in the operating activities. The cash flows from investing activities and financing activities will then be presented in the same manner as under the direct method.

5.2.2   Determine the net cash flow from investing activities

In determining the net cash flow from investing activities, care should be taken to make sure that all information related to the acquisition and disposal of property and equipment as well as short term investments are accounted for.

5.2.3 Determine the net cash flow from financing activities

In determining the net cash flow from financing activities, emphasis is laid on changes in the long term liabilities and owners' equity accounts. As such, all information related to financing activities such as the issue of shares, debentures, loans, and cash flows used to redeem shares or debentures or pay back long term debt should be taken into consideration.

5.2.4 Collate all the previous 3 net cash flows into the definitive SCF

Net operating cash flow
  plus
Net investing cash flow
  plus
Net financing cash flow
  equals
Net cash flow for the period
  plus
Beginning cash balance
  equals
Ending cash balance

In using either the direct or indirect method to establish the net cash flow from operating activities the net cash flow is expected to be the same. Accounting standard boards normally requires companies to use the direct method. In practice however, since the information needed while using the indirect method is much more easily available to the companies, most company management prefer using the indirect method.

The next section provides a worked example on the establishment of a SCF.

5.3 A worked example in the establishment of the SCF using the indirect method

The financial statements of the Skyline Hotel for the years 2007 and 2008 are provided below with some additional information. With this information, the SCF of the Skyline Hotel for the year 2008 will be developed. In addition to the financial statements below, the Skyline Hotel in the course of the year 2008 carried out the following transactions that will be significant in determining the SCF:
· Investments of an initial value of €125,000 were sold for €375,000 resulting in a gain on the sale of investments of €250,000
· All investment and equipment purchases during the year were made with cash.
· There was the conversion of long-term liabilities of €625,000 into capital shares in a non-cash transaction. There was no other issue of shares as well as no repurchase of shares.

Comparative balance sheets of the Skyline Hotel for the years ending December 31st 2007 and 2008

Skyline Hotel
Balance sheets

December 31, 2007 and 2008	2007	2008
Assets		
Current assets		
Cash	€ 12,500	€ 25,000
Accounts receivable	€ 75,000	€ 65,000
Inventory	€ 25,000	€ 30,000
Total current assets	**€ 112,500**	**€ 120,000**
Investments	**€ 125,000**	**€ 750,000**
Property and equipment:		
Land	€ 500,000	€ 500,000
Building	€ 25,000,000	€ 25,000,000
Equipment	€ 2,500,000	€ 2,750,000
Less: Accumulated depreciation	(€ 12,500,000)	(€ 13,750,000)
Total property and equipment	**€ 15,500,000**	**€ 14,500,000**
Total assets	**€ 15,737,500**	**€ 15,370,000**
Liabilities and owners' equity		
Current liabilities:		
Accounts payable	€ 15,000	€ 16,250
Accrued wages	€ 10,000	€ 11,250
Income taxes payable	€ 17,500	€ 15,000
Dividends payable	€ 25,000	€ 37,500
Total current liabilities	**€ 67,500**	**€ 80,000**
Long-term liabilities	€ 11,250,000	€ 9,375,000
Total liabilities	**€ 11,317,500**	**€ 9,455,000**
Owners' equity		
Capital	€ 2,500,000	€ 3,125,000
Retained earnings	€ 1,920,000	€ 2,790,000
Total owners' equity	**€ 4,420,000**	**€ 5,915,000**
Total liabilities and owners' equity	**€ 15,737,500**	**€ 15,370,000**

The condensed income statement of the Skyline Hotel for the year 2008

Sales	€	17,500,000
Cost of goods sold	€	2,500,000
Payroll expenses	€	6,125,000
Other expenses	€	6,000,000
Depreciation expense	€	1,250,000
Income taxes	€	625,000
Gain on the sale of investments	€	250,000
Net income	€	**1,250,000**

The Statement of retained earnings of the Skyline Hotel for 2008

Net income	€	1,250,000
Retained earnings – 12/31/2007	€	1,920,000
Dividends declared	€	380,000
Retained earnings – 12/31/2008	€	2,790,000

Using the indirect method, follow the four steps.

Step 1 Determine the net cash flows from operating activities
Using the indirect method, commence with the net income (taken from the income statement) of €1,250,000. Adjust this figure with items found in the income statement that did not provide or use cash. In this case, adjust for the depreciation expense (€1,250,000) and the gain on the sale of investment (€250,000) as follows:

Net Income		€ 1,250,000
Add the depreciation expense since it was subtracted in the income statement to arrive at the net income	+	€ 1,250,000
Deduct the gain on the sale of investments as this is an investment activity (to be reviewed later on)	–	€ 250,000

Proceed with the adjustments of both the current asset and current liability accounts that changed during the period as per the balance sheet information and following the basic rule of thumb. Note that since it is the change in the cash account that is being established, it is excluded in these adjustments.

Accounts receivable declined from €75,000 to €65,000 between 2007 and 2008. As a current asset, following the rule of thumb, the positive difference must then be added to the net income	+ €	10,000
Inventory increased between 2007 and 2008 by €5,000 and as such will be deducted	– €	5,000
Accounts payable increased between 2007 and 2008 by €1,250 and as this is a current liability, it will be added to the net income following the rule of thumb	+ €	1,250
Similarly accrued wages increased by €1,250 and will also be added to the net income	+ €	1,250
Finally income taxes payable decreased by €2,500 and as per the rule will be deducted from the net income	– €	2,500

Combining all of these adjustments will lead to the net cash flow from operating activities of the Skyline Hotel for 2008

Net cash flow from operating activities		
Net income		€ 1,250,000
Adjustments to reconcile net income to cash flows from operating activities		
Depreciation	€ 1,250,000	
Gain on sale of investments	(€ 250,000)	
Decrease in accounts receivable	€ 10,000	
Increase in inventory	(€ 5,000)	
Increase in accounts payable	€ 1,250	
Increase in accrued wages	€ 1,250	
Decrease in income taxes payable	(€ 2,500)	€ 1,005,000
Net cash flow from operating activities		**€ 2,255,000**

Step 2 Determine the net cash flow from investing activities

Based on the additional information at the beginning of this example, proceeds from the sale of investments came up to €375,000. This will be considered as a positive investing activity cash inflow.

A look at the balance sheet equally reveals that investments changed between 2007 and 2008 from €125,000 to €750,000. For the Skyline Hotel to have arrived at such investment levels at the end of 2008, they used up cash to acquire new investments to the sum of €625,000. Note equally that from the additional information; investments worth €125,000 were sold, indicating that an additional investment worth €125,000 would have been bought using cash to the tune of €125,000. Summing these figures together (€125,000 + €625,000), leads to the total usage of cash in 2008 for the purchase of new investments by the Skyline Hotel of €750,000.

Finally, the balance sheet of the Skyline Hotel reveals that equipment increased between 2007 and 2008 by €250,000. This equally indicates use of cash for the purchase of the new equipment.

Collating the above figures leads to the net cash flow from investing activities:

Sale of investments (a cash inflow)	€ 375,000
Purchase of investments (a cash outflow)	(€ 750,000)
Purchase of equipment (a cash outflow)	(€ 250,000)
Net cash flow from investing activities	**(€ 625,000)**

Step 3 Determine the net cash flow from financing activities

The balance sheet of the Skyline Hotel indicates two changes relevant to analyzing the movement of cash for financing activities. Note that the change in capital was due to a non-cash transformation of long term liabilities into shares.

First of all, there is the change in their long term liabilities. There is a decrease in these liabilities between 2007 and 2008 from €11,250,000 to

€9,375,000 indicating a possible cash usage of €1,875,000 to honour those debts. However note that from the additional information at the top of this example, long term liabilities worth €625,000 were converted into capital shares in a non cash transaction. This means that not all of the reduction in the long term liabilities led to the use of cash. So this amount of €625,000 has to be deducted from €1,875,000 to establish the exact amount of cash used in honouring their long term obligations. This leads to €1,250,000 as cash effectively used.

Change in long term liabilities between 2007 and 2008	€ 1,875,000
Conversion of long term liabilities into shares in 2008 (non-cash)	_ € 625,000
Cash actually used to honour the long term obligations	= € 1,250,000

Secondly, the statement of retained earnings indicated that dividends were declared during 2008 by the Skyline Hotel. The amount was €380,000. This figure will permit the establishment of what was really paid out as dividends to the shareholders in 2008. Declaring dividends does not mean that they have actually been paid out through cash disbursements to the shareholders. To establish what the shareholders actually received in the form of dividends, the current liabilities account called dividends payable must be analyzed. Between 2007 and 2008, dividends payable increased by €12,500 (€37,500 – €25,000). At the end of 2007, Skyline Hotel's shareholders still had €25,000 worth of dividends to collect from the company. Adding the amount of dividends declared in the course of 2008 (€380,000), and then deducting what will be paid out to the shareholders in 2009 (€37,500), leads to the amount of cash effectively disbursed in 2008 as dividends to the shareholders.

Dividends payable end 2007	€ 25,000
Dividends declared in 2008	+ € 380,000
Dividends payable end 2008	− € 37,500
Dividends actually received by the shareholders in 2008 in cash	= € 367,500

To round up, the net cash flow from financing activities of the Skyline Hotel is

Cash used to honour long term obligations	(€ 1,250,000)
Cash used to pay dividends	(€ 367,500)
Net cash flow from financing activities	**(€ 1,617,500)**

Step 4 Collating all the above activity cash flows leads to the statement of cash flow of the Skyline Hotel for 2008.

Skyline Hotel
Statement of cash flows for the year ended December 31st 2008
Net cash flow from operating activities

Net income			€ 1,250,000
Adjustments to reconcile net income to cash flows from operating activities			
Depreciation	€	1,250,000	
Gain on sale of investments	(€	250,000)	
Decrease in accounts receivable	€	10,000	
Increase in inventory	(€	5,000)	
Increase in accounts payable	€	1,250	
Increase in accrued wages	€	1,250	
Decrease in income taxes payable	(€	2,500)	€ 1,005,000
Net cash flow from operating activities			**€ 2,255,000**
Net cash flow from investing activities			
Sale of investments	€	375,000	
Purchase of investments	(€	750,000)	
Purchase of equipment	(€	250,000)	
Net cash flow from investing activities			**(€ 625,000)**
Net cash flow from financing activities			
Cash used to honour long term obligations	(€	1,250,000)	
Cash used to pay dividends	(€	367,500)	
Net cash flow from financing activities			**(€ 1,617,500)**
Net cash flow for 2008			**€ 12,500**
Cash at the end of 2007			**€ 12,500**
Cash at the end of 2008			**€ 25,000**

Glossary

Cash equivalents – these are short term and highly liquid investments.

Cash flow statement – measures the flow of money in and out of a business. One of four financial statements found in the annual report, it categorizes a company's cash receipts and disbursements for a given fiscal year by three major activities: operations, investments and financing.

Cash inflows – these represent the cash received in the course of an accounting period by a business.

Cash outflows – these represent the cash paid out in the course of an accounting period by a business

Direct method – this method requires bringing together the beginning cash level to the ending cash level. Under the direct method, cash and bank accounts are analyzed to identify cash flow during the period.

Financing activities – those activities that help to raise the financial resources received from owners and creditors, and the associated repayments of the resulting obligations.

Indirect method – this method starts with the net income for the period concerned. The net income is then adjusted for non cash movements found in the income statement.

Investing activities – the purchase and sale of operating equipment or other assets intended to produce revenue in the long run. Also include activities related to non-operating assets strictly intended for investment purposes, such as buying shares of other companies.

Operating activities – these represent the principal revenue producing activities associated with the day-to-day running of a business on an ongoing basis.

Multiple choice questions

5.1 Which of the following stakeholders will consider using a company's statement of cash flows to assess its ability to generate enough cash from its operations?
a creditors
b investors
c suppliers
d all of the above

5.2 Which of the following will not be included in a cash flow statement?
a a new long term loan
b interests paid in the period
c new dividends declared
d purchase of land

5.3 In the cash flow statement, which of the following will be used in assessing the net cash flow from financing activities?
a payments of accounts payable
b payments to acquire property and equipment
c repayment of long term debt
d tax payments

5.4 In the cash flow statement, transactions related to accounts receivable and accounts payable will be used when establishing the net cash flows related to:
a financing activities
b investing activities
c operating activities
d all of the above

5.5 Using the basic rule of thumb is assessing changes in working capital, a decrease in accounts payable is shown in the cash flow statement designed on an indirect basis as an _____ of cash in the _____ activities section.
a inflow; financing
b inflow; investing
c inflow; operating
d none of the above

Exercises

5.1 The activities listed below featured amongst those carried out by the Invast Hotels in the course of the last year.
· bought a new piece of land
· bought beverages
· bought food
· declared dividends
· exchanged some shares for a long-term note
· opened an account in a new bank to process salaries
· paid a distiller for whiskies
· paid interests on long-term loan

- paid taxes
- received interest income
- reclassified a long-term note as current notes payable
- recorded depreciation
- sold beverages on credit
- sold equipment

Classify each activity under its appropriate heading based on the following possibilities

a financing activity
b investing activity
c noncash transaction
d operating activity
e none of the above

5.2 The following table lists current asset and current liability accounts. Identify each as either a current asset or a current liability account. After identifying each account, determine how the change in the account balance is treated when using the indirect method. If cash increases fill in "add"; and if it decreases, fill in "deduct".

Account	Current asset or current liability	If it increases	If it decreases
Accounts receivable			
Accounts payable			
Inventories			
Notes receivable			
Prepaid expenses			
Notes payable			
Accrued expenses			
Marketable securities			
Interests payable			

5.3 The Europa Hotel carried out various activities as described below:

- In 2010, the Europa Motel declared dividends of €450,000. The dividends payable account was €55,000 at the beginning of the year and €32,000 at the end of the year. Determine the dividends paid by the motel in 2010.

- In 2010, the Europa Motel had cash sales of €1,800,000 and credit sales of €3,250,000. During the year, accounts receivable decreased by €85,000. Determine the cash received from the guests in 2010.

- In 2010, the Europa Motel had cost of food used of €900,000. During the year, food inventory decreased by €24,000 and the food suppliers accounts payable increased by €43,000. Determine the cash payments for food purchases in 2010.

- In 2010, the Europa Motel's long-term debts were €2,200,000 on January 1st 2010. These increased to €3,100,000 by December 31st 2010. In 2010, €850,000 of long-term debt was converted to common stock, and €450,000 of long-term debt was reclassified as current debt. Determine the cash received as long-term debt in 2010.

- In 2010, the income tax expense of the Europa Motel was €122,000. The income taxes payable account was €15,500 on January 1st 2010 and €25,000 on December 31st 2010. Determine the amount of income taxes paid during the year.

5.4 Prepare the statement of cash flow of the Constant Visits Restaurant based on its condensed balance sheets and additional information presented below:

Constant Visits Restaurant
Condensed Balance Sheets
December 31st

	2009	2010
Current assets		
Cash	€ 120,000.00	€ 160,000.00
Accounts receivable	€ 312,000.00	€ 280,000.00
Iventory	€ 160,000.00	€ 192,000.00
Total current assets	€ 592,000.00	€ 632,000.00
Property and equipment	€ 2,480,000.00	€ 2,520,000.00
less accumulated depreciation	€ 1,200,000.00	€ 1,280,000.00
Total assets	€ 1,872,000.00	€ 1,872,000.00
Current liabilities:		
Accounts payable	€ 120,000.00	€ 136,000.00
Dividends payable	€ 184,000.00	€ 96,000.00
Total current liabilities	€ 304,000.00	€ 232,000.00
Long term liabilities:		
Notes payable	€ 640,000.00	€ 640,000.00
Total long term liabilities	€ 640,000.00	€ 640,000.00
Common stock	€ 800,000.00	€ 880,000.00
Retained earnings	€ 128,000.00	€ 120,000.00
Total Liabilities & Owners' Equity	€ 1,872,000.00	€ 1,872,000.00

Additional information	
Dividends declared in 2010	€ 160,000.00
Old equipment which cost	€ 160,000.00
was sold at	€ 80,000.00
its net book value was	€ 40,000.00

Analyzing financial statements

6.1   **Purposes of analyzing statements**
6.2   **Horizontal analysis**
6.3   **Base-year analysis**
6.4   **Vertical analysis**

Financial reports result from a combination of facts contained in the statements to be analysed and the personal judgements of the analysts. These facts and personal judgements are all influenced by the accounting principles discussed in Chapter 1. These principles determine how the reports will have to be presented to the concerned stakeholders. Good financial analysis requires that the stakeholder for whom the analysis is being carried out is clearly identified with the purpose of the analysis. For the analysis to be considered valid, all the factors relevant to the business performance of the organization should be taken into account. These factors include amongst others, principally the size of the organization, the socio-political and economic conditions, the trends in the industry, the risks entailed in carrying out the business as well as changes in technology. In section 6.1 the purposes of analyzing financial statements are discussed, followed in section 6.2 by a description of how horizontal analysis is carried out. Section 6.3 introduces the two ways of carrying out base-year analysis and this chapter ends with a description of how vertical analysis is carried out in section 6.4.

6.1   Purposes of analyzing statements

Financial statements most of the time present a summary of a company's activities over a given period or as in the case of balance sheets at a given point in time. This summary of activities is done in monetary terms. The income statement presents the revenues and expenses related to a particular period, the balance sheet gives an insight into the financial worth of the organization at a given date. The SCF shows how cash was generated or used during a certain period within the organization while the statement of retained earnings indicates how the net profit generated is either distributed as dividends or ploughed back into the company as reserves.

For financial statements to be meaningful they have to be analyzed because just having the financial statement figures on their own does not generally answer all the questions of concerned stakeholders. Analyzing financial statements involves examining relationships between the financial figures and the tendencies that these figures show over time. A primary purpose of financial statement analysis is to review the past performances of a company and see how this can be used to predict the company's future performance. This particular purpose is considered as the forecasting function of financial statement analysis. Secondly, financial statement analysis permits a company to review its performances in order to be able to identify areas that need special attention. This is considered as the problem-solving function of financial statement analysis and it is historical in nature.

The relationship between financial statement figures are called financial ratios and these are discussed in chapter 7. In general, the more thorough the analysis that is carried out, the more realistic the information generated from the analysis will be. The following financial statements of the Europa Alliance Hotel Plc. (exhibits 6.1 – balance sheets, 6.2 – income statements, 6.3 – cash flow statements, 6.4 – other information, 6.5 – condensed F & B departmental statement) will be used in all the analyses that will follow in this chapter.

Exhibit 6.1 **Balance sheets of The Europa Alliance Hotel Plc. for the years ending December 31st 2010, 2011, and 2012**

Balance Sheet
Europa Alliance Hotel Plc.
For the year ending December 31st

	2010	2011	2012
Assets			
Current Assets			
Cash	€ 1,100,000.00	€ 1,155,000.00	€ 1,320,000.00
Marketable Securities	€ 3,300,000.00	€ 4,455,000.00	€ 7,975,000.00
Net Accounts Receivable	€ 5,500,000.00	€ 4,950,000.00	€ 7,700,000.00
Inventories	€ 770,000.00	€ 935,000.00	€ 825,000.00
Prepaid Expenses	€ 715,000.00	€ 660,000.00	€ 770,000.00
Total Current Assets	*€ 11,385,000.00*	*€ 12,155,000.00*	*€ 18,590,000.00*
Investments	€ 2,365,000.00	€ 1,925,000.00	€ 2,200,000.00
Property and Equipment:			
Land	€ 3,767,500.00	€ 3,767,500.00	€ 3,767,500.00
Buildings	€ 44,550,000.00	€ 46,750,000.00	€ 48,400,000.00
Furniture, and Equipment	€ 9,350,000.00	€ 10,450,000.00	€ 11,440,000.00
	€ 57,667,500.00	€ 60,967,500.00	€ 63,607,500.00
Less: Accumulated Depreciation	€ 14,300,000.00	€ 17,600,000.00	€ 20,955,000.00
China, glassware, silver, linen, and uniforms	€ 632,500.00	€ 1,127,500.00	€ 1,254,000.00
Total Property and Equipment	*€ 44,000,000.00*	*€ 44,495,000.00*	*€ 43,906,500.00*
Total Assets	**€ 57,750,000.00**	**€ 58,575,000.00**	**€ 64,696,500.00**
Liabilities and Owners' Equity			
Current Liabilities:			
Accounts Payable	€ 3,300,000.00	€ 2,942,500.00	€ 3,905,000.00
Accrued Income Taxes	€ 1,650,000.00	€ 1,760,000.00	€ 1,870,000.00
Accrued Expenses	€ 3,850,000.00	€ 4,686,000.00	€ 4,675,000.00
Current Portion of Long-term Debt	€ 1,375,000.00	€ 1,182,500.00	€ 1,320,000.00
Total Current Liabilities	*€ 10,175,000.00*	*€ 10,571,000.00*	*€ 11,770,000.00*
Long-term Debt:			
Mortgage Payable	€ 23,375,000.00	€ 22,550,000.00	€ 22,000,000.00
Deferred Income Taxes	€ 2,200,000.00	€ 2,354,000.00	€ 2,475,000.00
Total Long-term Debt	*€ 25,575,000.00*	*€ 24,904,000.00*	*€ 24,475,000.00*
Total Liabilities	**€ 35,750,000.00**	**€ 35,475,000.00**	**€ 36,245,000.00**
Owners' Equity:			
Common Stock	€ 3,025,000.00	€ 3,025,000.00	€ 3,025,000.00
Paid-in Capital in excess of par	€ 6,050,000.00	€ 6,050,000.00	€ 6,050,000.00
Retained Earnings	€ 12,925,000.00	€ 14,025,000.00	€ 19,376,500.00
Total Owners' Equity	*€ 22,000,000.00*	*€ 23,100,000.00*	*€ 28,451,500.00*
Total Liabilities and Owners' Equity	**€ 57,750,000.00**	**€ 58,575,000.00**	**€ 64,696,500.00**

Exhibit 6.2 **Income statements of The Europa Alliance Hotel Plc. for the years 2011 and 2012**

Income Statement
European Alliance Hotel Plc.
For the years

	2011	2012
Total Revenue	€ 71,500,000.00	€ 74,360,000.00
Rooms:		
Revenue	€ 42,900,000.00	€ 44,550,000.00
Payroll and Related Expenses	€ 7,425,000.00	€ 7,975,000.00
Other Direct Expenses	€ 3,437,500.00	€ 3,300,000.00
Departmental Income	*€ 32,037,500.00*	*€ 33,275,000.00*
Food and Beverage:		
Revenue	€ 23,650,000.00	€ 24,475,000.00
Cost of Sales	€ 7,810,000.00	€ 8,140,000.00
Payroll and Related Expenses	€ 9,625,000.00	€ 9,900,000.00
Other Direct Expenses	€ 2,387,000.00	€ 2,475,000.00
Departmental Income	*€ 3,828,000.00*	*€ 3,960,000.00*
Health Club:		
Revenue	€ 2,200,000.00	€ 2,310,000.00
Cost of Sales	€ 1,650,000.00	€ 1,705,000.00
Payroll and Related Expenses	€ 550,000.00	€ 577,500.00
Other Direct Expenses	€ 275,000.00	€ 247,500.00
Departmental Income	*(€ 275,000.00)*	*(€ 220,000.00)*
Rental and Other Income Revenue	€ 2,750,000.00	€ 3,025,000.00
Total Operated Departments Income	€ 38,340,500.00	€ 40,040,000.00
Undistributed Operating Expenses:		
Administrative & General	€ 5,775,000.00	€ 5,967,500.00
Marketing	€ 2,832,500.00	€ 3,025,000.00
Property Operations & Maintenance	€ 3,588,750,00	€ 3,712,500.00
Utility Costs	€ 4,413,750.00	€ 4,482,500.00
Total Undistributed Operating Expenses	*€ 16,610,000.00*	*€ 17,187,500.00*
Income After Undistributed Operating Expenses	€ 21,730,500.00	€ 22,852,500.00
Rent	€ 1,100,000.00	€ 1,100,000.00
Property Taxes	€ 1,100,000.00	€ 1,320,000.00
Insurance	€ 302,500.00	€ 330,000.00
Interest	€ 2,970,000.00	€ 3,300,000.00
Depreciation	€ 3,300,300.00	€ 3,355,000.00
Total Fixed Charges	*€ 8,772,500.00*	*€ 9,405,000.00*
Income Before Income Taxes	€ 12,958,000.00	€ 13,447,500.00
Income Taxes	€ 5,186,500.00	€ 5,379,000.00
Net Income	€ 7,771,500.00	€ 8,068,500.00

Exhibit 6.3 Statement of cash flows of The Europa Alliance Hotel Plc. for the years 2011 and 2012

Statement of Cash Flows
Europa Alliance Plc.
For the Years

	2011	2012
Cash Flows from Operating Activities		
Net Income	€ 7,771,500.00	€ 8,068,500.00
Adjustments to reconcile net income to net cash provided by operations:		
Depreciation expense	€ 3,300,000.00	€ 3,355,000.00
Inc./Dec. In accounts receivable	€ 550,000.00	(€ 2,750,000.00)
Inc./Dec. In inventories	€ 165,000.00	€ 110,000.00
Inc./Dec. In prepaid expenses	€ 55,000.00	(€ 110,000.00)
Inc./Dec. In accounts payable	(€ 357,500.00)	€ 962,500.00
Increase in income taxes	€ 110,000.00	€ 110,000.00
Inc./Dec. In accrued expenses	€ 836,000.00	(€ 11,000.00)
Inc./Dec. In deferred taxes	€ 154,000.00	€ 121,000.00
Net cash from operating activities	*€12,254,000.00*	*€ 9,856,000.00*
Cash Flows from investing activities		
Purchase of marketable securities	(€ 1,155,000.00)	(€ 3,520,000.00)
Sale of investments	€ 440,000.00	€ –
Purchase of buildings	(€ 2,200,000.00)	(€ 1,650,000.00)
Purchase of furniture	(€ 1,100,000.00)	(€ 990,000.00)
Purchase of china etc.	(€ 495,000.00)	(€ 126,500.00)
Purchase of investments	€ –	(€ 275,000.00)
Net cash from investing activities	*(€ 4,510,000.00)*	*(€ 6,561,500.00)*
Cash Flows from Financing Activities		
Payment of dividends	(€ 6,671,500.00)	(€ 2,717,000.00)
Payment of long-term debt	(€ 1,375,000.00)	(€ 1,182,500.00)
Borrowed long term debt	€ 357,500.00	€ 770,000.00
Net cash from financing activities	*(€ 7,689,000.00)*	*(€ 3,129,500.00)*
Net increase in Cash	€ 55,000.00	€ 165,000.00
Additional information		
Investments sold in 2011	€ 440,000.00	

Exhibit 6.4 **Statement of retained earnings and other information of The Europa Alliance Hotel Plc. for the years 2011 and 2012**

Statement of Retained Earnings and Other Information
Europa Alliance Hotel Plc.
For the Years

	2011	2012
Retained Earnings – beginning of the year	€ 12,925,000.00	€ 14,025,000.00
Net Income	€ 7,771,500.00	€ 8,068,500.00
Dividends Declared	€ 6,671,500.00	€ 2,717,000.00
Retained Earnings – end of the year	€ 14,025,000.00	€ 19,376,500.00
Other Information		
Room Sold	1,127,500.00	1,155,000.00
Paid Guest	1,292,500.00	1,320,000.00
Rooms Occupied by Two or More Guests	132,000.00	137,500.00
Complimentary Rooms	8,250.00	8,800.00
Shares of Common Stock Outstanding	3,025,000.00	3,025,000.00
Food Covers	3,052,500.00	3,080,000.00
Food Sales	€ 15,400,000.00	€ 16,500,000.00
Beverage Sales	€ 8,250,000.00	€ 7,975,000.00

Exhibit 6.5 **Condensed food and beverage department statement of The Europa Alliance Hotel Plc. for the year 2012**

Condensed Food and Beverage Department Statement
Europa Alliance Hotel Plc.
For the Year

	2012	
	Food	Beverage
Sales	€ 16,500,000.00	€ 7,975,000.00
Cost of Sales		
Beginning Inventory	€ 605,000.00	€ 330,000.00
Purchases	€ 6,600,000.00	€ 1,540,000.00
Less: Ending Inventory	€ 495,000.00	€ 330,000.00
Cost of Goods Used	€ 6,710,000.00	€ 1,540,000.00
Less: Employee Meals	€ 110,000.00	€ –
Cost of Goods Sold	€ 6,600,000.00	€ 1,540,000.00
Gross Profit	€ 9,900,000.00	€ 6,435,000.00
Expenses:		
Payroll and Related Expenses	€ 7,425,000.00	€ 2,475,000.00
Other Expenses	€ 1,650,000.00	€ 825,000.00
Total Expenses	€ 9,075,000.00	€ 3,300,000.00
Departmental Income	€ 825,000.00	€ 3,135,000.00

6.2   Horizontal analysis

Horizontal analysis essentially compares two financial statements over at least two periods (last month against this month), two dates (December 31st 2008 against December 31st 2009) or two reasons (budgeted amounts against actual results). If the information available covers many more dates or periods it is then possible to carry out a trend analysis which permits to discover long term business tendencies.

Another name for horizontal analysis is comparative analysis as it will cover the same elements over different periods, dates or reasons. This form of analysis is the most basic in financial statement analysis but at the same time necessary in the reporting of the financial information of a company.

The changes in horizontal analysis are expressed either in absolute form or in relative form. The absolute change will indicate the changes in the currency amounts between the two periods or dates for the specific item. The relative change which is also called the percentage change is derived from dividing the absolute change figure by the amount of the initial period or date. Exhibit 6.6 is an illustration of horizontal analysis using the Europa Alliance Hotel Plc. balance sheets as of December 31st 2010 and 2011.

To illustrate horizontal analysis, consider the value for buildings in the balance sheets. On 31/12/2010, buildings had a value of €44,550,000.00 and this changed to €46,750,000.00 on 31/12/2011.

The absolute difference is calculated as follows:

$$€46,750,000.00 - €44,550,000.00 = €2,200,000.00$$

The relative difference is calculated as follows:

$$\frac{€2,200,000.00}{€44,550,000.00} \times 100 = 4.94\%$$

It can thus be said that in terms of the gross value of their buildings, the Europa Alliance Hotel Plc. increased their buildings value by €2,200,000.00 in the course of the year 2011. On the other hand, it can equally be said that the Europa Alliance Hotel Plc. raised their buildings value by 4.94% between the two balance sheet dates.

A specialized vocabulary is used to indicate changes in horizontal analysis. If the change is positive, then it would be interpreted as an increase in the specific item between the two dates or simply stated that the movement was upward. On the other hand, if the change was negative, then it would be interpreted as a decrease in the specific item between the two dates or simply stated that the movement was downward. These two movements do not indicate gains or losses but simply differences in the amounts of the items between the two dates. If the amounts of the items are equal between the two dates (for

■ Exhibit 6.6 **Illustration of horizontal analysis indicating absolute and relative changes**

Comperative Balance Sheets
Europa Alliance Hotel Plc.
For the year ending December 31st

	2010	2011	Absolute Difference Amount	Relative Difference Percentage
Assets				
Current Assets				
Cash	€ 1,100,000.00	€ 1,155,000.00	€ 55,000.00	5.00%
Marketable Securities	€ 3,300,000.00	€ 4,455,000.00	€ 1,155,000.00	35.00%
Net Accounts Receivable	€ 5,500,000.00	€ 4,950,000.00	(€ 550,000.00)	−10%
Inventories	€ 770,000.00	€ 935,000.00	€ 165,000.00	21.43%
Prepaid Expenses	€ 715,000.00	€ 660,000.00	(€ 55,000.00)	−7.69%
Total Current Assets	*€ 11,385,000.00*	*€ 12,155,000.00*	*€ 770,000.00*	*6.76%*
Investments	€ 2,365,000.00	€ 1,925,000.00	(€ 440,000.00)	−18.60%
Property and Equipment:				
Land	€ 3,767,500.00	€ 3,767,500.00	€ –	0.00%
Buildings	€ 44,550,000.00	€ 46,750,000.00	€ 2,200,000.00	4.94%
Furniture, and Equipment	€ 9,350,000.00	€ 10,450,000.00	€ 1,100,000.00	11.76%
	€ 57,667,500.00	€ 60,967,500.00	€ 3,300,000.00	5.72%
Less: Accumulated Depreciation	€ 14,300,000.00	€ 17,600,000.00	€ 3,300,000.00	23.08%
China, glassware, silver, linen, and uniforms	€ 632,500.00	€ 1,127,500.00	€ 495,000.00	78.26%
Total Property and Equipment	*€ 44,000,000.00*	*€ 44,495,000.00*	*€ 495,000.00*	*1.13%*
Total Assets	**€ 57,750,000.00**	**€ 58,575,000.00**	**€ 825,000.00**	**1.43%**
Liabilities and Owners' Equity				
Current Liabilities:				
Accounts Payable	€ 3,300,000.00	€ 2,942,500.00	(€ 357,500.00)	−10.83%
Accrued Income Taxes	€ 1,650,000.00	€ 1,760,000.00	€ 110,000.00	6.67%
Accrued Expenses	€ 3,850,000.00	€ 4,686,000.00	€ 836,000.00	21.71%
Current Portion of Long-term Debt	€ 1,375,000.00	€ 1,182,500.00	(€ 192,500.00)	−14.00%
Total Current Liabilities	*€ 10,175,000.00*	*€ 10,571,000.00*	*€ 396,000.00*	*3.89%*
Long-term Debt:				
Mortgage Payable	€ 23,375,000.00	€ 22,550,000.00	(€ 825,000.00)	−3.53%
Deferred Income Taxes	€ 2,200,000.00	€ 2,354,000.00	€ 154,000.00	7.00%
Total Long-term Debt	*€ 25,575,000.00*	*€ 24,904,000.00*	*(€ 671,000.00)*	*−2.62%*
Total Liabilities	**€ 35,750,000.00**	**€ 35,475,000.00**	**(€ 275,000.00)**	**−0.77%**
Owners' Equity:				
Common Stock	€ 3,025,000.00	€ 3,025,000.00	€ –	0.00%
Paid-in Capital in excess of par	€ 6,050,000.00	€ 6,050,000.00	€ –	0.00%
Retained Earnings	€ 12,925,000.00	€ 14,025,000.00	€ 1,100,000.00	8.51%
Total Owners' Equity	*€ 22,000,000.00*	*€ 23,100,000.00*	*€ 1,100,000.00*	*5.00%*
Total Liabilities and Owners' Equity	**€ 57,750,000.00**	**€ 58,575,000.00**	**€ 825,000.00**	**1.43%**

example land in exhibit 6.6), then it is simply indicated that there was no change.

Despite its necessity in the reporting of the financial information of a company, horizontal analysis is weighed down with primarily two problems:

- First of all, it is difficult to recognize the effects of very rapid changes taking place in the organization's business. Since the figures may not really be comparable, this creates the need for adjustments to be made regularly when dealing with horizontal analysis in rapidly changing situations.

- Secondly, horizontal analysis cannot adequately take into account the effects of inflation. So to be able to make workable conclusions, adjustments have to be made to take into account the effects of changes caused by changing prices.

As a whole, horizontal analysis does not always provide answers to the analyst but will point the analyst in the right direction for further analysis.

6.3   Base-year analysis

This is a variation of horizontal analysis in which a certain period or date is fixed as a base period or date. Such a base is selected and all the comparisons are made with it. In general, the figures of the base period or date are indexed at 100. Exhibit 6.8 is an illustration of base year analysis using two different approaches:

- The index approach: this is done by using only indices to represent the changes between the items of the statements.
- The percentage approach: this is done by using percentages to represent the changes between the items of the statements.

Note that in exhibit 6.8 all the information related to December 31st 2010 (considered as the base date) have all been converted to 100.00 or 100.00%.

One of the best known European indices is the DAX (Deutscher Aktien IndeX – German stock index) which is a stock market index of the 30 major German companies that trade at the Frankfurt stock exchange. The base date for the DAX is December 30th 1987 and it started from a base value of 1,000. At the date of inserting this information in this section, it stood at 5704.24 (February 23rd 2010 – http://deutsche-boerse.com). Exhibit 6.7 shows the evolution of the DAX over the six months September 2009 until February 2010, and collected on February 23rd 2010. It showed a high degree of volatility with the lowest point during the period in early September 2009 (around 5300) and the highest point at the beginning of January 2010 at about 6050.

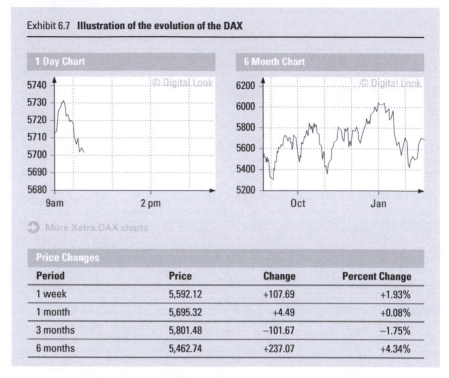

Exhibit 6.7 **Illustration of the evolution of the DAX**

Price Changes			
Period	**Price**	**Change**	**Percent Change**
1 week	5,592.12	+107.69	+1.93%
1 month	5,695.32	+4.49	+0.08%
3 months	5,801.48	−101.67	−1.75%
6 months	5,462.74	+237.07	+4.34%

To illustrate base year analysis, consider the value for investments in the balance sheet of the Europa Alliance Hotel Plc. in exhibit 6.8. The date of December 31st 2010 is indexed at 100.00 while December 31st 2011 is indexed at 81.40 which indicates that the level of investments on December 31st 2011 is 18.60 (100.00 – 81.40) points (or percentage points) less than that in the base year. As well, on December 31st 2012, the level of investments is 6.98 (100.00 – 93.02) points less than in the base year.

6.4 Vertical analysis

Vertical analysis (also known as common size analysis – when the vertical analysis is extended over more than one accounting period) is a form of analysis in which all the information found in the financial statements are reduced to percentages. This reduction is based on the following denominators:

· As it concerns balance sheets, the denominator is the total assets (or total liabilities + owners' equity).
· As it concerns income statements, the denominator is generally the total revenues of the organization. In cases where there are departmental revenues, such revenues will form the denominator for departmental analyses. In such organizations when analyzing the non-revenue generating service centres, the denominator is equally the total revenues of the organization.

Comperative Balance Sheets Using Base Year Analysis
Europa Alliance Hotel Plc.
For the year ending December 31st

	2010	2011	2012	Base Year = 2010			Base Year = 2010		
				2010	2011	2012	2010	2011	2012
				Using Indices			Using Percentages		
Assets									
Current Assets									
Cash	€ 1,100,000.00	€ 1,155,000.00	€ 1,320,000.00	100.00	105.00	120.00	100.00%	105.00%	120.00%
Marketable Securities	€ 3,300,000.00	€ 4,455,000.00	€ 7,975,000.00	100.00	135.00	241.67	100.00%	135.00%	241.67%
Net Accounts Receivable	€ 5,500,000.00	€ 4,950,000.00	€ 7,700,000.00	100.00	90.00	140.00	100.00%	90.00%	140.00%
Inventories	€ 770,000.00	€ 935,000.00	€ 825,000.00	100.00	121.43	107.14	100.00%	121.43%	107.14%
Prepaid Expenses	€ 715,000.00	€ 660,000.00	€ 770.000.00	100.00	92.31	107.69	100.00%	92.31%	107.69%
Total Current Assets	*€11,385,000.00*	*€12,155,000.00*	*€18,590,000.00*	*100.00*	*106.76*	*163.29*	*100.00%*	*106.76%*	*163.29%*
Investments	€ 2,365,000.00	€ 1,925,000.00	€ 2,200,000.00	100.00	81.40	93.02	100.00%	81.40%	93.02%
Property and Equipment:									
Land	€ 3,767,500.00	€ 3,767,500.00	€ 3,767,500.00	100.00	100.00	100.00	100.00%	100.00%	100.00%
Buildings	€44,550,000.00	€46,750,000.00	€48,400,000.00	100.00	104.94	108.64	100.00%	104.94%	108.64%
Furniture, and Equipment	€ 9,350,000.00	€10,450,000.00	€11,440,000.00	100.00	111.76	122.35	100.00%	111.76%	122.35%
	€57,667,500.00	€60,967,500.00	€63,607,500.00	100.00	105.72	110.30	100.00%	105.72%	110.30%
Less: Accumulated Depreciation	€14,300,000.00	€17,600,000.00	€20,955,000.00	100.00	123.08	146.54	100.00%	123.08%	146.54%
China, glassware, silver, linen, and uniforms	€ 632,500.00	€ 1,127,500.00	€ 1,254,000.00	100.00	178.26	198.26	100.00%	178.26%	198.26%
Total Property and Equipment	*€44,000,000.00*	*€44,495,000.00*	*€43,906,500.00*	*100.00*	*101.13*	*99.79*	*100.00%*	*101.13%*	*99.79%*
Total Assets	**€57,750,000.00**	**€58,575,000.00**	**€64,696,500.00**	**100.00**	**101.43**	**112.03**	**100.00%**	**101.43%**	**112.03%**
Liabilities and Owners' Equity									
Current Liabilities:									
Accounts Payable	€ 3,300,000.00	€ 2,942,500.00	€ 3,905,000.00	100.00	89.17	118.33	100.00%	89.17%	118.33%
Accrued Income Taxes	€ 1,650,000.00	€ 1,760,000.00	€ 1,870,000.00	100.00	106.67	113.33	100.00%	106.67%	113.33%
Accrued Expenses	€ 3,850,000.00	€ 4,686,000.00	€ 4,675,000.00	100.00	121.71	121.43	100.00%	121.71%	121.43%
Current Portion of Long-term Debt	€ 1,373,000.00	€ 1,182,500.00	€ 1,320,000.00	100.00	86.00	96.00	100.00%	86.00%	96.00%
Total Current Liabilities	*€10,175,000.00*	*€10,571,000.00*	*€11,770,000.00*	*100.00*	*103.89*	*115.68*	*100.00%*	*103.89%*	*115.68%*
Long-term Debt:									
Mortgage Payable	€23,375,000.00	€22,550,000.00	€22,000,000.00	100.00	96.47	94.12	100.00%	96.47%	94.12%
Deferred Income Taxes	€ 2,200,000.00	€ 2,354,000.00	€ 2,475,000.00	100.00	107.00	112.50	100.00%	107.00%	112.50%
Total Long-term Debt	*€25,575,000.00*	*€24,904,000.00*	*€24,475,000.00*	*100.00*	*97.38*	*95.70*	*100.00%*	*97.38%*	*95.70%*
Total Liabilities	**€35,750,000.00**	**€35,475,000.00**	**€36,245,000.00**	**100.00**	**99.23**	**101.38**	**100.00%**	**99.23%**	**101.38%**
Owners' Equity:									
Common Stock	€ 3,025,000.00	€ 3,025,000.00	€ 3,025,000.00	100.00	100.00	100.00	100.00%	100.00%	100.00%
Paid-in Capital in excess of par	€ 6,050,000.00	€ 6,050,000.00	€ 6,050,000.00	100.00	100.00	100.00	100.00%	100.00%	100.00%
Retained Earnings	€12,925,000.00	€14,025,000.00	€19,376,500.00	100.00	108.51	149.91	100.00%	108.51%	149.91%
Total Owners' Equity	*€22,000,000.00*	*€23,100,000.00*	*€28,451,500.00*	*100.00*	*105.00*	*129.33*	*100.00%*	*105.00%*	*129.33%*
Total Liabilities and Owners' Equity	**€57,750,000.00**	**€58,575,000.00**	**€64,696,500.00**	**100.00**	**101.43**	**112.03**	**100.00%**	**101.43%**	**112.03%**

Vertical analysis is very useful in that it can be used in comparing the financial statements of an organization with those of other organizations as well as with industrial averages. This comparison can be made between organizations of vastly different sizes since all the data is reduced to comparable percentages. Exhibit 6.9 is the illustration of the common size analysis of the Europa Alliance Hotel Plc. for the years 2011 and 2012.

Exhibit 6.9 **Ilustration of common size analysis**

Common Size Income Statement
Europa Alliance Hotel Plc.
For the years

			Common Size	
	2011	2012	2011	2012
Total Revenue	€ 71,500,000.00	€ 74,360,000.00	100.00%	100.00%
Rooms:				
Revenue	€ 42,900,000.00	€ 44,550,000.00	60.00%	59.91%
Payroll and Related Expenses	€ 7,425,000.00	€ 7,975,000.00	10.38%	10.72%
Other Direct Expenses	€ 3,437,500.00	€ 3,300,000.00	4.81%	4.44%
Department Income	*€ 32,037,500.00*	*€ 33,275,000.00*	*44.81%*	*44.75%*
Food and Beverage:				
Revenue	€ 23,650,000.00	€ 24,475,000.00	33.08%	32.91%
Cost of Sales	€ 7,810,000.00	€ 8,140,000.00	10.92%	10.95%
Payroll and Related Expenses	€ 9,625,000.00	€ 9,900,000.00	13.46%	13.31%
Other Direct Expenses	€ 2,387,000.00	€ 2,475,000.00	3.34%	3.33%
Departmental Income	*€ 3,828,000.00*	*€ 3,960,000.00*	*5.35%*	*5.33%*
Health Club:				
Revenue	€ 2,200,000.00	€ 2,310,000.00	3.08%	3.11%
Cost of Sales	€ 1,650,000.00	€ 1,705,000.00	2.31%	2.29%
Payroll and Related Expenses	€ 550,000.00	€ 577,500.00	0.77%	0.78%
Other Direct Expenses	€ 275,000.00	€ 247,500.00	0.38%	0.33%
Departmental Income	−*€ 275,000.00*	−*€ 220,000.00*	*−0.38%*	*−0.30%*
Rentals and Other Income Revenue	€ 2,750,000.00	€ 3,025,000.00	3.85%	4.07%
Total Operated Departments Income	€ 38,340,500.00	€ 40,040,000.00	53.62%	53.85%
Undistributed Operating Expenses:				
Administrative & General	€ 5,775,000.00	€ 5,967,500.00	8.08%	8.03%
Marketing	€ 2,832,500.00	€ 3,025,000.00	3.96%	4.07%
Property Operations & Maintenance	€ 3,588,750.00	€ 3,712,500.00	5.02%	4.99%
Utility Costs	€ 4,413,750.00	€ 4,482,500.00	6.17%	6.03%
Total Undistributed Operating Expenses	*€ 16,610,000.00*	*€ 17,187,500.00*	*23.23%*	*23.11%*
Icome After Undistributed Operating Expenses	€ 21,730,500.00	€ 22,852,500.00	30.39%	30.73%
Rent	€ 1,100,000.00	€ 1,100,000.00	1.54%	1.48%
Property Taxes	€ 1,100,000.00	€ 1,320,000.00	1.54%	1.78%
Insurance	€ 302,500.00	€ 330,000.00	0.42%	0.44%
Interest	€ 2,970,000.00	€ 3,300,000.00	4.15%	4.44%
Depreciation	€ 3,300,000.00	€ 3,355,000.00	4.62%	4.51%
Total Fixed Charges	*€ 8,772,500.00*	*€ 9,405,000.00*	*12.27%*	*12.65%*
Income Before Income Taxes	€ 12,958,000.00	€ 13,447,500.00	18.12%	18.08%
Income Taxes	€ 5,186,500.00	€ 5,379,000.00	7.25%	7.23%
Net Income	€ 7,771,500.00	€ 8,068,500.00	10.87%	10.85%

Limiting this particular review to the bottom line of the income statement (the net income) it is noticed that the net income for 2012 is substantially higher that the net income for 2011. However, looking at the situation vertically, the net income of 2012 is only 10.85% of their overall revenues of 2012. This percentage is slightly lower than the situation of 2011 which is 10.87%. Based on common size analysis, 2011 is a much more profitable year than 2012.

Glossary

Base year analysis – this is a variation of horizontal analysis in which a certain period or date is fixed as a base period or date. Such a base is selected and all the comparisons are made with this base.

Common size analysis – this is a variation of vertical analysis in which the financial data of more than one period is analyzed at the same time.

Comparative analysis – see horizontal analysis

Horizontal analysis – this is the comparison of financial statements for two or more accounting periods in terms of both absolute and relative differences for each item.

Vertical analysis – this is an analysis of the relationships amongst various financial items on a particular financial statement. These relationships are expressed as percentages of a certain total depending on which financial statement is being analyzed.

Multiple choice questions

6.1 The type of balance sheet analysis that will set total assets at 100% is called:
   a base year analysis
   b comparative analysis
   c horizontal analysis
   d vertical analysis

6.2 Which of the following will be included in common size balance sheets?
   a current assets as a percentage of current liabilities
   b current assets as a percentage of total assets
   c the absolute difference between the current assets
   d the relative difference between the current assets

6.3 The type of balance sheet analysis that compares the balance sheets of several periods with the balance sheet of one selected period is called:
   a base year analysis
   b common size analysis
   c horizontal analysis
   d vertical analysis

6.4 At the end of 2009, the income statement of the Fast Eaters Spot indicated revenues of €5,025,000 and at the end of 2010; it indicated revenues of €5,400,000. The absolute difference in revenues from the end of 2009 to the end of 2010 is determined to be:
   a (€375,000)
   b €375,000
   c 6.94%
   d 7.46%

6.5 At the end of 2009, the income statement of the Fast Eaters Spot indicated revenues of €5,025,000 and at the end of 2010; it indicated revenues of €5,400,000. The relative difference in revenues from the end of 2009 to the end of 2010 is determined to be:
   a (€375,000)
   b €375,000
   c 6.94%
   d 7.46%

Exercises

6.1 Prepare a comparative analysis for the Constant Visits Restaurant based on the information presented in their condensed balance sheets below:

Constant Visits Restaurant Condensed Balance Sheets December 31st				
		2009		2010
Current assets				
Cash	€	120,000.00	€	160,000.00
Accounts receivable	€	312,000.00	€	280,000.00
Inventory	€	160,000.00	€	192,000.00
Total current assets	€	592,000.00	€	632,000.00
Property and equipment	€	2,480,000.00	€	2,520,000.00
less accumulated depreciation	€	1,200,000.00	€	1,280,000.00
Total assets	€	1,872,000.00	€	1,872,000.00
Current liabilities:				
Accounts payable	€	120,000.00	€	136,000.00
Dividends payable	€	184,000.00	€	96,000.00
Total current liabilities	€	304,000.00	€	232,000.00
Long term liabilities:				
Notes payable	€	640,000.00	€	640,000.00
Total long term liabilities	€	640,000.00	€	640,000.00
Common stock	€	800,000.00	€	880,000.00
Retained earnings	€	128,000.00	€	120,000.00
Total Liabilities & Owners' Equity	€	1,872,000.00	€	1,872,000.00

6.2 The condensed income statement of the Three Corners' Restaurant for the years 2009 and 2010 are presented in the table below with information related to the number of customers served in those periods. Use the information to prepare common size income statements as well as comment on the restaurant's performance.

Three Corners' Restaurant Condensed income statement For the years				
		2009		2010
Revenues	€	616,250.00	€	659,750.00
Cost of sales	€	159,500.00	€	177,625.00
Salaries	€	184,875.00	€	216,050.00
Laundry	€	29,000.00	€	30,450.00
China, glass, silver	€	7,250.00	€	7,975.00
Other expenses	€	116.000.00	€	112.375.00
Total expenses	€	496,625.00	€	544,475.00
Income before taxes	€	119,625.00	€	115,275.00
Taxes (32%)	€	38,280.00	€	36,888.00
Net Income	€	81,345.00	€	78,387.00
Number of customers served		101,500		108,750

6.3 Using the current liabilities information of the Corporate Lunchroom for the years 2008 till 2011, prepare an index-based base year analysis using 2008 as the base year.

Corporate Lunchroom Current liabilities December 31st 2008, 2009, 2010 and 2011				
	2008	**2009**	**2010**	**2011**
Current liabilities				
Notes payable	€ 24,750.00	€ 32,500.00	€ 28,400.00	€ 35,200.00
Accounts payable	€ 12,500.00	€ 14,250.00	€ 13,500.00	€ 18,600.00
Accrued expenses	€ 2,500.00	€ 2,400.00	€ 2,650.00	€ 3,240.00
Advance deposits	€ 5,240.00	€ 2,500.00	€ 3,800.00	€ 5,200.00
Income taxes payable	€ 2,410.00	€ 3,105.00	€ 2,860.00	€ 3,150.00
Current maturities of long-term debt	€ 5,400.00	€ 5,400.00	€ 5,400.00	€ 5,400.00
Total current liabilities	**€ 52,800.00**	**€ 60,155.00**	**€ 56,610.00**	**€ 70,790.00**

6.4 Using the current liabilities information of the Corporate Lunchroom for the years 2008 till 2011, prepare a percentage-based base year analysis using 2009 as the base year.

Corporate Lunchroom Current liabilities December 31st 2008, 2009, 2010 and 2011				
	2008	**2009**	**2010**	**2011**
Current liabilities				
Notes payable	€ 24,750.00	€ 32,500.00	€ 28,400.00	€ 35,200.00
Accounts payable	€ 12,500.00	€ 14,250.00	€ 13,500.00	€ 18,600.00
Accrued expenses	€ 2,500.00	€ 2,400.00	€ 2,650.00	€ 3,240.00
Advance deposits	€ 5,240.00	€ 2,500.00	€ 3,800.00	€ 5,200.00
ncome taxes payable	€ 2,410.00	€ 3,105.00	€ 2,860.00	€ 3,150.00
Current maturities of long-term debt	€ 5,400.00	€ 5,400.00	€ 5,400.00	€ 5,400.00
Total current liabilities	**€ 52,800.00**	**€ 60,155.00**	**€ 56,610.00**	**€ 70,790.00**

Ratio analysis and types of ratios

7

7.1   Purpose and usefulness of ratio analysis
7.2   Classification of ratios
7.3   Performance review process
7.4   DuPont analysis

Ratio analysis has multiple definitions all of which relate to understanding the relationships between the accounting data of an organization. In Wall Street Words: An A to Z Guide to Investment Terms for Today's Investor, it is simply defined as "a study of the relationships between financial variables". On the contrary, the Farlex Financial Dictionary extends the definition by emphasizing on the significance of what ratios represent as such "ratio analysis is the study of the significance of financial ratios for a company". Ratio analysis is important in understanding the financial wellbeing of any organization. It permits intra- and inter-company evaluations as well as comparisons with industrial averages. Section 7.1 establishes the purpose and usefulness of ratio analysis followed by the various classifications of ratios in section 7.2. In section 7.3, the performance review process is introduced and the chapter ends with an introduction of one common method of performance analysis, the DuPont analysis in section 7.4.

7.1　Purpose and usefulness of ratio analysis

A ratio is simply a notation of the relationship between two or more things such as:

$$A = \frac{X}{Y}$$

in which,
A is the result
X is called the numerator, and
Y is called the denominator

It should be noted that it is the relationship which the ratio is expressing that must be understood. This understanding is of primary importance because without it, however precise the calculations are, they will have no meaning. Ratios permit the creation of new, much more meaningful and useful information that goes beyond the facts and figures found in financial statements.

On its own, a financial ratio says nothing. When put in its proper context, a financial ratio can permit an analyst to have a good overview of a company's performance and any upcoming trends. Additionally the ratios on their own will not be able to say whether a situation was acceptable or unacceptable except when these ratios are compared to other data and standards. This means that ratios have to be looked at in the context of other information and experiences. Note however that ratios permit analysts to cope with changes over time in absolute amounts as well as to compare organizations of different sizes.

In hospitality organizations the stakeholders (essentially the investors, creditors and the management) will have different perspectives when considering the ratios that result from the analysis of the financial statements. Investors would use the ratios to evaluate the performance of the hospitality organization. The ratios might permit them to be able to make judgments as to the dividends policy of the organization. The creditors make use of ratios to assess how solvent the organization is and if it will be able to pay back its debts in the future. Creditors will most of the time even use ratios to set conditions before credit is provided to the organization. The management will use ratios to help them evaluate the attainment of their objectives and monitor their performances.

Standards
A standard is generally considered to be a basis for comparison. This can be seen as a point of reference against which other things can be evaluated, and it might relate to quality levels, behaviour levels or units of measurements. Within the hospitality industry and when analyzing ratios, the standards commonly used can be split into three categories which are:

- Ratios from the past performance of the organization: this permits a company to compare its current performances with those of its past in order to discover if there are any significant changes.

- Planned ratios that are the budgeted ratios of the organization: differences in actual performances from the budgeted plans can equally be analyzed in order to enhance efficiency in the management of the organization.

- The averages of the industry: industrial averages, also called industrial benchmarks are used by organizations to evaluate the various aspects of their performances in relation to the best practices within their particular industry.

It should be noted that different results may be generated when comparing ratios against different standards; as such the purpose of the ratio analysis should be considered before any conclusions are made.

Expression of ratios
Ratios are commonly expressed in the following formats:

- As a decimal (0.54), representing for example, the profit margin.

- As a percentage (10.5%), this is simply, a decimal multiplied by a 100, representing for example the multiple occupancy percentage.

- On a per unit basis (€25.20) representing for example, the average food service cheque.

- As a turnover (1.5) representing for example, the number of guests visiting a restaurant during a given period compared to the number of seats in the restaurant.

- As coverage of so many times (1.5:1 – read as 1.5 is to 1) representing for example, the number of times the total liabilities are absorbed by the total assets.

The expression of ratios depends entirely on the particular ratio and the nature of the significant relationship that it is trying to express between the figures it is relating to. It is equally a function of how the information the ratios provide is to be used.

7.2   Classification of ratios

There are various categories of ratios which might differ depending on the industry being analyzed. Within the hospitality industry, it is common acceptance to make use of the following categories of ratios: liquidity, solvency, profitability, activity and operating. The structure of the subsections is as follows:

7.2.1   Liquidity ratios
7.2.2   Solvency ratios
7.2.3   Profitability ratios
7.2.4   Activity ratios
7.2.5   Operating ratios

7.2.1   **Liquidity ratios**

A liquidity ratio measures the availability of cash within the organization to pay its current debts. It is used to determine the organization's ability to pay off its short term obligations. The higher the value of the ratio, the better will be the margin of safety that the organization has to cover its short term obligations. A company's ability to transform its current assets into cash to take care of its debts is of primary importance when its creditors are seeking payment. These are the most common liquidity ratios that are in use within the hospitality industry.

Current ratio

The current ratio shows the direct relationship between the current assets and the current liabilities. It is expressed as shown in the formula:

$$\frac{\text{Current assets}}{\text{Current liabilities}}$$

The current ratio is normally expressed as coverage of so many times, for example 1.24 times or 1.24:1. Owners normally prefer a low current ratio because shareholders regard investments in current assets as less productive. On the other hand, creditors would prefer a higher current ratio because it gives them the assurance that the organization can pay back its debts in time.

Acid test ratio

The acid test ratio which is also known as quick ratio shows the direct relationship between the quick assets and the current liabilities. Quick assets are generally those current assets that can or will be converted into cash fairly soon. The common ones are cash, marketable securities and accounts receivable. Quick assets exclude inventories and prepaid expenses. It is expressed as shown in the formula:

$$\frac{\text{Current assets} - \text{inventories and prepaid expenses}}{\text{Current liabilities}}$$

The acid test ratio is expressed as coverage of so many times, for example 1.12 times or 1.12:1. It is equally viewed by the owners and creditors in the same way as the current ratio.

Operating cash flow ratio

The operating cash flow ratio shows the relationship between the net operating cash flow and the average current liabilities. It is expressed as shown in the formula:

$$\frac{\text{Net operating cash flow}}{\text{Average current liabilities}}$$

The operating cash flow ratio is normally expressed as a decimal (0.79) or percentage (79%), the users of accounting ratios prefer to see it high because it means that the organization has enough cash to pay off its current liabilities.

Accounts receivable turnover

The accounts receivable turnover indicates how well accounts receivable are collected within the organization. Calculating the accounts receivable turnover is a 2 step process:

Step 1 Calculate the average accounts receivable by looking for the mean of the accounts receivable for the period under analysis:

$$\frac{\text{Accounts receivable at the beginning of the year} + \text{Accounts receivable at the end of the year}}{2}$$

Step 2 Calculate the accounts receivable turnover by dividing the total revenues by the average accounts receivable:

$$\frac{\text{Total revenues}}{\text{Average accounts receivable}}$$

The accounts receivable turnover is expressed as coverage of so many times, for example 8.2 times. This ratio indicates how well accounts receivable are being collected. The higher the turnover figure compared to whatever benchmark is being used indicates that the organization is effectively collecting its revenues and that its customers are paying their bills on time. A higher figure equally indicates that the organization's credit and collection policies are sound and effective.

Average collection period

The average collection period is an outcome of the accounts receivable turnover ratio and it is calculated as follows:

$$\frac{\text{The number of days in the period}}{\text{Accounts receivable turnover}}$$

The average collection period is normally expressed in days such as 27 days. For any given period, the higher the accounts receivable turnover, the lower will be the average collection period. As an outcome of the accounts receivable turnover it is viewed by the stakeholders in the same manner.

Working capital turnover ratio

The working capital turnover ratio is also known as the net sales to working capital ratio. It indicates the organization's effectiveness in using its working capital. It is calculated as follows:

$$\frac{\text{Total revenue}}{\text{Average working capital}}$$

The average working capital is determined as follows:

$$\frac{(\text{Current assets} - \text{current liabilities in the beginning of the period}) + (\text{Current assets} - \text{current liabilities at the end of the period})}{2}$$

The working capital turnover ratio is normally expressed as coverage over a number of times, such as 14 times. In general, owners prefer a lower working capital turnover ratio whereas creditors would prefer a higher working capital turnover ratio.

7.2.2 Solvency ratios

Solvency ratios indicate the ability of a company to meet its obligations when they are due, including the principal and interest on their long term debts. There are principally 2 basic sources of funds to finance a company which are; funds received from the owners, and financing received through contracting debts with third parties, which may include finance houses, suppliers, employees and the state. Other terms for solvency ratios are leverage or gearing ratios. The owners may provide substantially all of the funds that a company needs or there will be a combination of owner participation and financing from third parties. The risk of insolvency of organization depends on the amount of funding brought in by the owners and by the other parties. Leverage refers to the amount of long term debt that is used to finance the assets of a company compared to the amounts of owners' equity. A company with significantly more debt than equity is considered to be highly leveraged.

Solvency ratios as a category are made up of ratios that can be split into 2 subgroups;
- those ratios which are based on the balance sheet (solvency ratio, debt to equity ratio, long term debt to total capitalization ratio);

- those based on the income statement (the number of times interest earned ratio, the fixed charge coverage ratio, and the debt service coverage ratio) as well as the operating cash flows to total liabilities ratio which is based on both the balance sheet and the SCF.

From the general perspective of management and with the expanded use of leases, management contracts, joint ventures, and other financing techniques, leverage ratios must be carefully evaluated before conclusions are drawn. Generally, if the interests on the borrowed funds are less than the earnings which can be generated from using these funds then it will be advantageous to make use of leverage.

Solvency ratio
The solvency ratio, as a specific ratio, indicates the organization's ability to take care of its long term obligations. The solvency ratio is calculated by using the following formula:

$$\frac{\text{Total assets}}{\text{Total liabilities}}$$

The solvency ratio is normally expressed as coverage of so many times, for example 2.34 times or 2.34:1. This ratio is a measure of the solvency of a company at a given point time, but it ignores the effects of future inflows of funds from the operations of the organization. The greater the leverage used by the organization the lower will be the solvency ratio. Creditors generally prefer a high solvency ratio as it gives them the assurance of having something paid back in the event of the liquidation and disposal of the organization's assets. On the contrary, owners would prefer lower solvency ratios because this will help them in maximising their returns on investment.

Debt to equity ratio

The debt to equity ratio shows the relationship between the total liabilities and total owners' equity. It is calculated by using the following formula:

$$\frac{\text{Total liabilities}}{\text{Total owners' equity}}$$

The debt to equity ratio is generally expressed as coverage of so many times such as, 1.52:1. It indicates the organization's ability to survive, and at the same time honour the repayment of its long term debts. It is viewed in the same way as the solvency ratio by the owners and creditors. Creditors use this ratio as an indicator of the risk involved in providing credit to the organization and as such will prefer a lower debt to equity ratio. Owners on the other hand, in their desire to maximise their returns on investment using leverage, will prefer a higher debt to equity ratio.

Long term debt to total capitalization ratio

The long term debt to total capitalization ratio shows the relationship between the long term debts and the available capital. It is calculated as follows:

$$\frac{\text{Long term debt}}{\text{Long term debt} + \text{owners' equity}}$$

The long term debt to total capitalization ratio is normally expressed as a percentage, such as 38%. This is a variation of the debt to equity ratio and it calculates the proportion of a company's long term debt compared to its available capital. The available capital is derived by adding the long term debt to the owners' equity. Using this ratio permits creditors and investors to assess the leverage used by the organization and are able to compare it to other organizations in their analysis of the organization's exposure to risk. Creditors generally prefer a lower percentage since this will indicate a reduced exposure to risk while owners will prefer a higher percentage because of their desire to earn higher returns using leverage.

Number of times interest earned ratio

The number of times interest earned ratio shows the relationship between the earnings before interest and taxes and the interest expense. It is calculated using the following formula:

$$\frac{\text{EBIT}}{\text{Interest expense}}$$

The number of times interest earned ratio is expressed as coverage of so many times such as 4.2 times, this ratio shows a company's past ability to meet its interest payments. It also indicates the margin of safety or the amounts which profits could decline and still meet the interest obligations of a company. All the major stakeholders (creditors, management and owners) prefer a relatively high ratio.

Fixed charge coverage ratio

The fixed charge coverage ratio is a variation of the number of times interest ratio by its inclusion of lease expenses. It is calculated as follows:

$$\frac{\text{EBIT} + \text{lease expenses}}{\text{Interest expense} + \text{lease expenses}}$$

The fixed charge coverage ratio, expressed as coverage of so many times such as 5.02 times is a variation of the number of times interest ratio because it considers lease (rental) expenses in both its numerator and denominator. It is given the same consideration like the number of times interest earned ratio by the main stakeholders. The larger the ratio, the safer the company is since it has a thicker cushion to pay its debts.

Debt service coverage ratio

The debt service coverage ratio shows the relationship between the operating incomes and the debt service payments. In its complete form it is calculated as follows:

$$\frac{\text{Net operating income} - \text{cash transfers to replacement reserves}}{\text{Debt service payments}}$$

The debt service coverage ratio is expressed as coverage of so many times such as 6.18 times and it measures the extent to which a company creates enough adjusted net operated income to cover its debts (both principal and interest).

In situations where there are no cash transfers to replacement reserves, the formula simply becomes

$$\frac{\text{Net operating income}}{\text{Debt service payments}}$$

All the major stakeholders would prefer to have a high debt service coverage ratio.

Operating cash flows to total liabilities ratio

The operating cash flows to total liabilities ratio combines information from the balance sheet as well as information from the statement of cash flow. It is calculated as follows:

$$\frac{\text{Operating cash flows}}{\text{Average total liabilities}}$$

The operating cash flows to total liabilities ratio is expressed as a decimal (0.315) or a percentage (31.5%). It introduces a dynamic notion into the assessment of solvency by bringing in operating cash flows (from the SCF) which covers a period of time into solvency analysis unlike the debt to equity ratio, equity ratio and the long term debt to capitalization ratio which comes from the balance sheets (fixed point in time). All the major stakeholders prefer this ratio to be relatively high.

7.2.3 Profitability ratios

Profitability ratios are used to measure the business' ability to generate earnings compared to its expenses and other relevant costs during its operations for a specific period of time. These ratios permit management and owners to compare their performances to that of others within the same property or across companies as well as compare to their own expectations as defined in their budgets. As a primary objective of most hospitality operations is to make profit which can be paid out through dividends or retained in the company as retained earnings, the assessment of a company's profitability is of primary importance. Creditors always want to notice increases in the company's profitability soon as this will reduce the risk the creditors bear.

Gross return on assets

The gross return on assets shows the relationship between the EBIT and the average total assets. It is calculated as follows:

$$\frac{\text{EBIT}}{\text{Average total assets}}$$

The gross return on assets is expressed as a percentage. It measures the effectiveness of management's use of the organisation's assets regardless of financing methods. It is useful in assessing the likelihood of obtaining more debt financing. It is assessed based on industry standards and individual company expectations.

Net return on assets

The net return on assets is the relationship between net income and average total assets. It is calculated as follows:

$$\frac{\text{Net income}}{\text{Average total assets}}$$

The net return on assets is equally expressed as a percentage. It evaluates the possibility of seeking for equity financing instead of debt financing. It is a general indicator of the company's profitability. The net return on assets can equally be calculated by multiplying the profit margin ratio by the asset turnover ratio. Its assessment is based on industry averages as well as the company's own profile developed through time.

Profit margin

The profit margin ratio shows the relationship between net income and total revenue. It is calculated as follows:

$$\frac{\text{Net income}}{\text{Total revenue}}$$

The profit margin is expressed as a percentage, it is equally known as the net income to sales revenue ratio. It measures management effectiveness in generating sales and controlling expenses. The higher the profit margin the better the situation.

Operating efficiency ratio

The operating efficiency ratio shows the relationship between the gross operating profit and the total revenue. It is determined as follows:

$$\frac{\text{Gross operating profit}}{\text{Total revenue}}$$

The operating efficiency ratio is expressed as a percentage. It is also called gross operating profit margin ratio or simply gross operating ratio. It measures the company's ability to generate sales and control its expenses. Since it is calculated before the deduction of management expenses, it is useful in comparing comparable properties operated by third party management companies with owner operated properties. The higher the outcome of the efficiency ratio, the better will be the situation.

Return on owners' equity

The return on owners' equity shows the relationship between the net income and the average owners' equity. It is derived as follows:

$$\frac{\text{Net income}}{\text{Average owners' equity}}$$

The return on owners' equity is expressed as a percentage. It shows the effectiveness of the management's use of equity funds. It compares the profits of the company to the investments brought in by the shareholders. If the company has different types of shares (common and preferred) the return on owners' equity can be modified as follows:

$$\frac{\text{Net income} - \text{preferred dividends}}{\text{Average owners equity}}$$

This now will be called the return on common shareholders' equity.

Earnings per share

The earnings per share in its simplest form, where there are no preferred shares, is calculated as:

$$\frac{\text{Net income}}{\text{Average outstanding shares}}$$

In situations where preferred shares exist the formula is modified as such:

$$\frac{\text{Net income} - \text{preferred dividends}}{\text{Average outstanding shares}}$$

The earnings per share is expressed in currency values. It serves as an indicator of a company's profitability. It is generally considered as the single most important element in determining share price and it is used in assessing the price-to-earnings valuation ratio.

Price-to-earnings valuation ratio

The price-to-earnings valuation ratio shows the relationship between the market value per share and the earnings per share. It is calculated as follows:

$$\frac{\text{Market value per share}}{\text{Earnings per share}}$$

The price-to-earnings valuation ratio evaluates a company's current share price to its earnings per share. This ratio is affected by how buyers and sellers view the stability of the company, its potential growth in earnings, and the risk of investing in the shares of the company.

Gross operating profit per available room (GOPPAR)
The gross operating profit per available room (GOPPAR) shows the relationship between the gross operating profit and the total rooms for sale. It is determined as follows:

$$\frac{\text{Gross operating profit}}{\text{Total rooms for sale}}$$

The gross operating profit per available room (GOPPAR) reflects the gross operating profits of the hotel as opposed to its revenues and it provides a clearer indication of its overall performance than the REVPAR (discussed in 7.2.5 below). GOPPAR takes into consideration management control and containment costs. It is useful in comparing gross operation profits across properties within the same competitive set.

Income before fixed charges per available room
The income before fixed charges per available room shows the relationship between the income before fixed charges and the available rooms. It is calculated as follows:

$$\frac{\text{Income before fixed charges}}{\text{Available rooms}}$$

The income before fixed charges per available room is expressed in units. It measures the management's ability to produce profits through sales while controlling all departmental costs, undistributed expenses and management fees.

Income before fixed charges margin
The income before fixed charges margin ratio shows the relationship between income before fixed charges and the total revenue. It is determined as follows:

$$\frac{\text{Income before fixed charges}}{\text{Total revenue}}$$

The income before fixed charges margin ratio is expressed in units. It measures the management's ability to produce profits through sales while controlling all departmental costs, undistributed expenses and management fees.

Net operating income per available room
The net operating income per available room shows the relationship between the net operating income and the available rooms. It is determined as follows:

$$\frac{\text{Net operating income}}{\text{Available rooms}}$$

The net operating income per available room is expressed in units. It measures the management's ability to produce profits through sales while controlling all departmental costs, undistributed expenses, management fees, property taxes, insurance and property rents.

Net operating income margin ratio

The net operating income margin ratio shows the relationship between the net operating income and the total revenue. It is calculated as follows:

$$\frac{\text{Net operating income}}{\text{Total revenue}}$$

The net operating income margin ratio is expressed in units. It measures the management's ability to produce profits through sales while controlling all departmental costs, undistributed expenses, management fees, property taxes, insurance and property rents.

Cash on cash return

The cash on cash return shows the relationship between the amount of cash that was used in the business during the period and the average owners' equity. It is calculated as follows:

$$\frac{\text{Adjusted net operating income} - \text{debt service}}{\text{Average owners' equity}}$$

The cash on cash return is expressed in percentages and it is one of the methods of estimating return on investments. The higher the return, the more satisfied are the investors.

7.2.4 Activity ratios

Activity ratios measure management's effectiveness and ability to convert its resources into cash or sales. They are equally called turnover or efficiency ratios. They help in measuring management's effectiveness in making use of the assets of the company.

Food inventory turnover ratio

The food inventory turnover ratio shows the relationship between the cost of food used and the average food inventory. It is determined as follows:

$$\frac{\text{Cost of food used}}{\text{Average food inventory}}$$

The food inventory turnover ratio is expressed as a number of times during the period. It shows how quickly the food inventory is used. The average food inventory which forms the denominator in the formula is calculated as follows:

$$\frac{\text{Inventory at the beginning of the period} + \text{inventory at the end of the period}}{2}$$

Generally the quicker the food inventory turnover the more desirable is the situation because food inventory costs a lot to maintain.

Beverage inventory turnover ratio

The beverage inventory turnover ratio shows the relationship between the cost of beverage used and the average beverage inventory. It is determined as follows:

$$\frac{\text{Cost of beverage used}}{\text{Average beverage inventory}}$$

The beverage inventory turnover ratio is expressed as a number of times during the period. It shows how quickly the beverage inventory is used. The average beverage inventory which forms the denominator in the formula is determined as follows:

$$\frac{\text{Inventory at the beginning of the period + inventory at the end of the period}}{2}$$

Generally the quicker the inventory turnover the more desirable is the situation because beverage inventory costs a lot to maintain.

Inventory holding period

The inventory holding period shows the relationship between the operating days in the period and the inventory turnover ratio for the period. It is calculated as follows:

$$\frac{\text{Operating days in the period}}{\text{Inventory turnover ratio for the period}}$$

The inventory holding period should be split between the two major types of inventory (food & beverages). Expressed in number of days, it represents the number of times during a given period that the specific inventory is theoretically brought down to zero.

Fixed asset turnover

The fixed asset turnover ratio shows the relationship between the total revenues and the average total fixed assets. It is determined as follows:

$$\frac{\text{Total sales revenue}}{\text{Average total fixed assets}}$$

The fixed asset turnover ratio is expressed as a number of times. It measures the effectiveness of the use of fixed assets in generating sales. The average total fixed assets shown in the formula is determined as follows:

$$\frac{\text{Total fixed assets in beginning of period + total fixed assets end of period}}{2}$$

In general within the hospitality industry, this ratio can range from 1.5 to more than 2 times a year. Restaurants could have ratios of more than 5 times a year if they are in rented properties. A high ratio indicates management's effectiveness in the use of fixed assets, whereas a low ratio indicates that management is not that effective and might to need to dispose some of its property. All stakeholders would want to have a high ratio.

Asset turnover

The asset turnover ratio shows the relationship between total sales and average total assets. It is calculated as follows:

$$\frac{\text{Total sales}}{\text{Average total assets}}$$

The asset turnover ratio is expressed as a number of times. It measures the effectiveness of the use of total assets in generating sales. The average total asset is calculated as follows:

$$\frac{\text{Total assets in beginning of period + total assets end of period}}{2}$$

A high asset turnover ratio indicates management's effectiveness in the use of its assets, whereas a low ratio indicates that management is not that effective and might need to dispose some of its property. All stakeholders would want to have a high ratio.

Paid occupancy percentage

The paid occupancy percentage shows the relationship between the rooms sold and the available rooms. It is determined as follows:

$$\frac{\text{Paid rooms occupied}}{\text{Available rooms}}$$

Available rooms are derived from the available number of rooms in the property multiplied by the number of days in the year. Expressed as a percentage, it is a major indicator of management's success in selling its rooms. It can be split between the general occupancy percentage, the transient occupancy percentage, group occupancy percentage, contract occupancy percentage, complimentary occupancy percentage and multiple occupancy percentage, some of which are shown below.

Complimentary occupancy percentage

The complimentary occupancy percentage is a variation of the paid occupancy percentage in which only the occupied complimentary rooms are assessed. It is determined as follows:

$$\frac{\text{Complimentary rooms}}{\text{Available rooms}}$$

Also expressed as a percentage, it shows the weight of the complimentary rooms in the overall rooms' sales.

Average occupancy per room

The average occupancy per room shows the relationship between the number of guests and the number of rooms occupied by guests. It is calculated as follows:

$$\frac{\text{Number of guests}}{\text{Number of rooms occupied by guests}}$$

The average occupancy per room is expressed in guest units and should be assessed in relation to industrial averages and company expectations.

Multiple occupancy percentage

The multiple occupancy percentage shows the relationship between the rooms occupied by two or more persons and the total number of rooms occupied by guests. It is calculated as follows:

$$\frac{\text{Rooms occupied by two or more persons}}{\text{Number of rooms occupied by guests}}$$

The multiple occupancy percentage is also called double occupancy and it is expressed as a percentage. As with all occupancy percentages, the higher the percentage the better will be the situation.

Food service seat turnover

The food service seat turnover shows the relationship between the total guests served and the number of seats available for the period. It can be calculated as follows:

$$\frac{\text{Total guests served (covers)}}{\text{Number of seats for the period}}$$

The food service seat turnover is expressed as a number of times covered and the higher the level the better the situation.

7.2.5 Operating ratios

Operating ratios measure the efficiency of a company's management by comparing its operating expenses to its sales. These operating ratios can be calculated on a daily, weekly, monthly or annual basis and are very useful for control purposes. The detailed information that is used to compute these ratios are generally reserved for internal management. Within the hospitality industry more than 200 operating ratios can be generated, but here, only a few are discussed.

Average daily rate (ADR)

The average daily rate (ADR) shows the relationship between the rooms' revenue and the number of rooms occupied. It is calculated as follows:

$$\frac{\text{Rooms revenue}}{\text{Rooms occupied}}$$

The average daily rate (ADR) is also called the average room rate. Hotels make use of this global rate despite the fact that within the same property room prices may vary considerably. In case of need, this rate can be calculated for each particular market segment.

Sales revenue per available room (REVPAR)

The sales revenue per available room (REVPAR) shows the relationship between the total rooms' revenue and the total number of available rooms. It is calculated as follows:

$$\frac{\text{Total rooms revenue}}{\text{Total available rooms}}$$

The sales revenue per available room (REVPAR) can be equally derived from the relationship between the paid occupancy percentage and the average daily rate (paid occupancy percentage × ADR).

Total REVPAR

The total REVPAR shows the relationship between the total property revenue and the number of available rooms. It is determined as follows:

$$\frac{\text{Total property revenue}}{\text{Available rooms}}$$

Total REVPAR introduces into the REVPAR analysis the contributions from the sale of non room items such as F & B products in the assessment of the REVPAR.

Sales revenue per available customer (REVPAC)

The sales revenue per available customer (REVPAC) shows the relationship between the total revenue from the hotel guests and the total number of guests. It is calculated as follows:

$$\frac{\text{Total revenue from hotel guests}}{\text{Total number of guests}}$$

The sales revenue per available customer (REVPAC) brings the idea of revenue assessment right down to the level of a single guest.

Labour cost percentage

The labour cost percentage shows the relationship between the overall labour costs and the total revenue. It is calculated as follows:

$$\frac{\text{Salaries + wages + bonuses + payroll taxes + fringe benefits}}{\text{Total revenue}}$$

In cases of multiple operated departments the labour cost percentages can be separated such as rooms labour cost percentage, F & B labour cost percentage. In such instances the salaries and its related components should result only from the specific department as well as the revenue should come only from that department. In cases of the non-operated departments, the labour cost percentages will be related to the total revenue of the property.

Food cost percentage

The food cost percentage shows the relationship between the cost of food sold and the food sales. It is determined as follows:

$$\frac{\text{Cost of food sold}}{\text{Food sales}}$$

The food cost percentage is one of the most important ratios in analyzing food service operations. It permits the company to determine how reasonable or not are their food costs – time-wise and industry-wise.

Beverage cost percentage

The beverage cost percentage shows the relationship between the cost of beverage sold and the beverage sales. It is determined as follows:

$$\frac{\text{Cost of beverages sold}}{\text{Beverage sales}}$$

The beverage cost percentage has the same significance like the food cost percentage to beverage services operations.

Average food service cheque

The average food service cheque shows the relationship between the total food revenue and the number of guests served. It is calculated as follows:

$$\frac{\text{Total food revenue}}{\text{Number of food covers}}$$

The average food service cheque can be calculated separately per meal period as well as separately per the different food service outlets. Covers represent the number of guests served in the food service outlet during a period.

Mix of sales

The mix of sales is the proportion of sales coming from the different departments or products within an establishment. It indicates the individual contribution of the various departments to the overall sales. Exhibit 7.1 illustrates the sales mix of a simple hotel. It shows for example that the rooms department contributes 55.93% of the total revenues.

Exhibit 7.1 **Illustration of the mix of sales**

Department	Sales	Percentage
Rooms	€ 44,550,000.00	55.93%
Food & Bevarage	€ 24,475,000.00	30.72%
Rentals and other incomes	€ 10,635,000.00	13.35%
Total	€ 79,660,000.00	100.00%

7.3 Performance review process

The main aim of a performance review is to provide an understanding of the business, and, together with an analysis of all the relevant information, provide an interpretation of the results. A performance review is generally undertaken using a standard format and methodology. The most effective performance review is provided from a balanced view of each of the activities of the organization, which necessarily involves close cooperation amongst all the departments.

A performance review using financial statements may be undertaken for a number of reasons, for example:

- to assist in investment decisions
- to identify possible takeover targets
- to evaluate the financial strength of potential or existing customers or suppliers

All performance reviews must use some sort of benchmark. Comparisons may be made against past periods and against budget; they may also be made against other companies and using general data relating to the industry within which the company operates.

The steps of the performance review process can be summarized as follows:

Step 1 Carry out a SWOT analysis which involves assessing the company's performance by listing the key features of the company from both an internal and an external perspective. Internally, the strengths and weaknesses of the company will be assessed and externally, the opportunities the company can take advantage of, and the threats the company is exposed to will be reviewed.

Step 2 Consider the major features of the company by reviewing in detail, based on all available financial statements, the various industrial and geographical sectors of the business, the trends within these sectors, and the business in general. Background information may be extracted from the applicable accounting policies, the annual report, the auditors' report, and details of any significant events that may have occurred in the period under analysis.

Step 3 Assess the profitability of the company by analysing the major profitability ratios as shown in 7.2.3.

Step 4 Assess the efficiency of the company by analysing the major operating and activity ratios (see 7.2.4 and 7.2.5), its operating cycle, its gearing as well as carrying out a vertical (common size) analysis (see 6.4) of its income statement.

Step 5 Assess the growth of the company by carrying out a comparative (horizontal) analysis (see 6.2) of the main financial statements which may provide indications as to the trends in the performance of the company.

Step 6 Assess the liquidity of the company by analysing the major liquidity ratios (see 7.2.1).

Step 7 Verify the financing of the company by analysing the major solvency ratios (see 7.2.2).

Step 8 Assess the company's management of financial risk which is more and more relevant in the current context of globalization combined with the complex nature in the types of products, services, operations and financing now available. Risk assessment can be analysed from the perspectives of types and areas of investment, exchange and interest rates, as well as levels of trade credit.

Step 9 Assess the company's investment policy to determine if it is carrying out enough capital investment to ensure its future continuous operations, profitability and sustainability. This can be assessed by verifying the various relationships between the company's capital expenditure to its sales, to the level of depreciation, and also to the levels of plant, property and equipment.

Step 10 Conclude the analysis and this will include a consideration of the company's SWOT analysis and the main performance features. It will consider growth and profitability and whether or not this is maintainable, as well as levels of finance and investment, and whether there is sufficient cash flow, and it should indicate the possible future plans of the company.

This performance review process finishes with the establishment a proper report to the management that will be able to give them an effective insight into the functioning of the company.

Limitations of the performance review process
There are some limitations to the performance review process as described above. The following points should be taken into account when comparing performance against other companies (and sometimes within the company itself – past periods), or when industrial averages are used:

- there may be a lack of uniformity in accounting definitions and techniques
- the balance sheet is only a snapshot in time, and only represents a single estimate of the company's position
- there may actually be no standards for comparison
- changes in the environment and changes in money values, together with short-term fluctuations, may have a significant impact
- the past should really not be relied on as a good predictor of the future

The overall essence will be for the performance review to be able to paint the correct picture of the performance of the company that should be able to permit its management make proper decisions.

7.4   DuPont analysis

DuPont analysis (also known as the DuPont identity, the DuPont model, the DuPont formula, or the DuPont method) is a method of performance measurement that was started by the DuPont Corporation (USA) in the 1920s. As ratios are not entirely independent, the performance on one is related to the performance of others.
The DuPont system of analysis is used to determine the return on assets (ROA) and the return on equity (ROE) by multiplying related ratios as will be shown in this section.

DuPont analysis shows that the ROA is affected by two things:

- The operating efficiency, which is measured by the profit margin, and
- The asset use efficiency, which is measured by the total asset turnover

$$ROA = \text{Profit margin} \times \text{Asset turnover}$$

This can be transformed, by using the various components of the ratios into:

$$ROA = \frac{\text{Net income}}{\text{Total revenue}} \times \frac{\text{Total revenue}}{\text{Average total assets}}$$

ROA measures how a firm uses its assets to generate profits. The profit margin reveals how the firm generates net income in relation to its revenue. The asset turnover reveals the firm's ability to generate sales with assets. A desired ROA can be achieved in a number of different combinations of profit margin and asset turnover ratios. For example, assume the desired ROA level is 14%. This can be achieved with different possible combinations of profit margin ratios and asset turnover ratios. Exhibit 7.2 is an illustration of this possibility in which the desired ROA of 14% is achieved through three different options.

Exhibit 7.2 **ROA from different options**

Option	Profit Margin	Asset Turnover	ROA
A	28.00%	0.5	14.00%
B	18.67%	0.75	14.00%
C	14.00%	1	14.00%

As with the ROA, DuPont analysis also shows that the ROE is on its own affected by three things:

· The operating efficiency,
· The asset use efficiency, and
· The financial leverage, which is measured by the equity multiplier

$$ROE = \text{Profit margin} \times \text{Asset turnover} \times \text{Equity multiplier}$$

This can be transformed, by using the various components of the ratios into:

$$ROE = \frac{\text{Net income}}{\text{Total revenue}} \times \frac{\text{Total revenue}}{\text{Average total assets}} \times \frac{\text{Average total assets}}{\text{Average owners' equity}}$$

Essentially, ROE is determined by multiplying the ROA by the equity multiplier. The greater the equity multiplier of a firm with a given ROA, the greater will be the ROE. The higher the ROE, the greater will be the financial risk associated with that higher ROE.

This analysis enables the analyst to understand the source of superior (or inferior) return by comparison with companies in similar industries (or between industries). The DuPont identity, however, is less useful for some industries, that do not use certain concepts, or for which the concepts are less meaningful. Variations may be used in certain industries, as long as they also respect the underlying structure of DuPont analysis. DuPont analysis is illustrated in exhibit 7.5 based on the data contained in exhibits 7.3 and 7.4.

Exhibit 7.3 **Condensed balance sheet of the Europa Alliance Hotel Plc. December 31st 2011**

**Balance Sheet – Europa Alliance Hotel Plc
on December 31st 2011**

Current assets	€ 12,155,000.00
Fixed Assets	€ 46,420,000.00
Total Assets	€ 58,575,000.00
Current Liabilities	€ 10,571,000.00
Long Term Liabilities	€ 24,904,000.00
Total Liabilities	€ 35,475,000.00
Common Stock	€ 3,025,000.00
Other Owners' Equity	€ 20,075,000.00
Total Owners' Equity	€ 23,100,000.00

Exhibit 7.4 **Condensed income statement of the Europa Alliance Hotel Plc. December 31st 2011**

**Income Statement – Europa Alliance Hotel Plc
FTY ending December 31st 2011**

Revenues	€ 71,500,000.00
Cost of Sales	€ 33,159,500.00
Indirect Expenses	€ 16,610,000.00
Fixed Charges	€ 8,772,500.00
Income Tax	€ 5,186,500.00
Net Income	€ 7,771,500.00

Exhibit 7.5 An Excel generated DuPont Analysis of the Europa Alliance Hotel Plc.
December 31st 2011

DuPont Analysis – Europa Alliance Hotel Plc. Decmber 31st 2011

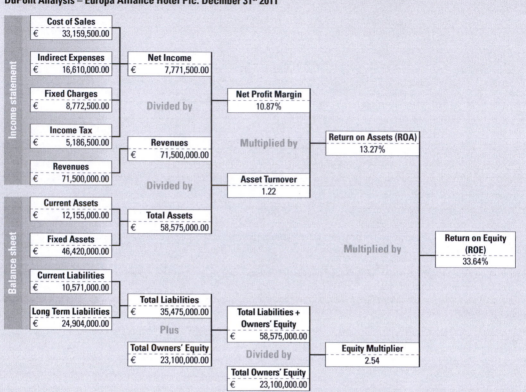

© Noordhoff Uitgevers bv

Glossary

Accounts receivable turnover – is the ratio of total revenue divided by the average accounts receivable. It measures how quickly guests pay their bills.

Acid test ratio – is the ratio obtained through dividing the liquid assets by current liabilities. It is one of the main indicators of the liquidity of a company.

Activity ratios – is the group of accounting ratios that measure a company's ability to convert its different balance sheet accounts into cash or sales.

Asset turnover – is the ratio that measures a company's ability to generate sales in relation to total assets. It is calculated through dividing the total revenue by the average total assets.

Average collection period – is the number of days it takes for a company to collect all its accounts receivable. It is calculated through dividing the accounts receivable turnover by the number of days in the period.

Average daily rate (ADR) – is the ratio that indicates the level of a hotel's performance. It is calculated through dividing the rooms revenue by the number of rooms sold. It is also called the average room rate.

Average food service cheque – is the average amount of guests consumption of food services. It is calculated through dividing the total food revenues by the total number of food covers.

Average occupancy per room – is the ratio that indicates the company's ability to use the room facilities. It is calculated through dividing the number of guests by the number of rooms occupied by guests.

Average room rate – see average daily rate

Beverage cost percentage – is the ratio that compares the cost of beverage sold to beverage revenues. It is calculated through dividing the cost of beverage sold during a given period by the beverage revenues of the same period.

Beverage inventory turnover – is the ratio that shows how quickly the beverage inventory is used. It is calculated through dividing the cost of beverage used by the average beverage inventory.

Cash on cash return – is the ratio that shows the relationship between the amount of cash that was used in the company during the period and the average owners' equity. It is calculated through dividing the adjusted net operating income less debt service by the average owners' equity.

Complimentary occupancy percentage – is the ratio that shows the relationship between the complimentary rooms and the available rooms. It is calculated through dividing the complimentary rooms by the available rooms.

Current ratio – is the ratio of the relationship between the current assets and the current liabilities. It is calculated through dividing the total current assets by the total current liabilities. It is one of the main indicators of the liquidity of a company.

Debt service coverage ratio – is the ratio that shows the extent to which a company creates enough adjusted net operating income to cover its debts. It is calculated through dividing the net operating income less cash transfers to replacement reserves by the debt service payments.

Debt to equity ratio – is the ratio that shows the company's ability to survive and as such honour the payments of its long term debts. It is calculated through dividing the total liabilities by the total owners' equity.

DuPont analysis – is a method of performance measurement used in determining the return on equity (ROE) and the return on assets (ROA).

Earnings per share – is the ratio that is a general indicator of the profitability of a company. It is calculated through dividing the net income by the average outstanding shares.

Equity multiplier – is the ratio that shows the amount of assets owned by the company for each equivalent monetary unit the owners have put into the company. It is calculated through dividing the average total assets by the average owners' equity. The equity multiplier is one of the measures of financial leverage and represents both profit and risk measurement. It is used to determine the return on equity (ROE) when it is applied to the return on assets (ROA). It also reflects how many assets can go into default before a company becomes insolvent.

Fixed asset turnover – is the ratio that measures the effectiveness of the use of fixed assets in generating revenues. It is calculated through dividing the total revenue by the average total fixed assets.

Fixed charge coverage ratio – is a variation of the number of times interest earned ratio because it takes into account lease expenses. It is calculated through dividing the earnings before interest and taxes (EBIT) plus lease expenses by interest and lease expenses.

Food cost percentage – is the ratio that compares the cost of food sold to food revenues. It is calculated through dividing the cost of food sold during a given period by the food revenues of the same period.

Food inventory turnover ratio – is the ratio that shows how quickly the food inventory is used. It is calculated through dividing the cost of food used by the average food inventory.

Food service seat turnover – is the measure of the number of seats turned over (number of guests) during a meal period. It is calculated through dividing the total guests served (covers) by the number of available seats for the meal period.

Gross operating profit per available room (GOPPAR) – is the ratio that provides a clearer indication of the overall performance of a hotel than the REVPAR because it takes into account management control and containment costs. It is calculated through dividing the gross operating profit by the total rooms for sale.

Gross return on assets – measures the effectiveness of the use of a company's assets by the management. It is calculated through dividing the earnings before interest and taxes (EBIT) by the average total assets.

Income before fixed charges margin ratio – is the ratio that measures the management's ability to produce profits through sales while controlling all departmental costs, undistributed expenses and management fees. It is calculated through dividing the income before fixed charges by the total revenue.

Income before fixed charges per available room – is variation of the income before fixed charges margin ratio in the sense that it is calculated through dividing the income before fixed charges by the available rooms.

Inventory holding period – is the ratio that shows the number of times in a given period that a specific inventory is theoretically brought down to zero. It is calculated through dividing the number of operating days in the period by the inventory turnover ratio.

Labour cost percentage – is the ratio that compares the labour costs per department to the revenues generated by the departments (for revenue centres), or to the total revenue (for service centres). It is calculated through dividing the overall labour costs by the related revenues.

Liquidity ratios – is the group of accounting ratios that measure a company's ability to honour its short term obligations.

Long term debt to total capitalization ratio – is a variation of the debt to equity ratio and it compares the company's long term debt to the available capital. It is calculated through dividing the long term debt by the long term debt and owners' equity.

Mix of sales – is the proportion of sales coming from the different departments or products within an establishment. It indicates the individual contribution of the various departments to the overall sales.

Multiple occupancy percentage – is also called double occupancy percentage and the ratio indicates the relationship between rooms occupied by more than one guest to the number of rooms occupied by guests. It is calculated through dividing the number of rooms occupied by two or more guests by the number of rooms occupied by guests.

Net operating income margin ratio – is the ratio that measures the company's ability to produce profit through sales while controlling all departmental costs, undistributed expenses, management fees, property taxes, insurance and property rents. It is calculated through dividing the net operating income by the total revenue.

Net operating income per available room – is a variation of the net operating income margin ratio and it is calculated through dividing the net operating income by the number of available rooms.

Net return on assets – is a ratio that shows the after tax earnings of assets and is an indicator of the profitability of a company. It is calculated through dividing the net income by the average total assets.

Number of times interest earned ratio – is the ratio that shows a company's past ability to honour its interest payments. It is calculated through dividing the earnings before interest on taxes by the interest expense.

Operating cash flow ratio – is a ratio that measures how well current liabilities are covered by the cash flow generated from a company's operations. It is calculated through dividing the net operating cash flow by the average current liabilities.

Operating cash flow to total liability ratio – is a variation of the operating cash flow ratio and it is calculated through dividing the operating cash flow by the average total liabilities.

Operating efficiency ratio – also called the gross operating profit ratio, it measures the company's ability to generate sales and control its expenses. It is calculated through dividing the gross operating profit by the total revenue.

Operating ratios – is the group of accounting ratios that helps a company's management to analyze their operations.

Paid occupancy percentage – is a ratio that shows the relationship between the rooms sold and the available rooms. It is calculated through dividing the rooms sold by the available rooms.

Price-to-earnings valuation ratio – is a ratio that evaluates a company's current share price in relation to its earnings per share. It is calculated through dividing the market value per share by the earnings per share.

Profit margin – is a ratio that measures the management's effectiveness in generating revenues and controlling its expenses. It is calculated through dividing the net income by the total revenue.

Profitability ratios – is the group of accounting ratios that show how effective the management has been.

Ratio – shows the arithmetic relationship between two or more elements.

Return on owners' equity (ROE) – is a ratio that shows how effective the management has been in their use of equity funding. It is a general indicator of the profitability of the company. It is calculated through dividing the net income by the average owners' equity.

Revenue per available customer (REVPAC) – is a ratio that shows the revenues received per guest served. It is calculated through dividing the total revenue from the hotel guests by the total number of guests.

Revenue per available room (REVPAR) – is a ratio that shows the revenues received per available room in the property. It is calculated through dividing the total rooms' revenue by the total available rooms.

Solvency ratio – is a ratio that measures the solvency of a company at the given point of time, by showing how far the company is able to meet its long term obligations. It is calculated through dividing the total assets by the total liabilities.

Solvency ratios – is the group of ratios that show how far a company is financed by debt and if it can honour its long term obligations.

Standard – is a basis for comparison which can be seen as a point of reference against which other things be evaluated.

Working capital turnover ratio – is a ratio that indicates the company's effectiveness in using its working capital. It is calculated through dividing the total revenues by the average working capital.

Multiple choice questions

7.1 Hospitality managers use ratios mainly to help them:
a clarify why the guests may not be loyal
b evaluate the attainment of their objectives and monitor their performances
c recognize specific problems and the solutions to them
d verify the effectiveness of the competition

7.2 Creditors will generally use ratio analysis to evaluate the _____ of a business.
a activity
b efficiency
c liquidity
d solvency

7.3 Which of the following categories of ratios shows how effective management has been in a particular period?
a activity
b liquidity
c profitability
d solvency

7.4 Using the information below, the multiple occupancy percentage is equal to:

Available rooms	220,000
Rooms occupied by guests	146,000
Number of guests	180,000
Rooms occupied by 2 or more guests	25,400

a 11.5%
b 14.1%
c 17.4%
d none of the above

7.5 DuPont analysis shows that the ROA is affected by:
a the operating efficiency and the equity multiplier
b the asset use efficiency and the equity multiplier
c the financial leverage and the equity multiplier
d none of the above

Exercises

7.1 Using this selection of some of the financial ratios of the New Standards Restaurant, write a short commentary on their liquidity position during the years analyzed.

	2008	2009	2010
Acid-test ratio	1.15:1	1.25:1	1.35:1
Current ratio	1.4:1	1.6:1	1.8:1
Inventory turnover	21 times	23 times	25 times
Accounts receivable turnover	23 times	20 times	17 times

7.2 Determine the food cost percentage of the Corporate Road stop during the month of March 2010 based on the following financial information:

Beginning food inventory	€	30,600.00
Ending food inventory	€	27,200.00
Food sales	€	408,000.00
Food purchases	€	139,400.00

7.3 The balance sheet and condensed income statement of the Sea View Motel are given below

The Sea View Motel
Balance sheet
December 31st 2009

Assets		
Current assets		
Cash	€	157,500.00
Accounts receivable	€	186,000.00
Inventories	€	10,500.00
Total current assets	€	354,000.00
Property and equipment:		
Land	€	93,000.00
Building (net)	€	465,000.00
Furniture & equipment (net)	€	138,000.00
Total property and equipment	€	696,000.00
Total assets	€	1,050,000.00
Liabilities and owners' equity		
Current Liabilities		
Accounts payable	€	270,000.00
Note payable	€	22,500.00
Current maturity of martgage payable	€	37,500.00
Total current liabilities	€	330,000.00
Long term liabilities		
Notes payable	€	75,000.00
Mortgage payable	€	150,000.00
Total long term liabilities	€	225,000.00
Total Liabilities	€	555,000.00
Owners' Equity		
Common stock	€	165,000.00
Retained earnings	€	330,000.00
Total owners' equity	€	495,000.00
Total liabilities and owners' equity	€	1,050,000.00

The Sea View Motel
Condensed Income Statement
For the year anded December 31st 2009

Revenues	€	2,325,000.00
Cost of goods sold	€	307,500.00
Operating expenses	€	1,215,000.00
Contribution margin	€	802,500.00
Undistributed operating expenses	€	183,000.00
Income after undistributed operating expenses	€	619,500.00
Interest	€	36,000.00
Other fixed charges	€	262,500.00
Income before taxes	€	321,000.00
Income tax (32%)	€	102,720.00
Net income	€	218,280.00

Using the data provided in the statements of the Sea View Motel, calculate the following ratios:
- Acid-test ratio
- Asset turnover (assume the total assets stayed the same during 2009)
- Current ratio
- Debt to equity ratio
- Number of times interest earned ratio
- Operating efficiency ratio
- Profit margin

7.4 Using the information contained in 7.3, carry out the following activities
- establish the complete DuPont analysis as shown in exhibit 7.5
- make a brief performance report about the Sea View Motel for 2009

Management of working capital

8

8.1 The importance of working capital management
8.2 The working capital cycle

Cash is the most fundamental business resource through which creditors, suppliers, employees, the state, shareholders and other stakeholders can be satisfied. Sources of cash include those placed in the business by the owners, those borrowed from third parties (individuals, other business establishments or lending institutions), and those generated by the business itself. In section 8.1 the importance of working capital management is discussed followed by the explanation and illustration of the working capital cycle in section 8.2.

8.1 The importance of working capital management

Working capital is defined as the surplus of current assets over current liabilities and indicates the amounts available to the business to conduct its revenue generating activities. It is expressed in the following formula:

Working capital = current assets – current liabilities

Decisions related to working capital and short term financing are called working capital management decisions and they are all meant to ensure that the business is able to continue its operations with sufficient cash that will be able to satisfy its current obligations as well as operational expenses. Profitable businesses generally generate cash but some businesses can be profitable but lack sufficient cash during certain periods of the operating cycle. It is very important to ensure that working capital in the business is properly controlled to eliminate problems such as: too much or too little inventory; too high or too little receivables; too high or too little payables; and lastly, too high or too little levels of cash.

Working capital analysis permits the evaluation of working capital during an operating period for the following reasons:

- Exposes the increases in the working capital by showing the various inflows that caused the increase.
- Exposes decreases in working capital by showing the various outflows that caused the decrease.
- Exposes the net changes to working capital during the period.
- Exposes the effectiveness of working capital controls during the period.
- Exposes to prospective lenders information that will permit them to make informed decisions related to the business.

As a general rule working capital should always be positive in the long run because if it was negative, the company would be financing its property and equipment with current liabilities.

8.2 The working capital cycle

The working capital cycle (also called the "cash cycle" or the "operating cycle") is used to determine the period of time which elapses from the point where cash is spent on any investment in current assets, until the point of the inflow of cash from the guests. Exhibit 8.1 illustrates in a simplified form the flow of cash within a well organised company.

Exhibit 8.1 **The Working Capital Cycle**

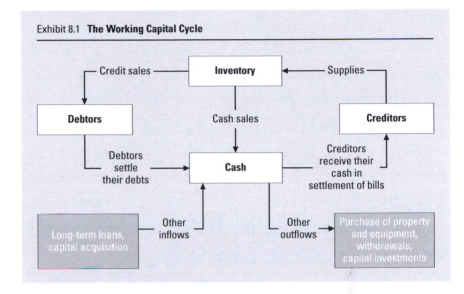

To illustrate the cycle, assume that the company is a restaurant. The cycle will begin with the restaurant acquiring F & B products as well as other operating supplies from their suppliers which have to be paid for in cash, either immediately (cash) or after some delay (creditors). These operating supplies as well as F & B products accumulate as inventory (inventory) which will eventually be transformed and sold to the guests. These guests will pay in cash, either directly (cash) or on account (debtors). All of these movements create inflows and outflows of cash for the restaurant. The cycle can be extended to take into account those other inflows and outflows of cash that would be considered for investment and financing purposes. The various components of the working capital cycle are summarily discussed below.

Cash management

The statement of cash flow was discussed in chapter 5 in which an introduction to cash management was equally stated (section 5.1). It is important to recall that net cash flow is not the same as the profit earned during a particular period. Any failure to recognise this fundamental difference between net cash flows and net profits can lead hospitality managers to bankruptcy. To avoid such failures it is necessary to establish cash budgets in which management will be able to identify periods in which they foresee cash deficits, as well as periods of cash surpluses. Consider a situation in which a hotel runs out of cash and cannot find a lender at short notice. It might find itself trying to liquidate some of its assets, arrange for some long-term financing, or miss on some of its due liability repayments.

Good cash management does not simply mean avoiding having too little cash. Too much cash can be detrimental to the profitability for the business. Since investors get into businesses to make profits in the form of return on investment, they expect to make more out of their investment than if they had kept the money in their own banks in the form of cash. If there is too much cash within a company, it will be advisable for management to try and invest it in such a way that it could generate returns for the company instead of staying idle in their bank accounts.

Accounts receivable management

Accounts receivable results from sales on account, or in other words, credit sales to customers. In order to push up sales, hospitality operations are called upon to make credit available to their guests. These accounts receivable are expected in the normal course of business to be transformed into cash within a short period of time. Extending credits to customers entails two types of costs:
- The absence of the monetary value of the completed sales, and
- The lost revenue if the accounts receivable becomes uncollectible

Due to these costs, the establishment should try to ensure that the credit period given to the customers is neither too long nor too short and this should be given only to creditworthy customers. If the accounts receivable are too high it means that the company is not collecting its cash quickly enough, which could lead to bottlenecks in the working capital cycle. On the other hand, if the level of accounts receivable is too low it may mean that the company is offering insufficient levels of credits to its customers, and as such not benefitting enough from its sales' potentials.

Accounts receivable are generally monitored using ratios as shown in 7.2.1 (accounts receivable turnover which indicates how well accounts receivable are collected within the organization, and the average collection period which relates the collection days to the accounts receivable turnover ratio). The analysis of the accounts receivable balance can be conducted by using what is called the account receivable ageing schedule which is a listing of the customers making up the total accounts receivable balance. It is normally prepared at the end of each month. Analysing the accounts receivable ageing schedule may help to easily identify sources of potential cash flow problems.

A typical accounts receivable ageing schedule consists of six columns and it is illustrated in exhibit 8.2.

- Column 1 lists the name of each customer with an accounts receivable balance;
- Column 2 lists the total amount due from the customers listed in column 1;
- Column 3 is the current column in which is listed the amounts due from customers for sales made during the current month;
- Column 4 shows the unpaid amount due from sales made in the previous month;
- Column 5 lists the amounts due from sales made two months earlier;
- Column 6 lists the amount due from sale over two months earlier.

Exhibit 8.2 **Sample accounts receivable ageing schedule**

Accounts Receivable Ageing Schedule
Hospitality Caterers United
June 30th 2009

1	2	3	4	5	6
Customer Name	Total Accounts Receivable	Current	1-30 days past due	31-60 days past due	Over 60 days past due
Customer ABC	€ 2,000.00	€ 400.00	€ 600.00	€ 600.00	€ 400.00
Customer DEF	€ 4,100.00	€ 4,100.00	€ –	€ –	€ –
Customer GHI	€ 1,200.00	€ 1,200.00	€ –	€ –	€ –
Customer JKL	€ 2,600.00	€ 1,300.00	€ 650.00	€ 650.00	€ –
Customer MNO	€ 500.00	€ –	€ 500.00	€ –	€ –
Customer PQR	€ 750.00	€ 750.00	€ –	€ –	€ –
Customer STU	€ 1,600.00	€ 1,600.00	€ –	€ –	€ –
Total	€ 12,750.00	€ 9,350.00	€ 1,750.00	€ 1,250.00	€ 400.00
Percentage	100%	73%	14%	10%	3%

The accounts receivable ageing schedule can be used to identify the customers that are extending their payment times. If the bulk of the overdue amount in receivables is attributable to one customer such as customer DEF in Exhibit 8.2, then steps can be taken to see that this customer's account is properly supervised to avoid undue surprises. Overdue amounts attributable to many customers at the same time may signal that the business needs to tighten its general credit policy towards new and existing customers. The ageing schedule also identifies any recent changes in the accounts making up the total accounts receivable balance. Changes in the makeup of the accounts receivable balances can be easily spotted between the months and the accounts receivable ageing schedule can sound an early warning and help protect the business from cash-flow problems.

Inventory management
Having low inventory levels is a very good way of conserving cash; however care has to be taken to ensure that neither too much nor too little inventory is held at any time. High levels of inventory will lead to the following problems:
· Higher insurance costs for inventory
· Higher handling costs
· Higher storage costs and space needs
· Higher maintenance costs
· Loss in quality and value
· More exposure to pilferage
· Unavailability for other investment purposes

Low levels of inventory can lead to the risk of not having enough in stock to satisfy current customer demands which might lead to loss of sales as well as the negative effects it might have on customer satisfaction. To determine correct inventory levels is really a matter of judgement based on the evaluation of the various inventory turnover ratios. Another way of inventory management is the use of the economic order quantity model which enables the estimation of the optimal order size for purchase orders and illustrated in exhibit 8.3.

■ Exhibit 8.3 **Using the economic order quantity model to determine optimal order size**

The economic order quantity (EOQ) is the most economical quantity of a product that should be purchased at one time. It is based on all the associated costs for ordering and maintaining the product.

The model determines the amount of goods to order to meet projected demand while minimizing inventory costs. The original version of the model assumed the following:
a) Demand for inventory is predictable.
b) The ordering costs do not vary with the size of order.

EOQ is computed as such:

$$Q = \sqrt{\frac{2CD}{H}}$$

in which:
Q = optimal order quantity
D = annual demand quantity of the product
C = fixed cost per order
H = annual holding cost per unit (also known as carrying cost)

Example:
The Spice & Taste Restaurant has a good wine list. On an average, Spice & Taste Restaurant sells 850 cases of wines each year and the average cost of each case is €80.00. Based on past observation, the cost of ordering and receiving one shipment of wine is €18.00. And the opportunity cost of any excess working capital is assumed to be 4% as this is the remuneration rate received by Spice & Taste Restaurant in their short term deposits with the bank. Based on this, the holding cost per case is calculated as 4% of €80.00 = €3.20. The EOQ of their wines inventory can be calculated as such:

$$Q = \sqrt{\frac{2 \times 80 \times 18}{3.20}}$$

$$Q = \sqrt{900}$$

$$Q = 30$$

This means that if the Spice & Taste Restaurant orders its wines in shipments of 30 cases its annual ordering and carrying costs will be minimized.

Current liabilities management
Current liabilities management is limited to principally dealing with accounts payable, accrued expenses and other current liabilities. The primary objective will be to delay, as much as it is possible, payments to third parties until these payments are due and required. However

care should be exercised to avoid late payment situations which might result in the company becoming blacklisted – that is registered in the list of companies with bad payment history. Blacklisting might result in greater difficulties in obtaining credit, as well as it might result in obtaining credit at penalty rates. Blacklisting also might lead to most of the company's payments to be requested on cash-only basis.

An accounts payable ageing schedule may help determine cash outflows for certain expenses in the near future – 30 to 60 days. This will give a good estimate of the cash outflows necessary to pay all the accounts payable on time. The cash outflows for every business can be classified into one of four possible categories: costs of goods sold; operating expenses; major purchases; and debt payments. The accounts payable ageing schedule can help determine how well the company is (or not) paying its invoices. While it is good cash-flow management to delay payment until the invoice due date, take care not to rely too heavily on trade credit and stretch the goodwill of the suppliers. Paying bills late can indicate that the company is not managing its cash flow the way a successful business should.

An accounts payable ageing schedule looks almost like an accounts receivable ageing schedule except that it lists what the company owes its various suppliers. It is thus a breakdown by supplier of the total amount in the accounts payable balance.

Exhibit 8.4 is an illustration of a sample accounts payable ageing schedule for the Hospitality Caterers United:

Exhibit 8.4 **Sample accounts payable ageing schedule**

	Accounts Payable Ageing Schedule **Hospitality Caterers United** **October 31st 2009**				
1	**2**	**3**	**4**	**5**	**6**
Supplier	**Total Accounts Payable**	**Current**	**1-30 days past due**	**31-60 days past due**	**Over 60 days past due**
Supplier 1	€ 840.00	€ 420.00	€ 210.00	€ 210.00	€ –
Supplier 2	€ 1,250.00	€ 1,000.00	€ 250.00	€ –	€ –
Supplier 3	€ 900.00	€ 500.00	€ 400.00	€ –	€ –
Supplier 4	€ 580.00	€ 580.00	€ –	€ –	€ –
Supplier 5	€ 1,400.00	€ 700.00	€ 700.00	€ –	€ –
Supplier 6	€ 1,525.00	€ 525.00	€ 500.00	€ 500.00	€ –
Supplier 7	€ 680.00	€ 680.00	€ –	€ –	€ –
Total	**€ 7,175.00**	**€ 4,405.00**	**€ 2,060.00**	**€ 710.00**	**€ –**
Percentage	**100%**	**61%**	**29%**	**10%**	**0%**

The accounts payable ageing schedule is a useful tool for analysing the makeup of the accounts payable balance. The schedule permits the company to detect problems in the management of payables early enough to protect the company from any major trade credit problems. For example in exhibit 8.4, if supplier 6 was an important supplier to Hospitality Caterers United, then the past due amounts listed for supplier 6 should be paid in order to protect the trade credit established. The accounts payable schedule can also be used to help manage and improve the company's cash flow. Based on the schedule in exhibit 8.4, Hospitality Caterers United will need to generate at least €4,405.00 in income to cover the current month's purchases on account.

As with all current liabilities, the general rule then is for management to pay their bills only when they are due except in situations where they might receive cash discounts for early payments. Cash discounts should be considered only when the assessment of the cash discounts and its resulting effective interest rate might lead to the lowering of the costs to the company. Payment of bills before their due dates result in higher business costs, but management should also take into account other factors such as the relationship with the suppliers. For those interested in assessing the effect of cash discounts for early payments, the effective interest rate is calculated by using the formula below:

$$\text{Effective interest rate} = \frac{\text{Discount Percentage}}{100\% - \text{Discount Percentage}} \times \frac{\text{Days in the year}}{\text{Days between end of discount period and final due date}}$$

It is beyond the scope of this chapter to go into any further analysis of effective interest rates.

Glossary

Accounts payable ageing schedule – is a listing of what the company owes to its suppliers at any given date. The total of the schedule should be equal to the balance of the accounts payable account on that given date.

Accounts receivable ageing schedule – is a listing of what customers owe the company at any given date. The total of the schedule should be equal to the balance of the accounts receivable account on that given date.

Accounts receivable management – is the management of the accounts receivable balances of a company in order to ensure that the amounts of credit extended to the customers, and the periods of credit allowed them are properly supervised. It helps to protect the company from cash flow problems.

Cash management – is the management of the cash balances of a company in order to maximize the availability of cash that is not invested in fixed assets or inventories, and to avoid the risk of insolvency. The most important tool in cash management is the use of the cash budget which will help the management to identify periods in which they foresee cash deficits or surpluses.

Current liabilities management – is the management of the current liabilities account balances of a company in order to ensure that the current liabilities are properly honoured when they are due.

Economic order quantity – is a model that permits the establishment of the most economic quantity of a product that should be ordered at one time. It ensures that the customers are adequately served while at the same time minimizing the inventory costs.

Inventory management – is the management of the inventory levels in order to avoid either too much or too little inventory being held at any given moment.

Trade credit – is the credit offered by suppliers without charging any interest.

Working capital – is the difference between the current assets and the current liabilities.

Working capital cycle – is the illustration of the flow of cash within a company from the moment cash is spent for the production of any good or service until the moment cash is received from consumers of the good or service.

Multiple choice questions

8.1 Only one of the following activities is relevant when referring to a company's management of its cash balances and its cash flow situation. Which one?
  a cash management
  b forecasting
  c internal control
  d pricing

8.2 The working capital cycle is
  a the flow of capital within a company
  b the flow of cash within a company
  c the flow of current assets within a company
  d none of the above

8.3 Only one of the statements below constitutes an assumption of the economic order quantity.
  Which one?
  a demand for inventory is unpredictable
  b ordering costs do not vary with the size of the order
  c ordering costs vary with the size of the order
  d supply of inventory is predictable

8.4 Costs that result from hospitality companies extending credit to their customers are of two types. The first is the absence of the monetary value of the sale and the second is:
  a the absence of the accounts payable
  b the absence of the accounts receivable
  c the lost revenue in case the accounts payable becomes uncollectible
  d the lost revenue in case the accounts receivable becomes uncollectible

8.5 One of the major advantages of an accounts payable ageing schedule is that it:
  a permits the company to detect problems in the management of its relations with its customers
  b permits the company to detect problems in the management of its relations with its owners
  c permits the company to detect problems in the management of its relations with its suppliers
  d all of the above

Exercises

8.1 Indicate the effects on cash of the following account movements that took place during the month of September 2010 in the activities of the Town University Hotel:

  · Accounts payable decreased by €23,400
  · Accounts receivable decreased by €14,200
  · Accrued expenses increased by €23,100
  · Inventory increased by €12,600

- Marketable securities decreased by €4,700
- Income taxes payable increased by €1,700
- Salaries and wages payable decreased by €3,500

8.2 The projected sales of the Four Junctions Café are as shown in the table that follows:

Period	Projected sales
March 2011	€ 180,000
April 2011	€ 210,000
May 2011	€ 195,000

In general, the café sells 25% in cash and 75% on credit. 25 % of the accounts receivable are collected during the month of sale, 65% in the month after the sale, and the last 20%, the following month. Use this information and determine the estimated cash receipts for May 2011.

8.3 The projected sales of the Logical Eating Spot are as shown in the table that follows:

Period	Projected sales
June 2011	€ 275,000
July 2011	€ 310,000
August 2011	€ 345,000
September 2011	€ 330,000
October 2011	€ 290,000
November 2011	€ 255,000

In general, their sales are 30% in cash and 70 on credit. The accounts receivable are collected in the following manner:

Month of sale	15%
Month after	55%
Second month after	18%
Third month after	11%
Bad debts	1%
Total	100%

Use this information and determine their estimated cash receipts for November 2011.

8.4 You have been asked to determine the economic order quantity for the Munching Moose Motel's wine purchases. From past experience, the average cost of each case is €75.00 and the cost of ordering and receiving each wine shipment is €15.64. The opportunity cost of any excess working capital of the motel is 4%.

a calculate the holding cost per case of wine

b how many cases should the motel order per shipment in view of minimizing its ordering and carrying costs?

Cost Management

9.1 The nature of costs and assumptions

9.2 Types of costs

9.3 Activity-based costing

9.4 Allocating indirect (overhead) costs to the operating departments

9.5 Separating mixed-costs between their fixed and variable elements

For managers to be able to choose between the alternative opportunities open to them, they need information related to the future costs and revenues and the way in which these change at different levels of operation. Costs represent the money measurements of the efforts that a company has to make in order to achieve its objectives. Consequently, costs play a very important role in management decision making. In section 9.1 the nature of costs and the basic assumptions related to costs are discussed, followed by the description of the basic types of costs in section 9.2. Section 9.3 introduces the notion of activity-based costing, and this is followed in section 9.4 with a discussion on the allocation of indirect costs. The various methods of separating mixed-costs into their fixed and variable elements are explained in section 9.5.

9.1 The nature of costs and assumptions

At the most basic level, costs can be defined as the sacrifices made in order to achieve a specific goal. Cost can have many meanings depending on the context in which it is used. In management accounting, cost is considered as an expense that is incurred in order to increase revenues. For most hospitality operations as much as 90% of all revenues are used to pay for costs. For this reason, cost management is very important. One way of controlling costs in order to improve net income is through cost budgeting and analysis. Before proceeding with the types of costs, it is necessary to note that accountants generally employ cost functions that are linear. This is based on a certain number of assumptions which will be summarized below:

- Fixed costs are assumed to remain constant over different levels of production activity
- Variable costs are assumed to vary with different levels of production activity but are constant per unit of output
- It is assumed that all costs can be separated into either fixed or variable
- It is assumed that the levels of efficiency and productivity remain constant over all production activity levels
- It is assumed that costs behaviour can be explained by causing changes on any one of the related independent variables.

Costs may have been incurred in the past, as well be a cost for the future. In such a case the alternative use of resources may play an important role in the decision to go ahead with possibly incurring that future cost.

9.2 Types of costs

Before any analysis of costs is done within an organization, a comprehensive understanding of its costs structure is necessary. This understanding can only result from knowing all the types of costs that can exist within an organization. Following is a basic description of the various types of costs.

Standard cost
Standard cost is the measure of how much a product or service should normally cost based on a given volume or sales. These costs have to be established by each organization based on past experiences because the many factors that influence standard costs differ from organization to organization. The establishment of standard costs provides the basis for decision making, permits costs analysis and control, and permits the measurement of inventory and cost of goods sold. Standard costs serve as benchmarks against which actual costs are compared. Differences between standard costs and actual costs are called variances, and these are discussed in section 14.5 of chapter 14 – Budgeting and variance analysis.

Fixed cost

Fixed costs are those expenses that do not change in relation to the volume of the business within a specific period or production level. Examples of fixed costs include management salaries and fire insurance expenses. In the long run these costs can change but in the short run they are not expected to change.

Variable cost

Variable costs are those expenses that change proportionately to changes in the volume of the business. Very few costs will have a directly linear relationship to the changes to the volume of the business, however within the hospitality industry two good examples of variable costs are the cost of food sold and the cost of beverage sold. If for example the food cost percentage is 25% this means that if the total food sales for the period are €85,000.00 then cost of food sold will be €21,250.00. This relationship will be assumed to be the same even if the total food sales for the period were €170,000.00 or €40,000.00.

Semi-fixed and semi-variable costs

Some costs cannot be finely split into their fixed or variable components. These are expenses that contain both fixed costs components and variable costs components. The fixed costs component is the part that will need to be paid whatever the level of business activity. The variable cost component is the part that will vary proportionately to the business activity. Examples include utilities and maintenance costs. Cost of electricity is a good example. It has both fixed and variable components. Electricity is essential for the basic operation of the business for light and heat. With demand increases more energy is required to keep up with the increase in demand. Cost of electricity will as such rise accordingly as production activities increase. In some literature these costs are also called mixed-costs.

Direct cost

Direct costs are those costs that can be traced to a particular operating department and is the responsibility of that department. In general most direct costs are variable costs. The cost of linen and laundry within the rooms division is an example, as well as the salaries and wages of the rooms division employees.

Indirect cost

Indirect costs are costs that are not directly identified and are not traceable to a particular operating department. Such costs cannot be charged to any particular department. Indirect costs can either be fixed or variable and some examples are general administration expenses, taxes and security costs. Indirect costs are equally called undistributed or overhead costs.

Joint cost

Joint costs are those costs that are shared and are the responsibility of two or more departments. These costs will have to be appropriately allocated to the responsible departments. For example if an employee in the main kitchen is producing food for the banqueting department, then this employee's salary will have to be allocated appropriately to the F & B and the banqueting departments. The main issue here is to seek for a rational way of allocating these costs to the departments. Cost allocation is discussed in section 9.4 of this chapter.

Controllable and non-controllable costs

Controllable costs are those costs that the department heads can directly influence in the short run. An example will be the F & B manager's ability to determine the amount of money to be spent on wines. On the other hand, this F & B manager will not be able in the short run to influence the amounts paid for rents. Those costs that cannot be influenced are therefore called non-controllable costs.

Discretionary cost

These are costs that managers can choose to avoid, mainly for budgetary reasons, in the short run and are mainly of a fixed character. Such avoidance decisions are normally made by the general manager. Avoiding these costs has little effect on operations in the short run, but in the long run they cannot be avoided because sales might eventually become seriously affected. Examples of discretionary costs are advertising, maintenance and employee training programmes.

Relevant and non-relevant costs

Relevant costs are costs that change depending on decisions that are made, as well as affecting these decisions. For a cost to become relevant it should be in the future and it should differ between the possible alternatives. An example would be the possibility of replacing an old oven in the kitchen by a combi-steamer. The relevant costs will be the costs of a new combi-steamer (minus any trade-offs of the old oven, the cost of training the employees to use the new combi-steamer as well as all maintenance related costs of the combi-steamer). In such a situation the labour cost of the kitchen employees will not be affected and as such do not form part of the decision making process. These employees' labour costs will be considered as non-relevant costs in making the decision to acquire the combi-steamer.

Sunk cost

Sunk costs are costs that have been incurred and as such cannot be recovered. An example of a sunk cost derived from the example in relevant cost above could be the following. Assume that prior to making the decision to buy the new combi-steamer, management had requested and paid for the services of a consultant to produce a report on the advantages of using a combi-steamer instead of a conventional oven. The amount of money paid for the consultant's services will be considered a sunk cost and it should not make any difference to the decision to acquire the new combi-steamer. This cost should equally not be included in the assessment of the cost of the combi-steamer.

Opportunity cost

Opportunity cost, also called the economic opportunity loss is a very important concept in economics. It represents the value of the forgone next best alternative that results from a decision. Opportunity costs are not assessed only in monetary terms but equally in terms of anything of value. As an example, still in line with our combi-steamer, the opportunity cost of acquiring the combi-steamer will be the monetary value attributed to acquiring the conventional oven. Another example without monetary terms would be in the situation that during a particular weekend, the hotel guests have the opportunity to either attend on the Saturday night a musical, or experience a special sunset evening at the beach. To the guest who attends the musical, the opportunity cost will be missing out on the experience of the special sunset evening at the beach.

9.3 Activity-based costing

Activity-based costing (ABC) is a costing approach that assigns resource costs to cost objects such as products, services, or customers based on activities performed for the cost objects. The premise of this costing approach is that an organization's products or services are the results of activities, and activities use resources which incur costs. By controlling activities managers ensure that costs are controlled at their source. Costs of resources are assigned to activities based on the activities that use or consume resources, and the costs of activities are assigned to cost objects based on activities performed for the cost objects. ABC recognizes the causal or direct relationships between resource costs, cost drivers, activities, and cost objects in assigning costs to activities and then to cost objects. A wise manager will not concentrate on how to calculate product or service costs but will concentrate more on why the costs were there in the first place. When designing an activity based costing system this should be used as a departure point.

In order to design an activity based costing system it is important to remember that the objectives should be met at the minimum cost and complexity. To be successful, the final activity based costing system should provide the right kind of information at the right level of detail. In addition to this the design of the system should be as simple as possible without being too simple, since it may report inaccurate costs if it is too simple. The answer is to strike a balance between simplicity and complexity. In addition to this, performance measures should be identified at process level and for key activities. They should be used to monitor and evaluate activities or processes and must be used to promote consistent improvement. This should be done without unnecessarily complicating the design of the system. Seven assumptions underlie the design of an activity-based costing system and they are the following:

- All activities within an organization consume resources
- Producing products or services makes use of activities
- The business model is focused on consumption rather than spending
- There could be many causes to the consumption of the resources of the organization

- The organization can be able to internally identify and measure a wide variety of activities
- The costs pools in the organization should be homogeneous
- The costs in each pool are variable

Taking into consideration these assumptions, there are a number of different approaches possible when introducing an activity-based costing system. The introduction of such a system usually entails the following three steps:

Step 1 identifying resource costs and activities

The first step in designing an ABC system is to conduct an activity analysis to identify the resource costs and activities of the firm. Most firms record resource costs in specific accounts in the accounting system. Examples of these accounts include supplies, purchasing, materials handling, warehousing, office expenses, furniture and fixtures, buildings, equipment, utilities, and salaries and benefits.

Step 2 assigning resource costs to activities

The second step is for the organization to choose resource consumption cost drivers based on cause-and-effect relationships. Typical resource consumption cost drivers include the number of (1) labour hours for labour intensive activities; (2) employees for payroll-related activities; and (3) surface area for general maintenance and cleaning activities. The cost of the resources can be assigned to activities by direct tracing or estimation. Direct tracing requires measuring the actual usage of resources by activities. For example, fuel consumed by an oven can be traced directly by reading the gas meter attached to the oven. When direct tracing is not available, department managers and supervisors need to estimate the amount or percentage of time (or effort) employees spend on each identified activity.

Step 3 assigning activity costs to cost objects (products, services or customers)

The last step is to assign costs of activities to cost objects based on the appropriate activity consumption cost drivers. Outputs are the cost objects for which firms or organizations perform activities. Typical outputs for a cost system are products and services; however, outputs also can include customers, projects, or business units. For example, the outputs of a bar-restaurant may be number and types of coffee cups served, or amount of waiters serving during a banquet. Firms use activity consumption cost drivers to assign activity costs to cost objects. Activity cost drivers should explain why the cost of a cost object goes up or down. Typical activity consumption cost drivers are purchase orders, receiving reports, and direct labour-hours.

In ABC, the greatest accuracy in costing is achieved by recognising five different levels of activities: the unit level activities; the batch level activities; the service level activities; the company level activities and lastly the customer level of activities. The design of an ABC system is a complicated and complex process that needs the cooperation of many different functional heads within the organization. To simply match the level of the activity driver with the activity does not always ensure that the desired level of accuracy is achieved. A part of the answer may be found in involving the correctly motivated individuals at the correct time with a strong mandate and then to let the team establish the correlation between the performance of the activity and the activity driver.

ABC is suitable for market-oriented sectors such as the lodging industry. It has been proposed that ABC is the most effective and accurate costing method for customer profitability analysis – CPA in a hotel environment. There are certain types of customers who consume far more costs than others, for example, the longer the stay of the customer, the lower the overhead costs per room night incurred (check-in and check-out costs, for instance). However, the use of ABC in the hotel industry is still limited because although there is considerable knowledge of the theory of ABC, there is still a low understanding of how it should be used in the hospitality industry.

Exhibit 9.1 shows an illustration of how the three steps of the ABC process can be applied within the hospitality industry.

Exhibit 9.1 **Illustration of the three steps of the ABC Process in the hospitality industry**

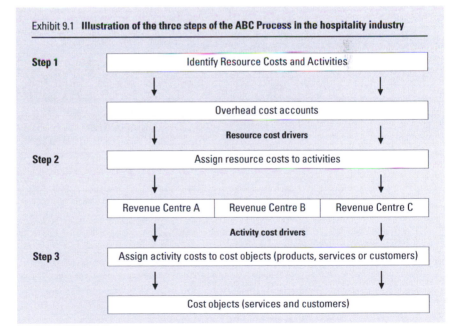

An important factor in adapting an activity-based costing system is the information required for such a system. With advances in data management systems and computing it is nowadays much easier for companies to adopt activity-based costing systems.

9.4 Allocating indirect (overhead) costs to the operating departments

Cost allocation is the distribution of overhead expenses and costs by management among the profit and sales revenue centres of an operation. It is based on the principle of responsibility accounting. Cost allocation has the advantage that it permits the management to make better decisions since their decisions are made based on fully allocated income statements. The structure of the subsections is as follows:

9.4.1	Responsibility accounting
9.4.2	Determining allocation bases
9.4.3	Common methods of cost allocation
9.4.4	Illustration of the direct method of cost allocation
9.4.5	Illustration of the step method of cost allocation

9.4.1 Responsibility accounting

Responsibility accounting is a system of accounting that separates revenues and costs into areas of departmental responsibility in order to assess performance attained by the departments to which the authority has been given. The important point is that department heads or managers should be held accountable for their performance and the performance of the employees in their departments. An argument in favour of allocating indirect expenses to departments is that, although departmental managers are not responsible for controlling those costs, they should be aware of what portion of the costs is related to their departments since this could have an impact on departmental decision making, such as establishing selling prices at a level that covers all costs and not just direct costs. The main reasons for creating responsibility centres are:
- It allows the top-level management to delegate responsibility and authority to department heads so they can achieve departmental operating goals compatible with the overall company's goals.
- It provides the top-level management with the necessary information to measure the performance of each department in achieving its operating goals.

Within a single organization practicing responsibility accounting, departments can be identified as cost centres, sales revenue centres, profit centres, or investment centres.

A cost centre
A cost centre is one that generates no direct revenue (such as the maintenance department). In such a situation, the department manager is held responsible only for the costs incurred.

A sales revenue centre
A sales revenue centre receives sales revenue, but has little or no direct costs associated with their operation. For example, a major resort hotel might lease out a large part of its floor space to retail stores. The rent income provides revenue for the department, all of which is profit.

A profit centre

A profit centre is one that has costs but also generates sales revenues that are directly related to that department such as the rooms division where the manager is responsible for generating revenue from guest room sales. The manager of a profit centre should have some control over the sales revenue it can generate.

An investment centre

An investment centre will usually exist in large or chain organizations with units located in several different places. Each unit is given full authority over how it operates and is held responsible for the results of its decisions. Such decentralized units are measured by the rate of return their general managers achieve on the investment in the centre.

The overhead costs are all the expenses, other than the direct expenses generated by the specific revenue or profit centre of the operation. These are considered to be indirect costs. Examples include the following:

- Undistributed operating expenses (for example administration and general, marketing and sales, property operations and maintenance, and utility costs)
- Management fees
- Fixed charges (for example insurance, rent, depreciation, and interest)

9.4.2 Determining allocation bases

A major issue in the allocation of costs to the various departments is the selection of a rational allocation base. To help in solving this issue, the 9th edition of the USALI (omitted in the 10th edition) suggested certain bases as shown in exhibit 9.2. An allocation base is the factor that determines how much of an overhead expense will be allocated to a department. For example the administration and general expenses of a hotel could be allocated on the basis of the number of employees in each department.

The bases, as suggested in exhibit 9.2 should be considered to be just what they are. Each management will have to make its own decisions based on their own experiences and realities of their own companies. Once an allocation base has been selected, it should be consistently used in order to ensure meaningful internal future comparisons of the income statements.

There are generally two approaches to selecting the allocation bases – the SABA and the MABA. SABA stands for the single allocation base approach. In this method, a single allocation base is used to allocate all the overhead costs among the departments. In most SABA cases, the surface area occupied by the various departments is used in the allocation process. However, contrary to the SABA is the MABA which stands for multiple allocation base approach. In the MABA, multiple allocation bases are used in the allocation process. However it should

Exhibit 9.2 **Suggested allocation bases**

Costs and Expenses	Suggested Allocation Base
Rent	Percentage applicable to source of revenue Surface area in m^2
Property Taxes	Surface area in m^2
Insurance	Surface area in m^2 Surface area in m^2 + equipment value
Interest	Surface area in m^2 Surface area in m^2 + equipment value
Depreciation – Building	Surface area in m^2
Depreciation – Equipment	Surface area in m^2 Department assets record
Depreciation – Capital Leases	Surface area in m^2 Department use of leased equipment
Telephone	Number of extensions
Payroll Taxes and Employee Benefits	Number of employees Detailed payroll records Salaries and wages
Administrative and General	Accumulated costs Number of employees
Data processing	Accumulated costs Number of employees
Marketing	Departmental revenue percentage
Guest Entertainment	Departmental revenue percentage
Energy costs	Sub-metres Surface area in m^3
Property Operations and Maintenance	Job orders Number of employees Surface area in m^2
Human Resources	Number of employees
Tranportation	Number of employees

be noted that these bases have to be defined in advance by the management of the property for the sake of consistency. In general, the MABA is preferable to the SABA, because it allocates overhead costs on the basis of some pre-observed relationship between the service and the profit and revenue centres.

9.4.3 Common methods of cost allocation

Cost allocation is carried out using three common methods – the direct method, the step method, and the formula method. In the direct method, all the overhead costs are allocated directly from the service centres to the profit centres. As such, no parts of the overhead costs are allocated to the service centres. The step method of cost allocation requires a two-step process whereby in the first step, the fixed costs are first of all allocated to both the profit and service centres. This is then followed in the second step by the allocation of the costs of the service centres (including their own parts of the allocated fixed costs) to the profit centres. The formula method equally requires two steps in the allocation process. In the first step, similar to those of the step method, the allocation of the fixed costs is carried out. The second step introduces the full consideration of the services carried out by the service centres to each other. This is however a complex method that requires the use of advanced computational techniques and is beyond the scope of this text to illustrate. To illustrate the direct and step methods of cost allocation using the MABA, the unallocated income statement of the Blue Ribbon Roadside Inn shown in exhibit 9.3 will be used.

Exhibit 9.3 Unallocated income statement of the Blue Ribbon Roadside Inn

The Blue Ribbon Roadside Inn
Unallocated Income Statement
For the year ending December 31st 2009

Department	Net Revenues	Cost of Sales	Payroll and Related Expenses	Other Expenses	Departmental Income
Rooms	€ 565,000.00	€ –	€ 225,000.00	€ 102,000.00	€ 238,000.00
Food and Beverage	€ 1,590,000.00	€ 725,000.00	€ 440,000.00	€ 75,000.00	€ 350,000.00
Total	€ 2,155,000.00	€ 725,000.00	€ 665,000.00	€ 177,000.00	€ 588,000.00
Undistributed Operating Expenses					
Administration and General			€ 96,000.00	€ 18,000.00	€ 114,000.00
Sales and Marketing			€ 75,000.00	€ 16,000.00	€ 91,000.00
Human Resource Management			€ 69,000.00	€ 3,000.00	€ 72,000.00
Property Operations, Maintenance and Utility Costs			€ 58,000.00	€ 15,000.00	€ 73,000.00

Total Undistributed Operating Expenses	€ 350,000.00
Income Before Fixed Charges	€ 238,000.00
Fixed Charges	
Insurance	€ 40,000.00
Depreciation	€ 125,000.00
Total Fixed Charges	€ 165,000.00
Income Before Income Taxes	€ 73,000.00
Income Taxes	€ 24,000.00
Net Income	€ 49,000.00

The bases used by the management of the Blue Ribbon Roadside Inn to allocate all of their overhead expenses are shown in exhibit 9.4

Exhibit 9.4 **Allocation bases used by the Blue Ribbon Roadside Inn**

Allocation Bases used by the Blue Ribbon Roadside Inn

A & G	Number of employees
S & M	Departmental revenue percentage
HRM	Number of employees
POM & UC	Surface area in m²
Insurance	Book value of fixed assets
Depreciation	Surface area in m²

To complete the basic information required to establish the allocation bases, the management of the Blue Ribbon Roadside Inn provides the following additional data about their operations as shown in exhibit 9.5

Exhibit 9.5 **Additional information required to establish allocation bases**

Department	Book value of fixed assets	Surface area (m²)	Number of employees
Rooms	€ 4,000,000.00	2000	6
Food and Beverage	€ 2,500.000.00	1500	14
A & G	€ 200,000.00	200	3
S & M	€ 80,000.00	100	2
HRM	€ 70,000.00	100	2
POM & UC	€ 550,000.00	300	3
Total	**€ 7,400.000.00**	**4200**	**30**

9.4.4 Illustration of the direct method of cost allocation

To illustrate the direct method of cost allocation using the MABA of the unallocated income statement of the Blue Ribbon Roadside Inn, exhibit 9.6 shows how the various overhead costs of administration and general (A & G), sales and marketing (S & M), human resource management (HRM), property operations and maintenance plus utility costs (POM & UC), insurance as well as depreciation have been allocated.

As shown in exhibit 9.6, the first action is to determine the proportions of the various bases that will be given to the profit centres. For example, the administration and general expenses are to be allocated using the number of employees in the profit centres (rooms division, and food and beverage). In these two departments, the total number of employees comes up to 20. Consequently the rooms division will be allocated 30% (which is 6 divided by 20) of the A & G expenses, and all the other expenses that will be allocated on the basis of number of employees. Similar calculations will then be made for all the other

Exhibit 9.6 **Allocation of the overhead costs of the Blue Ribbon Roadside Inn using the MABA**

Costs to be allocated	Amount to be allocated	Allocation bases	Proportions to		Amounts allocated to	
			Rooms	Food and Beverage	Rooms	Food and Beverage
A & G	€ 114,000.00	Number of employees	30%	70%	€ 34,200.00	€ 79,800.00
S & M	€ 91,000.00	Departmental revenu percentage	26%	74%	€ 23,858,47	€ 67,141,53
HRM	€ 72,000.00	Number of employees	30%	70%	€ 21,600.00	€ 50,400.00
POM & UC	€ 73,000.00	Surface area in m^2	57%	43%	€ 41,714.29	€ 31,285.71
Insurance	€ 40,000.00	Book value of fixed assets	62%	38%	€ 24,615.38	€ 15,384.62
Depreciation	€ 125,000.00	Surface area in m^2	57%	43%	€ 71,428.57	€ 53,571.43
Total	€ 515,000.00				€ 217,416.71	€ 297,583.29

bases bearing in mind that the denominators in the calculations will be limited only to the sums of the parts related to the profit centres. The next action is to use these percentages to allocate the overhead costs to the profit centres. For example, the costs of HRM allocated to the food and beverage department is determined as follows:

$$€72,000.00 \times 70\% = €50,400.00$$

The final action will be to design an allocated income statement based on the new figures. Exhibit 9.7 shows the allocated income statement of the Blue Ribbon Roadside Inn based on the direct method of cost allocation using the MABA.

Exhibit 9.7 **Fully allocated income statement of the Blue Ribbon Roadside Inn – direct method**

The Blue Ribbon Roadside Inn
Fully Allocated income Statement
For the year ending December 31st 2009

Department	Net Revenues	Cost of Sales	Payroll and Related Expenses	Other Expenses	Departmental Income	Allocated Expenses	Departmental Income After Allocation
Rooms	€ 565,000.00	€ —	€ 225,000.00	€ 102,000.00	€ 238,000.00	€ 217,416.71	€ 20,583.29
Food & Beverage	€ 1,590,000.00	€ 725,000.00	440,000.00	€ 75,000.00	€ 350.000.00	€ 297,583.29	€ 52,416.71
Total	€ 2,155,000.00	€ 725,000.00	665,000.00	€ 177,000.00	€ 588,000.00	€ 515,000.00	€ 73,000.00
				Income Taxes			€ 24,000.00
				Net Income			€ 49,000.00

If after allocation, all the profit centres remain profitable as in the case of the Blue Ribbon Roadside Inn – Direct Method shown in exhibit 9.7, then there is little that management can do but to continue operating in such a positive environment. If on the contrary, after cost allocation a profit centre is shown to be unprofitable, then management has the ability to make certain decisions based on at least the following four factors:

- The level of income of the underperforming department
- The extent to which the overhead costs allocated to the underperforming department are fixed
- The extent to which the existence and performance of the underperforming department affects the other profit centres
- The operating alternatives available for the underperforming department

9.4.5   Illustration of the step method of cost allocation

The step method of cost allocation using the MABA of the unallocated income statement of the Blue Ribbon Roadside Inn is made up of two steps. The first step is to allocate the fixed charges to all the departments of the company – both the service centres and the profit centres. The common fixed charges include rents, property taxes, interests, insurance, depreciation and amortization.

In the case of the Blue Ribbon Roadside Inn the fixed charges to be allocated first to all the centres are:

- Insurance of €40,000.00 which will be allocated based on the book value of the fixed assets (BV of FA), and
- Depreciation of €125,000.00 which will be allocated based on the surface areas in square metres occupied

Step 1 is illustrated in exhibit 9.8.

Exhibit 9.8 **Step 1 – Allocating the fixed charges of the Blue Ribbon Roadside Inn**

Step 1 Cost to be allocated	Allocation Base	Amount				
Insurance	BV of FA	€ 40,000.00				
Depreciation	Surface area in m^2	€ 125,000.00				

Department	Book Value of Fixed Assets	Surface area in m^2	BV of FA %	SA %	Insurance allocation	Depreciation allocation
Rooms	€ 4,000,000.00	2000	54.05%	47.62%	€ 21,621.62	€ 59,523.81
Food & Beverage	€ 2,500,000.00	1500	33.78%	35.71%	€ 13,513.51	€ 44,642.86
Adm & Gen	€ 200,000.00	200	2.70%	4.76%	€ 1,081.08	€ 5,952.38
Sales & Marketing	€ 80,000.00	100	1.08%	2.38%	€ 432.43	€ 2,976.19
HRM	€ 70,000.00	100	0.95%	2.38%	€ 378.38	€ 2,976.19
POM & UC	€ 550,000.00	300	7.43%	7.14%	€ 2,972.97	€ 8,928.57
Total	€ 7,400,000.00	4200	100.00%	100.00%	€ 40,000.00	€ 125,000.00

Exhibit 9.8 shows how the various profit and service centres will be affected by the allocation of insurance and depreciation (fixed costs).

Step 2 starts by using the predefined bases to sequentially calculate the various proportions to be used in allocating the service centre costs to the remaining service centres and the profit centres. In the example of the Blue Ribbon Roadside Inn, the service centre costs will be allocated based on the following sequence: A & G; POM & UC; HRM; and lastly S & M. This order is based on the perception of the volume of services transferred from the service centres to the profit centres. Exhibit 9.9 shows the various proportions based on the data set of the Blue Ribbon Roadside Inn.

Exhibit 9.9 **Sequential allocation proportions based on the data set of the Blue Ribbon Roadside Inn**

Step 2 – Part 1		Sequential Allocation Proportions						
	Allocation Base	Rooms	F & B	A & G	POM & UC	HRM	S & M	Control
A & G	Number of employees	22.22%	51.85%	0.00%	11.11%	7.41%	7.41%	100.00%
POM & UC	Surface area in m²	54.05%	40.54%	0.00%	0.00%	2.70%	2.70%	100.00%
HRM	Number of employees	27.27%	63.64%	0.00%	0.00%	0.00%	9.09%	100.00%
S & M	Departmental revenu percentage	26.22%	73.78%	0.00%	0.00%	0.00%	0.00%	100.00%

Based on the proportions shown in exhibit 9.9, the overhead costs of the service centres are then allocated sequentially to the other centres until all the service centre costs are completely allocated. For example since the A & G expenses are to be initially allocated, the A & G column has only 0.00% whereas all the other departments have proportions as contained in the A & G row from 22.22% for rooms, through 51.85% for F & B, 11.11% for POM & UC and 7.41% for both HRM and S & M. Applying these proportions now to the existing costs in a sequential manner leads to complete allocation of the costs as shown in exhibit 9.10.

Exhibit 9.10 **Sequential allocation of the Blue Ribbon Roadside Inn Service Centre Costs**

Step 2 – Part 2 Department	Unallocated Service Centre costs	Allocated per Step 1	Initial Costs to be Allocated	Allocating Costs of A & G	Allocating Costs of POM & UC	Allocating Costs of HRM	Allocating Costs of S & M	Total
Rooms	€ –	€ 81,145.43	€ –	€ 26,896.32	€ 48,571.24	€ 23,658.70	€ 32,033.74	€ 212,305.43
Food & Beverage	€ –	€ 58,156.37	€ –	€ 62,728.43	€ 36,428.43	€ 55,203.64	€ 90,148.04	€ 302,694.57
Adm & Gen	€ 114,000.00	€ 7,033.46	€ 121,033.46	€ –	€ –	€ –	€ –	€ –
POM & UC	€ 73,000.00	€ 3,408.62	€ 76,408.62	€ 13,448.16	€ –	€ –	€ –	€ –
HRM	€ 72,000.00	€ 3,354.57	€ 75,354.57	€ 8,965.44	€ 2,428.56	€ –	€ –	€ –
Sales & Marketing	€ 91,000.00	€ 11,901.54	€ 102,901.54	€ 8,965.44	€ 2,428.56	€ 7,886.23	€ –	€ –
Total	€ 350,000.00	€ 165,000.00	€ 375,698.20	€ 121,033.46	€ 89,856.79	€ 86,748.57	€122,181.78	€ 515,000.00
			New POM & UC €	89,856.79				
			new HRM €	86,748.57				
			new S & M €	122,181.78				

In exhibit 9.10, the first service centre costs allocated are those of the A & G. The amount to be allocated of the A & G is equal to the costs allocated to A & G in Step 1 (€7,033.46) plus its own costs of €114,000.00 making a total of €121,033.46. Based on the proportions already established in exhibit 9.9 (Step 2 – Part 1) the amount of €121,033.46 is then allocated to the remaining service centres (POM & UC, HRM and S & M), as well as the profit centres (Rooms and F & B). The next step in the sequence is to allocate the costs of the POM & UC. However, for this to be carried out, the newly allocated portion of the costs of the A & G should be added to the initial costs of the POM & UC before proceeding. This total is shown in exhibit 9.10 as new POM & UC of €89,856.79 eventually. Similar actions are then carried out with the remaining service centre costs (new HRM and new S & M).

As was shown when the direct method was illustrated, a fully allocated income statement is then established that will show the final performance of the profit centres. Exhibit 9.11 is the fully allocated income statement of the Blue Ribbon Roadside Inn based on the step method.

Exhibit 9.11 **Fully allocated income statement of the Blue Ribbon Roadside Inn – step method**

The Blue Ribbon Roadside Inn
Fully Allocated Income Statement
For the year ending December 31st 2009

Department	Net Revenues	Cost of Sales	Payroll and Related Expenses	Other Expenses	Departmental Income	Allocated Expenses	Departmental Income After Allocation
Rooms	€ 565,000.00	€ –	€ 225,000.00	€ 102,000.00	€ 238,000.00	€ 212,305.43	€ 25,694.57
Food & Beverage	€ 1,590,000.00	€ 725,000.00	€ 440,000.00	€ 75,000.00	€ 350,000.00	€ 302,694.57	€ 47,305.43
Total	€ 2,155,000.00	€ 725,000.00	€ 665,000.00	€ 177,000.00	€ 588,000.00	€ 515,000.00	€ 73,000.00
				Income Taxes			€ 24,000.00
				Net Income			€ 49,000.00

The effects on the departmental incomes of the two allocation methods can be easily noticed by comparing the incidences of the allocation methods on the profit centres' departmental incomes. This is illustrated in exhibit 9.12.

Exhibit 9.12 showed that based on the step method of cost allocation, the departmental income of the rooms division became better than when the direct method was used, and the opposite goes for the performance of the food and beverage department. Any decisions made by the management based on after-allocation performance should take into account the factors earlier stated in this section.

© Noordhoff Uitgevers bv

Exhibit 9.12 **Comparing the effects of the two methods on the departmental incomes**

Comparison of the effect on the profit centres

Department	MABA Direct	MABA Step Method
Rooms	€ 20,583.29	€ 25,694.57
Food & Beverage	€ 52,416.71	€ 47,305.43

Recall that they relate to levels of income, how fixed the overhead costs are, the service relationships between the departments and lastly the available operating alternatives.

To conclude, in assessing both allocation methods the following observations can be made:

- The direct method is simple and easy to understand. It however omits the allocation of overhead costs to the service centres themselves.
- The step method uses more time and energy in its establishment. It resolves the problem of the direct method with the initial attribution of all the fixed costs to all the departments of the operation. However it omits to consider the reciprocal provision of services between the service centres themselves. This is solved via the formula method which is, as earlier indicated, beyond the scope of this book.

9.5 Separating mixed-costs between their fixed and variable elements

When called to make certain pricing, marketing and expansion decisions, management should be able to determine the fixed and variable components in each mixed-cost. Mixed-costs (see section 9.2) are those costs that cannot be finely split into their fixed or variable components. To assist managements in separating these mixed-costs, three common methods used are the high/low two-point method, the scatter diagram, and lastly regression analysis.

To illustrate all these methods of separating mixed-costs, information about the monthly room sales and the POM & UC expenses of the Blue Ribbon Roadside Inn for the year 2009 will be used and this is shown in exhibit 9.13. The POM activities of the Blue Ribbon Roadside Inn are outsourced and all POM & UC expenses are considered to be mixed costs.

Exhibit 9.13 **Monthly breakdown of room sales and POM & UC expense of the Blue Ribbon Roadside Inn for 2009**

The Blue Ribbon Roadside Inn

2009

Month	Rooms Sold	POM & UC Expense
January	450	€ 4,520.00
February	470	€ 4,680.00
March	520	€ 5,300.00
April	580	€ 5,750.00
May	600	€ 6,100.00
June	680	€ 6,900.00
July	720	€ 7,300.00
August	750	€ 7,450.00
September	690	€ 6,800.00
October	650	€ 6,600.00
November	590	€ 6,000.00
December	510	€ 5,600.00
Total	**7210**	**€ 73,000.00**

The structure of the section is as follows:

9.5.1   High/low two-point method
9.5.2   Scatter diagram
9.5.3   Regression analysis

9.5.1   High/low two-point method

The high/low two-point method is the simplest of the approaches used in estimating fixed and variable elements in mixed-costs. It is also called the high-low method or the maximum-minimum method. The high/low two-point method uses data from only two periods in the time span of the organization's operations. In the case of the Blue Ribbon Roadside Inn, the month of January with 450 rooms sold is the low point in 2009 whereas August with 750 rooms is the high point in 2009. The high/low two-point method will be illustrated using the following 5 steps:

Step 1 – Calculate the differences in the total mixed-cost and activity between the high and low periods

Month	Rooms Sold	POM & UC Expense
August (high)	750	€ 7,450.00
January (low)	450	€ 4,520.00
Difference	**300**	**€ 2,930.00**

The difference in rooms sold between the high and low periods in 2009 is 300, while that in the cost category POM & UC is €2,930.00.

Step 2 – Divide the mixed-cost difference by the activity difference to determine the variable cost per unit

$$\text{Variable cost per room sold} = \frac{\text{Mixed cost difference}}{\text{Rooms sold difference}}$$

$$\text{Variable cost per room sold} = \frac{\text{POM \& UC expense difference}}{\text{Rooms sold difference}}$$

$$\text{Variable cost per room sold} = \frac{\text{€2,930.00}}{300}$$

$$\text{Variable cost per room sold} = \text{€9.766667 (rounded to 9.77)}$$

This result indicates that for every additional room sold by the Blue Ribbon Roadside Inn, they will incur a POM & UC variable expense of €9.77.

Step 3 – Determine the total variable costs for the periods of high or low activity

Total Variable POM & UC Expenses

Month	Rooms Sold	Total Variable POM & UC Expense
August (high)	750	€ 7,325.00
January (low)	450	€ 4,395.00

This is done by multiplying the rooms sold for the periods by the variable cost per room. For the month of August 750 x €9.77 = €7,325.00.

Step 4 – Determine the total fixed costs for the periods of high or low activity

Determining the Total Fixed Costs

Month	POM & UC Expense	Total Variable POM & UC Expense	Total Fixed POM & UC Expense
August (high)	€ 7,450.00	€ 7,325.00	€ 125.00
January (low)	€ 4,520.00	€ 4,395.00	€ 125.00

This is done by deducting the total variable POM & UC expense for each period from the POM & UC expense for that period. Such as for January the total POM & UC expense was €4,520.00 less the total variable expense of €4,395.00 which gives a fixed cost of €125.00 for the low period.

Step 5 – Determine the total values for the year

	The Blue Ribbon Roadside Inn 2009		
Month	POM & UC Expense	Total Fixed POM & UC Expense	Total Variable POM & UC Expense
January	€ 4,520.00	€ 125.00	€ 4,395.00
February	€ 4,680.00	€ 125.00	€ 4,555.00
March	€ 5,300.00	€ 125.00	€ 5,175.00
April	€ 5,750.00	€ 125.00	€ 5,625.00
May	€ 6,100.00	€ 125.00	€ 5,975.00
June	€ 6,900.00	€ 125.00	€ 6,775.00
July	€ 7,300.00	€ 125.00	€ 7,175.00
August	€ 7,450.00	€ 125.00	€ 7,325.00
September	€ 6,800.00	€ 125.00	€ 6,675.00
October	€ 6,600.00	€ 125.00	€ 6,475.00
November	€ 6,000.00	€ 125.00	€ 5,875.00
December	€ 5,600.00	€ 125.00	€ 5,475.00
Total	€ 73,000.00	€ 1,500.00	€ 71,500.00

It is thus seen that out of the total POM & UC expense of €73,000.00 the fixed cost amounted to €1,500.00 only. A very large proportion of the POM & UC expense was made up of variable elements.

The high/low two-point method is quick and simple to use and can also be calculated using graphs by plotting the cost (vertical axis) and sales (horizontal axis) data of the high and low periods and by drawing and extending the line linking the two observed intersection points to the vertical axis. The high/low two-point data of the POM & UC expenses of the Blue Ribbon Roadside Inn is plotted in a graph and shown in exhibit 9.14. If the graph is accurately drawn, the same monthly figure of approximately €125.00 is obtained.

The high/low two-point method has some limitations:
· It assumes that the extreme periods are a fair reflection of the high and low points for the year
· either one or both of the sets of figures may not be typical of the relationship between sales and the expenses for the year
· Distortions can be built into the figures

These limitations notwithstanding, the ease of the use of the high/low two-point method makes it quite popular with small businesses.

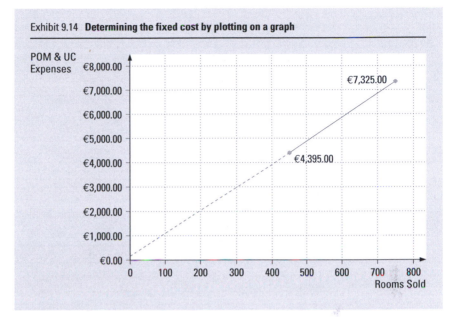

Exhibit 9.14 **Determining the fixed cost by plotting on a graph**

9.5.2 Scatter diagram

To help improve on the lack of accuracy of the high/low two-point method in determining the fixed costs of an organization, the scatter diagram can be used. This is much more detailed and involves the following steps:

Step 1
Establish and plot a graph showing the independent variable on the horizontal axis and the dependent variable on the vertical axis. In the case of the Blue Ribbon Roadside Inn, the number of rooms sold is the independent variable whereas the POM & UC expenses are the dependent variable because these expenses vary with the number of rooms sold.

Step 2
Draw a straight line through the points ensuring that an equal number of points are located above and below the line. Extend this line to meet with the vertical axis. The point where the line meets the vertical axis is considered to be the fixed costs for the period. Using this monthly fixed cost level, the annual fixed costs can then be assessed.

Based on these two steps and using the Blue Ribbon Roadside Inn data exhibit 9.15 is drawn. The line might vary depending on who draws it, but it should represent the best possible fit. In exhibit 9.15, there are 5 points below or just below the line, 1 point cut by the line, and 6 points above or barely above the line. The projected line in exhibit 9.15 meets the expenses (vertical) axis around the value of €250 which is then assumed to be the monthly fixed costs in the total POM & UC expenses. The annual fixed POM & UC expenses is then

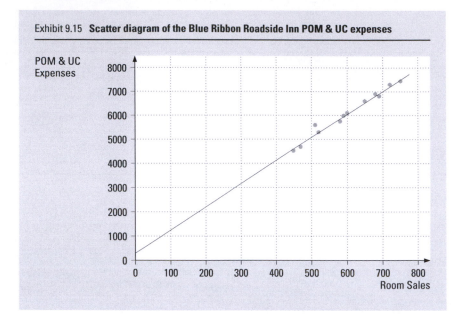

Exhibit 9.15 **Scatter diagram of the Blue Ribbon Roadside Inn POM & UC expenses**

calculated to be €3,000.00 and the total variable POM & UC expenses for 2009 is equal to €70,000.00 (€73,000.00 minus €3,000.00). Per room sold, the variable POM & UC expenses is equal to €9.71 which is:

$$\frac{€70,000.00}{7,210}$$

The scatter diagram is an improvement over the high/low two point method but it is also time consuming and only an approximation instead of the exact measurement of the real value of the fixed costs. To correct this situation, regression analysis can be used.

9.5.3 Regression analysis

Regression analysis is the mathematical approach that permits perfectly fitting a straight line to any given set of data. Its main objective is to explore the relationship between a given variable (usually called the dependent variable) and one or more other variables (usually called the independent variables). With regression analysis, the outcome of a given key business indicator can be predicted based on the interactions with other related business drivers. The formula used in regression analysis makes it unnecessary to draw a graph, plot points, and draw a line through them. Mathematically, the simple linear regression model is represented by the following equation whose goal is to find the equation of the straight line:

$$y = a + bx$$

in which
"a" is the intercept, and
"b" is the regression coefficient (slope).

The formula for calculating "a" is:

$$\frac{\sum x^2 \sum y - \sum x \sum xy}{n \sum x^2 - \left(\sum x\right)^2}$$

The formula for calculating "b" is:

$$\frac{n \sum xy - \sum x \sum y}{n \sum x^2 - \left(\sum x\right)^2}$$

The Greek symbol Σ means "the sum of" thus for example Σx means the sum of all x values.

To separate the costs in the Blue Ribbon Roadside Inn POM & UC expenses using regression analysis, the first thing to do is to recognize which of the data values represent the "a" in the straight line equation. In the straight line equation

$$y = a + bx$$

in which
y represents the total POM & UC expenses for any of the periods,
a, the fixed cost for that period,
b the slope of the straight line, and
x the number of rooms sold in each period.

Using the formula for calculating a, exhibit 9.16 shows the values for the Blue Ribbon Roadside Inn for 2009.

Exhibit 9.16 **Using Regression Analysis to determine the fixed costs of the Blue Ribbon Roadside Inn**

The Blue Ribbon Roadside Inn
2009

Month	Rooms Sold	POM & UC Expense		
	x	y	x^2	xy
January	450	€ 4,520.00	202,500	€ 2,034,000.00
February	470	€ 4,680.00	220,900	€ 2,199,600.00
March	520	€ 5,300.00	270,400	€ 2,756,000.00
April	580	€ 5,750.00	336,400	€ 3,335,000.00
May	600	€ 6,100.00	360,000	€ 3,660,000.00
June	680	€ 6,900.00	462,400	€ 4,692,000.00
July	720	€ 7,300.00	518,400	€ 5,256,000.00
August	750	€ 7,450.00	562,500	€ 5,587,500.00
September	690	€ 6,800.00	476,100	€ 4,692,000.00
October	650	€ 6,600.00	422,500	€ 4,290,000.00
November	590	€ 6,000.00	348,100	€ 3,540,000.00
December	510	€ 5,600.00	260,100	€ 2,856,000.00
Total	$\Sigma x = 7210$	$\Sigma y = 73,000.00$	$\Sigma x^2 = 4,440,300$	$\Sigma xy = 44,898,100.00$

Replacing the values contained in exhibit 9.16 in the formula to calculate "a" – the monthly fixed costs shows that the monthly fixed cost in POM & UC is €328.28.

$$\text{Monthly fixed costs} = \frac{(73,000)(4,440,300) - (7,210)(44,898,100)}{12(4,440,300) - (7,210)(7,210)}$$

Monthly fixed costs = €328.28

Based on these monthly fixed costs, the annual fixed cost is determined to be €3,939.35 (that is €328.28 × 12 months). The total variable POM & UC expenses for 2009 is equal to €69,060.65 (€73,000.00 minus €3,939.35). Per room sold, the variable POM & UC expenses is equal to €9.58, which is

$$\frac{€69,060.65}{7,210}$$

A comparative analysis of the results obtained using the three methods of the fixed/variable breakdown of the Blue Ribbon Roadside Inn's POM & UC expenses for 2009 can be made as shown in exhibit 9.17

Exhibit 9.17 **Comparing the three methods**

The Blue Ribbon Roadside Inn POM & UC Expense for 2009				
Method	**Fixed component**	**Variable component**	**Variable unit cost**	**Total**
High/low two point method	€ 1,500.00	€ 71,500.00	€ 9.77	€ 73,000.00
Scatter diagram	€ 3,000.00	€ 70,000.00	€ 9.71	€ 73,000.00
Regression analysis	€ 3,939.35	€ 69,060.65	€ 9.58	€ 73,000.00

Exhibit 9.17 shows a big difference between the fixed costs established by the high/low two point method and the regression analysis of up to €2,439.35. Regression analysis is known to be the most accurate of the methods and can be easily done using programmable calculators or spreadsheet programmes such as Excel.

Glossary

Activity-based costing – the costing approach that assigns resource costs to cost objects based on activities performed for the cost objects.

Allocation base – is that factor that determines how much of an overhead expense will be allocated to a department.

Controllable costs – these are costs that the departmental managers can directly influence in the short run.

Cost allocation – is the process of distributing overhead expenses among the various departments.

Cost centre – is that department that generates no direct revenues.

Cost objects – these are the outputs such as products, services or customers for which companies perform their activities

Discretionary costs – these are costs that departmental managers can choose to avoid in the short run.

Direct costs – are those costs that can be traced to a particular operating department and is the responsibility of that department

Fixed costs – are those costs that do not change in relation to the volume of business within a specific period or production level.

High/low two-point method – this is the simplest approach to estimating the fixed and variable elements of a mixed cost.

Indirect costs – are those costs that are not directly identified and not traceable to a particular operating department.

Investment centre – these are decentralized units within very large or chain organizations that have full authority over how they operate and are responsible for their decisions.

Joint costs – are those costs that are shared and are the responsibility of two or more departments

Mixed costs – these are costs that cannot be finely split into their fixed or variable elements. These are also called semi-fixed or semi-variable costs.

Multiple allocation base approach (MABA) – this is the use of different allocation bases to allocate different overhead costs among departments.

Non controllable costs – are those costs that cannot be influenced by the departmental heads.

Opportunity cost – this represents the value of the foregone next best alternative that results from a decision in a situation involving several alternatives.

Overhead costs – see indirect costs.

Profit centre – is that department that has costs but also generates sales revenue that is directly related to the department.

Regression analysis – is a mathematical approach that permits perfectly fitting a straight line to any given set of data.

Relevant costs – are those costs that change depending on decisions that are made, as well as affecting those decisions.

Sales revenue centre – is that department that receives sales revenues but has little or no direct costs associated with their operations.

Scatter diagram – this is a graphic approach used in determining the fixed and variable elements of a mixed cost.

Semi-fixed and semi-variable costs – see mixed costs

Single allocation base approach (SABA) – is the allocation of overhead costs among departments using a single allocation base.

Standard costs – is the measure of how much a product or service should normally cost based on a given volume or sales.

Sunk costs – are those costs that have already been incurred and as such cannot be recovered.

Variable costs – are those costs that change proportionately to changes in the volume of the business.

Multiple choice questions

9.1 Which of the following types of costs is the measure of how much a product or service should normally cost?
    a direct cost
    b discretionary cost
    c fixed cost
    d standard cost

9.2 Which cost does not change in a specific period or production level as activity changes?
    a fixed
    b indirect
    c joint
    d variable

9.3 Which of the following statements is false?
    a cost centre managers are responsible for the costs of all the departments
    b cost, sales revenue, profit and investment centres result from responsibility accounting
    c department heads are responsible for the direct costs of their departments
    d sales revenue centres have little or no direct costs

9.4 Which of the following types of costs is generally allocated among profit centres of a hospitality operation?
    a discretionary costs
    b incremental costs
    c indirect costs
    d standard costs

9.5 A sunk cost is:
    a a cost that is incurred and recoverable
    b a cost that is incurred and unrecoverable
    c a quantifiable future cost
    d shared and joint responsibility of two or more departments

Exercises

9.1 Classify the following expenses into their principal cost types (multiple types per expense item is a possibility)

    a Cost of beverages sold
    b Cost of food sold
    c Depreciation
    d General manager's salary
    e Guest supplies
    f Income taxes
    g Laundry expenses
    h Property fire insurance
    i Property taxes
    j Repair and maintenance
    k Rooms division salaries
    l Telephone expense

9.2 The quarterly POM expenses and occupancy percentages of the Sweet Sour Restaurant for 2010 are as detailed in the accompanying table:

	POM expenses	Occupancy
31 March 2010	€ 28,980.00	62%
30 June 2010	€ 31,740.00	68%
30 September 2010	€ 29,900.00	72%
31 December 2010	€ 32,200.00	66%

Using the high/low two point method, calculate the following based on the provided information:

a the monthly fixed element in the POM expenses for 2010
b the monthly variable element in the POM expenses per occupancy percentage for 2010
c knowing that the POM expenses will rise by 4% in 2011, what will be the expected monthly POM expenses for 2011 with an average occupancy of 71%

9.3 The owner of the Ocean Front Restaurant needs an analysis of the salary expenses in the restaurant and provides you with the following data:

The Ocean Front Restaurant Salaries 2010		
	Customers	Salaries
January	6400	€ 23,250.00
Febrary	3840	€ 15,675.00
March	5920	€ 27,750.00
April	7120	€ 28,500.00
May	7040	€ 28,500.00
June	7680	€ 30,375.00
July	8000	€ 30,750.00
August	6240	€ 27,750.00
September	6080	€ 27,000.00
October	4960	€ 23,250.00
November	4640	€ 22,875.00
December	4800	€ 24,975.00

Using the high/low two point method, calculate the following based on the provided information:

a the variable salary expense per customer
b the annual total variable cost
c the fixed monthly component in the salary expense of the restaurant
d the annual fixed cost

9.4 The monthly sales of the Sushi Delight at different performance levels are given in the accompanying table.

Sushi Rolls	19200.00	38400.00	57600.00
Cost of sales	€ 28,800.00	€ 57,600.00	€ 86,400.00
Salaries	€ 22,400.00	€ 32,000.00	€ 41,600.00
Supplies	€ 3,840.00	€ 7,680.00	€ 11,520.00
Utilities	€ 2,304.00	€ 2,688.00	€ 3,072.00
Other operating costs	€ 9,600.00	€ 19,200.00	€ 28,800.00
Rent	€ 6,400.00	€ 6,400.00	€ 6,400.00
Depreciation	€ 1,280.00	€ 1,280.00	€ 1,280.00
Total costs	€ 74,624.00	€ 126,848.00	€ 179,072.00

You are asked to carry out the following activities:

a use the variable, fixed or mixed classification of costs to classify the costs of the Sushi Delight
b establish the regression equation of monthly total costs for the Sushi Delight
c use the regression equation to estimate the total costs of the Sushi Delight if sales were 51,200 sushi rolls

Pricing and Revenue Management

10

10.1 The importance of pricing and the relationship between price and quantity
10.2 Approaches to pricing
10.3 Pricing rooms
10.4 Pricing food and beverage products
10.5 Menu engineering
10.6 Revenue management

Pricing is defined as the method companies use to set the selling prices for their products and services, and it is a very important aspect of the decision making process within hospitality operations. Because of this, pricing theory will entail that hospitality operations price their rooms, F & B and other products in such a way that they control their costs and maximize their incomes but at the same time ensure that the service experience of their customers are not negatively affected. Section 10.1 deals with the importance of pricing and the relationship between pricing and quantity. In section 10.2 the various approaches to pricing are discussed and section 10.3 shows the various methods of setting room rates. In section 10.4 the methods of pricing Food and Beverage products are explained, while section 10.5 introduces the concepts of Menu Engineering. In the last section 10.6, the concept of Revenue Management is introduced.

10.1 The importance of pricing and the relationship between price and quantity

Pricing is a very challenging aspect of the decision making process within hospitality operations. This results from the great diversity in the number and types of meals that have to be priced as well as the different room types and configurations that have to be priced. Pricing is furthermore challenging due to the service nature of the industry and the interactions between the guests and the servers that lead to different experiences even if the service delivery was exactly the same.

Pricing is just one of the ways through which the hospitality operation can influence the demand for its products and services. For example revenues can be increased through advertisement, expanding the sales and marketing personnel as well as improving their product presentation and service delivery. Modifying pricing policies may not turn out to be the best way possible to increasing sales and improving net incomes. It should be noted that this chapter is about pricing which is just one of the factors that can be used to influence sales and net income levels.

The relationship between price and quantity is principally explained by the principle of price elasticity. In this specific instance the notion discussed is that of price elasticity of demand. Price elasticity of demand is that measure of the responsiveness in the quantity demanded for a product or service as a result of changes in the price of that product or service. The price elasticity of demand is measured as the ratio of percentage changes between the quantity demanded and changes in its price.

The basic formula in the determination of the price elasticity of demand is as follows:

$$\text{Price elasticity } n = \frac{\%\Delta Q}{\%\Delta P}$$

in which:
n = price elasticity
% = percentage
Δ = change
Q = quantity
P = price

This formula always result in a negative value, however by convention, the negative values are ignored.

The various levels of the price elasticity of demand are summarily discussed below:

Perfect inelasticity (n = 0)
If the result is exactly equal to zero it is said that the demand is perfectly inelastic which means that whatever changes affect the price, the demand is not affected.

Relative inelasticity ($-1 < n < 0$)
If the result is between zero and minus one, it is said to be relatively inelastic which means that the relative change in the quantity demanded is less than the relative change in the price.

Unit elasticity ($n = -1$)
If the result is exactly equal to minus one then it is said to be unitary elastic which means that the relative change in the quantity demanded is exactly equal to the relative change in price.

Relative elasticity ($-\infty < n < -1$)
If the result is smaller than minus one then it is said to be relatively elastic which means that the change in quantity demanded is slightly higher than the change in price.

Perfect elasticity ($n = -\infty$)
If the result is near infinity it indicates that the demand is perfectly elastic which means that the slightest change in price would lead to an infinite change in the quantity demanded.

10.2   Approaches to pricing

There are many different approaches to pricing used within the hospitality industry and some of them are summarily explained below. More details about room-specific or menu-specific approaches are dealt with in sections 10.3, 10.4 and 10.5.

Rule of thumb method
The rule of thumb is a method in which the prices are set at a certain rate based on the initial costs. For example prices are set at 60% of the cost of goods sold.

Intuitive method
In this informal method prices are simply established based on intuition. No research about costs, profits, competition and the market as a whole would have been carried out. Prices are set in the hope that they are correct and the guests will accept them.

Trial and error method
In this informal method prices are tentatively set to evaluate the effect it would have on sales and net incomes. The price is finally set at levels where the net incomes are apparently maximized.

Price cutting method
In competitive situations, prices are set at levels below those of the competition. This is an informal method and generally risky because in case the competition reacts by similar reductions in price, this might lead to a price war.

High price method
Similarly in competitive situations prices might be set higher than the competition due to product differentiation. Also informal, it is equally

risky in the sense that if the guests cannot easily make the price-quality relationship, they might tend to move elsewhere.

Competitive method
In this informal method prices are set at the same level as those of the competition. However, some non price factors such as location and atmosphere can lead to differentiation. In situations where there is a dominant operator in the market who normally sets the price trend, this is called 'follow-the-leader' method.

Mark-up method
Specific to restaurants the mark-up is the difference between the costs of the products and the selling price. The mark-up generally includes the related costs such as labour, utilities, supplies and the expected profit.

10.3 Pricing rooms

The supply of rooms is generally fixed in the short term and rooms are characterized by the fact that if its sales revenue for a particular day is not received then it is lost forever. For these reasons, the pricing of rooms should be done in such a way that the fixed costs of the rooms can be recovered as well as the maximum occupancy levels can be obtained. There are various methods of setting room rates as will be described in the following subsections. The structure of the subsections is as follows:

10.3.1	The rule of a thousand approach
10.3.2	The bottom up approach
10.3.3	Relative room size approach
10.3.4	Differential room pricing
10.3.5	Room rate discounting

10.3.1 The rule of a thousand approach

This is a basic rule of thumb approach in which the price of a hotel room is set at one thousandth ($1/_{1000}$) of the investment costs incurred in the development of the room. Assume that the total cost of building a 75-room hotel is €12,500,000.00 and that 30% of this investment relates to other non-rooms related hotel activities. Then the price of one room will be assessed as such:

$$\text{Total rooms investment} = €12,500,000.00 \times 70\% = €8,750,000.00$$

$$\text{Cost of one room} = \frac{€8,750,000.00}{75} = €116,666.67$$

$$\text{Room selling price} = \frac{€116,666.67}{1,000} = €116.67$$

Using this method, the hotel will sell its rooms at an average rate of €116.67.

This method fails to address issues such as seasonality and all the other services that the guest might pay for within the hotel. As well, it does not consider the time at which the investment was made in the hotel, and also what the competition does.

10.3.2 The bottom up approach (Hubbart formula or required rate of return)

This approach involves determining what room rate must be charged in order to generate the annual revenue that will be sufficient to cover all costs and taxes as well as to meet the owners' expected profit levels. This is a bottom up approach that was developed for the American Hotel & Motel Association and it is commonly referred to as the 'Hubbart formula'. It is called bottom up approach because it progresses from the bottom line of the income statement (net income) upwards towards sales revenues which make up the first item in the income statement.

The Hubbart formula can be summarized as:

$$\frac{\text{Operating costs} + \text{required return} - \text{Income of other departments}}{\text{Expected number of room nights}} = \text{Average room rate}$$

In using the Hubbart formula, the following steps should be respected:

Step 1	Calculate the total amount invested in the hotel.
Step 2	Decide on the required annual rate of return on the investment (this may be a percentage of the amount invested)
Step 3	Estimate the overhead expenses.
Step 4	Combine steps 2 and 3 to find the required gross operating income.
Step 5	Estimate the probable profits from all other sources (i.e. restaurants, bars etc).
Step 6	Deduct step 5 from step 4 to find out how much profit you need to make from room sales.
Step 7	Estimate rooms department's expenses (include fixed and variable costs based on forecasted occupancy)
Step 8	Add steps 6 and 7 to find out how much you need to make from the rooms
Step 9	Estimate the number of room nights you are likely to achieve per year (based on forecasted occupancy)
Step 10	Divide step 8 by step 9 to find out the average room rate you should charge.

■ Exhibit 10.1 **Illustration of the application of the Hubbart formula**

Afilen Hotels Plc. operates a 300-room hotel. The capital invested is €22,500,000 and the company is expecting a net profit of 10% after paying tax at the rate of 30%. They expect an average occupancy rate of 68%. Rooms departmental expenses are expected to amount to €3,000,000 and profits from other departments are expected to be €1,400,000. The overhead expenses are:

Administrative and General	1,140,000
Sales & Marketing	825,000
Utilities	500,000
POM	570,000
Depreciation	1,640,000
Insurance, licences and property taxes	740,000
Interest	850,000

Step 1	Total investment = €22,500,000
Step 2	10% of €22,500,000 = €2,250,000 (pre tax income = €3,214,286)
Step 3	Overhead expenses = €6,265,000
Step 4	The required gross operating income (€3,214,286 + €6,265,000) = €9,479,286
Step 5	Profits from other sources are expected to amount to €1,400,000
Step 6	Total room revenue needed of €8,079,286
Step 7	Add the departmental cost of €3,000,000 to the needed amount of €8,079,286
Step 8	The hotel needs to make €11,079,286 from room sales.
Step 9	300 rooms × 365 days = 109,500 = 100% room occupancy Therefore = 74,460 = 68% room occupancy
Step 10	Average room rate = $\dfrac{€11,079,286}{74,460 \text{ Room nights}}$ = €148.79

The Hubbart formula can be used for varying occupancy percentages. This can be done by simply reviewing steps 7 to 9.

10.3.3 Relative room size approach

One of the main problems with both the rule of a thousand and bottom-up approaches is that they only produce an average room rate. This would have been a nice thing if the hotel had only one room type, but in reality this is not always the case. The relative room size approach permits the establishment of room rates that would take into effect the relative sizes of the various rooms within the hospitality operation.

Let's assume that one of the properties belonging to Afilen Hotels Plc. has two different room types. 50 rooms of Type A and 100 rooms of Type B. Type A rooms measure 40 square metres and Type B rooms measure 30 square metres. The occupancy percentage of the room types are 65 and 70 percent for Types A and B respectively.

The hotel expects to make revenue of at least €6,205,000 for the next year in which it will be operating all the 365 days of the year. With the above information, at what rates should the rooms be priced?

Step 1
Assess the surface area of the rooms sold daily

	Number of rooms		m²		Occupancy		Total m² sold
Type A	50	×	40	×	65%	=	1,300
Type B	100	×	30	×	70%	=	2,100
							3,400

Step 2
Determine the average revenue required per day:
This is done by dividing the expected annual sales by the number of days of operation.

$$\text{Expected annual sales} = \frac{6,205,000.00}{365} = €17,000.00$$

Step 3
Determine the average rate to charge each square meter of room space:
This is done by dividing the average daily revenue by the total square metres sold.

$$\frac{\text{Average daily revenue}}{\text{Total square metres sold daily}} = \frac{€17,000.00}{3,400.00 \text{ m}^2} = €5.00$$

Step 4
The last step is to determine the specific rates to charge each room type as follows:

This is done by multiplying the room size by the price per square metre:

	Room size		Price per m²		Room charge
Type A	40	×	€5.00	=	€200.00
Type B	30	×	€5.00	=	€150.00

The Type A rooms should be charged €200.00 and the Type B rooms at €150.00.

To cross check if, based on the above occupancy levels and room rates, the expected revenue will be attained the following can be done:

	Number of rooms		Occupancy		Rate		Annual operating days		Total revenue
Type A	50	×	65%	×	€200.00	×	365	=	€ 2,372,500.00
Type B	100	×	70%	×	€150.00	×	365	=	€ 3,832,500.00
									€ 6,205,000.00

From the above verification it is noticed that the total revenue equals the initial expected revenue for next year for Afilen Hotels Plc.

10.3.4 Differential room pricing

In situations where the hotel has different types of rooms, the pricing methods are as well adapted to the specific room types. Following are examples of how the room rates are determined under different situations. In 10.3.4.1 the calculation of single and double rates are shown, while 10.3.4.2 shows how the effects of seasonality are integrated in the calculation of the room rates.

10.3.4.1 Calculating single and double rates
After having looked at the effect of the room size and room pricing the analysis can be extended further into the establishment of single and double rates.

Assume that Afilen Hotels Plc. has another property with 180 rooms and an overall occupancy percentage of 72%. The 180 rooms are distributed between the three room types as follows:

	Code	Number of Rooms	Occupancy Rate
Single, single occupancy	S	60	68%
Double, single occupancy	D-s	90	20%
Double, double occupancy	D-d		60%
Executive, single occupancy	E-s	30	9%
Executive, double occupancy	E-d		48%
Total		180	

Proceed by attributing weights for the various occupancy levels types. These weights are established based only on the management's judgement. In this example, the following weights are attributed:

	Weight
Single, single occupancy	1
Double, single occupancy	1.5
Double, double occupancy	1.9
Executive, single occupancy	1.9
Executive, double occupancy	2.5

At this point the average revenue target per day based on an ADR of €175.00 has to be calculated.
The average revenue per day would be

$$\text{ADR} \times \text{occupancy percentage} \times \text{number of rooms} =$$
$$= €175.00 \times 72.17\% \times 180 = €22,732.50$$

Code	Rooms	Occ. %	Average occupied rooms	Weight	AO × Weight	Revenue expected	Room rate*
Single, single occupancy	60	68%	40.8	1	40.8	€ 4,384.65	€ 107.47
Double, single occupancy		20%	18	1.5	27	€ 2,901.61	€ 161.20
Double, double occupancy	90	60%	54	1.9	102.6	€11,026.12	€ 204.19
Executive, single occupancy		9%	2.7	1.9	5.13	€ 551.31	€ 204.19
Executive, double occupancy	30	48%	14.4	2.5	36	€ 3,868.81	€ 268.67
	180				211.53	€22,732.50	

* These room rates can be rounded up for convenience purposes

in which:
Average occupied rooms: number of rooms multiplied by the occupancy percentage for the type of room.

AO × weight: average occupied rooms × weight

Revenue expected: AO × weight divided by the total AO × weight as percentage of the total average revenue target per day.

Room rate: revenue expected divided by the average occupied rooms.

Realise now that based on the combination of the number of rooms, the occupancy percentages, the given weights and the expected revenue the various room rates have been determined. Thus for the three room types, single, double and executive the following rates will be charged:

Single room	€ 107.47
Double room, single occupancy	€ 161.20
Double room, double occupancy	€ 204.19
Executive, single occupancy	€ 204.19
Executive, double occupancy	€ 268.67

10.3.4.2 Integrating the effects of seasonality

A further step in understanding differential room pricing is to bring in the notion of the effects that seasonality has on hotel occupancy. Hotels normally experience two seasons: a high season and a low season. Exhibit 10.2 shows the integration of the effects of seasonality using the Afilen Hotels Plc. example that was explained in 10.4.3.1. This seasonality effect is brought in by attributing weights to the various seasons. The selection of these weights is simply a matter of judgement. In this particular example a weight of 4 will be given to the low season and a weight of 6 will be given to the high season.

Exhibit 10.2 **The effect of seasonality on room rates calculation**

Code	Rooms	Occ. %	Average occupied rooms	Weight	Seasonal weights	AO × Weight	Revenue expected	Room rate
Low season								
S	60	63%	37.8	1	4.0	151.2	€ 1,811.24	€ 95.83
D-s	90	18%	16.2	1.5	4.0	97.2	€ 1,164.37	€ 143.75
D-d		50%	45	1.9	4.0	342	€ 4,096.85	€ 182.08
E-s	30	6%	1.8	1.9	4.0	13.68	€ 163.87	€ 182.08
E-d		30%	9	2.5	4.0	90	€ 1,078.12	€ 239.58
High season								
S	60	73%	43.8	1	6.0	262.8	€ 3,148.10	€ 143.75
D-s	90	22%	19.8	1.5	6.0	178.2	€ 2,134.67	€ 215.62
D-d		70%	63	1.9	6.0	718.2	€ 8,603.38	€ 273.12
E-s	30	12%	3.6	1.9	6.0	41.04	€ 491.62	€ 273.12
E-d		66%	19.8	2.5	6.0	297	€ 3,557.79	€ 359.37

In this instance the AO × weight = average occupied rooms × room weight × seasonal weight

Exhibit 10.2 clearly brings out the differences caused by the low and high season effects on the room rates asked by the Afilen Hotels Plc. In the low season the following rates will be charged:

Single room	€ 95.83
Double room, single occupancy	€ 143.75
Double room, double occupancy	€ 182.08
Executive, single occupancy	€ 182.08
Executive, double occupancy	€ 239.58

This is sharply in contrast to what the Afilen Hotels Plc. will charge during the high season as shown below:

Single room	€ 143.75
Double room, single occupancy	€ 215.62
Double room, double occupancy	€ 273.12
Executive, single occupancy	€ 273.12
Executive, double occupancy	€ 359.37

10.3.5 Room rate discounting

The discounting of room rates is generally practiced in the hospitality industry. Discounting room rates simply means reducing the room price to levels below the rack rate. The rack rate is defined as the maximum rate that will be quoted for a room. This is practiced due to the specific characteristics of rooms, that cannot be carried over to the next day if not sold, and the effect of seasonality. Discounting rates for rooms prevents the hotel from achieving its maximum potential average room rate as well as the maximum potential total sales revenue. Discounting can be done in cases of large convention groups, regular guests, corporate and government travellers. Discounts are a normal cost of business in order to maintain occupancy levels. The reductions in rooms revenue is most of the time balanced by the extra sales that will be achieved from the guests' making use of the hotel's other paying facilities such as F & B products, spa and health, telecommunication, etc.

One of the peculiarities of a hotel room is the difference between the variable cost of an occupied room and the room rate. For example a guest room with a rack rate of about €175.00 with a variable cost of €25.00 leads to a contribution to the fixed costs of €150.00. In case the room rate is discounted to €120.00, this will still lead to a contribution of the fixed costs of €95.00. Thus an additional income of €95.00 is obtained from selling the room that would have otherwise been unoccupied. Theoretically the hotel can reduce its rate to a level just above the variable costs per room and still make some additional contributions to the fixed costs. However, this does not mean that selling all rooms at such low levels would be a good long-run decision. In the long-run, it is necessary that only those rooms that could not have been sold should be discounted. It is of importance to take all measures necessary to sell the hotel rooms at the rack rate before any discounting. Considering the price sensitivity of the particular group of guests the hotel should be able to determine its discount policy. The more price-sensitive they are, the more they can have access to discounted rates and vice versa.

To help in the process of making discounting decisions, hotels generally prepare what is called a discount grid. The grid generally shows the effect of various room rate discounts on the total room sales revenue. To develop a grid, the variable costs of selling each additional room should be known and these are normally easy to determine by hotel managements.

In order for a hospitality operation to achieve this, the equivalent room contribution margin and equivalent occupancy (EO) should be determined. This is done as follows:

$$\text{Equivalent occupancy (EO)} = \frac{\text{original occupancy} \times (\text{rack rate} - \text{marginal cost})}{[\text{rack rate} \times (1 - \text{discount percentage})] - \text{marginal cost}}$$

This can be summarized as:

$$EO = \frac{\text{original occupancy} \times \text{current contribution margin}}{\text{revised contribution margin}}$$

To better understand the notion of equivalent occupancy and its effect on the discount rate, assume the following:

A hotel has a rack rate of €175.00 with a marginal cost of €25.00. Assuming an occupancy level of 70% and an expected discounting of 10%, the equivalent occupancy can be calculated as follows:

$$EO = \frac{70\% \times (€175 - €25)}{[€175 \times (1 - 10\%)] - €25}$$

$$EO = \frac{0.7 \times €150}{(€175 \times 0.9) - €25}$$

$$EO = \frac{€105}{€157.5 - €25}$$

$$EO = \frac{€105}{€132.5} \text{ thus the EO} = 0.7924528 \text{ or } 79.24528\%$$

To verify the effectiveness of the concept of equivalent occupancy (EO), exhibit 10.3 will be used. In exhibit 10.3, it is assumed that the hotel has 200 rooms, a rack rate of €175.00 and currently has an occupancy rate of 70%.

■ Exhibit 10.3 **Verifying the effectiveness of the equivalent occupancy concept**

Revenue before discounting
    = 200 rooms × 70% occupancy × €175 rack rate = €24,500.00

Total variable cost
    = 200 rooms × 70% occupancy × €25 variable cost = €3,500.00

Net rooms revenue = €24,500 – 3,500 = €21,000

After discounting at 10% the occupancy will be 79.24528%

Revenue after discounting
    = 200 rooms × 79.24528% occupancy × €157.5 = €24,962.26

Total variable cost
    = 200 rooms × 79.24528% occupancy × €25 variable cost = €3,962.26

Net discounted rooms' revenue
    = €24,962.26 – €3,962.26 = €21,000.00

Exhibit 10.3 clearly illustrates that while discounting and based on the equivalent occupancy concept the net rooms' revenue remains the same.

Similar calculations as has been done in exhibit 10.3 can be made for various occupancy levels and discount percentages. These results can be transformed into a grid called the discount grid. An example of a discount grid based on a rack rate of €175.00 with variable costs of €25.00 is shown in exhibit 10.4

Exhibit 10.4 **Discount table for a €175 rack rate with a variable cost of €25**

Rack rate		€175.00					
Variable cost		€ 25.00					
		Required EO levels to maintain profitability if rates are discounted.					
	5%	10%	15%	20%	25%	30%	35%
100%	106.2%	113.2%	121.2%	130.4%	141.2%	153.8%	169.0%
95%	100.9%	107.5%	115.2%	123.9%	134.1%	146.2%	160.6%
90%	95.6%	101.9%	109.1%	117.4%	127.1%	138.5%	152.1%
85%	90.3%	96.2%	103.0%	110.9%	120.0%	130.8%	143.7%
80%	85.0%	90.6%	97.0%	104.3%	112.9%	123.1%	135.2%
75%	79.6%	84.9%	90.9%	97.8%	105.9%	115.4%	126.8%
70%	74.3%	79.2%	84.8%	91.3%	98.8%	107.7%	118.3%
65%	69.0%	73.6%	78.8%	84.8%	91.8%	100.0%	109.9%
60%	63.7%	67.9%	72.7%	78.3%	84.7%	92.3%	101.4%
55%	58.4%	62.3%	66.7%	71.7%	77.6%	84.6%	93.0%
50%	53.1%	56.6%	60.6%	65.2%	70.6%	76.9%	84.5%
45%	47.8%	50.9%	54.5%	58.7%	63.5%	69.2%	76.1%
40%	42.5%	45.3%	48.5%	52.2%	56.5%	61.5%	67.6%
35%	37.2%	39.6%	42.4%	45.7%	49.4%	53.8%	59.2%
30%	31.9%	34.0%	36.4%	39.1%	42.4%	46.2%	50.7%
25%	26.5%	28.3%	30.3%	32.6%	35.3%	38.5%	42.3%
20%	21.2%	22.6%	24.2%	26.1%	28.2%	30.8%	33.8%
15%	15.9%	17.0%	18.2%	19.6%	21.2%	23.1%	25.4%

Note that this grid will serve only for a €175 rack rate with a variable cost of €25.

Based on exhibit 10.4, it means that if the average occupancy of the hotel is about 60% for example, and it needs to apply a discount of 15%, then in order to maintain its level of profitability the rooms' occupancy will have to rise to 72.7%.

10.4   Pricing food and beverage products

Food service operations must establish appropriate selling prices for their menu items. In establishing the prices of Food and Beverage products, two groups of pricing methods are used. First of all are the subjective pricing methods which are mostly based on assumptions and guesses. On the contrary, the objective pricing methods ensure that the property's profit requirements, as well as the value guests attach to the entire dining experience are incorporated into the selling price. The food pricing approaches examined in this chapter are:

10.4.1   Subjective pricing methods
10.4.2   Objective pricing methods

10.4.1 Subjective pricing methods

These are methods that are simply based on the manager's assumptions or guesses about what the prices should be, and as such apply such prices. Some examples of such methods are described below:

10.4.1.1 The reasonable price method
This method uses a price that the food service manager thinks will represent a value to the guest. The manager presumes to know – from the guest's perspective – what charge is fair and equitable.

10.4.1.2 The highest price method
In this method, the manager sets the highest price that he or she thinks guests are willing to pay.

10.4.1.3 The loss leader method
In this method, an unusually low price is set for an item (or items). The manager assumes that guests will be attracted to the property to purchase the low-priced item(s) and that they will then select other items while they are there. Beverage or food prices on some items are set low to bring guests into the property, but purchases of other items are necessary for the operation to meet profit requirements. This pricing method is sometimes used as an "early bird" or senior citizen discount to attract specific segments of the market.

10.4.1.4 The intuitive price method
When prices are set by intuition alone, the manager makes little more than a wild guess about the selling price. Closely related to this approach is a trial-and-error pricing plan – if one price doesn't work, another is tested. The intuitive price method differs from the reasonable price method in that there is less effort to determine what represents value from the guests' perspective.

These subjective pricing methods may be common in the food service industry simply because they have been used in the past, because the manager setting prices has no information about product costs or profit requirements to work with, and/or because the manager is not familiar with more objective methods. In today's market, with increased consumer demands for value in dining, and with higher purchase prices for products needed by the property, these plans seldom work.

10.4.2 Objective pricing methods

Objective pricing methods based upon data in the approved operating budget help the manager transfer budget plans into selling prices. Before any objective pricing method can be used, three basic cost procedures must be in place and consistently used:

- Standard recipes must be available – Standard recipes dictate the type and amount of each ingredient required to produce a menu item. Also, they indicate the portion size to be served. A standard recipe must be available for each item when a selling price is being developed.

- Pre-costing with current costs – Each affected recipe must be pre-costed with current market cost data to determine the cost to produce one portion of each component of the menu item being priced.

- Standard recipes must be consistently used – Many operations have standard recipes available but do not consistently use them. If recipes are not used, there is no reason to have them or to cost them.

The following five objective food pricing methods are discussed below:

10.4.2.1   Using a mark-up multiplier
10.4.2.2   Contribution margin pricing method
10.4.2.3   Ratio pricing method
10.4.2.4   Simple prime costs method
10.4.2.5   Specific prime costs method

10.4.2.1   Using a mark-up multiplier
In using the mark-up multiple to determine food and beverage prices, the mark-up is the difference between the costs of the products and the selling price. There are several ways of using the mark-up in establishing food and beverage prices and these include the simple mark-up by a multiplier, the ingredients mark-up, prime ingredient mark-up, mark-up with accompaniment costs pricing methods. The rules on determining the multiplier will be explained at the end of this section.

Simple mark-up by a multiplier
The simple mark-up generally includes the related costs such as labour, utilities, supplies and the expected profit. This approach is equally called cost-plus-pricing and it involves indentifying costs that can be traced to the F & B food item that is to be priced. It is much easier to mark-up beverages than to mark-up food items. Beverages (with the exception of cocktails) generally contain at most not more than two or three ingredients. On the other hand, meals contain many ingredients and determining the cost of the meal can be very difficult. This difficulty could be for such reasons as the kitchen labour component as well as seasonal, weekly or daily price fluctuations. Three of such methods are the ingredients mark-up pricing, prime-ingredient mark-up pricing, and the mark-up with accompaniment costs.

Ingredients mark-up pricing method
The ingredients mark-up pricing method attempts to consider all product costs: food costs when pricing food items, and beverage costs when pricing beverages. The steps to pricing with this method are as follows:

Step 1	Determine the ingredients' costs
Step 2	Determine the multiplier to use in marking up the ingredients' costs
Step 3	Establish a base selling price by multiplying the ingredients' costs by the multiplier to calculate a final selling price
Step 4	Determine if the base selling price will be accepted within the market

A base selling price is not necessarily the final selling price. The simple output from formulas may not be an appropriate final selling price. Rather, a base selling price is considered a starting point from which other factors must be assessed and the price adjusted accordingly. These other factors are addressed later under important pricing considerations.

The multiplier determined in step 2 is generally based on the desired food (or beverage) cost percentage. For example, if the desired food cost percentage is 33% percent, the multiplier would be 3.03, determined as follows:

$$\text{Multiplier} = \frac{1}{\text{Desired food cost percentage}}$$

$$3.03 = \frac{1}{33\%}$$

To illustrate the ingredients mark-up approach to pricing, exhibit 10.5 below based on a mark-up multiple of 3.03 shows the ingredients and costs of a beef filet dinner.

Exhibit 10.5 **Ingredients mark-up pricing method**

Ingredient	Quantity	Cost
Beef tenderloin	200 grams	€ 4.00
Salt and black pepper	1	€ 0.10
Garlic clove	1	€ 0.05
Clarified butter	10 grams	€ 0.20
Champignons	80 grams	€ 0.40
Brandy	5 ml	€ 0.50
Lemon juice	5 ml	€ 0.10
Chicken liver pâté	80 grams	€ 0.80
Cream	20 ml	€ 0.60
Horse-radish	5 grams	€ 0.20
Total cost price		€ 6.95
Mark-up		3.03
Selling price		€ 21.06

Exhibit 10.5 shows that based on the total cost price of €6.95 the restaurant will expect to sell the dish at €21.06 which can be rounded to €21.00. If this price appears reasonable based on the market for beef filet dinners, then the item is sold for about €21.00.

Prime-ingredient mark-up method

The prime-ingredient mark-up pricing method differs from the ingredients mark-up method in that only the cost of the prime ingredient is marked-up. In addition, the multiplier used must be greater than the multiplier used when considering the total cost of all ingredients.

If the prime ingredient approach was used in exhibit 10.5, then the cost price of the beef tenderloin (€4.00) would be multiplied by a mark-up multiple different from the one that was used (3.03) based on the experience and arbitrary assumptions of the management. For example a mark-up multiple of 5 can be used. This will lead to an expected selling price of €20.00 based on the information contained in exhibit 10.5.

If the cost of the beef tenderloin in this example increases to €4.50 for the dinner portion, the new price would be €22.50 (€4.50 × 5).

The prime-ingredient approach assumes that the costs of all ingredients change in proportion to the prime ingredient. That is, when the prime ingredient's cost increases 10%, then other ingredients' costs are assumed to increase also by 10%.

Mark-up with accompaniment costs

Using the mark-up with accompaniment costs pricing method, managers determine ingredient costs based only upon entrée items and then add a standard accompaniment or "plate" cost to this amount before multiplying by a multiplier. This plate cost is an average cost for all non- entrée and other relatively inexpensive items including salads, vegetables, bread, butter, and non-alcoholic beverages. For example

Entrée Costs		€	3.50
Plate Cost	+	€	2.00
Estimated Food Cost		€	5.50
Multiplier	×		3.03
Base Selling Price		€	16.67

Note that the "plate" cost, covering the estimated food cost of all items other than the entrée cost, is added to the entrée cost before the multiplier is used.

An advantage of this method is its simplicity. Careful calculations for only the expensive entrée costs are necessary. Time can be saved by combining all other food costs into an estimated plate cost. A disadvantage may be that plate costs are not truly representative of food costs associated with these other items. Managers must also establish a reasonable and objective multiplier that relates to profit requirements. If this is not done, the mark-up with accompaniment costs pricing method is no better than the subjective pricing methods.

Determining the mark-up multiplier

The mark-up pricing methods just discussed are simple to use and, for that reason, are commonly used in the food service industry. They however have a significant disadvantage which involves determining the multiplier. For many managers, it is a subjective decision based primarily upon experience and "rule of thumb". To help in this regard, the following formulas can be used:

Ingredients mark-up pricing method

$$\text{Multiplier} = \frac{1}{\text{Desired food cost percentage}}$$

Prime ingredient mark-up method

$$\text{Multiplier} = \frac{\text{Total food revenue}}{\text{Total entrée cost}}$$

Mark-up with accompaniment method

$$\text{Multiplier} = \frac{1}{\text{Desired Food Cost Percentage}}$$

The little time required to generate and use this multiplier based on the operating budget makes it especially cost effective for many small-volume operations. Using the multiplier has some disadvantages such as omitting the impact of the sales mix, and not reflecting the higher or lower labour, energy, or other costs associated with the production of specific menu items. Rather, they either assume that all operating costs relate in some direct way to food costs or that these cost differences can be ignored. The mark-up pricing methods using a multiplier also assume that all food costs associated with producing a menu item are known. In fact, many other costs may be excluded from the cost of ingredients used as the base for the multiplier.

10.4.2.2 Contribution margin pricing method

The term contribution margin refers to the amount left after a menu item's food cost is subtracted from its selling price. The contribution margin is the amount that the sale of a menu item "contributes" to pay for all non-food costs allocated to the food service operation and to help with profit requirements. With a contribution margin pricing method, managers can set base selling prices for menu items by following two steps:

Step 1 Determine the average contribution margin required per guest by dividing all non-food costs plus required profit by the number of expected guests

Step 2 Determine the base selling price for a menu item by adding the average contribution margin required per guest to the item's standard food cost

Assume that the approved operating budget for the year provides the manager with the following data: all non-food costs are €225,000.00, the required profit is set at €35,000.00 and 25,000 guests are expected to be served. The manager can calculate the base selling price for a menu item with a standard food cost of €7.50 as follows:

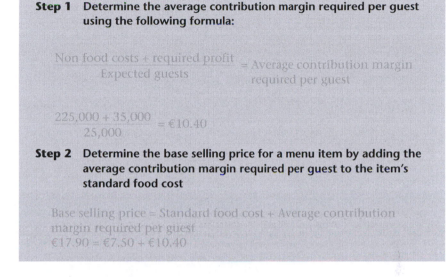

Step 1 Determine the average contribution margin required per guest using the following formula:

$$\frac{\text{Non food costs} + \text{required profit}}{\text{Expected guests}} = \text{Average contribution margin required per guest}$$

$$\frac{225,000 + 35,000}{25,000} = €10.40$$

Step 2 Determine the base selling price for a menu item by adding the average contribution margin required per guest to the item's standard food cost

Base selling price = Standard food cost + Average contribution margin required per guest

€17.90 = €7.50 + €10.40

Advantages of this method are its ease and practicality when reasonably accurate information is available from the operating budget. It is also useful in those operations where costs associated with serving each guest are basically the same, with the exception of varying food costs. Also, this method tends to reduce the range of selling prices on the menu, since the only difference is reflected in the actual food cost incorporated into the selling price. A potential disadvantage of this method is that it assumes that each guest should pay the same share of the property's non-food costs and profit requirements.

10.4.2.3 Ratio pricing method

The ratio pricing method determines the relationship between food costs and all non-food costs plus profit requirements and uses this ratio to develop base selling prices for menu items. The method is made up of the following three steps:

Step 1 Determine the ratio of food costs to all non-food costs plus required profit by dividing all non-food costs plus profit by food costs

Step 2 Calculate the amount of non-food costs plus profit required for a menu item by multiplying the standard food cost of the menu item by the ratio calculated in step 1

Step 3 Determine the base selling price of a menu item by adding the result of step 2 to the standard food cost of the menu item

Assume that the approved operating budget of a restaurant (with no alcoholic beverage sales) provides the following information: food costs are €117,000.00, all non-food costs (labour and other costs) are €225,000.00, and the required profit is €35,000.00. Using the ratio pricing method, the manager establishes a base selling price for a menu item with a standard food cost of €7.50 as follows:

Step 1 Determine the ratio of food costs to all non-food costs plus required profit by dividing all non-food costs plus profit by food costs

$$\frac{\text{All non-food costs} + \text{Required profit}}{\text{Food Cost}} = \text{Ratio}$$

$$\frac{€225,000.00 + €35,000.00}{€117,000.00} = 2.22$$

This ratio means that for each €1 of revenue required to cover food costs, €2.22 of additional revenue is needed to pay for non-food costs and meet profit requirements

Step 2 Calculate the amount of non-food costs plus profit required for a menu item by multiplying the standard food cost of the menu item by the ratio calculated in step 1

$$\text{Standard food cost} \times \text{Ratio} = \text{Amount of non-food costs and profit}$$
required for menu item
$$€7.50 \times 2.22 = €16.67$$

This is accomplished by multiplying the standard food cost of the menu item by the ratio calculated in step 1. Therefore, if the standard food cost of the menu item is €7.50, the amount of non-food costs and profit required is €16.67 (€7.50 × 2.22).

Step 3 Determine the base selling price of a menu item by adding the result of step 2 to the standard food cost of the menu item

This is done by adding the result of step 2 to the standard food cost of the menu item. The base selling price for the item with a €7.50 food cost would be €24.17 (€7.50 + €16.67)

The ratio method of menu pricing is simple to use and can be based on operating budget requirements. However, it does have several disadvantages. In an operation offering both food and beverages, it is necessary to separate non-food costs and profit requirements between the two revenue centres. Also, under this pricing method, each meal assumes an equal share of non-food costs and profit. The ratio pricing method does not compensate for higher labour costs associated with the preparation of labour-intensive menu items.

10.4.2.4   **Simple prime costs method**
The prime costs refer to the most significant costs in a food service operation: product (food and beverage) and labour. A simple prime costs pricing method involves assessing the labour costs for the food service operation and factoring these costs into the pricing equation.

The steps of the simple prime costs pricing are as follows:

Step 1 Determine the labour cost per guest by dividing labour costs by the number of expected guests
Step 2 Determine the prime costs per guest by adding the labour cost per guest to the menu item's food cost
Step 3 Determine the menu item's base selling price by dividing the prime costs per guest by the desired prime costs percentage

Exhibit 10.6 shows how the steps of the simple prime costs pricing method are used to determine the base selling price.

■ Exhibit 10.6 **Application of the simple prime costs pricing method**

Assume that the food service manager has obtained the following data:

Menu item food cost	€ 7.50
Labour costs	€ 155,000.00
Number of expected guests	25,000
Desired prime costs percentage	66%

The food cost for the menu item is the standard cost derived by costing the item's standard recipe. Labour costs and estimated guests are obtained from the approved operating budget. The desired prime costs percentage combines projected food and labour cost percentages.

Step 1 Determine the labour cost per guest by dividing labour costs by the number of expected guests

$$\text{Labour cost per guest} = \frac{\text{Labour costs}}{\text{Number of expected guests}}$$

$$€6.20 = \frac{€155,000.00}{25,000.00}$$

Step 2 Determine the prime costs per guest by adding the labour cost per guest to the menu item's food cost

Prime costs per guest = €13.70

Step 3 Determine the menu item's base selling price by dividing the prime costs per guest by the desired prime cost percentage

$$\text{Base selling price} = \frac{\text{Prime costs per guest}}{\text{Desired prime cost percentage}}$$

$$€20.76 = \frac{€13.70}{66\%}$$

Exhibit 10.6 shows that the food service manager would then adjust the base selling price in relation to other factors, such as the operation's target markets and the competition. Advantages of this method are its focus on both food and labour costs and the fact that it is easy to use. An obvious disadvantage is the need to assign an equal labour cost to each menu item, even though the actual labour costs for menu items may vary greatly. This problem is reduced in the specific prime costs pricing method.

10.4.2.5   Specific prime costs method

With the specific prime costs pricing method the food service manager develops multipliers for menu items so that the base selling prices for the items cover their food costs and their fair share of labour costs. Items with extensive preparation have higher labour costs and should have higher mark-ups. Conversely, items not requiring extensive preparation have lower labour costs that can be reflected in a lower mark-up.

The manager first divides all menu items into two categories: those that do and those that do not involve extensive preparation labour. The definition of extensive preparation labour is left to the manager to determine. For example, perhaps stew made from scratch is considered labour-intensive to prepare, while a steak that only has to be broiled is considered non-labour-intensive. Typically, all items are assumed to require approximately the same amount of labour for service and cleanup; these labour costs are shared by both categories of menu items.

Next, the manager allocates appropriate percentages of total food costs and labour costs to each category of menu items. Let's assume that the manager's analysis of menu items sold during a recent period showed that:

60 percent of the total food costs are expended for items requiring extensive preparation (Category A items).
40 percent of total food costs are expended for items requiring little preparation (Category B items).
55 percent of all labour costs are incurred for preparation of all menu items (both Category A and Category B items).
45 percent of all labour costs are incurred for service, cleanup, and other non-preparation activities.

Given this information, Exhibit 10.7 demonstrates the calculations to be made using the specific prime costs pricing method.

Note that line items from the approved operating budget are listed in column (1) – Budget items. These line items include: food cost, labour cost, all other costs, and profit. Operating budget percentages for each line item are noted in column (2). These figures represent percentages of forecasted revenue. For example, the operating budget specifies a 35 percent food cost – 35 percent of expected revenue will go toward paying food costs. These percentages are re-allocated in column (3) for menu items that involve extensive preparation labour (Category A)

Exhibit 10.7 **Calculations for specific prime costs pricing**

Calculations for specific prime costs pricing

Budget item	Operating budget percentage	Category A (Extensive preparation) items	Category B (Non-extensive preparation) items
(1)	(2)	(3)	(4)
Food cost	35%	60% of 35% = 21%	40% of 35% = 14%
Labour cost	30%	55% of 30% = 17%	
		60% of 13% = 8%	40% of 13% = 5%
All other costs	20%	60% of 20% = 12%	40% of 20% = 8%
Profit	15%	60% of 15% = 9%	40% of 15% = 6%
Total	100%	67%	33%
Multiplier	100% ÷ 35% = 2.9	67% ÷ 21% = 3.2	33% ÷ 14% = 2.4

and in column 4 for items that do not involve extensive preparation labour (Category B).

Recall that the manager's previous analysis of menu items sold during a recent period showed that the food costs required to produce Category A items (involving extensive preparation) equalled 60 percent of the food costs incurred for the period. An adjusted food cost percentage for labour-intensive menu items of 21 percent can be calculated by multiplying the 35 percent total food cost by 60 percent ($.35 \times .6 = .21 \times 100 = 21$ percent). Similarly, an adjusted food cost percentage for non-labour-intensive menu items of 14 percent is calculated by multiplying the 35 percent total food cost by 40 percent ($.35 \times .4 = .14 \times 100 = 14$ percent).

The manager now needs to allocate the total labour cost percentage (30 percent as shown in column 2) between preparation and non-preparation labour items. In this particular case, the manager decides to allocate all of the preparation labour to Category A menu items because little or no labour expense is incurred for Category B menu items. Recall that the manager's previous analysis showed that 55 percent of all labour cost is incurred for the preparation of menu items. Since all of this labour cost will be allocated to Category A menu items, the manager multiplies 30 percent (the percentage of revenue representing total labour costs) by 55 percent (the percentage of total labour costs for preparing menu items) and the result, rounded to 17 percent ($.30 \times .55$) of the total labour cost is charged to menu items involving extensive preparation.

The remaining 13 percent of the total labour costs (30 percent labour costs from the operating budget minus 17 percent labour costs for preparation of menu items) is allocated between both Category A and Category B menu items, since this is the cost of labour incurred for service, cleanup, and other activities that should be shared equally. However, sharing equally does not necessarily mean a 50/50 split. Because food costs have been allocated on the 60/40 basis, this approach is also used to allocate non-preparation labour. Therefore, 8 percent of labour costs are charged to Category A menu items {.60 × .13 = .08 (rounded) × 100 = 8 percent}. This labour cost is identified in column 3. The remaining 5 percent of non-preparation labour cost (13 percent – 8 percent = 5 percent) is allocated to Category B menu items. This labour cost is identified in column 4.

All other costs (20 percent of forecasted revenue as shown in column 2) and profit (15 percent of forecasted revenue as noted in column 2) are also allocated on the 60/40 basis between Category A and Category B menu items.

At this point in the process, the manager can determine several multipliers. Multipliers are set by adding the individual cost percentages (food cost, labour cost, all other costs, and profit) and dividing by the desired food cost percentage.

For example, a multiplier based on the 35 percent desired food cost from the current operating budget (column 2) is 2.9. This is calculated by dividing 100 percent (the total cost and profit percentage shown at the bottom of column 2) by the budgeted food cost percentage of 35 percent {1 divided by .35 equals 2.9 (rounded)}.

The multiplier for menu items requiring extensive preparation (column 3) is calculated by dividing 67 percent (the total cost and profit percentage shown at the bottom of column 3) by the desired food cost percentage of 21 percent for this category of menu items {.67 divided by .21 equals 3.2 (rounded)}.

The multiplier for menu items requiring little preparation (column 4) is calculated by dividing 33 percent (the total cost and profit percentage shown at the bottom of column 4) by the desired food cost percentage of 14 percent for this category of menu items {.33 divided by .14 equals 2.4 (rounded)}.

Note that the multiplier for items involving extensive preparation (3.2) is higher than that for items in the non-extensive preparation category (2.4). Assume that the food cost of a menu item involving extensive preparation is €7.50. The food service manager determines a base selling price for that item by multiplying €7.50 by 3.2. This yields a base selling price for the menu item of €24.00. Note that the resulting base selling price (€24.00) is higher than if the item's food cost was marked up by only 2.4 (the mark-up for menu items that require little preparation), which would yield an €18.00 base selling price. This lower price reflects the fact that there is much less labour required to produce the menu item.

While the specific prime costs pricing method establishes base selling prices for the items to cover their fair share of labour costs, there are several disadvantages to this pricing method. Significant time may be spent in classifying menu items into extensive-preparation and non-extensive-preparation categories. Time will also be spent performing the necessary calculations. Also, this pricing method forces managers to assume that the relationships among all other operating costs vary in the same proportion as food costs. While this is often a reasonable assumption, there may be costs, such as higher energy costs, associated with preparing some items that reduce the accuracy of this method.

Important pricing considerations

This section has suggested that the result of menu pricing calculations is a base selling price. This is because the simple output of formulas used in the examples may not be an appropriate final selling price for a menu item. Rather, it is a starting point from which other factors must be assessed.

The concept of value (price relative to quality) is always important. Guests pay for more than just the product (food and beverage) when they visit the operation. Quality of service, cleanliness of the facility, and atmosphere are also part of the dining experience and should, even if subjectively, be factored into the selling price decision.

The basic law of supply and demand is another factor to be considered. Ultimately, the price that can be charged is established by the guests themselves as they decide whether to return to the property.

Volume concerns must also be considered. As fewer guests are served, overhead charges per guest increase; selling prices must be higher. The reverse is also true: more guests may allow the manager to reduce overhead costs in the pricing decision.

The price charged by the competition for a similar product is another concern. The more an operation can differentiate its products from those of the competition, the more freedom the operation has in setting a selling price.

For example, perhaps two properties offer a similar steak dinner. While the price charged for the steak is important, there are other factors that may influence people to visit one property or the other. Perhaps one property provides entertainment, while the other offers an attractive atmosphere. Emphasizing the differences between the property's own products and services and those offered by other businesses is one way to remain competitive.

One technique that can be used to attract guests from competitors is lowering menu prices. This may succeed in bringing more people into an operation, but only if the lower priced items are considered by guests as substitutes for what the competition offers. If there are no significant differences between what one operation offers and what the competition offers, then guests may see price as the main factor in selecting one property over the others. However, if there are non-price-related differences that are important to guests (such as atmosphere, entertainment, etc.) this technique may not work.

Raising prices is also a way of responding to pressures from the competition. With higher prices, fewer menu items will need to be sold for the operation to meet profit requirements. However, raising a menu item's selling price may be effective only if the increased revenue from the price increase makes up for the revenue lost as demand falls off and current guests begin to buy other menu items as substitutes. In fact, in some cases, a more effective strategy for increasing total revenue may be lowering a menu item's selling price. Lowering prices may increase the volume of unit sales, and this increase may produce an increase in total revenue.

10.5 Menu engineering

One other method of menu analysis and food pricing is called menu engineering. This concept of menu engineering was first established in a book by Kasavana, M. L. and Smith, D. I. called *Menu Engineering – A Practical Guide to Menu Analysis*, 4th revised edition (Okemos, Michigan: Hospitality Publications Inc., 2002). For this purpose a worksheet as illustrated in exhibits 10.8 and 10.9 has to be established for each meal period (breakfast, lunch, dinner), as well as for each menu category (starters, entrées, desserts) within each meal period. The emphasis is on the contribution margin of each menu item combined with its popularity and as such food cost percentages are ignored.

The contribution margin is considered as high or low when compared to the average contribution margin for all items sold. For example, if the average contribution is €12.00 for all items, an item with a contribution margin of €10.50 is considered to be low, whereas an item with a contribution margin of €15.00 is considered to be high. In the same line, each menu item is further classified by its popularity. This is defined as either high or low by comparing the sales revenue mix percentage to the average sales mix percentage. The formula is:

$$\frac{\text{Quantity sold of each menu item}}{\text{Total quantity sold of all menu items}}$$

Average popularity would be 100% divided by the number of menu items. So in a situation of 10 menu items, the average popularity of each item would be expected to be 10% of all items sold. However, Kasavana and Smith state that in real life it will be unreasonable to expect that every menu item will achieve the minimum level of sales and therefore suggested that the minimum popularity of each menu item should be only 70% of the average popularity number. In this case the formula is transformed as such.

$$70\% \times \frac{\text{Quantity sold of each menu item}}{\text{Total quantity sold of all menu items}}$$

So according to Kasavana and Smith, in a situation where there are 10 menu items, if the item sells more than 7% of the total items sold, it would be considered to have a high popularity and vice versa.

The popularity and profitability for each menu item can be classified under four categories: Stars, puzzles, plough horses and dogs.

The last column in the menu engineering worksheet as shown in exhibit 10.8 indicates profit factors. The average profit factor for all items is always equal to one. Since the average is always equal to one, it means that if some menu items have factors higher than one, these will be equally counterbalanced by other menu items that will have profit factors lower than one. A balanced menu will be one in which the profit factors of all the items are very close to one. Because of this it is not necessarily a nice thing to assume that an item with a very high profit factor is a good situation.

Exhibit 10.8 **Menu engineering worksheet**

Menu engineering worksheet

Restaurant name:

Date:
Meal period:

A	B	C	D	E	F	G	H	L	P	R	S	T
Menu item name	Number sold	Menu mix %	Food cost	Selling price	CM (E-D)	Menu costs (D × B)	Menu revenues (E × B)	Menu CM (F × B)	CM category	Menu mix % category	Menu item classifi-cation	Profit factor
	N					$I = \Sigma G$	$J = \Sigma H$	$M = \Sigma L$		Average CM = M ÷ Menu items		

Totals

Additional computations: $K = I \div J$ $O = M \div MN$ $Q = (100 \div items) (70\%)$

Exhibit 10.9 is an illustration of the dinner menu items worksheet of the Beach and Sand Restaurant.

The information contained in exhibit 10.9 can be plotted in a graph as shown in exhibit 10.10. The basic information needed will be the number of menu items sold (plotted on the y-axis), and the contribution margin per menu item (plotted on the x-axis). Plotting this basic data on the graph clearly shows the demarcation lines between the menu item classifications (plough horses, dogs, stars, and puzzles).

Stars are considered to be the most profitable items on the menu. For these menu items, rigid specifications for quality, portion size and presentation should be maintained. These items should be in a highly visible position on the menu because of their relative popularity. Their prices can easily be raised without affecting their popularity and as such increasing profit. Their prices should never be reduced because the quantity sold will likely not be affected but total contribution margin will be reduced. If the demand for stars is more elastic, a price

Exhibit 10.9 **Completed menu engineering worksheet**

Menu engineering worksheet

Restaurant name:

Date:
Meal period:

A	B	C	D	E	F	G	H	L	P	R	S	T
Menu item name	Number sold	Menu mix %	Food cost	Selling price	CM (E-D)	Menu costs (D × B)	Menu revenues (E × B)	Menu CM (F × B)	CM category	Menu mix % category	Menu item classification	Profit factor
Steak 200gr	350	16.92%	6.95	23.144	16.2	2433	8100.23	5667.73	Low	High	Plough horse	1.55
Steak 400gr	152	7.35%	8.8	29.304	20.5	1338	4454.21	3116.61	High	High	Star	0.85
Steak 600gr	120	5.80%	10.6	35.298	24.7	1272	4235.76	2963.76	High	Low	Puzzle	0.81
Salmon	308	14.89%	7.2	23.976	16.8	2218	7384.61	5167.01	Low	High	Plough horse	1.41
Lamb	270	13.06%	10.4	21.6	11.2	2808	5832.00	3024.00	Low	High	Plough horse	0.82
Chicken	112	5.42%	6.9	22.977	16.1	772.8	2573.42	1800.62	Low	Low	Dog	0.49
Game	212	10.25%	8.7	28.971	20.3	1844	6141.85	4297.45	High	High	Star	1.17
Pork	184	8.90%	8.1	26.973	18.9	1490	4963.03	3472.63	High	High	Star	0.95
Ribs	140	6.77%	7.5	24.975	17.5	1050	3496.50	2446.50	Low	Low	Dog	0.67
Sole	220	10.64%	9.2	30.636	21.4	2024	6739.92	4715.92	High	High	Star	1.29

	N					I = ΣG	J = ΣH	M = ΣL	Average CM = M ÷ Menu items			
Totals	2068					17249	53921.529	36672.23	3667.2229			

Additional Computations:

						K = I ÷ J	O = M ÷ N	Q = (100 ÷ items) (70%)
						31.99%	17.73319	7.00%

Exhibit 10.10 **Graphical representation of the menu engineering results contained in exhibit 10.9**

reduction might increase the sales revenue derived from these items with a similar effect on profits.

Plough horses (in some cases also called cash cows) are those items that are popular, even though they do not yield a high contribution margin. They are normally items popular with price-sensitive guests. These items should be kept on the menu, but the management should try to increase their contribution margin without affecting demand. One of the ways to do this is to raise the prices of the items. A second way is to try to decrease the cost of ingredients by reviewing the recipes and agreements with the suppliers. If their contribution margins cannot be increased, they should be reduced to a lower position on the menu. Note that it will not be a nice idea to lower their prices since their contribution margins are already low.

Puzzles are those items that are low in popularity but yield a higher than average contribution margin. Management should generally consider taking them off the menu. However, caution should be exercised before such a decision is taken. The elements that might affect their popularity such as price and quality could be examined to determine if they remain on the menu or not. They could be renamed, better packaged or better positioned on the menu. Their prices could equally be reduced especially if it has a relatively high contribution margin and an elastic demand. Caution should be exercised with price reductions in order not to take business away from the stars which will reduce the contribution margin.

Dogs are the losers in the business because they are both unpopular and have low contribution margins. These items may have to be eliminated or their price increased to see whether they can at least reach the status of puzzles. Dogs are the least desirable items of the menu. If their situation cannot be improved, they should be replaced with new items. Sometimes, it might be necessary not to remove it because it might be what some regular guests consume. In order not to dissatisfy these guests, an increase in price can be considered in the hope that it will move into the puzzle category.

Explanation of the menu engineering worksheet

Column A Menu item name: This contains the list of all the items in the menu categories.

Column B Number sold (the menu mix MM): this contains the records of the quantity of each menu item sold for the period. The total is recorded at the bottom of the column in Box N.

Column C Details the percentages of the menu mix. It is a vertical analysis of the items in column B as a percentage of the total found in box N.

Column D Food cost: This shows the food cost of each menu item.

Column E Selling price: This shows the selling price of each menu item.

Column F Contribution margin (CM): This indicates the CM of each menu item. It is calculated by deducting the food costs from the selling price. In other words it is column E minus D.

Column G Menu costs: This lists the total cost for each menu item. It is calculated by multiplying the number sold by the sold (B) by its food cost (D).

Column H Menu revenues: This lists the total sales for each menu item. It is calculated by multiplying the numbers sold (B) by the selling price (E).

Box I Is the sum of column G and it represents the total cost of all the menu items sold.

Box J Is the sum of column H and it represents the total revenue generated from the sale of the menu items

Box K Represents the overall food cost percentage. It is calculated by dividing I by J, and it is a percentage.

Column L Menu contribution margin: indicates the total CM for each menu item. It is calculated by multiplying column B by column F.

Box M Is the sum of column L.

Box N Is the sum of column B.

Box O Represents the average contribution margin for all the items. It is calculated by dividing M by N. It is used to compare the CM of each item to see if it is higher or lower than the average.

Column P Contribution margin category: Is used to fill in the High or Low score for each menu item after its contribution margin is compared with the result in Box O.

Box Q This indicates the average popularity of all the menu items. Based on the main observation by Kasavana and Smith as noted earlier in this section, this is then reduced to 70% of the popularity. It is calculated as such: (100 divided by the items) × (70%).

Column R Menu mix percentage category: This indicates either a high or a low based on the comparison between each item's menu mix percentage (C) with the result in box Q.

Column S Menu item classification: Lists the menu items into one of the four categories (stars, plough horses, puzzles and dogs).

Column T Profit factor: This shows the comparison between each item's total contribution margin to the average contribution margin for each item. It is calculated in two steps:

Step 1 Divide the menu's total contribution margin by the number of items on the menu. That is Box M divided by the number of menu items

Step 2 Divide each item's total contribution margin by the average contribution margin.

10.6 Revenue management

Revenue management (at times also referred to as yield management) is generally referred to as the process of selling the right product to the right guests at the right time for the right price. Revenue management is based on the two notions of price discrimination and market segmentation. Price discrimination helps to achieve sales increases in two ways. Higher prices charged to relatively price inelastic segments of the market can lead to higher revenues. At the same time, charging discounted prices to price elastic segments of the market can lead to higher sales volumes which might offset the revenue effect of the reduced prices. Common to many industries, revenue management is considered more of an art than a science, in which businesses are motivated to maximize the profitability of each unit sold under existing demand and market conditions. Some common examples of revenue management practices are clearance sales, seasonal pricing, preferred customer pricing, volume discounts, and "early bird" specials. The advantages of revenue management become clearer but at the same time more complicated when dealing with perishable goods and services such as hotel rooms. An unsold hotel room is revenue lost forever. The major challenge to hospitality companies is to sell as many perishable rooms as possible while at the same time maximizing the ADR.

Nowadays, revenue management is considered by most hospitality operations as both a business philosophy and a process oriented approach crucial to their ability to increase revenues and maximize profits. Most major hotel chains have adopted revenue management practices. They use sophisticated revenue management systems such as RevparGuru that are integrated with their distribution channels. Examples of such channels are GDS (Amadeus and Sabre) and internet-based distribution systems ranging from 3rd party websites such as Expedia, Orbitz or Travelocity to opaque or auction sites such as Hotwire and Priceline. Hotel operations need to review total customer worth of guest bookings through these channels since these services are costly and have an incidence on the contribution margins. Some of these operations have revenue managers at the property level, regional revenue managers, and even revenue management departments at their corporate head quarters. The hotels generally receive benchmarking data from a wide variety of sources that most of the times are integrated into their reservation systems, for example Market Vision and Travel Click. The existence of sophisticated revenue management systems coupled with the expansion of internet technology cannot however eliminate the great importance of human judgement in the revenue management decision making process. Effective revenue management should be based on a strategic approach that will help good decision making based on the best available information.

Demand forecasting will allow a revenue manager to anticipate business and as such appropriately establish the rates before reservations are made. It is essential in this process for the managers to understand as well the demand composition of the guests' base. This is called market segmentation. Some examples of market segments within the hospitality industry are: individual business week, individual business weekend, business group, leisure individual weekend, leisure group, and government. Each particular market segment will have its own demand pattern as well as price ranges. Revenue managers can then make their decisions based on their comprehensive understanding of each particular segment as well as the time period concerned.

Hotel management's main objective is to maximize sales revenue, also referred to as yield, from the available rooms. Two of the main statistics used to assess rooms' sales (the occupancy percentage and the ADR) unfortunately have certain limitations. The occupancy percentage does not indicate if revenues are maximized. The ADR can be raised at the expense of sending away potential guests unwilling to pay the increased rates. To mitigate these limitations, the yield statistic which relates the actual sales to the potential sales is a better measure of a room's department manager's performance. The yield statistic thus presents a more meaningful and consistent measure of a hotel's performance. The yield formula is:

$$\text{Yield} = \frac{\text{(Actual sales)}}{\text{(Potential sales)}} \times 100$$

A potential sale is defined as the room sales that will be generated if 100% occupancy is achieved and each room is sold at its rack rate. For example, if a hotel has 200 rooms and a rack rate of €175, then the potential sales would be 200 × €175 = €35,000 per day. If on a particular day, rooms' revenue was €28,200 then the yield would be:

$$\text{Yield} = \frac{\text{(€28,200)}}{\text{(€35,000)}} \times 100 = 80.57\%$$

Note that the yield can also be calculated by multiplying the actual occupancy percentage by the average rate ratio. The formula is

$$\text{Average rate ratio} = \frac{\text{Actual average rate}}{\text{Average maximum potential rate}}$$

For indicative purposes only, listed below are some commonly used yield formulas:

$$\text{Potential average single rate} = \frac{\text{Single room revenues at rack rate}}{\text{Number of rooms sold as singles}}$$

$$\text{Potential average double rate} = \frac{\text{Double revenues at rack rate}}{\text{Number of rooms sold as doubles}}$$

$$\text{Multiple occupancy percentage} = \frac{\text{Rooms occupied by two or more persons}}{\text{Rooms occupied by guests}}$$

Rate spread: Potential average double rate – potential average single rate

Potential average rate: (Multiple occupancy percentage × rate spread) + potential average single rate

$$\text{Room rate achievement factor} = \frac{\text{Actual average rate}}{\text{Potential average rate}}$$

Yield statistic: occupancy percentage × room rate achievement factor

$$\text{Identical yield percentage} = \text{Current occupancy percentage} \times \frac{\text{Current rate}}{\text{Proposed rate}}$$

Glossary

Bottom up approach (Hubbart formula) – is an approach that involves determining the average room rate which must be charged in order to generate the annual revenue that will be sufficient to cover all costs and taxes as well as to meet the owners' expected profit levels.

Contribution margin pricing – is a pricing approach in which menu items are priced taking into consideration an analysis of the contribution margin of the item. The contribution margin is the difference between the food costs and its selling price. This pricing method helps in determining the specific contribution of each menu item towards covering for all the non-food costs in the operation as well as in generating profits.

Differential room pricing – is an approach that takes into consideration the different room types on the hospitality operations before the room type rates are established.

Equivalent occupancy – is that level of occupancy that is required to maintain a constant level in the total revenues less the variable costs if the rack rate is discounted.

Mark-up – is the amount that is added to the cost of goods sold in order to produce the desired profit. It is established with the purpose of covering all the costs that have to be incurred in the production of the good or service.

Menu engineering – is a method of menu analysis and food pricing in which prices are regularly reviewed based on their popularity and profitability.

Price elasticity of demand – is an expression of the degree to which customers respond to price changes. Price elasticity of demand is measured as the ratio of percentage changes between the quantity demanded and changes in its price. Price elasticity of demand values determine the sensitivity or not of the customers, and this sensitivity ranges from perfect inelasticity in which whatever the change in price, demand will not be affected; to perfect elasticity in which the slightest change in price will lead to an infinite change in the quantity demanded.

Prime costs – are the most significant costs in a food service operation and primarily consist of the direct material costs (of the food and beverage products) plus the associated labour costs in producing the menu item.

Ratio pricing – is an approach in which using standard food costs, a base selling price for menu items is established taking into account the ratio of the relationship between food costs and all non-food costs plus profit requirements.

Relative room size approach – is an approach that permits the establishment of room rates based on taking into account the effect the relative sizes of the various rooms within the hospitality operation.

Revenue management – is that management process in which capacity and sources of revenues are carefully and skilfully managed, controlled and directed while taking into account the constraints of demand and supply. It is generally referred to as the process of selling the right product to the right guests at the right time for the right price and in some circles commonly referred to as yield management.

Room rate discounting – in order to mitigate the negative effects of some of the peculiarities of the room as a product, room rate discounting is practiced and it simple means reducing the room prices to levels below the rack rate. This practice however prevents the hotel from achieving its maximum potential average room rate as well as the maximum potential total sales revenue, but is considered necessary in order to maintain occupancy levels.

Rule of a thousand approach – is a basic approach in which the price of a hotel room is set at one-thousandth ($^{1}/_{1000}$) of the value of the investment costs that were incurred towards the development of the room.

Rule of thumb – is a simple but at times useful principle or method which is based on more on the experiences of the decision makers rather than on precisely accurate measures

Multiple choice questions

10.1 When demand is inelastic, how will a price increase affect total revenues?
 a total revenues will decrease
 b total revenues will increase
 c total revenues will increase, and then decrease
 d total revenues will decrease, and then increase

10.2 Which of the following is a formal approach to pricing?
 a price cutting approach
 b high price approach
 c rule of a thousand approach
 d competitive approach

10.3 Informal approaches to pricing do not take into account:
 a the associated costs.
 b location and atmosphere.
 c prices set by the competition.
 d the intuition of the managers.

10.4 The prime ingredient cost of an organic grilled chicken dinner is €5.35. The desired food cost percentage for organic grilled chicken is 24%. The mark-up multiplier is 4.25. Using the prime-ingredient mark-up method, the price of the organic grilled chicken will be:
 a €22.29
 b €23.72
 c €22.74
 d €17.71

10.5 Menu engineering classifies a menu item that is low in contribution margin and high in menu mix category as a:
 a puzzle
 b plough horse
 c star
 d dog

Exercises

10.1 Last year, the King's Cottage's ADR was €75 and its occupancy percentage was 72%. The management hopes to achieve an ADR this year of €80 based on an expected occupancy level of 70%. Determine the price elasticity of demand of the King's Cottage's rooms.

10.2 The Way Ahead is a 40-room roadside motel and it expects its occupancy in 2011 to be 75%. The capital invested in the motel is €1,280,000 and the owners expect an after-tax net profit of 14%. The tax rate is 30%. From vending machines and parking charges, they expect to make about €65,000 in 2011. The direct expenses of running the rooms are expected to be €400,000, while the overhead expenses for 2011 are expected to be as follows:
 · Administration and general expenses €225,000
 · Sales and marketing expenses €68,000

- POM €72,000
- Interest €75,000
- Depreciation €150,000
- Insurance €64,000
- Other expenses €155,000

Based on this information,

a what should be the ADR of the Way Ahead in 2011?

b what should be the single and double room rates if the motel operates at 24% double occupancy and has a difference of €15 between its single and double rates? Assume one common room size all with the same rates.

10.3 Peter & Petra's Place is a proposed 45-room motel with a fully equipped restaurant that will cost them €1,750,000 to build. The projected occupancy rate is 75% for the year. Peter and Petra desire a 14% after-tax net profit. The tax rate is 30%. The estimated overhead expenses, not including income taxes, are €650,000. The estimated direct expenses of the rooms department are €8.50 for each room sold and they expect a double occupancy rate of 45%.

Based on this information,

a determine the ADR using the Hubbart formula and assume the restaurant produced nothing

b determine the single and double rates if there is a €16 price difference between the single and double rooms

c determine to what extent the ADR can be lowered and still meet Peter and Petra's financial expectations if the restaurant makes a departmental profit of €45,000 each year

10.4 The Sunset Delight is a new 75-seat, lunch and dinner only, restaurant that will operate 5 days a week. The owners invested €375,000 in all the equipment and held €25,000 as initial working capital. The tax rate is 30%. Their estimates for the first year of operation are as follows:

- Depreciation on equipment   15%
- Fixed salary elements   €95,200
- Insurance   €2,400
- Menu selling prices   170% over cost of food sold
- Other variable costs   5.5% of total revenue
- Rent   €30,000
- Expected after-tax net profit   14%
- Variable salary elements   26% of total revenue
- Lunch revenue   35% of total revenue
- Lunch seat turnover   1.8
- Dinner revenue   65% of total revenue
- Dinner seat turnover   1.5

Calculate the average food service cheque per meal period that will cover all costs taking into account the expected after-tax net profit.

Cost-volume-profit analysis

11.1   Definition, assumptions and limitations
11.2   Contribution margin
11.3   Breakeven analysis

Cost-volume-profit analysis (CVP), a short run and marginal analysis is a set of analytical tools that are used to determine the levels of sales needed to be carried out at any desired level of profit. The analytical tools could be in either a graphic or equation form.

When management is trying to decide on a new business activity (for example starting a new catering outlet), certain questions may arise such as:

- 'How many units will have to be sold in order to break even?'
- 'How much will we need to sell in order to achieve our target profit level?'
- 'What is the amount of additional sales needed to cover the cost of the new activity while providing the needed level of profit?'

On the other hand, when decisions have to be made related to current activities, the following types of question may arise:

- 'What will happen to profit if sales are increased by 15%?'
- 'How much more would we have to sell in order to maintain our current level of profit if we increase our marketing costs by 10%?'
- 'What increases in sales will be required to cover the cost of a 5% increase in salaries while providing the needed level of profit?'

To help in understanding cost-volume-profit analysis and to be able to answer questions like these, this chapter is organized in the following way. Section 11.1 sets the foundation of this understanding by defining CVP analysis as well as explaining the underlying assumptions and limitations. In section 11.2 the concept of the contribution margin is further developed, and section 11.3 shows in detail the various calculations related to breakeven analysis.

11.1   Definition, assumptions, and limitations

In order to be able to answer such and similar questions, CVP analysis helps management to make the informed and rational decisions.

CVP analysis is based on several assumptions, the most common of which are that:

- Mixed costs can be divided into their variable and fixed elements with a reasonable level of accuracy.
- Identified fixed costs will remain unchanged during the period under consideration.
- Variable costs will increase or decrease in a linear relationship with sales revenue during the period under consideration.
- All costs can be attributed to the individual operated departments with the analysis limited to specific situations, operating divisions, or departments.
- The mix of sales remains constant during the period under consideration.
- Revenues have a linear relationship to the volume of sales.
- All units produced during the period under consideration are sold.
- The economic conditions will be relatively stable during the period under consideration.

CVP analysis equally has certain limitations of which the principal ones are:
- Only quantitative factors are taken into consideration to the exclusion of important qualitative factors such as employee morale.
- Joint costs cannot be attributed to individual operated departments.
- The result of CVP analysis is only an estimate to help management make decisions.
- CVP analysis does not take into consideration the possible effects of the decisions made either internally (employee analysis) or externally (guests, social, and environmental analyses)

These limitations notwithstanding, CVP analysis and the establishment of the breakeven point, forms an important measure for many organizations.

11.2   Contribution margin

In the previous chapter the contribution margin was introduced (section 10.4.2.2). Now, it will be further explained. The primary focus in CVP analysis is trying to determine future levels of profitability which requires an understanding of how much costs and profits will be affected following any changes in sales.
The CVP analysis is generally presented in the form of a contribution margin income statement in which the details of the variable and fixed costs are separately indicated. The USALI formatted income statement for internal purposes is designed on such lines. The contribution to fixed costs is referred to as the contribution margin.

The contribution margin (CM) = revenues – direct operating expenses (also called the variable costs)

This can also be expressed as a percentage of the revenues in what is called the contribution margin ratio (CMR).

$$\text{Contribution margin ratio (CMR)} = \frac{CM}{Revenues}$$

The CMR represents the part of sales that is contributed towards the fixed costs and or profits.

11.3 Breakeven analysis

The major premise on which CVP analysis is done is called breakeven analysis. Some authors do even use the terms interchangeably. Breakeven analysis relates to the determination of a single point (the breakeven point) at which no gains or losses will be made in a business. The breakeven point is consequently the point at which the net income is exactly equal to zero. At this point, all the costs or expenses and revenue are equal. With breakeven analysis, the margin of safety is calculated, which is the amount that revenues exceed the breakeven point. The margin of safety is the amount by which revenues can fall while still staying above the breakeven point. The structure of the section is as follows:

11.3.1   Establishing the breakeven point
11.3.2   Single service analysis
11.3.3   Other considerations in breakeven analysis

11.3.1 Establishing the breakeven point

Breakeven analysis is a supply-side analysis which only analyzes the costs of the sales excluding any analysis on how demand may be affected at different price levels.

The breakeven point can be expressed as an equation as follows:

Profit = total revenue – total costs = zero

This equation can be broken down into its constituent elements as follows:
$$0 = (X \times S) - \{(V \times X) + F\} = P$$

in which:
X = quantity sold
S = sales price
V = variable cost
F = fixed cost
P = profit

This can be further simplified to:
$$0 = SX - VX - F$$

in which:

SX = total revenue
VX = total variable cost

Assuming a situation of the sale of a single product, the equation can be rearranged to solve for any one of its four variables as follows:

Fixed costs at breakeven:

$$F = SX - VX$$

Variable cost per unit at breakeven:

$$V = S - \frac{F}{X}$$

Selling price at breakeven:

$$S = \frac{F}{X} + V$$

Quantity sold at breakeven:

$$X = \frac{F}{S - V}$$

The best way to understand the breakeven analysis is by using examples and for this purpose multiple considerations will be made. The first one will be analyzing the single service after which other considerations will be taken into account.

11.3.2   Single service analysis

Afilen Hotels Plc. manages two hotels along the southern coast – the Blue Beach Hotel, and the White Beach Hotel. In the Blue Beach Hotel, the rooms' division manager would like to determine the levels of occupancy that will permit the hotel attain breakeven in the following year.
The information at his disposal is:

· There are 220 rooms in the hotel
· The hotel will be open for 365 days
· Annual fixed costs related to the Rooms Division are €6,475,002.00
· The ADR is €165.00
· The per-room variable cost is €24.00

In keeping in line with the formulas provided in the section 11.3.1, this information can be transformed as follows:
X = 220 rooms
F = €6,475,002.00
V = €24.00
S = €165.00

The contribution margin (CM) of the Blue Beach Hotel is

$$CM = S - V = €165.00 - €24.00 = €141.00$$

The breakeven number of rooms (X) for the Blue Beach Hotel will thus be:

$$X = \frac{F}{CM} = \frac{€6,475,002.00}{141} = 45,922 \text{ Rooms}$$

With this breakeven number of 45,922 rooms, the breakeven level of occupancy can be determined as such:

$$\frac{\text{Required number of rooms at breakeven}}{\text{available room nights}} \times 100$$

Consequently for the Blue Beach Hotel:
Required number of rooms at breakeven = 45,922
Available room nights = 220 × 365 = 80,300
thus

$$\text{Breakeven level of occupancy} = \frac{45,922}{80,300} = 57.19\%$$

(rounded to two decimal places)

The ADR at breakeven is verified as follows:

$$ADR = \frac{F}{X} + V$$

$$\frac{€6,475,002.00}{€45,922.00} + €24.00 = €165.00$$

The variable cost per unit at breakeven is verified as follows:

$$V = S - \frac{F}{X}$$

$$€165.00 - \frac{€6,475,002.00}{€45,922.00} = €24.00$$

The fixed costs at breakeven is verified as such:

$$F = SX - VX$$

$$(€165.00 \times 220 \times 0.5719 \times 365) - (€24.00 \times 220 \times 0.5719 \times 365)$$

$$= €7,577,130.00 - €1,102,128.00$$

$$= €6,475,002.00$$

Exhibit 11.1 is a graphical representation of the breakeven point based on the Blue Beach Hotel's information. The number of rooms sold is indicated in the x-axis (horizontal axis), while the currency values (€) are indicated in the y-axis (vertical axis). If the total sales revenue line and also the total cost line for all levels of activity are drawn in, the breakeven point can be determined.

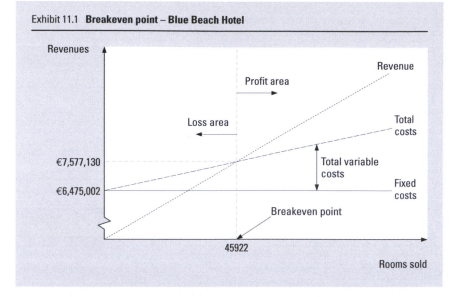

Exhibit 11.1 **Breakeven point – Blue Beach Hotel**

As breakeven occurs at that activity level where total cost equals total sales, breakeven is represented by the point where the sales and total cost lines cross each other. In the exhibit 11.1, this breakeven point (45,922 rooms sold) is highlighted by the vertical dotted line. The breakeven revenue (€7,577,130.00) is highlighted by the horizontal dotted line. Any level of sales to the right of the vertical dotted line will result in a profit. Any level of sales to the left of the line will result in a loss.

An extension of the basic breakeven analysis is the use of the concept of the safety margin. The safety margin represents the excess of expected or actual sales over the breakeven sales. The margin of safety can be expressed in terms of revenues (€), units (for example rooms), as well as in occupancy percentages.

> Margin of safety in revenues = current (or expected) sales revenue
>   – sales revenue at breakeven level
> Margin of safety in units = current (or expected) units sold
>   – units required to breakeven
> Occupancy % safety margin = current (or expected) occupancy %
>   – occupancy % required to break even

Assume now that the revenues of the Blue Beach Hotel for the period came up to €9,750,345.00. This represents the sale of 59,093 rooms and consequently an occupancy level of 73.59%.
The margin of safety in revenues = €9,750,345.00 – €7,577,130.00 = €2,173,220.00. This means that sales could fall by up to this amount before the Blue Beach Hotel incurs a loss.
Similarly the margin of safety in rooms is 13,171 (59,093 – 45,922), and in occupancy percentage is 16.4% (73.59% – 57.19%).

11.3.3 Other considerations in breakeven analysis

The previous example made use of the basic breakeven situation. In the following sections, examples of variations in the breakeven analysis will be shown. The structure of the subsection is as follows:

11.3.3.1 First situation – two room types
11.3.3.2 Second situation – two room types plus additional services
11.3.3.3 Third situation – integrating desired profit levels

11.3.3.1 First situation – two room types
To illustrate examples of variations in breakeven analysis, now, assume that the second of the Afilen Hotels Plc. hotel (the White Beach Hotel) provides the following information:

- 120 single rooms
- 100 double rooms
- The hotel will be open for 365 days
- ADR single room €160.00
- Per-room variable cost single room is €24.00
- ADR double room €190.00
- Per-room variable cost double room is €32.00
- Annual fixed costs related to the White Beach Hotel's Rooms Division are €7,255,360.00
- The historical sales mix is 4 double rooms to every 5 single rooms sold

The breakeven analysis will be done as follows:

Determine the various contribution margins of the rooms

CM single rooms = €136.00 (€160.00 – €24.00)

CM double rooms = €158.00 (€190.00 – €32.00)

Establish sales packages and calculate the CM of the package
Based on the historical sales mix (4 double rooms for every 5 single rooms) the CM from the sale of one package is:

$(5 \times$ CM of the singles$) + (4 \times$ CM of the doubles$)$

$(5 \times$ €136.00$) + (4 \times$ €158.00$)$ = €680.00 + €632.00 = €1,312.00

The amount of €1,312.00 represents then the contribution margin from the sale of one package.

Calculate the breakeven based on the established packages

Using the standard formula of

$$X = \frac{F}{CM}$$

the breakeven in number of packages is:

$$\frac{€7,255,360.00}{€1,312.00} = 5,530 \text{ packages}$$

This implies that the White Beach Hotel will have to sell 5,530 packages to breakeven. This can be translated into single and double rooms as follows:

Each package = 5 singles and 4 doubles

5,530 packages = (5 × 5,530) singles and (4 × 5,530) doubles

Thus the White Beach Hotel will have to sell 27,650 single rooms and 22,120 double rooms to break even.

11.3.3.2   Second situation – two room types plus additional services
Building on the previous situation, now, assume that the White Beach Hotel plans to establish a breakfast-service-only restaurant and needs to know what the effect will be on their breakeven level. The additional estimated information is:
- The average breakfast price will be €20.00
- The average variable cost for the breakfast will be €6.00
- The fixed costs of the White Beach Hotel will increase by €1,412,290.00
- 40 percent of the single room guests will eat breakfast
- 25 percent of the double room guests will eat breakfast (note that all double room sales bring in two guests)

The determination of the different contribution margins of the room nights will now be as follows:

Determine the contribution margins of the rooms taking into account their breakfast effect

CM single rooms = €136.00 + (0.4 × 14) = €141.60

CM double rooms = €158.00 + (0.25 × 2 × 14) = €165.00

Establish sales packages and calculate the CM of each package
Based on the historical sales mix (4 double rooms for every 5 single rooms) the CM from the sale of one package is

(5 × CM of the singles) + (4 × CM of the doubles)

(5 × €141.60) + (4 × €165.00) = €708.00 + €660.00 = €1,368.00

Calculate the breakeven based on the established packages

Using the standard formula of

$$X = \frac{F}{CM}$$

the breakeven in number of packages is calculated as follows:

The expected annual fixed costs (F) is

€7,255,360.00 + €1,412,290.00 = €8,667,650.00

Thus

$$\frac{€8,667,650.00}{€1,368.00} = 6,336 \text{ packages}$$

This implies that the White Beach Hotel will have to sell 6,336 packages to breakeven. This can be translated into single and double rooms as follows:

Each package = 5 singles and 4 doubles
6,336 packages = (5 × 6,336) singles and (4 × 6,336) doubles, thus the White Beach Hotel will have to sell 31,680 single rooms and 25,344 double rooms to breakeven.

These breakeven volumes can be verified to make sure that the established levels really lead to zero profit:
Contribution from the single rooms = number of rooms sold × CM single rooms
Contribution from the double rooms = number of rooms sold × CM double rooms
Contribution from the single rooms' breakfast = number of rooms sold × CM breakfast × ratio of single breakfast
Contribution from the double rooms' breakfast = number of rooms sold × CM breakfast × ratio of double breakfast
Thus,
Contribution from the single rooms =
31,680 × €136.00   €4,308,481.00
Contribution from the double rooms =
25,344 × €158.00   €4,004,353.00
Contribution from the single rooms' breakfast =
31,680 × €14.00 × 0.4   €177,408.00
Contribution from the double rooms' breakfast =
25,344 × €14.00 × 0.25 × 2 €177,408.00

These contributions are summed up and then the fixed cost deducted from the solution as follows:

Singles contribution	+	4308481.00
Double contribution	+	4004353.00
Singles breakfast contribution	+	177408.00
Double breakfast contribution	=	177408.00
Total CM	−	8667650.00
Fixed costs		8667650.00
Profit		0

This zero profit result indicates that the White Beach Hotel will break even with sales of 31,680 single rooms and 25,344 double rooms when they integrate the breakfast-service-only restaurant.

11.3.3.3 Third situation – integrating desired profit levels

Now, assume that the Management of the Blue Beach Hotel (see 11.3.2) desires to buy an adjoining 18-hole golf course at the end of the next year's operations. For this to be realized, they expect to generate enough profit that will permit them to make the purchase. For the management to know what will be the exact effect of these expectations on their breakeven volumes, they have to first of all decide which approach to use in the analysis. There are two approaches possible:

- Decide on a pre-income tax analysis
- Decide on a post-income tax analysis

Pre-income tax analysis

Recall that the basic data of the Blue Beach Hotel is as follows:

- There are 220 rooms in the hotel
- The hotel will be open for 365 days
- Annual fixed costs related to the rooms division are €6,475,002.00
- The ADR is €165.00
- The per-room variable cost is €24.00

Now, assume that for the management to be able to make the purchase of the golf course at the end of the year, they need to attain a pre-income tax profit level of €1,657,455.00. With this expectation, the breakeven volume will be calculated as such:

The contribution margin (CM) of the Blue Beach Hotel is

$$CM = S - V = €165.00 - €24.00 = €141.00$$

The required breakeven number of rooms (X) for the Blue Beach Hotel will now become:

$$X = \frac{F + \text{desired profit}}{CM}$$

$$\frac{€6,475,002.00 + €1,657,445.00}{€141.00} = 57,677 \text{ rooms}$$

The Blue Beach Hotel will have now to sell extra 11,755 rooms (57,677 – 45,922) in order to be able to generate enough profit that will permit them to carry out the purchase of the golf course.

Post-income tax analysis

Assuming now that incomes are taxed at 35%, the breakeven volume will be computed as follows:

$$X = \frac{\left[\dfrac{F + \text{Post-Income Tax Desired Profit}}{1 - \text{Tax rate}} \right]}{CM}$$

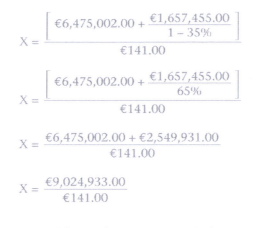

$$X = \frac{\left[€6,475,002.00 + \dfrac{€1,657,455.00}{1 - 35\%} \right]}{€141.00}$$

$$X = \frac{\left[€6,475,002.00 + \dfrac{€1,657,455.00}{65\%} \right]}{€141.00}$$

$$X = \frac{€6,475,002.00 + €2,549,931.00}{€141.00}$$

$$X = \frac{€9,024,933.00}{€141.00}$$

X = 64006.62 This can be rounded to 64,007 rooms.

The Blue Beach Hotel will have now to sell extra 18,085 rooms (64,007 – 45,922) in order to be able to generate enough post-income tax profit that will permit them to carry out the purchase of the golf course.

Glossary

Breakeven analysis – see cost-volume-profit analysis.

Breakeven point – is the point at which all the costs or expenses and the revenue are equal. At this point the net income is exactly equal to zero.

Contribution margin – is the difference between the costs of a product or service and its selling price. It represents the revenues less all direct operating expenses.

Contribution margin ratio (CMR) – is the proportion of sales revenue that is contributed towards the fixed costs and or profits.

Cost-volume-profit (CVP) analysis – is a set of analytical tools that are used to determine the levels of sales needed to be carried out at any desired profit level. It is commonly called breakeven analysis.

Margin of safety – is the excess of expected or actual sales over the breakeven sales.

Multiple choice questions

11.1   After the break-even point in number of rooms, rooms revenue generated during the particular period will:
 a be considered as pure profit
 b cover the fixed costs of the extra room sales
 c increase at a faster rate than the variable costs of the extra room sales
 d increase in proportion to the extra room sales

11.2   Which of the following does not belong amongst the common assumptions in cost-volume-profit analysis?
 a Fixed costs do not change during the period under consideration
 b Mixed costs can be reasonably divided into their fixed and variable elements
 c Revenues vary indirectly with fixed costs
 d Variable costs have a linear relationship with revenues during the period under consideration

11.3   The Munching Moose Motel expects to sell 10,666 room nights during a period with a per-room variable cost of €27. If total fixed costs of the period are expected to be €351,978, what would the ADR be at the breakeven point?
 a €60
 b €65
 c €70
 d €75

11.4   The Red Sands Hotel's breakeven point is achieved when 17,750 rooms are sold during a period. Its average daily rate (ADR) is €80, and the per-room variable cost sold is €32. The total fixed costs for the period equal:
 a €568,000
 b €852,000
 c €1,420,000
 d none of the above

11.5   A motel has an average daily rate (ADR) of €50. The fixed costs for each of the 2,200 rooms sold during a period were €15. If it has a variable cost percentage of 20%, what is the contribution margin per room sold?
 a €15
 b €35
 c €40
 d €50

Exercises

11.1   A restaurant with an average food service cheque of €18 per guest has the following average monthly figures:
Revenues € 850,000
Variable costs € 380,000
Fixed costs € 182,000

Using this information, determine the following:
a the breakeven level of revenue
b their operating income if revenues fell to €750,000
c the breakeven number of guests
d the number of guests if revenues fell to €750,000

11.2 The Gouda Split Restaurant is made up of a café and a bar. The café's variable cost is 45% and it provides 62% of the total revenues. The bar's variable cost is 36%. Determine the following:

a the café's contribution margin
b the bar's contribution margin
c the combined contribution margin
d the additional revenues needed if the management expects an increase of €75,000 in net operating income

11.3 Jan Marcus recently invested €350,000 in equipment to run a rented bistro. The income tax rate is 30%. The projected variable expenses are as follows:

Cost of food   24% of revenue
Salaries and wages   32% of revenue
Other expenses   12% of revenue

The projected annual fixed expenses are as follows:

· Depreciation   € 35,000
· Insurance   €   3,000
· Rent   € 18,000
· Salaries and wages € 72,000
· Other   € 34,000

Using this information, determine the following:

a the breakeven level of sales
b the breakeven level of sales if Jan Marcus wants to earn 14% on €350,000

11.4 The Sunnyside Motel's rooms department has annual revenues of €3.000,000 with accompanying variable costs of €900,000. The motel's food department has annual revenues of €1,000,000 with variable costs of €800,000. The fixed expenses of the motel are €1,100,000. The total revenues of the Sunnyside Motel come up to €4,000,000. Proceed with the following activities:

a calculate the breakeven point. Assume that the ratio of revenues from the rooms and food departments stay the same at all levels of activity
b in order to boost restaurant revenues, the owners plan to carry out an advertising campaign that will cost €5,000. Assuming room revenues stay the same; determine the extra food revenues that need to be made to compensate for the advertising costs.

Internal control

12

12.1 Need for internal control
12.2 Special characteristics of the hospitality industry from an internal control perspective
12.3 Principles of internal control
12.4 Basic internal control proposals
12.5 Bank reconciliation

For the managers within hospitality operations to effectively carry out their duties, they need information which is provided by the management accounting system. This information should at all times be current as well as accurate. Management will use the information to make decisions and implement procedures that will help to safeguard the assets of the organization, enhance their efficiency, increase sales, and also maximize their profitability. The responsibility for internal control lies in all the employees of the organization. It is ultimately top management's responsibility to ensure that controls are in place. However, that responsibility will have to be delegated to each area of operation. This delegation of responsibility in larger organizations is usually done through the establishment of organizational charts. An organizational chart which generally establishes lines of communication and levels of authority and responsibility within the organization is considered to be the base of any good internal control system. Exhibit 12.1 is the top-level organization chart of the Mövenpick Hotel Amsterdam City Centre.

In exhibit 12.1 for example notice the lines of responsibility moving from the executive sous-chef, through the executive chef via the director of F & B, the hotel manager before reaching the general manager. You will notice further that there are four different levels of authority as separated by the different colour shades in the organizational chart. Smaller or owner-operated organizations have fewer levels of responsibility and consequently fewer control points. In such organizations, the managers or owners are most of the time present, and they generally handle those sensitive operations such as the receipt of cash and the disbursement of cash or other payment

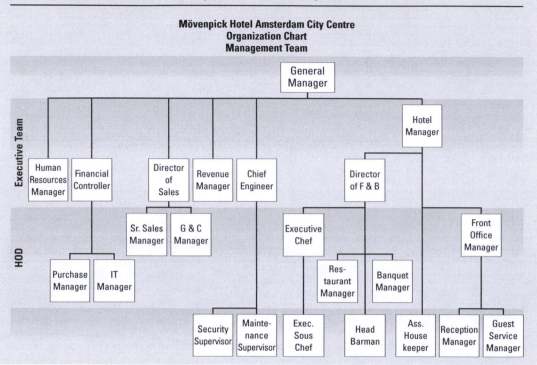

Mövenpick Hotel Amsterdam City Centre
Organization Chart
Management Team

activities. Internal control in this chapter is studied in the following manner. Section 12.1 establishes the reasons why internal control is a must for any organization, while section 12.2 gives those special characteristics that make internal control problematic within the hospitality industry. Section 12.3 introduces the reader to those common elements of internal control applicable to any type of industry; while section 12.4 based on the hotel internal control guide lists in a summary fashion basic internal control proposals. To end the chapter section 12.5 introduces the internal control activity of bank reconciliation.

12.1   Need for internal control

Internal control is that aspect of management that deals with the prevention of fraud and embezzlement. Internal control is principally a function of top management but also concerns everyone in the organization. The American Institute of Certified Public Accountants (AICPA) has defined internal control as follows:

> **Internal control comprises the plan of organization and all of the coordinate methods adopted within a business to safeguard its assets, check the accuracy and reliability of its accounting data, promote operational efficiency, and encourage adherence to prescribed managerial policies. This definition is possibly broader than the**

meaning sometimes attributed to the term. It recognizes that a system of internal control extends beyond those matters which relate directly to the functions of the accounting and financial departments. A well-developed system of internal controls might include budgetary controls, standard costs, periodic operating reports, statistical analyses, a personal training program and an internal staff audit.

Four central objectives, sub-divided into two control sub-groups can be derived from the above definition:

1   Accounting controls
- Safeguard assets – requires the prevention of theft as well as their proper maintenance, and spoilage reduction.
- Ensure the accuracy and reliability of accounting data – this is needed in order to help management make the correct decisions as well as prevent legal actions and fines from government.

2   Administrative controls
- Promote operational efficiency – to ensure that their products and services will be delivered without incurring unnecessary costs.
- Encourage the observation of management's policies – to ensure that all the employees keep to the internal rules and regulations of the organization.

Internal control systems are made up of the following two requirements:
- The existence of methods and procedures for the employees at all levels to follow. These methods and procedures ensure that employees keep to the management policies, operate efficiently, and also protect the organization's assets from waste, theft, and embezzlement.
- The existence of reliable forms and reports that will measure employee efficiency and effectiveness and lead to problem identification. These reports must be accurate, timely, and cost effective because it will make no sense to have a control system that will be costlier to implement than the possible losses to be incurred in case of its non-implementation.

Controls are of two types:
- Preventive controls, which are designed to discourage errors or irregularities such as assigning a cash bank to each waiter, and
- Detective controls, which are designed to discover errors or irregularities after they have occurred as well as monitor preventive controls such as the activities of the night auditor.

12.2   Special characteristics of the hospitality industry from an internal control perspective

Businesses of all types have much the same type of problems related to internal control. The hospitality industry however has certain characteristics that make it more exposed to fraud and embezzlement. This greater exposure makes it more difficult for internal control to be implemented. These general characteristics can be summarized as follows:

Volume of cash transactions

Despite the expansion of electronic means of settling transactions using credit and debit cards and the use of charge accounts, many transactions still have to be carried out using cash especially in the bars and restaurants. Some of these outlets also operate all day and night and this would require many shift changes. These revenue departments do accumulate lots of cash in the course of the day and this makes it easier for the cash to be stolen.

Size of the business

Most hospitality properties are considered to be small even if they are part of a large chain. The various revenue departments most of the time operate separately. This separation makes it difficult for the properties to have enough resources that will enable them establish robust control systems that economies of large scale can create.

Employee turnover and job status

Most of the jobs in the industry are carried out by relatively low-skilled employees (clerks, waiters, cashiers etc) receiving lower wages and considered lower in social status ranking. Generally filled with part-timers and students in their search for better employment elsewhere, the turnover rates are quite high, training levels as well as loyalty levels are low. These conditions render it more difficult for comprehensive and long lasting internal control procedures to be established.

Items in inventory

Items found in hospitality inventory are generally those items that employees would normally need for their own use – beverage and food items as well as lodging. Additionally, some of these items are of high value relative to their size or weight and can be easily consumed on the spot or hidden to be taken away later. Products such as quality wines, seafood, steak, and expensive containers of food products are valuable to dishonest employees who might remove them for their personal use or for sale to third parties.

12.3 Principles of internal control

The principles of internal control – sometimes referred to as elements of internal control – apply to all types of businesses.

Institute management leadership and supervision

The management board should establish the policies at the highest level and these should be communicated and enforced at all levels. Employees are generally honest but may yield to temptations in the absence of good internal control systems. Management's involvement in the internal control process will lead the way for the employees to follow. It should be about 'doing what we do' and not only doing 'what we tell you to do'.

Establish preventive instead of detective control procedures

From the adage 'prevention is better than cure' it is preferable to eliminate the opportunity for theft and embezzlement than to play the detective after the crime has been committed. In the long run, prevention is more cost effective and productive, and with proper preventive procedures, nothing will be left for detection.

Create effective monitoring of the control system

All existing control systems must be constantly monitored to ensure that they still provide the needed output, and also be flexible enough to be modified in case of need. To have employees spend time and energy to fill in forms that are not checked is both expensive and discouraging. If a reporting form needs to be changed or is redundant, then it should be modified, or replaced entirely with a more adequate one.

Maintain adequate records

An important consideration for effective internal control is to have good written records. These forms, reports and records include such forms as registration cards, time cards, folios, guest cheques, payroll cheques, purchase orders and receiving reports. These documents should be designed in such a way that all the users can easily understand them. To make the control process easier, these documents should be pre-numbered and they should be only prepared at the time of the transaction to reduce the possibility of errors. When pre-numbered documents are issued, the employee receiving the documents should be required to sign for them to establish responsibility and accountability for the documents. The accounting department should oversee all documents, even though they are actually used by employees in other departments. With good forms, reports and records, employees will be more careful, and theft and fraud reduced to a minimum. The types of forms, reports, and other records used in the internal control system will depend entirely on the size and type of establishment.

Establish written procedure manuals

Each job or activity within the hospitality industry can be described in written form in what is called the procedure manual. This manual should list the details of each position, describing how and when to carry out each activity. This will permit the employees to know what the policy and procedures are. These written procedures are particularly important in the hospitality industry, where employee turnover is relatively high and continuous employee training to support the system of internal control is necessary. The procedure manuals help maintain consistent job performance especially as new employees are concerned, as well as in cases where employees are called to temporarily fill in for absent colleagues.

Design the organizational chart

In very small operations, one owner/manager can effectively supervise all the employees; however most operations are divided into various functional areas such as general management, human resources, sales and marketing, production, finance and accounting, and property operations and maintenance. The organizational chart shows the organizational structure of the operation indicating the relationships and relative ranks of its parts and positions or jobs. The employees must know the organizational chart and respect the chain of command except in exceptional situations like management fraud where the employees may be called to skip some of the links in the chain.

Establish fixed responsibilities

Responsibility for a specific task or activity should always be given to a single person who will then be fully informed of his or her duties and obligations. This attribution of responsibility will permit management to know exactly where to start investigations in cases of problems. However, this principle should also be viewed from the employee's perspective. Since the employees are responsible for their actions, they need these conditions to allow them carry out their responsibilities effectively and no one should be allowed to interfere in the actions except after proper delegation of the duties.

Establish proper authorization procedures and create audit trails

All business transactions must be properly authorized by the supervisory persons. Management's authorization can be in two forms: general or specific. General authorization is provided to the employees for the normal performance of their duties such as selling the items on the menus at the listed prices. Specific authorization will be needed in case where there are to be deviations to the general authorization such as putting a limit to the amount of fixed assets that can be purchased beyond which, the CEO must approve by a written authorization. The audit trail will document each transaction from the time that it was initiated through to the final recording of the transaction in the operation's general ledger. A good audit trail creates the possibility of tracking transactions from start to finish.

Maintain a division of duties

Also referred to as separation of duties or segregation of duties, it is the most important principle of internal control. This principle means that no one involved in any transaction should have complete control over the transaction. This is done by separating the custody of assets from the recordkeeping or accountability of those assets. This segregation of duties prevents theft and fraud and at the same time detects theft and fraud. This principle can only be thwarted in cases of collusion whereby two or more employees decide to defraud the establishment by acting together.

Split responsibilities in related transactions

Responsibility for related transactions should be separated so that the work of one employee is verified by the work of another. This keeps one person from having too much control over assets and may prevent their theft. Splitting responsibilities in related transactions does not mean that there will be unnecessary and costly duplication of work but to have two tasks that must be carried out for control reasons done by two separate employees. The additional costs of the second person's time conducting the verification will normally be more than recovered in the increased net income that will result from the reduction of losses due to undetected errors.

Establish careful selection, training and supervision procedures for employees

In the hospitality industry, it is very important to have competent, trustworthy and well-trained employees to ensure sustainable and profitable operations. This will entail that hospitality establishments should have good systems for the pre-employment screening of job applicants, selecting the employees, providing adequate employee orientation, on-the-job training, and periodic evaluation. Personnel at all levels must be trained properly for them to be able to accomplish their activities. The employees must know what their activities entail and also how to carry them out. The employees should be able to recognize the importance of their particular activities and jobs in the overall objectives of the establishment. Supervisory personnel should have the skills necessary to maintain the standards of the establishment and motivate the personnel under their supervision. The establishment should equally have adequate reward policies for the employees with clearly defined future possibilities in cases of continued employment.

Limit the number of employees with access to assets

The number of employees who have access to assets such as cash and inventory should be limited. The more the number of employees with access to cash or inventory, the greater the risk of losses – whether by theft or through simple mismanagement. Responsibility for an asset cannot be fixed in a single employee if all other employees have unlimited and uncontrolled access to the asset. Additionally, the quantities of such assets should be maintained at the barest minimum. Limiting access and maintaining low quantity levels may lead to some operational conflicts. There should be the balancing act of ensuring that there are always enough quantities to prevent running out of stock. The limitation of access to assets should also not be so cumbersome that they severely restrict efficient operations.

Rotate employees and schedule mandatory vacations

Wherever feasible, employees in especially in the accounting, cash-handling and other clerical positions should be rotated. Employees who know they are not going to be doing the same job for a long time will be less likely to be dishonest and job rotation prevents employees from becoming bored from constantly carrying out the same tasks. Rotation builds flexibility into job assignments and gives the employees a better understanding of how the jobs relate to each other. Scheduling mandatory vacations for all employees should be part of management's human resources' policies. Employees may be discouraged from theft or fraud if they know that during their vacation some other person will have control of the assets under their control and that, if theft or fraud has occurred, it may be discovered during such a vacation. In situations where theft or fraud has not yet occurred, the new person may discover weaknesses in the control system that was not previously apparent. This may then lead to the creation of new preventive internal control measures.

Perform surprise checks by other employees as well as carry out independent performance checks

Random but expected checks of cash, merchandise and inventories should be frequently carried out by independent employees. Such checks should be frequent but not routine and systematic. Top management should get occasionally involved in the process. In most hospitality operations, the independent performance checks are carried out by the internal auditors. The internal audit is the appraisal of the operating and accounting controls of an organization to ensure that internal control procedures are being followed and assets are adequately safeguarded. The internal auditors are responsible for appraising the effectiveness of the operating and accounting controls, and for verifying the reliability of forms, records, reports, and other supporting documentation to ensure that internal control policies and procedures are being followed and assets are adequately safeguarded. All companies should undergo periodic external audits carried out by independent external auditors. The external auditors do not only verify the financial statements, but equally study and test the internal accounting control system. The stronger the internal accounting control system, the more it can be relied upon and all other things being equal, a strong internal control system will require less external auditing.

Establish performance standards and evaluate the results

Standards and standard costs were introduced in chapter 9 (see 9.2) and it was indicated that their establishment provides the basis for decision making, permits costs analysis and control, and permits the measurement of inventory and cost of goods sold. These are all necessary conditions for the establishment of a good internal control system. It is also necessary to establish a good reporting system that will be able to show that all aspects of the business are functioning properly. Establishing the standards and reporting about them properly will ensure that management can verify if actual results are in line with the expected standards of performance.

Establish forms, budgets and internal reports

In order to be able to properly evaluate the results, forms and reports providing information about all aspects of the business have to be designed. These forms and reports will provide management with the information needed to determine if the standards are respected and to take corrective actions in cases of discrepancies as well on how to improve the standards. Budgets will help to ensure that the management goals are attained. Examples of internal reports include the daily operations' report, the weekly forecasts, the future bookings' report and the annual budget.

Set up physical controls and use machines

Physical controls will include security devices and measures for safeguarding the assets of the property such as CCTV cameras, safes, locked storerooms, and locked storage compartments as well as mechanical and electronic equipment used in the execution and recording of transactions. Machines vastly reduce the possibilities of theft or fraud and they should be set up wherever possible. Installing machines if an employee is no longer required to perform a task manually equally has the advantage of reducing labour costs and enhancing efficiency. Common machines include the front office billing and audit equipment, bar and restaurant cash registers, point-of-sale systems (POS), and mechanical or electronic drink-dispensing bar equipment.

Bond those employees who have access to cash, records, or stores
Employees with access to cash, records, or stores as well as top management should be bonded through an insurance policy called the fidelity bond. The fidelity bond protects the operation from losses incurred by employee dishonesty because the establishment is reimbursed up to the face value of the insurance policy for the loss suffered.

12.4 Basic internal control proposals

In this section basic internal accounting control proposals based on the Hotel Internal Control Guide are simply indicated. It should be noted that each hospitality operation should review the various areas and determine which control proposals will be most suited to its needs. As this is a basic text on management accounting, it will be out of the scope of this book to go in detail into all the proposed control measures in all the areas of a hospitality operation. Those interested in further details can consult the Hotel Internal Control Guide published by the Committee on Financial Management of the AHMA.

Front of house internal control proposals
A Room revenue
   I   Establishing prices
        1 Authorize room rates to be charged
        2 Communicate approved room rates to appropriate parties
        3 Authorize deviations from approved rates
   II   Accepting reservations
        1 Obtain complete and accurate reservation information
        2 Accept reservations in accordance with established policies
   III Checking in the guest
        1 Receive reservation information in a timely manner
        2 Established approved methods of payment
        3 Obtain necessary guest information
        4 Train front desk personnel
        5 Obtain evidence of guest check-in
        6 Maintain current room status information
   IV Recording room revenue
        1 Bill all occupied rooms
        2 Post charges in a timely and accurate manner
        3 Provide a statement of charges to the guest
        4 Authorize rebates and allowances
   V   Checking out the guest
        1 Close out guest records in the guest ledger
        2 Update the current room status

B Food and beverage revenue
    I   Planning and pricing the menu
1. Plan, price, and periodically update menu items and product lists
2. Authorize prices to be charged
3. Authorize officers' cheques, complimentary meals and discounts
4. Document guest reservation procedures
5. Establish staffing guidelines based on forecasted business
6. Establish seating rotation procedures
7. Establish and maintain adequate par stocks
8. Establish and implement suggestive-selling techniques
9. Establish and implement hospitality training programmes
10. Set up a shopping service – establish an independent review of guest service and control procedures

    II   Recording revenue
1. Establish order/entry procedures and train staff in the proper use of the POS system
2. Authorize and account for void cheques and transactions/adjustments
3. Verify cash transactions and settlements
4. Prove the mathematical accuracy of F & B cheques and verify the posting of revenues and settlements
5. Calculate beverage sales potentials
6. Independently control guest/cover counts
7. Establish additional cheque controls for the restaurant buffet
8. Audit banquet cheques
9. Establish procedures for banquet cash bars
10. Balance, post, and verify all F & B transactions by night and income auditor
11. Record minibar consumption daily
12. Authorize steward sales

    III   Minimizing general risks
1. Establish a food safety programme
2. Establish an alcohol awareness programme

C Telephone revenue
    I   Establishing prices
1. Select a telephone switch
2. Select a long-distance carrier and rate structure
3. Select a call-accounting vendor
4. Establish a mark-up margin

    II   Recording revenue
1. Post charges in a timely and accurate manner
2. Reconcile total charges from the call-accounting vendor report to the total posted telephone charges
3. Establish procedures for operator-assisted calls
4. Provide a statement of charges to the guest
5. Authorize rebates and allowances
6. Establish procedures for manual systems
7. Restrict the outside operator without restricting emergency calls

III Reviewing the long-distance invoice to guest charges
    1 Review the mark-up margin
    2 Review potential operator-assisted calls (e.g., overseas, third-party charges) to guest postings
    3 Review for unusual charges (e.g., 0900 numbers)
    4 Review the call-accounting configuration
    5 Review the call-accounting database

D Other revenue
  I Services provided by an external vendor
    1 Selecting services and vendors
      a Determine whether to provide service internally or contract outside the hotel
      b Authorize a vendor
      c Obtain a written contract with the vendor
      d Establish a commission rate
      e Review the vendor's insurance limits
    2 Recording revenue
      a Establish procedures for how charges will be accepted from the vendor
      b Post charges in a timely and accurate manner
      c Provide a statement of charges to the guest
      d Authorize rebates and allowances
    3 Reviewing the vendor invoice to guest charges
      a Reconcile the vendor invoice to guest postings and allowances
      b Review the commission rate for accuracy
      c Audit concessionaires and outside vendors
      d Ensure that the vendor has the necessary licenses and permits
  II Services provided internally
    1 Establishing prices
      a Select a recording method for sales and receipts (e.g., separate utlet or all through the front desk)
      b Develop a system to accumulate applicable expenses
      c Authorize rates to be charged for services
    2 Recording revenue
      a Bill all applicable services
      b Post charges in a timely and accurate manner
      c Provide a statement of charges to the guest
      d Authorize rebates and allowances
    3 Controlling expenses
      a Train appropriate personnel
      b Compare revenue with related expenses

E Cashiering
  I Maintaining cash receipts – house funds
    1 Provide a secure storage area
    2 Limit access to cash monies
    3 Define the terms and conditions for maintenance of the house fund
    4 Establish accountability for the house fund
    5 Perform periodic, independent bank counts
  II Maintaining cash receipts – cash banks
    1 Provide a secure storage area
    2 Limit access to cash monies

3   Define the terms and conditions for maintenance of cash banks
4   Establish accountability for operating banks
5   Perform periodic, independent bank counts
III Maintaining cash receipts – cash transactions
1   Post all guest payments immediately upon receipt
2   Establish a cheque log for cheques received in the mail
3   Establish accountability
4   Provide receipts for payments on accounts to guests
IV Maintaining cash receipts – cheque cashing
1   Establish standards for cheque-cashing approval
2   Establish cheque-cashing procedures
3   Train cashiers to be alert to characteristics that may indicate a bad cheque
V   Maintaining cash receipts – petty cash
1   Define criteria for the use of petty cash
2   Establish standards for authorizing the use of petty cash
3   Record the payment of petty cash
4   Record expenses represented by petty cash payments on a timely basis
VI Maintaining cash receipts – paid outs
1   Establish standards authorizing a paid out
2   Establish accountability
3   Post all paid outs in a timely and accurate manner
VIIi Maintaining cash receipts – deposits
1   Establish a system of deposits
2   Establish accountability
3   Ensure the accuracy and timeliness of cash deposits
4   Account for and secure cash deposits
VIII Maintaining cash receipts – cheque payments
1   Accept cheques for payment of accounts, advance deposits, and miscellaneous income in accordance with established policies
2   Post cheque payments in a timely and accurate manner
3   Provide a credited folio as a receipt of payment to the guest
IX Maintaining cash receipts – credit card transactions
1   Apply all credit card payments to guest accounts
2   Approve credit cards
3   Post payments in a timely and accurate manner
4   Provide a credited folio as a receipt of payment to the guest
X   Controlling food and beverage revenue
1   Bill all food and beverage charges
2   Post charges in a timely and accurate manner
3   Provide a statement of charges to the guest
XI Controlling banquet and meeting room revenue
1   Bill all banquet and meeting room charges
2   Post charges in a timely and accurate manner
3   Provide a statement of charges to the guest
XII Controlling miscellaneous revenue
1   Bill all miscellaneous charges
2   Post charges in a timely and accurate manner
3   Provide a statement of charges to the guest

XIII Controlling adjustments
1 Authorize all adjustments
2 Post all adjustments in a timely and accurate manner

Back of house internal control proposals
A Purchasing
I Ordering
1 Establish and authorize purchase specifications
2 Communicate requirement to vendors
3 Select the optimal vendor(s) and establish bid procedures
4 Implement the use of authorized purchase orders or contracts, and requests
5 Establish and maintain purchase procedures
II Receiving
1 Advise the receiver as to the goods expected
2 Check the quality and quantity of goods or services received
3 Record the receipt of goods or services and establish procedures for errors, returns, and goods received without invoice
4 Communicate the receipt to stores and accounts payable
5 Match the receiver's report and related purchase documentation
III Paying vendors
1 Ensure that purchases are properly recorded, valued, classified, and accounted for
1 Authorize the disbursement voucher
3 Restrict access to critical forms, records, and processing areas
4 Ensure that cash disbursements are valid, accounted for, properly recorded, in the correct amount, and classified
B Inventories
I Controlling the storeroom
1 Establish storeroom controls for inventory items – based on the size of the hotel and the availability of sufficient storage space (food and beverage; general supplies; guest supplies; engineering supplies; non-circulating operating equipment – china, glass, silver, and linen
2 Use forms and procedures to record the receipt and issue of inventory stores
3 Maintain physical protection; safeguard assets
II Controlling inventory count and valuation
1 Perform an inventory count and adjust physical records accordingly; ascertain the reasons for the differences
2 Reconcile the perpetual record to the general ledger control account monthly, where applicable
III Controlling operating equipment
1 Establish a procedure for the control of and accounting for reserve and in-use operating equipment
C Food and beverage costs
I Purchasing and receiving
1 Establish purchase specifications to maintain consistency in food and beverage purchases

2 Establish guidelines for determining the quantities of food and beverage purchases
3 Establish procedures for the creation and maintenance of purchasing records
4 Establish procedures for receiving food and beverage items
5 Establish procedures for goods received without invoice, for delivery errors, and for returns

II Storing and issuing
1 Establish physical controls and standards for the storage and retention of perishable and non-perishable food and beverage items
2 Secure storage areas; restrict access to authorized personnel
3 Establish requisition procedures
4 Establish procedures for transfers from one storeroom to another, and between storerooms and food and beverage outlets

III Controlling daily and month-end F & B cost reconciliations/potentials and yields
1 Establish procedures for monitoring and controlling daily and monthly food and beverage costs
2 Establish procedures for calculating and monitoring of food and beverage pars, standards, yields, and potentials
3 Establish procedures for recording the sales values and cost equivalents for A & G or S & M food and beverage cheques of officers and other employees. Include the guidelines and authorization for application

IV Controlling banquets
1 Establish procedures to monitor banquet food and beverage costs

D Personnel administration
I Complying with government requirements
1 Require new employees to complete the necessary immigration forms
2 Require minors to have work permits
3 Comply with minimum wage requirements
4 Comply with workers' compensation laws
5 Comply with the equal employment opportunity requirements
6 Maintain the necessary work related insurances

II Following company guidelines
1 Require applicants to complete job application forms
2 Conduct reference and background checks on candidates
3 Establish fair wage guidelines
4 Monitor employees' eligibility for insurance benefits
5 Monitor employees' eligibility for paid vacation time
6 Conduct an annual review of each employee
7 Complete a termination checklist
8 Conduct exit interviews
9 Keep detailed employment and termination records

E Payroll
I Authorizing wages, salaries, withholdings, and deductions
1 Hire and retain employees only at rates, benefits, and perquisites determined in accordance with management's general or specific authorization

  2 Determine payroll withholdings and deductions based on evidence of appropriate authorization

II Preparing and recording

  1 Compensate company employees only at authorized rates and only for services rendered (hours worked) in accordance with management's authorization

  2 Correctly compute gross pay, withholdings, deductions, and net pay based on authorized rates, services rendered, and properly authorized withholding exemptions and deductions

  3 Correctly accumulate, classify, and summarize payroll costs and related liabilities in the appropriate accounts and periods

  4 Make comparisons of personnel, payroll, and work records at reasonable intervals for the timely detection and correction of errors

III Controlling disbursements

  1 Remit net pay and related withholdings and deductions to the appropriate employees and entities, respectively, when due

  2 Make disbursements only for expenditures incurred in accordance with management's authorization

  3 Make adjustments to cash accounts only in accordance with management's authorization

  4 Record disbursements at correct amounts in the appropriate period and properly classify disbursements in the accounts

  5 Restrict access to cash and cash disbursement records to minimize opportunities for irregular or erroneous disbursements

IV Separating functions and physical safeguards

  1 Assign function so that no single individual is in a position to both perpetuate and conceal fraud in the normal course of duties

  2 Limit access to personnel and payroll records to minimize opportunities for errors and irregularities

V Reconciling banks

  1 Make comparison of detail records, control, accounts, and bank statements at reasonable intervals for the detection and appropriate disposition of errors or irregularities

Administration internal control proposals

A General accounting and financial reporting

I Ensuring the accuracy and completeness of the financial data provided to various parties

  1 Authorize accounting principles

  2 Authorize entries and adjustments

  3 Authorize the issuance of specific financial statements

  4 Prepare general journal entries

  5 Summarize general ledger balances

  6 Combine departmental information accurately

  7 Prepare appropriate disclosures

  8 Protect records from hazards and misuse

B Loss prevention and risk management
- I Keeping guests and employees safe
  1. Promote safety awareness
  2. Fill out incident reports accurately and submit time on a timely basis
- II Restricting access to the property
  1. Protect the perimeter
  2. Designate an employee entrance and exit
  3. Restrict access to interior areas
- III Protecting the guestroom
  1. Establish physical security in guestrooms
  2. Inform guests of guestroom safety features
- IV Controlling keys
  1. Issue keys only to employees requiring access
  2. Document key issuance
  3. Rekey locks
- V Protecting against fires and planning for emergencies
  1. Educate all employees in fire prevention and safety
  2. Maintain adequate fire protection equipment
  3. Institute an emergency response and evacuation plan
- VI Evaluating the loss prevention programme
  1. Establish a protection committee
  2. Perform periodic safety audits
- VII Reducing internal theft
  1. Verify applicant information
- VIII Limiting property liability and loss
  1. Provide safe-deposit-box protection
  2. Obtain cost-effective insurance coverage
  3. Assign insurance coordination responsibilities to a qualified individual

C Computer systems
- I Control access to computer systems and applications
- II Protect sensitive company information from accidental or intentional misuse or disclosure
- III Establish a security administration function for each major system
- IV Include security awareness training in the employees' training programme
- V Establish an appropriate environment for the equipment in the computer room
- VI Purchase sufficient insurance coverage for all computer assets
- VII Cover all major hardware with preventative maintenance contracts, and arrange for the use of backup equipment in an emergency
- VIII Ensure the reliable installation, maintenance, and physical security of all telecommunications
- IX Make sure all acquisitions of software and hardware are fully justified, approved, and compatible with the existing environment
- X Implement controls over all software and hardware changes
- XI Make sure computer systems are used effectively and for their intended purposes

D Administration

I Controlling annual forecasts
1 Forecast revenue for each revenue centre by month, based on forecasted occupancy
2 Forecast expenses based on the occupancy volumes used to generate revenues
3 Review and compare monthly forecasts of revenues and expenses

II Controlling capital expenditures
1 Obtain, in writing, all approvals necessary to proceed with projects
2 Prepare forms necessary for the initiation of projects: purchase orders, major expense forms, contracts, etc.
3 Document any change of the original project, purchase order, or contract
4 Ensure the proper payments for planned projects
5 Compare the budget to actual expenditures and planned expenditures
6 Prepare an overview of capital expenditures made in the previous seven years
7 Prepare a list of all projects that may be desired or needed
8 Prepare the funding amounts to be spent on projects
9 Prioritize the project listing by importance to the ongoing operation and the objectives of management

12.5 Bank reconciliation

Bank reconciliation is an internal control activity that brings together the cash balance in the organization's bank statement with the cash balance according to the accounting records within the organization. It helps to detect any accounting, bookkeeping or banking errors. Based on the internal control principle of separation of duties, the bank reconciliation should be carried out by employees who have no role in cash receipts or cash disbursements. On a regular basis (depending on the amount of transactions carried out in the organization's account with the bank) a bank statement is issued by the bank to the organization. The bank statement will show the beginning and ending cash balances, deposits, cashed cheques, transfers received and other transactions. In most cases, the ending cash balance in the organization's accounting record will not match the amount shown in the bank statement for the period even though they might all be correct.

The essence of the bank statement reconciliation is to bring the organization's bank statement balance into equality with the cash balance per the books. Adjustments are made to the bank balance by adding or deducting information shown in the cash balance per the books but not yet handled by the bank. In general, bank omissions will be deposits in transit and outstanding cheques.
Bank reconciliation is carried out in steps. It is made in two parts leading to an adjusted bank balance and also an adjusted book balance. These balances should become equal. Exhibit 12.2 shows a format for bank reconciliation.

Exhibit 12.2 **Format for bank reconciliation**

| **Bank reconcilation** | | | **Date** |

Ending balance per bank statement
+ Deposits in transit
− Outstanding cheques
= **Adjusted bank balance**

Ending balance per books
+ Unrecorded interest earned
− Unrecorded bank service charges
− Unrecorded withdrawals
− Unrecorded cheques with insufficient
 funds
± Bookkeeping errors
= **Adjusted book balance**

List of outstanding cheques

Date issued	Cheque number	Amount
	Total	

The ± bookkeeping errors in the format (exhibit 12.2) are explained as follows:

- Deduct the amount if the cheque actually issued is more than the amount recorded in the chequebook
- Add the amount if the cheque actually issued is less than the amount recorded in the chequebook
- Deduct the amount if the deposit entered in the books is more than the amount in the bank statement
- Add the amount if deposit entered in the books is less than the amount in the bank statement

To illustrate how the bank reconciliation is carried out, the following example is provided:

The Red Herring Restaurant has received its bank statement for the month ending July 31st 2009, which shows the following:

Ending balance	€	15,156.30
Service charge	€	10.15
Insufficient funds cheque	€	40.00

Upon verifying the accounting records, the accountant notes that:

The 31st July current account balance in their books is €14,556.45. A deposit of €1,050.00 made on Friday, July 31st is not showing on the bank statement. Three cheques of €550.00, €840.00 and €310.00 issued respectively on July

28th 2009, July 29th 2009, and July 30th 2009 with numbers 147856, 147857, and 147858 do not also feature in the bank statement. The completed bank reconciliation of the Red Herring Restaurant for July 31st 2009 will look as in exhibit 12.3:

Exhibit 12.3 **Bank reconciliation – Red Herring Restaurant July 31st 2009**

Red Herring Restaurant
Bank reconciliation – July 31st 2009

Ending balance per bank statement		€	**15.156,30**
Deposits in transit	plus	€	1.050,00
Outstanding cheques	less	€	1.700,00
Adjusted bank balance	equals	€	**14.506,30**
Ending balance per books		€	**14.556,45**
Unrecorded bank service charges	less	€	10,15
Unrecorded cheques with insufficient funds	less	€	40,00
Adjusted book balance	equals	€	**14.506,30**

List of outstanding cheques

Date issued	Cheque number		Amount
28-07-2009	147856	€	550,00
29-07-2009	147857	€	840,00
30-07-2009	147858	€	310,00
Total		**€**	**1.700,00**

Note that the Red Herring Restaurant's adjusted bank balance is now exactly equal to the adjusted book balance, and this is all that bank reconciliation is about.

Glossary

Accounting controls – these are those controls that are meant to safeguard the assets and ensure the accuracy and reliability of the accounting data of the company

Administrative controls – these are those controls that are meant to promote the operational efficiency as well as encourage adherence to the company's managerial policies.

Bank reconciliation – this is an internal control activity of bringing together the cash balance in the company's bank statement with the cash balance according to the accounting records within the company.

Detective controls – these are those controls that are designed to discover errors or irregularities after they have occurred as well as monitor preventive controls.

Organizational chart – this is a chart showing the lines of communication and levels of authority and responsibility within an organization.

Preventive controls – these are those controls that are designed to discourage errors or irregularities.

Multiple choice questions

12.1   Which one of the following managerial accounting functions is used to encourage the observation of management's policies?
a   accounting controls
b   administrative controls
c   capital budgeting
d   operations budgeting

12.2   Which one of the following internal control tools lists the details of each position, saying how and when to carry out each activity?
a   organization charts
b   job descriptions
c   division of duties
d   none of the above

12.3   In an internal control system, the primary purpose of splitting responsibilities in related transactions is to:
a   bond the members of the personnel
b   evaluate the results, forms and reports
c   prevent any employee from having too much control over the assets
d   rotate the members of the personnel

12.4   Which of the following is not an effective procedure for controlling cash receipts?
a   define criteria for the use of petty cash
b   limit access to cash
c   provide a secure storage area
d   train appropriate personnel

12.5   The principal purpose of bank reconciliation is to:
a   control cash forecasts
b   control the cashier
c   equalize cash balances
d   restrict access to the bank

Exercises

12.1   Classify the actions listed below into their control types (accounting or administrative, as well as preventive or detective) and explain the reasons for your selection. There is the possibility of a control action having dual functions.

	Accounting or Administrative	Preventive or Detective
Cash receipts are deposited on a daily basis		
Meat is stored in the cold store at the proper temperatures		
Supplier invoices are cross-checked each month with delivery statements		
Surprise checks by external auditors		
The internal auditor prepares the bank reconciliation at regular intervals		
The motel uses a cash register		
The time clock is in front of the manager's office		
The work of the housekeepers is checked by a supervisor		

12.2 Kristine van de Leeuw received last year the best housekeeper's award. Now, the general manager has offered to pay her the same rates as the hotel for her to work 6 hours weekly at his private residence during her time off work at the hotel. You are requested to critique this assignment handed to Kristine by the general manager.

12.3 The June 30th 2010 bank statement of the Blue Golf Café showed a balance of €22,556.30 with service charges of €75.42, unrecorded interests of €25.14 and an insufficient funds cheque of €480.00. The owner/manager notes that the balance in the café's books reads €25,706.58. A deposit of €5,420.00 made on Tuesday, June 29th 2010 is not showing on the bank statement. Three cheques of €1,340.00, €1,800.00 and €1,200.00 issued on June 28th 2010 with numbers 58404, 58405, and 58406 do not also feature in the bank statement. The internal records show that a withdrawal was made on Monday, June 21st by the owner/manager for an amount of €1,540.00.

Prepare the bank reconciliation of the Blue Golf Café for June 30th 2010

12.4 The March 31st 2010 bank statement of the Slippery Road Motel showed a balance of €17,589.00 with service charges of €38.12, and an insufficient funds cheque of €210.00. The accountant notes that the balance in the motel's books is €18,712.12. A deposit of €1,750.00 made on the evening of Tuesday, March 30th 2010 is not shown in the bank statement. Two cheques of €475.00 and €400.00 issued on March 29th and March 30th respectively with numbers 2341 and 2342 have also not been presented at the bank for payment.

Prepare the bank reconciliation of the Slippery Road Motel for March 31st 2010.

Forecasting

13

13.1   Nature and limitations of forecasting
13.2   Understanding historical data patterns
13.3   Approaches to forecasting
13.4   Selecting forecasting methods
13.5   Forecasting in hospitality industry practice

Forecasts are the financial documents that are used to update the operating budget of an organization. Forecasts are flexible and provide the possibilities open to the management to carry out modifications in the operating budget during the operating cycle. This permits the management to take into consideration changes caused by the economic and market conditions as well as adapting to current trends. Forecasts are used to update the budget so that it reflects current business levels and conditions. Forecasting involves using current information and combining this information with established ratios and formulas to estimate or project future business levels and operations. Forecasting is the key management tool used to plan the details of the daily operations in the very short term such as tomorrow, next week or next month. For example, weekly activity forecasts will be used to predict and develop weekly part-time employee schedules. In section 13.1 the nature and limitations of forecasting are discussed; while section 13.2 introduces the four main patterns in historical data. Section 13.3 introduces the two main approaches to forecasting, and the factors that determine the selection of forecasting methods are discussed in section 13.4. Section 13.5 closes the chapter with a brief discussion on the practically of forecasting within the hospitality industry.

13.1 Nature and limitations of forecasting

As an important management tool, it is necessary to understand the nature and limitations of forecasting. These can amongst others include the following:
- Forecasting deals with the future and the reliability of forecasting is generally inversely proportional to how far the future is from the time the forecast is made. Forecasting sales for the next day is generally easier to carry out than to forecast the sales for the next year. The further away the forecast period is from the date of the forecast, the greater will be the difficulty in making the forecast as well as the greater will be the possibility that the actual results will differ from the forecasted figures. It should be noted however that forecasts can always be revised as time goes by to take into consideration the changing circumstances.

- As forecasting is concerned with the future, it as such involves uncertainty. Managers in the hospitality industry face uncertainties in their daily management activities. Facing uncertainties then should not be a problem to them. This implies that management must gather all the required information available and make judgments based on such information. Mathematical forecasting cannot replace experience and individual judgment and are thus expected to play a greater role in management decision making.

- Most forecasting methods rely on historical data, which though they may not be good indicators of future activity are considered to be good starting points. Management should in such cases adjust the forecasts by using common sense, experience and good judgement as noted in the previous paragraph.

- The use of forecasting techniques generally leads to precise mathematical results that are only as good as the data that was used in establishing the forecasts in the first place. For example, if the forecast for occupied rooms are not good, then the forecast for housekeeping expenses will not be reliable.

- Since by their nature forecasts are generally less accurate than desired, the management of the organization should consider using more sophisticated forecasting models or tools when their costs are justified, carry out frequent updates of the forecasts, and also plan more carefully based on the forecasts.

- Most of the models used in forecasting do not consider variables that can be directly controlled by management. For example, a forecast of restaurant sales based on historic sales revenue will have to be adjusted in case the management has a planned marketing campaign during the period that will have a positive impact on their sales.

- Due to all the preceding factors, the organization's management must plan to cover for the deviations between the forecast and the actual result. They do this by automatically building in a deviation factor of as much as 10%. For example, if actual sales historically have exceeded forecasted sales by an average of 5%, then management should make all necessary provisions to cover such a deviation for the projected activity.

13.2   Understanding historical data patterns

Forecasting is based on the assumption that a pattern exists in the available historical information that can be used in determining the future forecasts. The job of the forecaster will then to try as much as possible to link this historical information with the most appropriate forecasting tool available in order to come up with the forecasts. Historical data can be plotted into a graph which will enable the underlying pattern to be recognized. Generally, four types of historical patterns can be recognized: seasonal, cyclical, trend, and random variations.

The seasonal pattern
The seasonal pattern exists when the series of data fluctuates in a regular direction according to a particular period. This period could be within a day (lunch as opposed to dinners); during the week (week days as opposed to weekends); during the month (weekly variations within the month caused for example by the spending patterns of the inhabitants of the area in relation to their income flows); as well as the year (high season as opposed to low season). Management should be able to factor in such seasonal variations in their forecasts.

The cyclical pattern
The cyclical pattern results from the recurring and fluctuating levels of activity that a business or economy will experience over a long period of time. The five stages of the business cycle are growth, peak, recession, trough and recovery. Due to their irregularity, frequency, magnitude and duration variations it is much more difficult to make forecasts based on the cyclical pattern. When plotted on a graph, it is similar to the seasonal pattern except for the length of the pattern.

The trend pattern
The trend is the overall projection of the long-term forecast of the activity that is being analyzed. Trends represent the general movement of a market or of an activity. This movement is either upwards or downwards. In general, it is best to move with the trends. This means that if the trend is upward, then forecasts should reflect that upward tendency and also caution should be exercised about making forecasts in situations where the trend is downward. Trends can vary in length from short, to intermediate, to long term.

Random variations
Historical data are also affected by random variations. Random variation simply indicates the absence of any pattern in the historical data. Statistical tools such as random factor analysis are normally used to try and understand if the outlying data is caused by an underlying trend or just simply a random event. If the random data is caused by an underlying trend, that trend will need to be addressed and remedied accordingly. For example, consider a random event such as a

volcano eruption. Sales of breathing masks may skyrocket, and if someone was just looking at the sales data over a multi-year period this would look like an outlier, but analysis would attribute this data to this random event.

These patterns can be placed for a visual effect in a graph, as shown in exhibit 13.1.

Exhibit 13.1 **Graphical representation of historical data patterns**

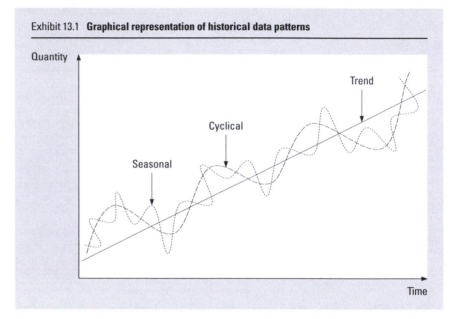

Exhibit 13.1 is a graphical representation of the seasonal, cyclical and trend historical data patterns (excluding randomness) showing how the three of them relate to each other when time and output are plotted on a graph. Time is plotted on the x-axis whereas quantity is plotted on the y-axis.

13.3   Approaches to forecasting

Forecasting is carried out in many different ways which range from very simple methods to very advanced methods. The simple approach, also called informal approach, is usually based on intuition and most of the time reserved for very limited and specific circumstances. Informal approaches involve the use of basic extrapolations of recent trends to make judgments on what the future outcome will be. The formal approaches can be sub classified into two major categories – the qualitative forecasting methods and the quantitative forecasting methods. For the purposes of this book, more emphasis will be placed on the use of quantitative methods but a brief review of some qualitative methods follows. The structure of the section is as follows:

13.3.1   Qualitative forecasting methods
13.3.2   Quantitative forecasting methods

13.3.1   Qualitative forecasting methods

Qualitative forecasting methods are based on the educated opinions of appropriate persons depending on the situation under analysis. The most common qualitative forecasting methods are:

The Delphi method
This is a forecasting method developed by a panel of experts who anonymously answer a series of questions; their answers are fed back to the panel of experts, who may then change their original responses until they arrive at a consensus on the future events as they would affect the organization's activities. Generally considered to be very time consuming and expensive but advances in groupware technology makes this method more and more feasible.

Market research
This is any organized effort to gather information about markets or customers. This is often carried out using panels, questionnaires, test markets, surveys, etc the outcomes of which will guide the management in making their decisions about their future activities. Market research is often differentiated from marketing research, which is the process of the systematic gathering, recording, and analysis of data about issues relating to the marketing of products and services. Marketing research is split into two sets of categorical pairs defined either by the target market (consumer or business) or by the method (qualitative or quantitative).

Product life-cycle analogy
In this method, the forecasts are made based on the life-cycles of similar products, services, or processes. The forecasts are estimated based on the position of the product in the four stages of its life-cycle – introduction, growth, maturity, or decline.

Expert judgment
This is generally an in-house forecasting method in which the experts or knowledgeable persons make the forecast. It can be split into two sub categories – the jury of executive opinion, and the sales force estimate. The jury of executive opinion will mean that the top executives within the organization prepare the forecasts. On the other hand, the sales force estimate is a bottom-up approach that brings together the forecasts of the various sales units and managers.

13.3.2   Quantitative forecasting methods

Quantitative forecasting methods are those forecasting methods that seek to predict the future outcomes based on the use of complex mathematical and statistical modelling, measurement and research. By assigning a numerical value to the variables, the forecasters try to come up with the possible future outcomes. Quantitative forecasting methods have some specific limitations. In the first instance, they cannot be used in the case of very limited or no available past data. Secondly, they are based on the assumption that past observed trends will continue. Quantitative forecasting methods are further divided into two sub categories, the time series approach and the causal approach which will now be briefly reviewed in this subsection as follows:

13.3.2.1   Time series forecasting methods
13.3.2.2   Causal forecasting methods

13.3.2.1   Time series forecasting methods

Time series forecasting methods are based on the analysis of historical data. A time series is a set of observations measured at successive times or over successive periods. It is assumed that past patterns in the data can be used to forecast future data points. For the purposes of this text, only the basic models will be looked into.

Naïve method

The naïve method is based on using a recently observed data as the basis of the forecast. This can be made simply by considering for example, the sales of yesterday or last month as a predictor for the sales of today or next month. This generally does not take into account the effect of seasonality. Seasonality can be taken into consideration if the forecast is made based on similar days or periods such as sales of low season periods used as predictors of the sales of the future low season periods.

Simple moving averages

Simple moving averages are made in the desire to eliminate as much as possible the effects of randomness. In this model, the forecast is based on the arithmetic mean of a given number of past data points. In this model, the forecast is made by calculating an average of actual data from a specified number of prior periods. With each new forecast, the data from the oldest period is dropped and replaced with the data of the most recent period; thus, the data analyzed is constantly moving over time. The basic formula is

$$\text{Simple moving average} = \frac{\text{total for each of the previous } n \text{ periods}}{N}$$

in which
n represents the number of periods used in the moving average
N represents the total number of periods

The larger the number of periods used, the less likely it is that any random causes will affect the moving average. In this way, to make a monthly forecast, a 12-month moving average can be used. The 12 monthly figures for the past year are added together and then divided by 12. For example, suppose that for the past year a restaurant's monthly guest visits were as shown in exhibit 13.2.

The forecast for 13th month will be the sum of all the guests served in the last 12 months (18009) divided by the number of months (12).

$$\frac{18009}{12} = 1500.75$$

Exhibit 13.2 **Restaurant monthly guests' visits**

Month	Guests served
1	1444
2	1500
3	1192
4	1098
5	1388
6	1555
7	1682
8	1805
9	1862
10	1650
11	1445
12	1388

The result is 1500.75, and this can be rounded to 1501 guests expected to be served in the 13th month. At the end of the 13th month, a new moving average is calculated for the 14th month by deleting from the total guest count of the 1st month and including the guest count for the immediately past 13th month. This is an easy way of forecasting and updating the database is normally an easy task for hospitality operations.

If the actual guest visits for the 13th month were 1378, then the forecast for the 14th month will become:

$$\frac{18009 - 1444 \ (1^{st} \text{ month}) + 1378 \ (13^{th} \text{ month})}{12} = 1495.25$$

And this can equally be rounded to 1495 guests as forecast for the 14th month.

The primary limitation to this method is that it gives the same importance (or weight) to each of the data values gathered over the number of periods. This limitation is taken care of in the next models.

Weighted moving averages

Weighted moving averages are often used when adjustments to the general formula become needed. There is first of all the linearly weighted moving average, which is a type of moving average that assigns a higher weighting to recent data than does the simple moving average. This average is calculated by taking each of the data over the given time period and multiplying them by its position in the data series. Once the positions of the time periods have been accounted for, they are summed together and then divided by the sum of the number of time periods.

For example, in a 12-month linearly-weighted moving average, the last month's data is multiplied by 12, the previous month's by 11, and so on until month 1 in the period's range is reached and this last month is multiplied by one. These results are then added together and divided by the sum of the multipliers (12 + 11 + 10 + 9 + 8 + ... + 3 + 2 + 1 = 78). The linearly weighted moving average was one of the first responses to placing a greater importance on recent data. The popularity of this moving average has been diminished by the exponential moving average, but none the less it still proves to be very useful.

Secondly, there is the exponential moving average which is a type of moving average that is similar to the linearly weighted moving average, except that more weight is given to the latest data. The exponential moving average is also known as "exponentially weighted moving average". This type of moving average reacts faster to recent data changes than the linearly weighted moving average. Exhibit 13.3 shows forecasts for the 13th month based on the data in exhibit 13.2, and using both the linearly weighted moving average and the exponentially weighted moving average. Recalling that the real figures for the 13th month were 1378, see how much closer the exponentially weighted moving average forecast of 1483 is to the real figure compared to the other previously used methods in this chapter.

Exhibit 13.3 **Forecasting compared – linearly weighted moving average versus exponentially weighted moving average**

Month	Guests served	Linear weights	Guests × linear weights ÷ Total	Exponential weights	Guests × exponential weights ÷ Total
1	1,444	1	18.51	1	0.35
2	1,500	2	38.46	2	0.73
3	1,192	3	45.85	4	1.16
4	1,098	4	56.31	8	2.15
5	1,388	5	88.97	16	5.42
6	1,555	6	119.62	32	12.15
7	1,682	7	150.95	64	26.29
8	1,805	8	185.13	128	56.42
9	1,862	9	214.85	256	116.40
10	1,650	10	211.54	512	206.30
11	1,445	11	203.78	1024	361.34
12	1,388	12	213.54	2048	694.17
	Total	**78**	**Total**	**4095**	
		Forecast	**1,548**		**1,483**

Exponential smoothing
Exponential smoothing uses a smoothing constant and recent actual and forecasted activity to estimate the future activity. Exponential smoothing forecasting approaches are very useful only when reasonably accurate and short-term forecasts are required. There are several exponential smoothing methods and in this book, only the basic approach is illustrated. To calculate the smoothing constant in this basic case, only two types of readily available data are required: the forecasts from the two past periods, and the actual activity during the earlier of the past two periods.

$$\text{Smoothing constant} = \frac{\text{Period 2 forecast} - \text{period 1 forecast}}{\text{Period 1 actual data} - \text{period 1 forecast}}$$

The example below results in a smoothing constant of 0.33.

Period	Forecast	Actual Output
1	2490	2520
2	2500	
Smoothing constant		0.33

If the activities of the operation have been relatively stable in the last periods, then the smoothing constant will be generally small. If on the contrary, the activities are experiencing rapid growth, then the smoothing constant would be expected to be large.

Based on such a predetermined smoothing constant, forecasts for any preceding period can be determined using the following formula:

New forecast = past forecast + smoothing constant × (actual output in the past period – past forecast)

For example, assuming that in the table above, the actual output in period 2 was 2560 and using the smoothing constant of 0.33 the forecast for period 3 will be determined as follows:

Period 3 forecast = $2500 + 0.33(2560 - 2500) = 2520$

13.3.2.2 Causal forecasting methods

Causal forecasting methods are based on a known or recognized relationship between the factor to be forecast and other external or internal factors. Causal forecasting uses historical data on independent variables, such as promotional campaigns, economic conditions, and competitors' actions, to carry out the predictions. There are many different methods. The most commonly used is regression analysis (both simple and multiple) based on a mathematical equation that relates a dependent variable to one or more independent variables that are believed to influence the dependent variable. Secondly, econometric models are used and these are systems of interdependent regression equations that describe some sector of economic activity. Thirdly, there are the input-output models which describe the flows from one sector of the economy to another, and so predict the inputs required to produce outputs in another sector. Lastly is simulation modelling which is the manipulation of a model in such a way that it operates on time or space to compress it, thus enabling one to perceive the interactions that would not otherwise be apparent because of their separation in time or space. In this chapter only the basic simple linear regression analysis model will be presented.

Regression analysis

Regression analysis has already been introduced in chapter 9 (see 9.5.3). Simple linear regression analysis is illustrated using the data in exhibit 13.4 that is an extension of the hypothetical restaurant example in exhibit 13.2. New data related to the guests served who consumed wine during the months is now incorporated. With this data, the number of guests who will consume wines can be predicted based on the knowledge of the number of guests to be served in the period.

Exhibit 13.4 **Data set to illustrate simple linear regression forecasting**

Months	Guests x	Drank wine y
1	1444	930
2	1500	980
3	1192	775
4	1098	720
5	1388	900
6	1555	1010
7	1682	1100
8	1805	1150
9	1862	1220
10	1650	1080
11	1445	940
12	1388	980

Using the formula $y = a + bx$,
in which
y represents the guests who drank wine
x represents the number of guests served in the restaurant
a is the quantity of wine sold to guests who did not eat in the restaurant
b is the average wine consumption by the restaurant guests

Based on the data in exhibit 13.4, and carrying out the necessary calculations to determine "a" and "b" (done in this case using the Excel spreadsheet program), the regression equation becomes:

$$y = 38 + 0.63(x)$$

This formula indicates that 38 clients who did not dine in the restaurant bought wine every month, and that amongst those who were regularly served in the restaurant, 63 out of every 100 bought wine while dining.

Based on this equation and assuming that the forecast for the 13th month was 1483 restaurant guests, the forecast for those who will drink wine will be determined as follows:

Forecast for wine sales = $38 + 0.63(1483) = 972.29$ which can be rounded to 972.

While quantitative forecasting methods and techniques are widely used and, when used correctly, provide an effective and defensible method on which to base conclusions about the "reasonably-foreseeable" future, they are often data intensive and may require considerable effort to determine if they will be useful in any evaluation. In general, econometric and statistical techniques are most applicable on large-scale systems where large datasets can be easily obtained and individual events do not obscure broader trends. Although widely available desktop software packages can make the task of econometric and statistical analysis less time consuming, trained professional judgment is required to ensure that statistical measures are accurately applied, interpreted, and summarized.

13.4 Selecting forecasting methods

The main objectives for any organization to select a forecasting method should be based on the need to maximize the accuracy of the forecasts and also to minimize the bias related to using the method. With this in mind, and as concerns time series forecasting methods, it is necessary to select the method that will give the smallest bias; give the smallest mean absolute deviation; give the smallest tracking signal; and support the management's beliefs about the underlying patterns.

Additionally, other relevant factors to be considered while selecting a forecasting method include:

- The frequency with which the forecasts will be updated
- The turnaround required for the required forecast
- The size and complexity of the hospitality operation
- The forecasting skills of the people involved in the forecasting activities
- The purposes for which the forecasts are made

Studies show that the lowest forecasting errors result from the use of trend projections, moving averages, and regression analysis rather than judgmental methods. The forecasting method used should not be the issue, but how effective the forecasts are and their practical value in the operation. In a small hospitality operation that can adapt quickly to changing circumstances, most forecasting will be done using simple methods, such as adjusting the sales for the coming month by a certain percentage increase or decrease over last year's or last month's, or by using the fairly simple moving average method. Larger enterprises will probably use more complex methods, such as regression analysis.

Even though the regression analysis method requires more work, it does not require tedious manual calculations because most calculators are programmed to perform the arithmetic once each series of X and Y variables have been entered. Spreadsheets can be used for budgeting, forecasting, and variance analysis. Once sales revenue forecasts have been completed, they can be used to help determine the quantities of items such as food and beverages to be purchased and when they should be purchased.

13.5   Forecasting in hospitality industry practice

Forecasting involves using current information and combining this information with established ratios and formulas to estimate or project future business levels and operations. These ratios are based on existing relationships between revenues and expenses. These ratios can be applied aggressively or conservatively depending on the current management strategy.

The income statement of the organization is the main focus of forecasting for hospitality managers as it presents the historical record of their day-to-day activities. In the forecasting process, the actual financial performances of the past are projected to the future through the development of an operations budget based on whatever forecasting method is used in the organization. Though not found in the income statements, forecasts are included in the internal management reports that are generally reviewed daily and weekly. This includes reviewing actual revenues and labour costs and comparing them to the forecast, the budget, and last year's figures. Any changes or differences are explained in variation reports called critiques.

The fact that weekly forecasts are not generally included in the monthly or accounting period income statement does not mean they are not important. It means that they are used primarily as an internal management tool to plan, operate, and analyze the daily and weekly operations. In fact, operations managers spend more time with the weekly financial information than with the income statement. This is because they use the forecasts daily in their operations, critique the variations daily and weekly, and make any necessary changes that will improve performance. Effectively using the weekly forecasts and other internal management reports generally leads to better financial performance on the monthly or period income statements.

Forecasting includes projecting future revenues and scheduling future expenses to maintain productivity and profit margins. The forecasting is primarily based on volumes as expressed in rooms sold or guests served. The amount of activity in a hotel or restaurant will require an established level of wages and other operating expenses to deliver the expected products and services. As business volumes increase, additional wages and operating expenditures will be necessary to properly deliver these expected levels of service. Likewise, when business levels decrease, these wage and operating expenses will also need to be reduced to maintain productivities and avoid unproductive waste in wage and operating costs. It is important for the operations managers to possess adequate forecasting skills that will enable them to adjust operating expenses with expected levels of business.

Glossary

Causal forecasting approaches – are forecasting approaches based on historical data in which there is the assumption that there is a recognized relationship between the dependent and independent variables.

Cyclical pattern – is that pattern that results from the recurring and fluctuating levels of activity that a business or economy will experience over a long period of time.

Delphi method – this is a qualitative forecasting method that involves a panel of expert who anonymously answer a series of questions in a continuous feedback system until they come to a consensus on the future events.

Exponential smoothing – this is a forecasting method that uses a smoothing constant and recent actual and forecasted activity to estimate the future activity.

Market research – this is a qualitative forecasting method that revolves around the organized gathering of information about markets or customers.

Naïve method – this is the most basic time series forecasting method in which a recently observed data is used as the basis of the forecast.

Product life-cycle analogy – this is a qualitative forecasting method in which the forecasts are made based on the life-cycles of similar products, services, or processes.

Qualitative forecasting methods – these are forecasting methods based on the educated opinions of appropriate persons and emphasize human judgment.

Quantitative forecasting methods – these are forecasting methods that try to predict future outcomes based on the use of mathematical and statistical modelling, measurement and research.

Seasonal pattern – is that pattern that exists when the series of data fluctuates in a regular direction according to a particular period.

Simple moving averages – these are forecasts made by calculating an average of actual data from a specified number of prior periods. With each new forecast, the data from the oldest period is dropped and replaced with the data from the most recent period.

Smoothing constant – this is a value used in exponential smoothing that is determined by using forecasts from two consecutive past periods and the actual data from the earlier of these two periods.

Time series forecasting methods – these are forecasts methods that are based on the analysis of historical pattern assuming that past patterns can be used to predict future outcomes.

Trend pattern – is that pattern that represents the overall projection of the long term forecasts of the activity that is being analyzed.

Weighted moving averages – these are forecasts made by introducing weights to moving averages.

Multiple choice questions

13.1 Which one of the following statements about forecasting is true?
   a advanced forecasting methods produce results that are more reliable than desired
   b as forecasting is about the future, historical data are useless
   c forecasting is about certainty
   d the reliability of forecast is inversely proportional to how far the future is from the time the forecast is made

13.2 Which of the following types of patterns would be noticed if a graph showing fluctuations in a business, which were consistent from year to year during the same period of the year?
   a cyclical pattern
   b random variations
   c seasonal pattern
   d trend pattern

13.3 Which of the following is a quantitative forecasting method?
   a market research
   b naïve method
   c product life-cycle analogy
   d the Delphi method

13.4 The Starfish diner uses a four-week moving average approach to forecast its dinner sales. If sales for the last four weeks were €21,400, €23,600, €22,700, and €24,300, what would be the sales forecast for the next week?
   a €22,500
   b €22,750
   c €23,000
   d €24,000

13.5 The Sizzling Café forecasted sale of 2,700 and 2,600 muffins respectively for periods one and two. The actual sale of muffins in period one was 2,600. Calculate the smoothing constant that the Sizzling Café should use to forecast its sale of muffins for the next period.
   a 0.5
   b 1
   c 1.5
   d 2

Exercises

13.1 The Pizzeria Italia forecasts its pizza sales based on the monthly pizza sales of the previous year adjusted by a 2% monthly growth rate. The current average prices per pizza are €0.75 higher than the prices practiced in the previous year. The Pizzeria Italia's sales during the last four months of 2010 were as follows:

Month	Pizzas sold	Average price
September	14500	€ 6.55
October	15200	€ 6.35
November	15950	€ 6.85
December	14700	€ 6.90

Forecast their pizza sales of for the last four months of 2011

13.2 The Sandy Beach Hotel's revenues during 2010 are shown below. It is common knowledge that the accountants of the hotel use exponential moving averages as a forecast tool. You are asked to provide their forecast for the first month of 2011.

Months	Revenues
January	€ 2,234,691.50
February	€ 2,153,904.00
March	€ 2,281,956.50
April	€ 2,275,976.50
May	€ 2,479,860.00
June	€ 2,419,726.50
July	€ 2,129,765.50
August	€ 2,072,300.00
September	€ 2,377,176.50
October	€ 2,482,160.00
November	€ 2,318,538.00
December	€ 1,902,226.50

13.3 The number of guests and the number of persons who took breakfast at the Europa Hotel in 2010 are as shown below:

Months	Guests	Breakfasts served
January	2,525	2,950
February	2,400	2,525
March	2,750	3,175
April	2,725	3,075
May	3,025	3,375
June	2,975	3,200
July	2,875	3,200
August	3,000	3,350
September	2,950	3,150
October	2,850	3,125
November	2,525	2,875
December	2,275	2,513

You are required to:

a determine the regression equation that can be used to forecast the number of persons who will take breakfast based on the number of hotel guests.

b forecast the number of persons who will take breakfast in January 2011 if they expect to have 2600 guests.

13.4 The accountant at the 100-room Afilen Hotel has developed regression equations to forecast restaurant sales based on the number of expected guests. The monthly equations are as follows:

Breakfast – Forecast meals = 680 + 0.75 guests
Lunch – Forecast meals = 850 + 1.40 guests
Dinner – Forecast meals = 1250 + 0.51 guests

The expected occupancy for the month of December 2010 is 75% and their expected multiple occupancy is 35%. The average food service cheque per meal period is as follows:

Breakfast   €10.50
Lunch   €18.75
Dinner   €23.50

You are requested to calculate the restaurant's forecast meal period sales, both in number of guests as well as in revenues for December 2010.

Budgeting and variance analysis

14.1   **The budget and the budget process**

14.2   **Objectives of budgeting**

14.3   **Approaches to budgeting**

14.4   **Types of budgets**

14.5   **Variance analysis**

The operating budget is a business plan that has been converted into monetary terms. Such a plan can be the forecasted revenue and related expenses for the next months. The budget could also be in non-monetary terms, such as the number of house-keeping staff needed next week. A business that does not have a budget or a plan will make decisions that do not contribute to the profitability of the business because managers lack a clear idea of the goals of the business. Forecasting (see chapter 13) and budgeting systems are expected to reflect realistic expectations. However, in real practice, differences will arise between actual and projected performances. It is thus necessary that the budgeting process should include control systems that permit immediate feedback for corrective actions to be taken within organizations. Section 14.1 defines the budget and introduces the budget process. Section 14.2 highlights the objectives of budgeting. In section 14.3, different approaches to budgeting are illustrated, while section 14.4 defines the various types of budgets and section 14.5 discusses the variance analysis.

14.1 The budget and the budget process

The budget is a listing of the amount of all estimated revenues which a company expects to receive as well as a listing of all the related costs and expenses that will be incurred in obtaining the estimated revenue during a particular period of time.

The budget helps:
- To provide organized estimates of future unit sales, sales revenues, expenses, net income, staffing requirements, or equipment needs, broken down by operating period and department.
- To provide management with both short-term and long-term goals; this can be used to plan all future activities.
- To provide information for control so that the actual results can be evaluated against the budget plans and in case of differences, adjustments are made to correct the situation

The budgeting process is essentially about planning for the future. Planning can be split into three types:

Long-range planning (also referred to as strategic planning)
Long range planning is about providing long-term vision and goals to the organization. It is a planning process that attempts to coordinate the use of resources over time. Such plans could include making decisions about future expansion or the creation of new markets and products.

Operational planning
Operational planning is a sub-set of long-range planning. The operational plan describes short-term ways of achieving milestones and explains how, or what portion of, a strategic plan will be put into operation during a given operational period. An operational plan is the basis for, and justification of an annual operating budget request. A good operational plan should contain: clear objectives; activities to be delivered; quality standards; desired outcomes; staffing and resource requirements and implementation timetables.

Project planning
Project planning covers the detailed activities on how to accomplish a given project such as opening a new catering outlet. Project planning is part of project management, which relates to the use of schedules such as Gantt charts to plan and subsequently report progress about the project. Good project planning involves the following steps: scope definition; determination of methods to complete the project; creation of a work breakdown structure; identification of the critical paths using activity network diagrams; and the estimation and allocation of the related revenues and expenses. Once established and agreed, the plan becomes known as the baseline which is used to measure the project's progress.

14.2 Objectives of budgeting

A budget serves five main purposes – communication, coordination, planning, control, and evaluation.

Communication
In the budgeting process, managers in every department justify the resources they need to achieve their goals. They explain to their superiors the scope and volume of their activities as well as how their tasks will be performed. The communication between superiors and subordinates helps affirm their mutual commitment to company goals. In addition, different departments and units must communicate with each other during the budget process to coordinate their plans and efforts.

Coordination
Different units in the company must also coordinate the many different tasks they perform. For example, the number and types of packages to be marketed must be coordinated between the service and revenue centres to ensure that the tasks are all performed appropriately.

Planning
A budget is the plan for the operations of an organization for a period of time. Many decisions are involved, and many questions must be answered. Old plans and processes are questioned as well as new plans and processes. Managers decide the most effective ways to perform each task. They ask whether a particular activity should still be performed and, if so, how. Managers ask what resources are available and what additional resources will be needed.

Control
Once a budget is finalized, it is the plan for the operations of the organization. Managers have authority to spend within the budget and responsibility to achieve revenues specified within the budget. Budgets and actual revenues and expenditures are monitored constantly for variations and to determine whether the organization is on target. If performance does not meet the budget, action can be taken immediately to adjust activities. Without constant monitoring, a company does not realize it is not on target until it is too late to make adjustments.

Evaluation
One way to evaluate a manager is to compare the budget with actual performance. Did the manager reach the target revenue within the constraints of the targeted expenditures? Of course, other factors, such as market and general economic conditions, affect a manager's performance. Whether a manager achieves targeted goals is an important part of managerial responsibility.

14.3   Approaches to budgeting and types of budgets

There are various approaches to budgeting and whichever one is used in the organization, for the sake of consistency, it should be maintained. It can be changed if the management has reasons to do so, but such a change should be adequately disclosed. Summarily, these are some of the common approaches to budgeting:

Fixed or static budgeting approach

The term static budget refers to the budget total that is set at the beginning of a budgeting period and that is geared to only one level of activity – the budgeted level of activity. The static budget is appropriate for the budgeted level of activity but is not realistic for other levels of activity, especially in cases where variable costs are significant. If activity is 5% higher than budgeted, then some costs are likely to be 5% higher than budgeted as well. The budget total is usually divided into 12 equal parts for the months of the year.

The primary weakness of this type of budgeting is that it does not allow for monthly or seasonal variations. For example, suppose the rooms' department budget in a hotel is based on the average year-round rooms' occupancy of 75%. Operating costs (e.g., payroll, supplies, linen, and laundry) are based on this level of occupancy. If actual occupancy dropped to 70% because of unforeseen economic conditions, it might be difficult for the rooms' department manager to know, in the short run, what the new payroll level should be. The same is true for all other expenses. Despite the fact that this is the simplest type of budget to determine, most managers feel it is too difficult to compare, evaluate and relate to department's actual performance since it does not allow for variations in levels of activity.

Flexible budgeting approach

A flexible budget is prepared based on several levels of activity within the relevant range and it is used to plan and control spending. The flexible budget will show the cost formula for each variable cost and total cost (possibly including fixed costs) at all the predetermined levels of activity. The relevant range of activity represents the range of volume or production from a low level to a higher level. For example, the rooms department sales revenue could be forecasted at several levels such as 55%, 65%, and 75% occupancy levels (or as many levels as are appropriate). As the actual year progresses, it can be determined at which level the operation is going to fit best, and the appropriate expense levels will have already been determined for this level. In such situations, adjustments are much more easily made.

The two primary disadvantages of the flexible budgeting approach is that it requires more preparation and maintenance time and that it establishes a range of activities instead of pinpointing the actual volume of activity.

Variable budgeting approach

The variable budgeting approach permits managers to directly link the budget plans to the actual performance volumes. This is done through the establishment of various formulas to enable the generation of a control budget directly related to the actual performance volumes. This is done by using predetermined standards or budgeted rates and multiplying these rates by the actual volume, which helps in eliminating variances that may be caused by volume differences. The variable budgeting approach requires that all the costs elements are properly identified into one of the following three categories – fixed, variable or mixed. The variable budgeting approach is effective in departments in which it is difficult to budget work load volumes such as in the F & B department, but is less effective in departments that have relatively fixed or routine output volumes such as in housekeeping or property operations and maintenance. The variable budgeting approach can be a very effective management tool but it also requires lots of preparation, maintenance time and cost.

Incremental budgeting approach

The incremental budgeting approach assumes that for most functions, the base budget of the prior year is generally representative of base needs in the current year. In this case, last year's budget is used as a starting point for the new budget. To this base budget, a certain number of pre-programmed increases are then made based on such elements like the expected inflation, changes in salary levels, and the expected variations in the overall market situation. This approach to budgeting is steady in nature, characterized by gradual changes which are clearly visible. It is easy to synchronize between different other budgetary documents. The approach is simple and easily comprehensible, and helps the managers to operate consistently in their individual departments. Some of the major drawbacks to this approach include the assumption that the current methodology and cost structure is the way forward, and it encourages a "spend it or lose it" attitude. An incremental budget tends to become obsolete quickly, when it does not associate with the existing activity level, as well as any changes in the resource priorities, from those which are originally set, tend to create discontent and confusion

Kaizen budgeting approach

Kaizen is a very simple concept, formed from two Japanese characters: "kai", meaning "change"; and "zen", meaning "good". Therefore, "kaizen", means, "change for the better", or "continuous improvement". The creator of the concept of kaizen, or continuous improvement, was Dr. W. Edwards Deming. The kaizen budgeting approach explicitly incorporates continuous improvement during the budget period into the budget numbers. The approach is based on analyzing every part of a process down to the smallest detail, seeing how every part of the process can be improved, looking at how employees' actions, equipment, and materials can be improved and lastly looking at ways of saving time and reducing waste. Kaizen is based on the belief that the people doing a particular job will often know better than everyone else, including their superiors, how that job can be improved; and that they should be given the responsibility for making those improvements. The emphasis in the kaizen budgeting approach is on many small improvements, rather than on quantum leaps. The budget numbers are based on changes that are yet to be implemented, rather than on current practices or methods. For example the cleaning time per room could be budgeted in this approach as follows:

Budgeted cleaning time per room
1st quarter 2010: 28 minutes
2nd quarter 2010: 27 minutes
3rd quarter 2010: 26 minutes
4th quarter 2010: 25 minutes

The effects of these reduced labour times would result in corresponding reductions in the labour expense which is one of the primary cost drivers in the rooms department. Unless the kaizen goals are met, the actual hours will exceed the budgeted hours in the latter quarters of the year. Managers will explore reasons for not meeting these goals and will make the necessary adjustments to meet these goals. The success of the kaizen budgeting approach depends not only on achieving the numbers, but also on delivering the anticipated improvements.

Zero-base budgeting approach
Zero-base budgeting is an approach that requires each manager to justify the entire budget request in detail and places the burden of proof on the manager to justify why authorization to spend any money at all should be granted. It starts with the assumption that zero will be spent on each activity – thus the term "zero-base". What a manager is already spending is not accepted as the starting point. Managers are asked to prepare for each activity or operation under their control a "decision package" that includes an analysis of costs, alternative courses of action, measures of performance, and expected benefits. The zero-base budgeting approach claims that in building the budget from zero, two types of alternatives should be considered by managers:

· different ways of performing the same activity, and
· different levels of effort in performing the activity

Success in implementing zero-base budgeting requires linkage of zero-base budgeting to the long range planning process, sustained support and commitment from executive management, innovation among the managers who make up the budget decision packages, sale of the procedure to the employees who must perform the work necessary to keep the concept vigorous. Sound budgeting procedure should always require a careful evaluation of all operating facts each time the budget is prepared. Zero-base budgeting procedure is new and unique, mainly in the approach rather than in the basic planning and control philosophy. It is built on the concept that what one expects in the future will be dependent on the ability to persuade the rest of the management team that it is deserved.

Some advantages of the zero-base budgeting approach are:
· results in an efficient allocation of resources
· encourages managers to find out cost effective ways to improve operations

- detects inflated budgets
- is useful for service department where the output is difficult to identify
- increases staff motivation by providing greater initiative and responsibility in decision making
- increases communication and coordination within the organization
- identifies and eliminates wastage and obsolete operations

Some its disadvantages are:

- that managers are forced to justify every detail related to expenditure
- that it is difficult to implement using spreadsheets
- that it is very time-consuming
- that it is necessary to train managers at all levels on the concept otherwise it cannot be successfully implemented
- that it is difficult to administer and communicate the budgeting process because more managers are involved in the process

Activity-based budgeting approach

The activity-based budgeting approach, which is also known as the performance-based budgeting approach focuses on the budgeted cost of activities necessary to produce and sell products and services. In this approach, the construction of the budget recognises the fact that all costs in the business are generated by the activities of the business. Activity-based budgeting is an important element of activity-based management that developed from the first approaches to activity-based costing. Activity-based management is based on the premise that since people are involved in activities, and activities consume resources, the control of activities allows the control of costs at their sources. Activity-based budgeting thus provides an understanding of the linkages between the drivers behind the activities. The desire is then to control the cost drivers. For each identifiable activity, the cost of a unit is measured, the demand is measured, a budgeted cost is set for each unit of activity, and the budget is designed around activity terms. The approach involves forecasting workloads of business processes (activities) and expressing them in financial terms to improve performance and achieve specific goals. This approach allows for identification of value-adding activities as well as their impact on key performance indicators (KPIs).

Some advantages of the activity-based budgeting approach are it:

- permits managers to recognize the horizontal flow of products, services and activities within the organization
- ensures an optimum allocation of scarce resources in the organization
- allows managers to focus on those activities that might offer opportunities for cost savings
- allows managers to assign costs to activities rather than averaged over a number of products or services
- permits the analysis of the real cost drivers that might lead to better cost focus and targeted customer pricing

Some of its disadvantages are that:

- much effort is required in order to measure and analyse the activities
- it assumes that activities are linked across departments forming cross-functional processes
- it assumes a causal and linear relationship between the activities and the overhead costs which might be erroneous since many factors may drive the costs such as the sharing of costs amongst the activities and the methods used in cost allocation

14.4 Types of budgets

Hospitality operations have different kinds of budgets (operations budget, capital budget, department budgets (profit and service centres), cash budget as well as the master budget just to name a few). Budgets can generally be either long-term or short-term. A long-term budget would be a plan for a period beyond 1 year to about 5 years. Such long-term budgets are also called strategic budgets. Short-term budgets could be for a day, a week, a month, a quarter, or a year. Brief explanations of the various types of budget follow.

Operations budgets
An operations budget, also called the revenue and expense budget, is the management's plans of generating revenues and incurring expenses over a specific period. For example, the revenue forecast of a motel for a month.

Capital budgets
A capital budget is a plan for the acquisition of new – as well as the replacement of old – plant, property and equipment. For example, the five years' development plans to increase the number of rooms in a property.

Department budgets
A department budget contains the planned activities of a single department. For revenue and profit centres, the department budget will include all its planned revenues as well as planned expenses for the given period as the case may be. With service centres on the contrary, the department budget will only show the projected expenses for the given period. Department budgets are normally prepared for a year and then sub-divided into months.

Cash budgets
A cash budget (also called cash flow budget) is the forecast of future cash receipts and expenditures for a particular time period, generally in the short term. It helps managements to determine when revenues will be sufficient to cover expenses and when the company will need to seek outside financing.

Master budgets

After all the organization's objectives, goals and strategies have been identified, the master budget is developed to express the plans in monetary terms. It is the most comprehensive of all budgets and it serves as a tool for communication and coordination within the organization. It is generally prepared for a year. An illustration of the interconnections between the various budgets within the master budget of a mid-sized hotel is shown in exhibit 14.1

Exhibit 14.1 **Parts of the master budget of a hospitality organization**

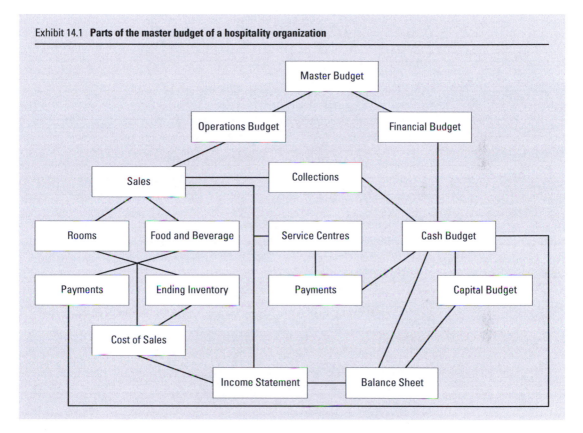

Exhibit 14.1 brings out clearly the two main parts within the master budget: the operations budget and the financial budget. The operations budget begins with the sales budget and ends with the budgeted income statement. The financial budget includes the capital budget along with the cash budget and the budgeted balance sheet. Collections and payments link the operations and financial budgets together along with all the budgeted changes in balance sheet accounts.

In very small owner-operated operations, the budget will be prepared by the owner with or without an external accounting helper. At this level the budget might be a written plan or an unwritten mental plan of the owner. In larger operations, many individuals get involved in the budget preparation process (department managers and their employees). In very organized bottom-up operations, a budget committee will exist consisting of the department managers, the financial controllers, and the general manager who gives the final approval. The committee coordinates the preparation of the budget to ensure that the final budget package is meaningful.

14.5 Variance analysis

A variance is the difference between a budgeted amount and the actual amount. A variance is considered to be either favourable or unfavourable. A favourable variance is when the actual amount is better than the budgeted amount, and is considered unfavourable if the actual amount is worse than the budgeted amount. The structure of the section is as follows:

14.1.1   Identifying and attributing variances
14.1.2   Variance analysis overview
14.1.3   Analyzing variances to ascertain causes

14.5.1 Identifying and attributing variances

The method of determining if a variance is favourable or unfavourable depends on whether it is a sales item or an expense item. A sales variance is favourable if actual sales are greater than budgeted sales. An expense variance is unfavourable if actual expenses are greater than budgeted expenses. Exhibit 14.2 illustrates favourable and unfavourable variances and shows alternative ways of displaying the variances.

Exhibit 14.2 **Favourable and unfavourable variances and shows alternative display format**

Scenario 1:

	Budget	Actual	Variance	
Revenues	€ 150,000.00	€ 165,000.00	€ 15,000.00	favourable
Food Costs	€ 56,000.00	€ 51,000.00	€ 5,000.00	favourable
Interest Expense	€ 2,500.00	€ 3,200.00	€ 700.00	unfavourable

Scenario 2:

	Budget	Actual	Variance	
Revenues	€ 150,000.00	€ 142,000.00	€ 8,000.00	unfavourable
Food Costs	€ 56,000.00	€ 65,000.00	€ 9,000.00	unfavourable
Interest Expense	€ 2,500.00	€ 2,200.00	€ 300.00	favourable

Logic to determine variances:
More actual sales = favourable
More actual expenses = unfavourable

	Alternative Format to Display Budget Variances		
	Budget	Actual	Variance*
Revenues	€ 150,000.00	€ 165,000.00	€ 15,000.00
Food Costs	€ 56,000.00	€ 51,000.00	€ 5,000.00
Interest Expense	€ 2,500.00	€ 3,200.00	(€ 700.00)

* Positive numbers indicate a favourable variance. Negative numbers indicate an unfavourable variance

There are no uniform rules for showing favourable and unfavourable variances. Companies may use different terms to reflect variance conditions. For instance, the label "better" might be used to indicate a favourable variance and the label "worse" used to indicate an unfavourable variance. One common practice is to show favourable variances as positive numbers and unfavourable variances as negative numbers (usually enclosed in parentheses).

14.5.2 Variance analysis overview

Due to the very simple and direct way that variance analysis has been illustrated in the text "Accounting for Hospitality Managers – Prof. Raymond Cote"; this section will adopt his approach in its entirety (with some little modifications). Merely knowing that a budget variance is favourable or unfavourable does not provide enough information to manage and control a hospitality operation. Even favourable variances (or no variances) might result from a hidden problem. A department manager should find out why a variance has occurred in order to manage the department efficiently and profitably while providing the level of guest service prescribed by company policy. Variance analysis is possible only if the supporting data used in preparing the budget has been retained and systematically indexed. For example, it is not enough to show that the budgeted revenue were €30,000.00 for a month. It is important to show in the working papers that a €30,000.00 revenue budget was computed using a €10.00 average food service cheque and 3,000 covers. Accurate variance analysis requires the maintenance of precise background data. A manager must properly interpret budget variances to perform appropriate corrective action. Variances occur because no budgeting method or procedure can precisely predict the future. An experienced hospitality manager generally recognizes which variances, large or small, should be investigated.

Generally, a revenue variance is due to price, quantity, or both. Price is the product selling price such as average room rate or average food service cheque. Quantity is the revenue volume stated in units, such as rooms or covers. Variance analysis might show that a favourable revenue variance is not necessarily a positive thing if actual revenues are higher because of price increases coupled with lower customer volume. Higher prices might turn customers away, beginning an unfavourable trend.

An unfavourable revenue variance might be due to a drop in customer volume or customers spending less because of economic conditions. Unfavourable rooms sales might result when too many rooms are out of order or an unrealistic average room rate is used in the forecasting process.

An expense variance is due to cost, quantity, or both. Cost is the unit purchase cost of an expense item. Again, quantity is the sales volume stated in units, such as rooms or covers.

A favourable expense variance could conceal future problems if the variance results from lower food cost due to buying lower quality or lower-than-expected payroll costs because of understaffing. Under-staffing could lead to diminished guest service. Lower purchase quality might be readily apparent to guests. These situations are critical to the success of any hospitality business because unsatisfied guests are not repeat guests.

An unfavourable expense variance could be due to overstaffing or staffing problems, excessive or unplanned overtime pay, and/or supplier cost increases. Finding the causes helps management take corrective action. The staffing and overtime problems might be due to unreliable staff or perhaps unsatisfactory supervision. Extraordinary supplier cost increases might be resolved by a meeting with the supplier or by a change in supplier.

14.5.3   Analyzing variances to ascertain causes

Several methods may be used to determine causes of variances. The uncomplicated procedures are just as precise as the sophisticated techniques. Since financial management is results oriented, a simple method is most satisfactory.

Price is related to a revenue variance, while cost is related to an expense variance. In either case, the quantity is always sales volume stated in covers, rooms, or other units of measurements. The same procedure can be used to determine the causes of revenue variances and expense variances: the formula merely interchanges the terms cost and price.

The acronym BAD PQ is used to aid your recall of the variance analysis procedure. This memory aid associates the letters BAD PQ with the following:
Budget
Actual
Difference (variance)
Price (or cost)
Quantity

The BAD PQ approach is formatted on the working paper as follows:
Price   Quantity
Budget
Actual
Difference

The next step involves entering the data in each field.
Price column:
Enter the budgeted unit selling price (or cost).
Enter the actual unit selling price (or cost).
Subtract the actual from the budgeted price (or cost).

Quantity column:
Enter the budgeted sales quantity (covers, rooms).
Enter the actual sales quantity (covers, rooms).
Subtract the actual from the budgeted quantity.

The causes of the variance may now be determined as follows:

Price difference × actual quantity = price cause
Quantity difference × budgeted price = quantity cause
The total of these two causes must agree with the total variance on
the budgetary report.
Note that the rules of algebraic multiplication are followed in the
multiplication process, as follows:
A positive number × a positive number = a positive result
(favourable)
A positive number × a negative number = a negative result
(unfavourable)

Below is a demonstration of the variance analysis process.

Determining causes of a revenue variance
Assume a rooms department monthly departmental budgetary report
shows, in part, the following:

	Budget	Month Actual	Difference	
Revenues	€ 195,000.00	€ 206,500.00	€ 11,500.00	Favourable
Guest supplies expense	€ 6,000	€ 6,195	€ 195	Unfavourable

At first glance, the favourable revenue variance might seem to
indicate that there is no need to analyze the variance. This example
will reveal that even favourable variances might conceal a weakness
that requires corrective action.

The manager's budget preparation working papers and current actual
statistics from the accounting department are shown in exhibit 14.3.

The revenue data from the manager's budgetary working papers and
from the accounting department are then entered (using the BAD PQ
format) as shown in exhibit 14.4.

The actual data is subtracted from the budgeted data to arrive at the
differences. The differences need to be labelled as favourable or
unfavourable, depending on whether revenue or expenses are
analyzed. When revenues are analyzed, the following logic is used:

Exhibit 14.3 **Manager's budget preparation working papers and accounting department statistics**

Information from manager's budget working papers

Revenue Forecast Computation:

Average Room Rate:	€	65.00
Rooms Sold		3,000
Budgeted Revenue:	€	195,000.00

Guest Supplies Expense Budget Computation:

Rooms Sold:		3,000
Unit Cost:	€	2.00
Budgeted Guest Supplies	€	6,000.00

Current Month's statistics reported from the accounting department:

Average Room Rate:	€ 70
Rooms Sold	2,950 (€70 × 2,950 = €206,500
Guest Supplies Unit Invoice Cost:	€2.10 (€2.10 × 2,950 = €6,195)

Exhibit 14.4 **Entering price and quantity data for revenue variance**

	Price		Quantity	
Budget	€ 65.00	ARR	3,000	Rooms Sold
Actual	€ 70.00		2,950	
Difference	€ 5.00	Favourable	50	Unfavourable

More customers than budgeted   = Favourable
Higher selling price than budgeted = Favourable

Exhibit 14.5 shows a mixed result. The price difference of €5.00 is favourable because the actual average room rate exceeded the budgeted rate. The quantity difference of 50 rooms is unfavourable because the actual rooms sold were fewer than those budgeted.

These differences are used to explain the price and quantity components of the total variance. Exhibit 14.5 shows the completed revenue variance analysis. The cause due to price is determined as follows (see next page).

Price cause	=	Price difference x actual quantity
	=	€5.00 × 2,950
	=	€14,750.00 favourable

The cause due to quantity is determined as follows:

Quantity cause	=	Quantity difference × budgeted price
	=	(50) × €65.00
	=	€(3,250.00) unfavourable

Exhibit 14.5 Completed revenue variance analysis

	Price			Quantity	
Budget	€ 65.00	ARR		3,000	Rooms Sold
Actual	€ 70.00			2,950	
Difference	€ 5.00	Favourable		50	Unfavourable

Determining the reasons for (causes of) the €11,500.00 Favourable Revenue Variance

Variance due to Price:

				Cause	
Price Difference	×	Actual Quantity	=	€ 14,750.00	Favourable Price
€5	×	65			

Variance due to Quantity:

Quantity Difference	×	Budgeted Price			
(50)	×	€ 65.00	=	€ (3,250.00)	Unfavourable Quantity

Total of causes	**€ 11,500.00**	**Favourable (net)**
Proof: Variance on Budgetary Report	€ 11,500.00	

Summary

Favourable variance due to Price	€ 14,750.00
Unfavourable variance due to Quantity	€ (3,250.00)
Net Favourable Variance	€ 11,500.00

The causes of the variance are then explained as follows:

Favourable variance due to price	€ 14,750.00
Unfavourable variance due to quantity	€ (3,250.00)
Net favourable variance	€ 11,500.00

The €11,500.00 favourable variance matches the revenue variance shown earlier on the budgetary report.

Determining causes of an expense variance

Referring again to the above rooms department monthly departmental budgetary report, it may seem at first glance that the small (€195.00) unfavourable guest supplies expense is compensated for by the significant favourable revenue variance. This example will again emphasize the importance of properly interpreting budgetary reports and carefully analyzing variances.

The manager's budget preparation working papers and current actual statistics from the accounting department were shown in exhibit 14.3. The data from the manager's budgetary working papers and from the accounting department is then entered as shown in exhibit 14.6.

Exhibit 14.6 **Entering cost and quantity data for expense variance**

	Cost		Quantity	
Budget	€ 2.00	Unit Cost	3,000	Rooms Sold
Actual	€ 2.10		2,950	
Diffenrence	€ (0.10)	Unfavourable	50	Favourable

Notice that the BAD PQ format has now been altered to BAD CQ. The change simply reflects the terminology used in an expense analysis. The actual data is then subtracted from the budgeted data to arrive at the differences. The differences must be labelled as favourable or unfavourable. When expenses are analyzed, the following logic is used:

More guests than budgeted   = Unfavourable
Higher unit purchase cost than budgeted   = Unfavourable

While more guests are desirable in a revenue analysis, a higher guest figure has an opposite effect on an expense analysis. More guests imply an increase to expense; any increase to revenue or profit is ignored when an expense variance is analyzed.

Exhibit 14.6 shows a mixed result. The cost difference of €0.10 is unfavourable because the actual unit purchase cost exceeded the budgeted unit cost. The quantity difference of 50 rooms is favourable because the actual rooms sold were less than those budgeted. (Contrary to a revenue analysis, a lower guest figure is favourable in an expense analysis.)

These differences are used to explain the price and quantity components of the total variance. Exhibit 14.7 shows the completed expense variance analysis.

The cause due to cost is determined as follows:

Cost cause   =   Cost difference × actual quantity
           =   €(0.10) × 2,950
           =   €(295.00) unfavourable

A negative number multiplied by a positive number produces a negative result, which is translated as unfavourable.

The cause due to quantity is determined as follows:

Quantity cause   =   Quantity difference × budgeted cost
              =   50 × €2.00
              =   €100.00 favourable

Exhibit 14.7 Completed expense variance analysis

	Cost			Quantity	
Budget	€ 2.00	Unit Cost		3,000	Rooms Sold
Actual	€ 2.10			2,950	
Difference	€ (0.10)	Unfavourable		50	Favourable

Determining the reasons for (causes of) the €195 Favourable Expense Variance

Variance due to Price:

				Cause	
Cost Difference	×	Actual Quantity	=	€ (295.00)	Unfavourable Cost
€5	×	65			

Variance due to Quantity:

Quantity Difference	×	Budgeted Price			
(50)	×	€ 2.00	=	€ 100.00	Favourable Quantity

Total of causes	€ (195.00)	**Unfavourable (net)**
Proof: Variance on Budgetary Report	€ (195.00)	

Summary

Unfavourable variance due to Cost	€	(295.00)
Favourable variance due to Quantity	€	100.00
Net Unfavourable Variance	€	(195.00)

The causes of the variance are then explained as follows:

Unfavourable variance due to cost €(295.00)
Favourable variance due to quantity €100.00
Net unfavourable variance €(195.00)

The €195.00 unfavourable variance matches the guest supplies expense variance shown on the budgetary report.

Glossary

Activity-based budgeting approach – is that budgeting approach that focuses on the budgeted costs of activities necessary to produce and sell products and services.

BAD CQ – this is an acronym for budget, actual, difference, cost, and quantity, used as a mnemonic aid in determining causes of sales and expense variances.

BAD PQ – this is an acronym for budget, actual, difference, price, and quantity, used as a mnemonic aid in determining causes of sales and expense variances.

Budget – is a listing of the amount of all estimated revenues which a company expects to receive as well as a listing of all the related costs and expenses that will be incurred in obtaining the estimated revenue during a particular period of time

Capital budget – is a plan for the purchase of new, as well as the replacement of old plant, property, and equipment.

Cash budget – is generally a short term plan of future cash, cash receipts and expenditures.

Department budget – is a plan that contains the details of the activities of a single department.

Fixed budgeting approach – is that approach that sets the budget total at the beginning of the period and which is geared to only one level of activity.

Flexible budgeting approach – is that approach that sets the budget on several levels of activity within the relevant range.

Incremental budgeting approach – is that budgeting approach that uses the prior year's budget as a base to which pre-programmed increases are made to take care of elements like inflation, salary changes and the overall market conditions.

Kaizen budgeting approach – is that budgeting approach that explicitly incorporates continuous improvements during the budget period into the budget figures.

Long-range planning – is the creation of long term vision and goals for an organization.

Master budget – is the overall budget within any organization that takes into account the entire organization's objectives, goals and strategies. It is an organization's main financial planning tool.

Operational planning – these are the short term ways of achieving the milestones within a strategic plan in a given operational period.

Operations budget – is the management's plan within a specific period related to all its revenues and expenses.

Project planning – this involves the detailed activities on how to accomplish a given project.

Static budgeting approach – see fixed budgeting approach

Strategic planning – see long-range planning

Variable budgeting approach – is that budgeting approach that permits managers to directly link the budget plans to the actual performance volumes.

Variance – this is the difference between a budgeted amount and the actual amount, and it can be either favourable or unfavourable

Variance analysis – this is the process of identifying and investigating causes of significant differences between the budgeted amounts and the actual amounts.

Zero-base budgeting – is that budgeting approach that requires managers to prepare a budget starting at zero and to justify why any authorization to spend money should be granted.

Multiple choice questions

14.1 One of the following activities does not form part of the main purpose of budgeting. Which one?
 a communication
 b coordination
 c evaluation
 d supervision

14.2 The operations budget is the management's plan in a specific period that relates to its:
 a cash inflows and cash outflows
 b plant, property and equipment
 c revenues and expenses
 d all of the above

14.3 Which of the following budgeting approaches incorporates continuous improvements in the budgeting process?
 a flexible budgeting approach
 b incremental budgeting approach
 c kaizen budgeting approach
 d variable budgeting approach

14.4 The budgeting approach that identifies and eliminates wastage and obsolete operations is:
 a activity-based budgeting approach
 b fixed budgeting approach
 c static budgeting approach
 d zero-base budgeting approach

14.5 In analyzing revenue variances the main logic is as follows:
 a higher selling price than budgeted is unfavourable
 b lower selling price than budgeted is favourable
 c more actual customers than budgeted is favourable
 d more actual customers than budgeted is unfavourable

Exercises

14.1 The Simba snack bar has 160 seats and operates 6 days every week excluding Mondays. The seat turnover and average food service cheques per meal period and days are as shown below:

	Seat turnover			Average food service cheque		
	Breakfast	Lunch	Dinner	Breakfast	Lunch	Dinner
Tuesday	1.20	1.00	0.50	€ 6.50	€ 10.50	€ 16.80
Wednesday	1.10	1.20	0.60	€ 7.40	€ 12.30	€ 17.40
Thursday	1.40	1.30	0.50	€ 7.20	€ 13.20	€ 18.60
Friday	1.30	1.20	0.60	€ 7.60	€ 12.80	€ 19.40
Saturday	0.60	1.00	0.90	€ 6.40	€ 12.70	€ 23.20
Sunday	0.80	0.50	0.90	€ 5.80	€ 10.80	€ 16.40

The snack bar generates extra revenues from the vending machines installed by external companies and for which they receive annual sums of €5,500.00. You are requested to determine the operating budget of the snack bar and show the details per meal period. Assume that the first day of the year is a Monday and there are 365 days in the year.

14.2 The 75-seat Safari Restaurant's weekly and per meal period seat turnover is as depicted in the following table:

	Seat turnover		
	Breakfast	Lunch	Dinner
Monday	1.26	1.05	0.53
Tuesday	1.16	1.26	0.63
Wednesday	1.47	1.37	0.53
Thursday	1.37	1.26	0.63
Friday	0.63	1.05	0.95
Saturday	0.84	0.53	0.95

The average food service cheques per meal period are €6.50 for the breakfasts, €11.50 for the lunches and €17.50 for the dinners. Determine the operating budget for the month of June 2010 knowing that the first day of the month was a Tuesday.

14.3 The management of the Hilltop Rest House are in the process of preparing their budget for the next year using flexible budgeting at four different levels of sales. The levels of sales are 65%, 75%, 85%, and 95% of their full capacity. At full capacity their revenues are €7,300,000. Use the following to draw up the flexible budget of the Hilltop Rest House for the next year at the four levels of activity:

Cots of sales	24.00%	
Fixed salary element	€ 450,000.00	
Variable salary element	28.00%	
Sales and marketing	2.00%	
POM & UC	1.50%	
Depreciation	€ 265,000.00	
Taxes	30.00%	on pre-tax income

14.4 Determine the causes of the following variance:

	Budget	Actual	Variance
Food sales	€48,000	€38,000	€10,000 unfavourable

Information from manager's budget working papers:

Sales forecast computation
Average cheque   €12.00
Covers   4,000

Current month's statistics reported from the accounting department:

Average cheque   €10.00
Covers   3,800

Capital investment decisions

15.1 Types of capital budgeting decisions
15.2 Basic methods for making investment decisions
15.3 Simple and compound interest
15.4 Process of discounting
15.5 Understanding factor tables
15.6 Discounted cash flow (DCF) methods
15.7 Incidence of taxes on DCF analysis
15.8 Choosing between projects

Businesses are created with the aim of existing forever. For this to become possible, the business must be able to earn profits over a period of years. In this case, short term gains might have to be sacrificed in the interest of long term goals. Decisions that involve the acquisition of equipment, land, buildings, and vehicles are examples of decisions that businesses will periodically have to make that have an influence on their cash flows. In the hospitality industry, the largest investments that are normally made will be about land or building acquisition. However these are not decisions that are made on a day-to-day basis. Whether the opportunity involves building a new hotel, modernizing an old one, or extending a hotel, money must be made available and spent on what might be called a 'capital investment' that is expenditure incurred now in order to produce a stream of benefits over a period of years which will, it is hoped, result in the firm being in a more favourable position. Capital investment decisions differ from operating decisions by reason of the nature of the expenditure and the length of time before the full effect of the decision is felt.

Capital investment decisions may concern the following:

- The acquisition or replacement of long-lived assets, such as buildings and equipment.
- The investment of funds into another firm from which revenues will flow.

- A special project which will affect the firm's future earnings capacity.
- The extension of the range of activities of the firm.

Capital investment decisions encompass two aspects of long-range profitability: first, estimating the future net increase in cash inflows or net savings in cash outflows which will result from the investment; and second, calculating the total cash outflows required to effect the investment. Section 15.1 introduces two main types of capital budgeting decisions managers are called to make, and in section 15.2 the basic methods for making investment decisions are introduced. This is followed by a review of simple and compound interest in section 15.3, before the discounting process is introduced in section 15.4. The use of basic factor tables is explained in section 15.5, to be followed by a review of the primary discounted cash flow (DCF) methods in 15.6. How taxes affect the DCF analysis is discussed in section 15.7, and using DCF analysis in making decisions about alternative projects is shown in section 15.8.

15.1 Types of capital budgeting decisions

Capital investment decisions involving cash inflows and outflows beyond the current year are called capital-budgeting decisions. Managers encounter two types of capital-budgeting decisions

Acceptance-or-rejection decisions
In acceptance-or-rejection decisions, managers must decide whether they should undertake a particular capital investment project. In such a decision, the required funds are available or readily obtainable, and management must decide whether the project is worthwhile. The remainder of this chapter will principally be about acceptance or rejection decisions.

Capital-rationing decisions
In capital-rationing decisions, managers must decide which of the several worthwhile projects makes the best use of limited investment funds. For example, a parent corporation may limit funds provided to a subsidiary corporation, or a corporation may limit funds provided to a division. Under capital rationing, the combination of projects with the highest net present value should be selected. Capital rationing is illustrated in exhibit 15.1 since this will be the only place in which it will be discussed.

Exhibit 15.1 considers five proposed projects and calculates several possible combinations and their NPV's (see 15.6.2). In exhibit 15.1, projects B and C are considered to be mutually exclusive and only €360,000.00 is available for the projects. The optimum combination is the projects A, B, and E, because this yields the highest combined NPV. Other feasible combinations result in a lower NPV. If the business has little cash, it may have to borrow in order to invest in capital assets and projects. Borrowing costs money in the form of

Exhibit 15.1 **Capital rationing – five proposed projects**

Project	Project Cost	NPV
A	€ 144,000.00	€ 72,000.00
B	€ 168,000.00	€ 48,000.00
C	€ 120,000.00	€ 36,000.00
D	€ 240,000.00	€ 96,000.00
E	€ 48,000.00	€ 24,000.00

Combination	Total Investment	Total NPV
A, B, & E	€ 360,000.00	€ 144,000.00
A, C, & E	€ 312,000.00	€ 132,000.00
A & B	€ 312,000.00	€ 120,000.00
A & C	€ 264,000.00	€ 108,000.00
C & D	€ 360,000.00	€ 132,000.00
D & E	€ 288,000.00	€ 120,000.00

regular interest payments, and of course, it cannot be infinitely expanded (there is a point, for both businesses and individuals, beyond which it is neither sensible nor practical to borrow more money). Whether finance comes from the existing resources or from outside the business, management is likely to have to face difficult decisions about which assets and projects are to be preferred.

Over time, as managers make decisions about a variety of specific programs and projects, the organization as a whole becomes the sum total of its individual investments, activities, programs, and projects. The organization's performance in any particular year is the combined result of all the projects under way during that year.

15.2   Basic methods for making investment decisions

In analysing investment decisions many of the important facts are unknown. The first action then is to try and reduce this uncertainty as must as possible before the decision is made. Secondly it will be necessary to make sure that all the data are correctly assessed and quantified. All of these known and unknown data are transformed into monetary terms which are then used in making the investment decision. There are three factors that affect investment decisions:

· The net amount of the investment required.
· The expected net cash inflows.
· The rate of return of the investment.

The basic methods of making investment decisions include the payback period, the accounting rate of return and the average rate of return. While these simple methods ignore the time value of money (see 15.4) they are quick and simple to use.

Payback method

This method attempts to forecast how long it will take for the expected net cash inflows to pay back the net investment outflows. The payback period is calculated as follows:

$$\text{Payback period (years)} = \frac{\text{Net investment outflows}}{\text{Average net cash inflows}}$$

To illustrate the payback period assume that the Golden Nugget Restaurant is considering the purchase of new kitchen equipment that will reduce labour cost. In the first scenario, the basic investment data are the following:

Exhibit 15.2 **Investment data of the Golden Nugget Restaurant showing annuities**

Net investment outflows	€ 75,000.00
Estimated annual cash savings	€ 20,000.00
Estimated useful life	6 years
Salvage value	nil

In exhibit 15.2, the estimated annual cash savings are the same for all the years (called annuities). The payback period is calculated as follows:

$$\text{Payback period} = \frac{€75,000.00}{€20,000.00}$$

= 3.75 years or to be more exact 3 years 9 months

In this first scenario the Golden Nugget Restaurant will recover its investments in 3 years 9 months.
Now assume that the estimated cash savings were not the same for all the years such as shown in exhibit 15.3.

Exhibit 15.3 **Investment data of the Golden Nugget Restaurant with differential net cash flows**

Net investment outflow (project cost)	€ 75,000.00
Estimated cash saving in year 1	€ 12,500.00
Estimated cash saving in year 2	€ 17,500.00
Estimated cash saving in year 3	€ 20,000.00
Estimated cash saving in year 4	€ 25,000.00
Estimated cash saving in year 5	€ 30,000.00
Estimated cash saving in year 6	€ 35,000.00
Estimated useful life	6 years
Salvage value	nil

Exhibit 15.3 shows the differential net cash savings of the Golden Nugget Restaurant over the life of the investment. Based on this second scenario the payback period will be determined by deducting the succeeding estimated cash savings as shown in exhibit 15.4 from the project cost until the point where the overall cost would have been recovered.

Exhibit 15.4 **Calculating the payback period in situations of differential net cash flows**

Project cost	€ 75,000.00		
Less cash saving in year 1	€ 12,500.00	equal to	€ 62,500.00
Less cash saving in year 2	€ 17,500.00	equal to	€ 45,000.00
Less cash saving in year 3	€ 20,000.00	equal to	€ 25,000.00
Less cash saving in year 4	€ 25,000.00	equal to	0

It is shown in exhibit 15.4 that the payback period is exactly 4 years because in the course of that year the entirety of the investment costs are recovered.

The payback method has the advantage of simplicity. By advocating the selection of projects by reference only to the speed with which investment outflows are recovered, it recommends the acceptance of only the safest projects. It is a method which emphasizes liquidity rather than profitability, and its limitations may be stated to be as follows:

- It emphasizes the payback period rather than the useful life of the investment, and ignores the cash flows beyond the payback period. Hence, it focuses on breaking even rather than on profitability.
- It ignores the time profile of the net cash inflows, and any time pattern in the net investment outflows. Any salvage value would also be ignored. This method, therefore, treats all cash flows through time as having the same value, so that in the first example given above, the value of €75,000.00 invested now is equated with €75,000.00 of net cash inflows received over 3 years 8 months.

The problems of the payback method can be illustrated using the example that follows.

The Unity Star Resort is considering four different investment proposals each estimated to cost €140,000.00. The information about the various project proposals is indicated in exhibit 15.5:

Exhibit 15.5 **Assessing the problems of the payback method**

Project Code	A	B	C	D
Project costs	€ 140,000.00	€ 140,000.00	€ 140,000.00	€ 140,000.00
Cash inflows				
Year 1	€ 63,000.00	€ 77,000.00	€ 21,000.00	€ 70,000.00
Year 2	€ 77,000.00	€ 63,000.00	€ 42,000.00	€ 42,000.00
Year 3			€ 56,000.00	€ 28,000.00
Year 4			€ 70,000.00	€ 28,000.00
Year 5			€ 70,000.00	€ 21,000.00
Payback period	2 years	2 years	3 years 3 months 18 days	3 years

Basic payback method analysis would lead to the selection of either Project Code A or B but it would not be able to decide between the two projects because as it is shown in exhibit 15.5 they both have the same payback period.

To conclude, the payback period is often used as a screening device in conjunction with more sophisticated models, especially in high risk situations. Some operations will not consider evaluating proposed projects using the NPV or IRR approaches unless their initial review using the payback model suggests that the proposed project is doable.

Accounting rate of return (ARR)

The accounting rate of return method focuses on the incremental accounting income that results from a project and it is calculated by using the following formula

$$ARR = \frac{\text{Average incremental revenue} - \text{average incremantal expenses*}}{\text{Initial investment}}$$

* this includes depreciation and income taxes

To illustrate the accounting rate of return method, suppose the Unity Star Resort is considering opening a new spa and health centre and the investment information is as contained in exhibit 15.6.

Exhibit 15.6 **Proposed investment in a new spa and health centre by the Unity Star Resort**

Proposed investment in a new Spa and Health Centre by the Unity Star Resort

Investment cost € 157,500.00

Year	Revenues	Cost of sales	Operating Expenses	Depreciation	Income Before Taxes	Income Taxes 30%	Net Income
1	€ 150,000.00	€ 75,000.00	€ 38,000.00	€ 11,250.00	€ 25,750.00	€ 7,725.00	€ 18,025.00
2	€ 150,000.00	€ 75,000.00	€ 38,000.00	€ 22,500.00	€ 14,500.00	€ 4,350.00	€ 10,150.00
3	€ 150,000.00	€ 75,000.00	€ 38,000.00	€ 22,500.00	€ 14,500.00	€ 4,450.00	€ 10,150.00
4	€ 150,000.00	€ 75,000.00	€ 38,000.00	€ 22,500.00	€ 14,500.00	€ 4,350.00	€ 10,150.00
5	€ 150,000.00	€ 75,000.00	€ 38,000.00	€ 22,500.00	€ 14,500.00	€ 4,350.00	€ 10,150.00
6	€ 150,000.00	€ 75,000.00	€ 38,000.00	€ 22,500.00	€ 14,500.00	€ 4,350.00	€ 10,150.00
7	€ 150,000.00	€ 75,000.00	€ 38,000.00	€ 22,500.00	€ 14,500.00	€ 4,450.00	€ 10,150.00
8	€ 150,000.00	€ 75,000.00	€ 38,000.00	€ 11,250.00	€ 25,750.00	€ 7,725.00	€ 18,025.00
9	€ 150,000.00	€ 75,000.00	€ 38,000.00		€ 37,000.00	€ 11,100.00	€ 25,900.00
10	€ 150,000.00	€ 75,000.00	€ 38,000.00		€ 37,000.00	€ 11,100.00	€ 25,900.00
				€157,500.00			€148,750.00

In the accounting rate of return method, the average annual income will be calculated. As shown in exhibit 15.6 in the net income column (last column), the average annual income is equal to the sum total of €148,750.00 divided by the 10 years of the project life. The average annual income is €14,875.00.

$$\text{The accounting rate of return} = \frac{€14,875.00}{€157,500.00} = 9.44\%$$

Average rate of return (ARR)

A slight modification to the accounting rate of return is the average rate of return which compares the net annual return (net after depreciation and income taxes) to the average of the investment. The formula is:

$$ARR = \frac{\text{Average incremental revenue} - \text{average incremental expenses*}}{\text{Average investment}}$$

* this includes depreciation and income taxes

A project's average investment is defined as the average accounting book value of the investment over the life of the project. Using the example of the spa and health centre of the Unity Star Resort, the average investment will be determined as shown in exhibit 15.7.

Exhibit 15.7 **Establishing the average investment of a project**

Year	Book Value at Beginning of year	Depreciation	Book Value at End of Year	Average Book Value During Year
1	€ 157,500.00	€ 11,250.00	€ 146,250.00	€ 151,875.00
2	€ 146,250.00	€ 22,500.00	€ 123,750.00	€ 135,000.00
3	€ 123,750.00	€ 22,500.00	€ 101,250.00	€ 112,500.00
4	€ 101,250.00	€ 22,500.00	€ 78,750.00	€ 90,000.00
5	€ 78,750.00	€ 22,500.00	€ 56,250.00	€ 67,500.00
6	€ 56,250.00	€ 22,500.00	€ 33,750.00	€ 45,000.00
7	€ 33,750.00	€ 22,500.00	€ 11,250.00	€ 22,500.00
8	€ 11,250.00	€ 11,250.00	€ –	€ 5,625.00

To understand how to read the content of exhibit 15.7, note that:

- the "book value at end of year" is the "book value beginning of year" less "depreciation" of the year
- the "average book value during the year" is the "book value beginning of the year" plus the "book value end of the year" divided by 2

The average investment is equal to the sum of the average book value during the year for all the years divided by number of years of the project. Thus,

$$\frac{€630,000.00}{10} = €63,000.00$$

This leads to an average rate of return of 23.61% calculated as follows:

$$\frac{€63,000.00}{€157,500.00} = 23.61\%$$

In comparison, it is noted that average rate of return has produced a higher percentage than the previously calculated accounting rate of return.

Both methods are quite a simple way of screening investment proposals. They equally overcome one disadvantage of the payback method in that they attempt to calculate the profitability of the project. They equally have some disadvantages which can be summarized in the following way:

- They fail to consider the changing value of money through time
- They treat the value of future inflows as if they were the same today
- They ignore the differences that may occur through time in the rate of net cash inflows
- The disagreement about the single method of calculating the rate of return (average or accounting)

15.3   Simple and compound interest

Interest is the payment for the use of money over a specified period of time and it can be calculated either on a simple or a compound basis. This distinction is important because it will affect the amount of interest to be earned.

Simple interest is the interest payment computed on only the amount of the principal for one or more periods. For example, assume an investment of €10,000.00 at 10% interest for three years; the yearly interest payment would be €1,000.00 (€10,000.00 × 0.10). The total interest earned over the three years would simply be €3,000.00.

Compound interest on the other hand is computed on the amount of the principal plus any interest that would have been accumulated till that date. This means that, the accumulated interest of each period is added to the principal of the period before the interest of the next period is assessed. In this way interest is earned not only on the principal but equally on the interest earned on each preceding principal. Using the example above the compound interest over three years will be calculated as shown in exhibit 15.8.

Exhibit 15.8 **Compound interest illustration**

Year	Principal Amount at Beginning of Year	Annual Interest Income, 10%	Accumulated at End of Year
1	€ 10,000.00	€ 1,000.00	€ 11,000.00
2	€ 11,000.00	€ 1,100.00	€ 12,100.00
3	€ 12,100.00	€ 1,210.00	€ 13,310.00

In exhibit 15.8, it is now realized that the total interest earned over the three years becomes €3,310.00 which is higher than the interest earned using the simple interest method.

Compound interest can be calculated more than once each year. This could be daily, weekly, monthly, quarterly, or semi-annually. When interest is compounded more than once a year, the necessary adjustments are quite easy to carry out. For example, if interest is compounded semi-annually there will then be two interest periods in the year. The interest rate, which is stated in annual terms, must be adjusted accordingly. Thus, in the example as shown in exhibit 15.8, if the compounding was to be done semi-annually then the rate of 5% would be used for each half year. Interest compounded semi-annually based on the example contained in exhibit 15.8 is shown in exhibit 15.9.

Exhibit 15.9 **Interest compounded semi-annually**

		Interest compounted semi-annually		
Year	Period	Principal Amount at Beginning of Period	Annual Interest Income, 5%	Accumulated at End of Period
1	1	€ 10,000.00	€ 500.00	€ 10,500.00
	2	€ 10,500.00	€ 525.00	€ 11,025.00
2	3	€ 11,025.00	€ 551.25	€ 11,576.25
	4	€ 11,576.25	€ 578.81	€ 12,155.06
3	5	€ 12,155.06	€ 607,75	€ 12,762.82
	6	€ 12,762.82	€ 638.14	€ 13,400.96

Exhibit 15.9 shows the advantage of multiple compounding within the year of interest. It is noticed that the overall interest over the three year period on €10,000.00 rose from €3,310.00 in exhibit 15.8 to €3,400.96 in exhibit 15.9. The more the number of periods within the year that the interest is compounded, the higher the accumulated interest would become.

Compounding can be easily done using mathematical formulas. The formula to determine the accumulated amount of a single deposit is as follows:

Accumulated amount $= p(1 + i)^n$

in which
p = principal amount
i = rate of interest
n = number of compounding periods

Using the simple example of €10,000.00 compounded annually for 3 years at 10% as shown in exhibit 15.8, the accumulated amount can be determined as follows:

$$\text{€}10,000.00(1 + 0.1)^3 = \text{€}10,000.00(1.1)^3 = \text{€}10,000.00(1.331) = \text{€}13,310.00$$

Using this formula produces the same result as was done sequentially by year in exhibit 15.8.

15.4   Process of discounting

Discounting is the reverse of compounding. In the example and discussions of compounding it was noted that at a constant rate of 10%, €10,000.00 invested now is the equivalent of €13,310.00 by the end of year 3 (assuming annual compounding). Likewise it can be said that €13,310.00 at the end of year 3 (future amount) is equal to €10,000.00 now (present amount). The rate of interest in the discounting process is equally referred to as the rate of discount (discount rate).

The discounting formula is the inverse of the compounding formula and it is determined as follows:

$$P = F \frac{1}{(1 + i)^n}$$

in which
P = present amount
F = future amount
i = discount rate
n = number of years

For example, using the illustrated figures the present value can be determined as follows:

$$P = \text{€}13,310.00 \frac{1}{(1 + 0.1)^3}$$

$$P = \text{€}13,310.00 \frac{1}{(1.1)^3}$$

$$P = 13,310.00 \frac{1}{1.331}$$

$$P = \frac{\text{€}13,310.00}{1.331}$$

$$P = \text{€}10,000.00$$

The processes of compounding and discounting lead to future and present value analyses. However it will be nice at this stage to be able to distinguish between the two. The easiest way to do so is by using timelines. The opposing perspectives are shown in exhibit 15.10.

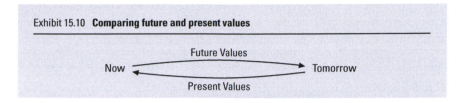

Exhibit 15.10 **Comparing future and present values**

Future Values

Now ⟷ Tomorrow

Present Values

Based on the directional arrows contained in exhibit 15.10, the timeline related to the compounding example of an investment of €10,000.00 at 10% interest for three years will be as shown in exhibit 15.11.

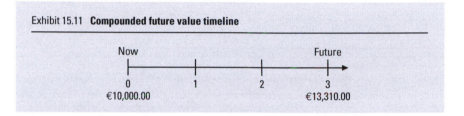

Exhibit 15.11 **Compounded future value timeline**

Now | Future
0 | 1 | 2 | 3
€10,000.00 | | | €13,310.00

In the opposite direction the time line related to the discounting example of €13,310.00 discounted at 10% will be as shown in exhibit 15.12.

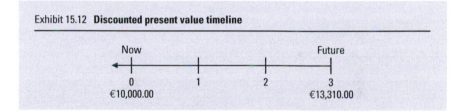

Exhibit 15.12 **Discounted present value timeline**

Now | Future
0 | 1 | 2 | 3
€10,000.00 | | | €13,310.00

Notice that the only change between the two timelines is in the direction of the arrow.

Compounding and discounting calculations can be made for any amount, rate of interest, and any number of years. It is however easier to use factor tables introduced in section 15.5.

15.5 Understanding factor tables

As an alternative to using formulas in the compounding and discounting of future and present amounts, factors that have already been pre-calculated and established in a table form can be used. These factors are simply derived from the formulas and they interpret the mathematical formulas. In this section four such factor tables will be introduced – table of future value factors for a single amount, table of future value factors for an annuity, table of present value factors for a single amount and lastly table of present value factors for an annuity.

1 Table of future value factors for a single amount

Exhibit 15.13 shows the various pre-calculated future value factors of €1.00 at rates ranging from 1% to 20% and for periods 1 to 20. To illustrate, the future value of an investment of €10,000.00 at 10% interest for three years can be calculated as follows:

Step 1 Seek for the factor to be used in establishing this future value
Step 2 Multiply the selected factor by the principal amount to get the future value

As such

Step 1 Seek for the factor to be used in establishing this future value
The factor to be used in establishing the future value will be found at the intersection between the number of periods in the scenario and rate of interest. In exhibit 15.13, and for this example, at the intersection between 10% and 3 years is the factor 1.331000.

Step 2 Multiply the selected factor by the principal amount to get the future value
The selected factor of 1.331000 will now be used to multiply the principal amount to get to the future amount. 1.331000 × €10,000.00 = €13,310.00.

Exhibit 15.13 **Future value factors of a single amount**

Future value interest factor of €1 per period at i% tor n periods, FVIF (i,n).

Period	1%	2%	3%	4%	5%	6%	7%	8%	9%
1	1.010000	1.020000	1.030000	1.040000	1.050000	1.060000	1.070000	1.080000	1.090000
2	1.020100	1.040400	1.060900	1.081600	1.102500	1.123600	1.144900	1.166400	1.188100
3	1.030301	1.061208	1.092727	1.124864	1.157625	1.191016	1.225043	1.259712	1.295029
4	1.040604	1.082432	1.125509	1.169859	1215506	1.262477	1.310796	1.360489	1.411582
5	1.051010	1.104081	1.159274	1.216653	1.276282	1.338226	1.402552	1.469328	1.538624
6	1.061520	1.126162	1.194052	1.265319	1.340096	1.418519	1.500730	1.586874	1.677100
7	1.072135	1.148686	1.229874	1.315932	1.407100	1.503630	1.605781	1.713824	1.828039
8	1.082857	1.171659	1.266770	1.368569	1.477455	1.593848	1.718186	1.850930	1.992563
9	1.093685	1.195093	1.304773	1.423312	1.551328	1.689479	1.838459	1.999005	2.171893
10	1.104622	1.218994	1.343916	1.480244	1.628895	1.790848	1.967151	2.158925	2.367364
11	1.115668	1.243374	1.384234	1.539454	1.710339	1.898299	2.104852	2.331639	2.580426
12	1.126825	1.268242	1.425761	1.601032	1.795856	2.012196	2.252192	2.518170	2.812665
13	1.138093	1.293607	1.468534	1.665074	1.885649	2.132928	2.409845	2.719624	3.065805
14	1.149474	1.319479	1.512590	1.731676	1.979932	2.260904	2.578534	2.937194	3.341727
15	1.160969	1.345868	1.557967	1.800944	2.078928	2.396558	2.759032	3.172169	3.642482
16	1.172579	1.372786	1.604706	1.872981	2.182875	2.540352	2.952164	3.425943	3.970306
17	1.184304	1.400241	1.652848	1.947900	2.292018	2.692773	3.158815	3.700018	4.327633
18	1.196147	1.428246	1.702433	2.025817	2.406619	2.854339	3.379932	3.996019	4.717120
19	1.208109	1.456811	1.753506	2.106849	2.526950	3.025600	3.616528	4.315701	5.141661
20	1.220190	1.485947	1.806111	2.191123	2.653298	3.207135	3.869684	4.660957	5.604411

The use of the future value factor table can be summarized in the following formula:

Future amount = Factor (from the table) × Present amount

This formula can then be used to solve a variety of related problems. Any two of the elements in the formula can be used to determine the missing element.

2 Table of future value factors for an annuity

An annuity represents a stream of equal payments that are made at regular intervals over a fixed period of time. Examples of annuities are regular payments into a deposit account, monthly mortgage payments and yearly insurance payments.

Exhibit 15.14 shows the various pre-calculated future value factors of an ordinary annuity of €1.00 at rates ranging from 1% to 20% and for periods 1 to 20. To illustrate the use of this factor table assume the following: the Mata Hari Spa & Health Centre wants to invest €25,000.00 at the end of each year for the next eight years; the investment will be compounded annually at an interest rate of 12%. The future value of such a stream of annuities will be determined as follows:

10%	12%	14%	16%	20%	Period
1.100000	1.120000	1.140000	1.160000	1.200000	1
1.210000	1.254400	1.299600	1.345600	1.440000	2
1.331000	1.404928	i.481544	1.560896	1.728000	3
1.464100	1.573519	Ī.688960	1.810639	2.073600	4
1.610510	1.762342	1.925415	2.100342	2.488320	5
1.771561	1.973823	2.194973	2.436396	2.985984	6
1.948717	2.210681	2.502269	2.826220	3.583181	7
2.143589	2.475963	2.852586	3.278415	4.299817	8
2,357948	2.773079	3.251949	3.802961	5.159780	9
2.593742	3.105848	3.707221	4.411435	6.191736	10
2.853117	3.478550	4.226232	5.117265	7.430084	11
3.138428	3.895976	4.817905	5.936027	8.916100	12
3.452271	4.363493	5.492411	6.885791	10.699321	13
3.797498	4.887112	6.261349	7.987518	12.839185	14
4.177248	5.473566	7.137938	9.265521	15.407022	15
4.594973	6.130394	8.137249	10.748004	18.488426	16
5.054470	6.866041	9.276464	12.467685	22.186111	17
5.559917	7.689966	10.575169	14.462514	26.623333	18
6.115909	8.612762	12.055693	16.776517	31.948000	19
6.727500	9.646293	13.743490	19.460759	38.337600	20

Exhibit 15.14 **Future value factors for an annuity**

Future value interest factor of an ordinary annuity of €1 per period at i% for n periods, FVIFA (i,n).

Period	1%	2%	3%	4%	5%	6%	7%	8%	9%
1	1.000000	1.000000	1.000000	1.000000	1.000000	1.000000	1.000000	1.000000	1.000000
2	2.010000	2.020000	2.030000	2.040000	2.050000	2.060000	2.070000	2.080000	2.090000
3	3.030100	3.060400	3.090900	3.121600	3.152500	3.183600	3.214900	3.246400	3.278100
4	4.060401	4.121608	4.183627	4.246464	4.310125	4.374616	4.439943	4.506112	4,573129
5	5.101005	5.204040	5.309136	5.416323	5.525631	5.637093	5.750739	5.866601	5.984711
6	6.152015	6.308121	6.468410	6.632975	6.801913	6.975319	7.153291	7.335929	7.523335
7	7.213535	7.434283	7.662462	7.898294	8.142008	8.393838	8.654021	8.922803	9.200435
8	8.285671	8.582969	8.892336	9.214226	9.549109	9.897468	10.259803	10.636628	11.028474
9	9.368527	9.754628	10.159106	10.582795	11.026564	11.491316	11.977989	12.487558	13.021036
10	10.462213	10.949721	11.463879	12,006107	12.577893	13.180795	13.816448	14.486562	15.192930
11	11.566835	12.168715	12.807796	13.486351	14.206787	14.971643	15.783599	16.645487	17.560293
12	12.682503	13.412090	14.192030	15.025805	15.917127	16.869941	17.888451	18.977126	20.140720
13	13.809328	14.680332	15.617790	16.626838	17.712983	18.882138	20.140643	21.495297	22.953385
14	14.947421	15.973938	17.086324	18.291911	19.598632	21.015066	22.550488	24.214920	26.019189
15	16.096896	17.293417	18.598914	20.023588	21.578564	23.275970	25.129022	27.152114	29.360916
16	17.257864	18.639285	20.156881	21.824531	23.657492	25.672528	27.888054	30.324283	33.003399
17	18.430443	20.012071	21.761588	23.697512	25.840366	28.212880	30.840217	33.750226	36.973705
18	19.614748	21.412312	23.414435	25.645413	28.132385	30.905653	33.999033	37.450244	41.301338
19	20.810895	22.840559	25.116868	27.671229	30.539004	33.759992	37.378965	41.446263	46.018458
20	22.019004	24.297370	26.870374	29.778079	33.065954	36.785591	40.995492	45.761964	51.160120

Step 1 Seek for the factor to be used in establishing this future value
Step 2 Multiply the selected factor by the single annuity to get the future value of the stream of annuities

As such

Step 1 Seek for the factor to be used in establishing this future value. The factor to be used in establishing the future value will be found at the intersection between the number of periods in the scenario and rate of interest. In exhibit 15.14, and for this example, at the intersection between 12% and 8 years is the factor 12.299693.

Step 2 Multiply the selected factor by the single annuity to get the future value of the stream of annuities.

The selected factor of 12.299693 will now be used to multiply the annuity of €25,000.00 to get to the future amount. 12.299693 × €25,000.00 = €307,492.32.

This future value analysis of annuities can be verified manually as shown in exhibit 15.15. At the end of year 8 they would have accumulated the sum of €307,492.32 based on an annual end of year investment of €25,000.00 and compounded at 12%.

10%	12%	14%	16%	20%	Period
1.000000	1.000000	1.000000	1.000000	1.000000	1
2.100000	2.120000	2.140000	2.160000	2.200000	2
3.310000	3.374400	3.439600	3.505600	3.640000	3
4.641000	4.779328	4.921144	5.066496	5.368000	4
6.105100	6.352847	6.610104	6.877135	7.441600	5
7.715610	8.115189	8.535519	8.977477	9.929920	6
9.487171	10.089012	10.730491	11.413873	12.915904	7
11.435888	12.299693	13.232760	14.240093	16.499085	8
13.579477	14.775656	16.085347	17.518508	20.798902	9
15.937425	17.548735	19.337295	21.321469	25.958682	10
18.531167	20.654583	23.044516	25.732904	32.150419	11
21.384284	24.133133	27.270749	30.850169	39.580502	12
24.522712	28.029109	32.088654	36.786196	48.496603	13
27.974983	32.392602	37.581065	43.671987	59.195923	14
31.772482	37.279715	43.842414	51.659505	72.035108	15
35.949730	42.753280	50.980352	60.925026	87.442129	16
40.544703	48.883674	59.117601	71.673030	105.930555	17
45.599173	55.749715	68.394066	84.140715	128.116666	18
51.159090	63.439681	78.969235	98.603230	154.740000	19
57.274999	72.052442	91.024928	115.379747	186.688000	20

Exhibit 15.15 **Mata Hari Spa & Health Centre proposed investment**

Mata Hari Spa & Health Centre Proposed Investment

Compound values at 12% with €25,000.00 invested at the end of each year

Year	Principal Amount at beginning of Year	Annual Interest Income, 12%	Accumulated at End of Year
1	€ –	€ –	€ 25,000.00
2	€ 25,000.00	€ 3,000.00	€ 53,000.00
3	€ 53,000.00	€ 6,360.00	€ 84,360.00
4	€ 84,360.00	€ 10,123.20	€ 119,483.20
5	€ 119,483.20	€ 14,337.98	€ 158,821.18
6	€ 158,821.18	€ 19,058.54	€ 202,879.73
7	€ 202,879.73	€ 24,345.57	€ 252,225.29
8	€ 252,225.29	€ 30,267.04	€ 307,492.32

3 Table of present value factors for a single amount

Exhibit 15.18 shows the various pre-calculated present value factors of €1.00 at rates ranging from 1% to 20% and for periods 1 to 20. To illustrate, assume that the Mata Hari Spa & Health Centre expects the following stream of net cash flows at the end of the next five years.

Exhibit 15.16 Mata Hari Spa & Health Centre expected net cash flows

Mata Hari Spa & Health Centre Expected Net Cash Flows

Year	Net Cash Flow End of Year
1	€ 75,000.00
2	€ 85,000.00
3	€ 95,000.00
4	€ 105,000.00
5	€ 115,000.00

Two sets of illustration will be done at this level.

Illustration 1: The Management of the Mata Hari Spa & Health Centre might want to know the value today of the €95,000.00 they will get in 3 years. They also know that the rate of discount is currently 8%. Using the present value factor table as shown in exhibit 15.18, they will seek for the factor at the intersection between 3 years and 8%, and then use this factor to multiply by the principal amount of €95,000.00. Thus, they will multiply €95,000.00 by 0.793832. The present value then is equal to €75,414.04. This means that the €95,000.00 they expect to get at the end of year 3 under the present conditions of an 8% discount rate is only worth €75,414.04 today. Similarly, they can calculate the present values for all the other expected net cash flows for each period under conditions of 8%.

Exhibit 15.18 Present value factors of a single amount

Present value interest factor of €1 per period at i% tor n periods, PVIF (i,n).

Period	1%	2%	3%	4%	5%	6%	7%	8%	9%
1	0.990099	0.980392	0.970874	0.961538	0.952381	0.943396	0.934579	0.925926	0.917431
2	0.980296	0.961169	0.942596	0.924556	0.907029	0.889996	0.873439	0.857339	0.841680
3	0.970590	0.942322	0.915142	0.888996	0.863838	0.839619	0.816298	0.793832	0.772183
4	0.960980	0.923845	0.888487	0.854804	0.822702	0.792094	0.762895	0.735030	0.708425
5	0.951466	0.905731	0.862609	0.821927	0.783526	0.747258	0.712986	0.680583	0.649931
6	0.942045	0.887971	0.837484	0.790315	0.746215	0.704961	0.666342	0.630170	0.596267
7	0.932718	0.870560	0.813092	0.759918	0.710681	0.665057	0.622750	0.583490	0.547034
8	0.923483	0.853490	0.789409	0.730690	0.676839	0.627412	0.582009	0.540269	0.501866
9	0.914340	0.836755	0.766417	0.702587	0.644609	0.591898	0.543934	0.500249	0.460428
10	0.905287	0.820348	0.744094	0.675564	0.613913	0.558395	0.508349	0.463193	0.422411
11	0.896324	0.804263	0.722421	0.649581	0.584679	0.526788	0.475093	0.428883	0.387533
12	0.887449	0.788493	0.701380	0.624597	0.556837	0.496969	0.444012	0.397114	0.355535
13	0.878663	0.773033	0.680951	0.600574	0.530321	0.468839	0.414964	0.367698	0.326179
14	0.869963	0.757875	0.661118	0.577475	0.505068	0.442301	0.387817	0.340461	0.299246
15	0.861349	0.743015	0.641862	0.555265	0.481017	0.417265	0.362446	0.315242	0.274538
16	0.852821	0.728446	0.623167	0.533908	0.458112	0.393646	0.338735	0.291890	0.251870
17	0.844377	0.714163	0.605016	0.513373	0.436297	0.371364	0.316574	0.270269	0.231073
18	0.836017	0.700159	0.587395	0.493628	0.415521	0.350344	0.295864	0.250249	0.211994
19	0.827740	0.686431	0.570286	0.474642	0.395734	0.330513	0.276508	0.231712	0.194490
20	0.819544	0.672971	0.553676	0.456387	0.376889	0.311805	0.258419	0.214548	0.178431

Illustration 2: Assume now that the Management of the Mata Hari Spa and Health Centre are conscious of the fact that interest rates could be rising year on year in the following order 8% for years 1 and 2, 10% for years 3 and 4 and finally 12% for year 5. Based on these, they will present the factors as shown in exhibit 15.17, as collected from exhibit 15.18 to establish the present values of the expected net cash flows.

Exhibit 15.17 **Mata Hari Spa & Health Centre expected net cash flows**

Present Values of Mata Hari Spa & Health Centre's Expected Net Cash Flows

Year	Net Cash Flow End of Year	Discount Rate to be Used	Discount Factor	Present Value
1	€ 75,000.00	8.00%	0.925926	€ 69,444.45
2	€ 85,000.00	8.00%	0.857339	€ 72,873.82
3	€ 95,000.00	10.00%	0.751315	€ 71,374.93
4	€ 105,000.00	10.00%	0.683013	€ 71,716.37
5	€ 115,000.00	12.00%	0.567427	€ 65,254.11

The selection of the correct factors is based on the ability to identify the correct rate of discount and relating it to its appropriate period.

10%	12%	14%	16%	20%	Period
0.909091	0.892857	0.877193	0.862069	0.833333	1
0.826446	0.797194	0.769468	0.743163	0.694444	2
0.751315	0.711780	0.674972	0.640658	0.578704	3
0.683013	0.635518	0.592080	0.552291	0.482253	4
0.620921	0.567427	0.519369	0.476113	0.401878	5
0.564474	0.506631	0.455587	0.410442	0.334898	6
0.513158	0.452349	0.399637	0.353830	0.279082	7
0.466507	0.403883	0.350559	0.305025	0.232568	8
0.424098	0.360610	0.307508	0.262953	0.193807	9
0.385543	0.321973	0.269744	0226684	0.161506	10
0.350494	0.287476	0.236617	0.195417	0.134588	11
0.318631	0.256675	0.207559	0.168463	0.112157	12
0.289664	0.229174	0.182069	0.145227	0.093464	13
0.263331	0.204620	0.159710	0.125195	0.077887	14
0.239392	0.182696	0.140096	0.107927	0.064905	15
0.217629	0.163122	0.122892	0.093041	0.054088	16
0.197845	0.145644	0.107800	0.080207	0.045073	17
0.179859	0.130040	0.094561	0.069144	0.037561	18
0.163508	0.116107	0.082948	0.059607	0.031301	19
0.148644	0.103667	0.072762	0.051385	0.026084	20

Exhibit 15.19 Present value factors of an annuity

Present value interest factor of an (ordinary) annuity of €1 per period at i% for n periods, PVIFA (i,n).

Period	1%	2%	3%	4%	5%	6%	7%	8%	9%
1	0.990099	0,980392	0.970874	0.961538	0.952381	0.943396	0.934579	0.925926	0.917431
2	1.970395	1.941561	1.913470	1.886095	1.859410	1.833393	1.808018	1.783265	1.759111
3	2.940985	2.883883	2.828611	2.775091	2.723248	2.673012	2.624316	2.577097	2.531295
4	3.901966	3.807729	3.717098	3.629895	3.545951	3.465106	3.387211	3.312127	3.239720
5	4.853431	4.713460	4.579707	4.451822	4.329477	4.212364	4.100197	3.992710	3.889651
6	5.795476	5.601431	5.417191	5.242137	5.075692	4.917324	4.766540	4.622880	4.485919
7	6.728195	6.471991	6.230283	6.002055	5.786373	5.582381	5.389289	5.206370	5.032953
8	7.651678	7.325481	7.019692	6.732745	6.463213	6.209794	5.971299	5.746639	5.534819
9	8.566018	8.162237	7.786109	7.435332	7.107822	6.801692	6.515232	6.246888	5.995247
10	9.471305	8.982585	8.530203	8.110896	7,721735	7.360087	7.023582	6.710081	6.417658
11	10.367628	9.786848	9.252624	8.760477	8.306414	7.886875	7.498674	7.138964	6.805191
12	11.255077	10.575341	9.954004	9.385074	8.863252	8.383844	7.942686	7.536078	7.160725
13	12.133740	11.348374	10.634955	9.985648	9.393573	8.852683	8.357651	7.903776	7.486904
14	13.003703	12.106249	11.296073	10.563123	9.898641	9.294984	8.745468	8.244237	7.786150
15	13.865053	12.849264	11.937935	11.118387	10.379658	9.712249	9.107914	8.559479	8.060688
16	14.717874	13.577709	12.561102	11.652296	10.837770	10.105895	9.446649	8.851369	8.312558
17	15.562251	14.291872	13.166118	12.165669	11.274066	10.477260	9.763223	9.121638	8.543631
18	16.398269	14.992031	13.753513	12.659297	11.689587	10.827603	10.059087	9.371887	8.755625
19	17.226008	15.678462	14.323799	13.133939	12.085321	11.158116	10.335595	9.603599	8.950115
20	18.045553	16.351433	14.877475	13.590326	12.462210	11.469921	10.594014	9.818147	9.128546

4 Table of present value factors for an annuity

Exhibit 15.19 shows the various pre-calculated present value factors for an annuity of €1.00 at rates ranging from 1% to 20% and for periods 1 to 20. To illustrate the use of the factor table of annuities assume that the Old-timers' Motel has a mortgage in which the annuity is €90,000.00 and has to be paid back in 10 years. The mortgage was taken at a rate of 6%. This can be shown as in exhibit 15.20:

Exhibit 15.20 Annual mortgage repayment schedule for the Old-timers' Motel

The Old-timers' Motel

Year	Annual Mortgage Repayment
1	€ 90,000.00
2	€ 90,000.00
3	€ 90,000.00
4	€ 90,000.00
5	€ 90,000.00
6	€ 90,000.00
7	€ 90,000.00
8	€ 90,000.00
9	€ 90,000.00
10	€ 90,000.00

10%	12%	14%	16%	20%	Period
0.909091	0.892857	0.877193	0.862069	0.833333	1
1.735537	1.690051	1.646661	1.605232	1.527778	2
2.486852	2.401831	2.321632	2.245890	2.106481	3
3.169865	3.037349	2.913712	2.798181	2.588735	4
3.790787	3.604776	3.433081	3.274294	2.990612	5
4.355261	4.111407	3.888668	3.684736	3.325510	6
4.868419	4.563757	4.288305	4.038565	3.604592	7
5.334926	4.967640	4.638864	4.343591	3.837160	8
5.759024	5.328250	4.946372	4.606544	4.030967	9
6.144567	5.650223	5.216116	4.833227	4.192472	10
6.495061	5.937699	5.452733	5.028644	4.327060	11
6.813692	6.194374	5.660292	5.197107	4.439217	12
7.103356	6.423548	5.842362	5.342334	4.532681	13
7.366687	6.628168	6.002072	5.467529	4.610567	14
7.606080	6.810864	6.142168	5.575456	4.675473	15
7.823709	6.973986	6.265060	5.668497	4.729561	16
8.021553	7.119630	6.372859	5.748704	4.774634	17
8.201412	7.249670	6.467420	5.817848	4.812195	18
8.364920	7.365777	6.550369	5.877455	4.843496	19
8.513564	7.469444	6.623131	5.928841	4.869580	20

The Management of the Old-timers' Motel can determine the present value of this stream of annuities by simply selecting from the present value factors of an annuity table (exhibit 15.19) the factor that is at the intersection between 6% and 10 years (7.360087), and multiply this factor by a single annuity of €90,000.00.

$$€90,000.00 \times 7.360087 = €662,407.83$$

This amount of €662,407.83 represents the combined present value of the 10 annuities of mortgage payments of €90,000.00 each. This can be verified using the present value factors for single amounts as contained in exhibit 15.18 and as shown in exhibit 15.21. It is noticed in exhibit 15.21 that the sum of the individual present values of the mortgage payments is exactly equal to the result of multiplying a single annuity of €90,000.00 by the factor 7.360087 derived from exhibit 15.19.

Exhibit 15.21 **Using single amount present value factors to verify the result of annuity factors**

The Old-timer' Motel

Year	Annual Mortgage Repayment	Present Value Discount Factors @ 6%	Present Value of Mortgage Repayment
1	€ 90.000.00	0.943396	€ 84,905.66
2	€ 90.000.00	0.889996	€ 80,099.68
3	€ 90.000.00	0.839619	€ 75,565.74
4	€ 90.000.00	0.792094	€ 71,288.43
5	€ 90.000.00	0.747258	€ 67.253.24
6	€ 90.000.00	0.704961	€ 63,446.45
7	€ 90.000.00	0.665057	€ 59,855.14
8	€ 90.000.00	0.627412	€ 56,467.11
9	€ 90.000.00	0.591898	€ 53,270.86
10	€ 90.000.00	0.558395	€ 50,255.53
		Total	**€ 662,407.83**

15.6 Discounted cash flow (DCF) methods

1 The notion of cost of capital and establishing a discount rate

In section 15.4 the discount rate was introduced. However on what bases are these rates established? In this section the analysis will be based on an investment project to be carried out by The Low Dyke Hotel. The overall project, which is about the acquisition of a floating restaurant, will cost the hotel €1,137,500.00 and the details are found in exhibit 15.22. Assume that The Low Dyke Hotel uses in its investment analysis a discount rate of 12%, this would represent an acceptable annual return for the activities of The Low Dyke Hotel. If the general bank interest rate in the economy is 5% per year, why would The Low Dyke Hotel expect to make more than that? The answer relates to risk.

Investing in a business is a riskier venture than leaving money in a bank. Normally, banks can be relied upon to survive and to carry on paying interest at the advertised rates; a normal savings account rate is more or less risk-free (there is always some level of risk; banks do occasionally fail as the bank failures of 2008/2009 have shown). A business investor is taking much more of a risk and therefore expects to be rewarded by a greater return in the form of interest or dividends. The 12% rate may be The Low Dyke Hotel's best guess at the risk-free rate plus a premium for the level of risk actually incurred by them. Another helpful way of looking at the problem is to consider the alternatives. If The Low Dyke Hotel invests in the new restaurant, it needs to either borrow €1,137,500.00 or take it out of existing resources. If there is an alternative use for that money that will yield 12% then the cost of money is (at least) 12%. The cost of money for a particular business is known as its cost of capital.

The evaluation of an investment project by DCF analysis requires a company to calculate its cost of capital. This is true in selecting the discount rate for any analysis by means of the net present value method, or for establishing an acceptable internal rate of return. A major problem in using the cost of capital lies in its different interpretations. From a lender's point of view, the cost of capital represents the cost to them of lending money which may be equated to the return they could have obtained by investing in a similar project with similar risks. This concept of the cost of capital is founded on its 'opportunity cost'. The opportunity cost approach to the assessment of the cost of capital is one which a company must always consider when evaluating an investment project. A company may find, for example, that investing funds somewhere else may produce higher returns than in an internal project. The main obstacle to a more widespread use of the opportunity cost concept is that of identifying investments of equal risks and hence measuring the opportunity cost.

DCF methods have gained widespread acceptance, for they recognize that the value of money is subject to a time preference, that is, that €1.00 today is preferred to €1.00 in the future unless the delay in receiving €1.00 in the future is compensated by an interest factor. This interest factor is expressed as a discount rate. DCF methods attempt to evaluate an investment proposal by comparing the net cash flows of the investment at their present value (section 15.5) with the value of funds to be invested. There are two widely used methods of DCF analysis: the net present value method and the internal rate of return method.

2 Net present value (NPV) method

The net present value is defined as the total present value (PV) of a time series of cash flows. It is a standard method used in appraising long term projects. The NPV measures the excess or shortfall of cash flows in present value terms.

The following four steps constitute a net present value analysis of an investment proposal:

Step 1	Prepare a table showing the cash flows during each year of the proposed investment.
Step 2	Compute the present value of each cash flow, using an appropriate discount rate.
Step 3	Compute the net present value, which is the sum of the present values of the cash flows.
Step 4	If the net present value (NPV) is equal to or greater than zero, accept the investment proposal. Otherwise, reject it.

To illustrate the NPV method, the investment proposal of The Low Dyke Hotel to acquire a new floating restaurant will be used. In addition the management of The Low Dyke Hotel considers 12% as their cost of capital.

In Step 1, a table as illustrated in exhibit 15.22 showing the cash flows during each year of the proposed investment is established.

Exhibit 15.22 Proposed acquisition of the Floating Oyster Restaurant by the Low Dyke Hotel

The Low Dyke Hotel
Proposed Acquisition of the Floating Oyster Restaurant

Project Cost   € 1,137,500.00
Linear Depreciation over 10 Years   € 113,750.00

	Years				
	1	2	3	4	5
Revenues	€ 1,000,000.00	€ 1,200,000.00	€ 1,400,000.00	€ 1,600,000.00	€ 1,800,000.00
Expenses:					
Labour	€ 255,000.00	€ 262.000.00	€ 339,000.00	€ 371,000.00	€ 403,000.00
Cost of Sales	€ 250,000.00	€ 300,000.00	€ 350,000.00	€ 400,000.00	€ 450,000.00
Supplies	€ 50,000.00	€ 60.000.00	€ 70,000.00	€ 80,000.00	€ 90,000.00
Utilities	€ 40,000.00	€ 48.000.00	€ 56,000.00	€ 64,000.00	€ 72,000.00
Depreciation	€ 113,750.00	€ 113.750.00	€ 113,750.00	€ 113,750.00	€ 113.750.00
Other Operating Expenses	€ 110,000.00	€ 120,000.00	€ 140.000.00	€ 160,000.00	€ 180,000.00
Income Taxes	€ 63,437.50	€ 103,687.50	€ 115,937.50	€ 143,937.50	€ 171,937.50
Net income	€ 117.812.50	€ 192,562.50	€ 215,312.50	€ 267,312.50	€ 319,312.50
Cashflow:					
Net Income	€ 117,812.50	€ 192,562.50	€ 215.312.50	€ 267.312.50	€ 319,312.50
Add: Depreciation	€ 113,750.00	€ 113,750.00	€ 113,750.00	€ 113,750.00	€ 113,750.00
Total	€ 231,562.50	€ 306,312.50	€ 329,062.50	€ 381,062.50	€ 433,062.50

In Step 2 the present value of each cash flow at 12% is calculated. Using discount factors for 12% over the various periods a table as illustrated in exhibit 15.23 is developed.

Exhibit 15.23 Calculation of the present value of each cash flow

Period	Cash Flow	DF @ 12%	Present Value
1	€ 231,562.50	0.892857	€ 206,752.23
2	€ 306,312.50	0.797194	€ 244,190.45
3	€ 329,062.50	0.711780	€ 234,220.19
4	€ 381,062.50	0.635518	€ 242,172.11
5	€ 433,062.50	0.567427	€ 245,731.29
6	€ 479,536.50	0.506631	€ 242,948.62
7	€ 527,312.50	0.452349	€ 238,529.40
8	€ 575,087.50	0.403883	€ 232,268.20
9	€ 622,862.50	0.360610	€ 224,610.46
10	€ 670,637.50	0.321973	€ 215,927.33

In Step 3, compute a table as illustrated in exhibit 15.24 showing the net present value, which is the sum of the present values of all the cash flows. This includes the original investment cost (this is a cash outflow). The original investment cost is indicated in Period 0 which means "now" (the date at which the investment will be carried out). As nothing changes now, the value of the cash outflow remains the same.

	6	7	8	9	10
	€ 2,000,000.00	€ 2,200,000.00	€ 2,400,000.00	€ 2,600,000.00	€ 2,800,000.00
	€ 447,500.00	€ 488,000.00	€ 528,500.00	€ 569,000.00	€ 609,500.00
	€ 500,000.00	€ 550.000.00	€ 600,000.00	€ 650,000.00	€ 700,000.00
	€ 100,000.00	€ 110,000.00	€ 120,000.00	€ 130,000.00	€ 140,000.00
	€ 80,000.00	€ 88.000.00	€ 96,000.00	€ 104,000.00	€ 112,000.00
	€ 113,750.00	€ 113.750.00	€ 113,750.00	€ 113,750.00	€ 113,750.00
	€ 196,000.00	€ 214,000.00	€ 232,000.00	€ 250,000.00	€ 268,000.00
	€ 196,962.50	€ 222,687.50	€ 248.412,50	€ 274,137.50	€ 299,862.50
	€ 365,787.50	€ 413,562.50	€ 461,337.50	€ 509,112.50	€ 556,887.50
	€ 365,787.50	€ 413,562.50	€ 461,337.50	€ 509,112.50	€ 556,887.50
	€ 113,750.00	€ 113,750.00	€ 113.750.00	€ 113,750.00	€ 113,750.00
	€ 479,537.50	€ 527,312.50	€ 575,087.50	€ 622,862.50	€ 670,637.50

Exhibit 15.24 **Computation of the net present value**

Period	Cash Flow	DF @ 12%	Present Value
0	(€ 1,137,500.00)	1	(€ 1,137,500.00)
1	€ 231,562.50	0.892857	€ 206,752.23
2	€ 306,312.50	0.797194	€ 244,190.45
3	€ 329,062.50	0.711780	€ 234,220.19
4	€ 381,062.50	0.635518	€ 242,172.11
5	€ 433,062.50	0.567427	€ 245,731.29
6	€ 479,536.50	0.506631	€ 242,948.62
7	€ 527,312.50	0.452349	€ 238,529.40
8	€ 575,087.50	0.403883	€ 232,268.20
9	€ 622,862.50	0.360610	€ 224,610.46
10	€ 670,637.50	0.321973	€ 215,927.33
		NPV	**€ 1,189,850.27**

In step 4, a decision has to be made following the rules as contained in exhibit 15.25.

Exhibit 15.25 **Illustration of rules concerning NPV outcomes**

	Positive	Acceptable, since it promises a return greater than the cost of capital
If the Net Present Value is	Zero	Acceptable, since it promises a return equal to the cost of capital
	Negative	Not acceptable, since it promises a return less than the cost of capital

In the case of The Low Dyke Hotel's proposed acquisition of the Floating Oyster Restaurant, the NPV is equal to €1,189,850.27 over the 10 years of the analysis and thus if all other conditions remain the same (*ceteris paribus*) it is an acceptable investment.

3 Internal rate of return (IRR) method

An alternative discounted cash flow method for analysing investment proposals is the internal rate of return method. An asset's internal rate of return is the true economic return earned by the asset over its life. Another way of stating the definition is that an asset's internal rate of return (IRR) is the discount rate that would be required in a net present value analysis in order for the asset's net present value to be exactly zero. Although a number of the principles applicable to the IRR method are similar to the NPV method, there is a notable difference in the final outcome and the decision criteria. In the application of the IRR method, it is necessary to calculate the exact DCF rate of return which an investment opportunity is expected to achieve, that is the rate of return at which the NPV is equal to 0, and compare this with the hurdle rate, which should be the project's cost of capital. If the expected rate of return exceeds the hurdle rate, the project should be undertaken. On the contrary, if the expected rate of return is less than the hurdle rate the project should be rejected.

Without a computer or a programmable calculator, the calculation of the internal rate of return is made by a trial and error technique called interpolation. The first step is to calculate two net present values, both as close as possible to zero. The closer to zero, the more accurate will be the end result. Ideally, in applying these two rates the result should be one NPV being positive and the other negative. It is then necessary to use interpolation to establish the rate where NPV is 0.

Using the example of The Low Dyke Hotel's proposed acquisition of the Floating Oyster Restaurant the internal rate of return will be determined in the following manner. Recall that at 12% the NPV is €1,189,850.27 over the 10 years of the analysis. It should be noted that the higher the discount rate used in a net present value analysis, the lower the present value of all future cash flows will be. This is true because a higher discount rate means that it is even more important to have the money earlier instead of later. Thus, a discount rate higher than 12% would be required to drive the proposed acquisition of the Floating Oyster Restaurant's net present value down to zero. Exhibit 15.26 indicates a positive NPV of €21,469.72 at a discount rate of 29% and also a negative NPV of €17,023.23 at a discount rate of 30%. Both amounts are relatively close to zero. This means that the real IRR is situated between 29% and 30%.

The interpolation method assumes that the NPV rises in a linear fashion between the two rates of return. The formula to apply is:

$$\text{Internal rate of return} = A + \frac{P}{(P + N)} \times (B - A)$$

Exhibit 15.26 **IRR interpolation**

Period	Cash flow	DF @ 29%	PV @ 29%	DF @ 30%	PV @ 30%
			IRR interpolation		
0	(€ 1,137,500.00)	1	(€ 1,137,500.00)	1	(€ 1,137,500.00)
1	€ 110,000.00	0.775194	€ 85,271.32	0.769231	€ 84,615.38
2	€ 150,000.00	0.600925	€ 90,138.81	0.591716	€ 88,757.40
3	€ 170,000.00	0.465834	€ 79,191.72	0.455166	€ 77,378.24
4	€ 210,000.00	0.361111	€ 75,833.39	0.350128	€ 73,526.84
5	€ 250,000.00	0.279931	€ 69,982.82	0.269329	€ 67,332.27
6	€ 280,000.00	0.217001	€ 60,760.28	0.207176	€ 58,009.34
7	€ 314,000.00	0.168218	€ 52,820.40	0.159366	€ 50,041.02
8	€ 348,000.00	0.130401	€ 45,379.69	0.122589	€ 42,661.14
9	€ 382,000.00	0.101086	€ 38,614.99	0.094300	€ 36,022.45
10	€ 416,000.00	0.078362	€ 32,598.40	0.072538	€ 30,175.87
		NPV	€ 21,469.72	**NPV**	(€ 17,023.23)

in which,

A is the (lower) rate of return with a positive NPV
B is the (higher) rate of return with a negative NPV
P is the absolute amount of the positive NPV
N is the absolute amount of the negative NPV

Now applying this formula to the data calculated for the project we can calculate the IRR:

$$IRR = 29\% + \frac{€21,469.72}{(€21,469.72 + €17,023.23)} \times (30\% - 29\%)$$

$$IRR = 29\% + \frac{€21,469.72}{€38,492.95} \times 1\%$$

$$IRR = 29\% + 0.5577571 \times 1\%$$

$$IRR = 29\% + 0.56\% \text{ (rounded to 2 decimals places)}$$

$$IRR = 29.56\%$$

As the IRR of 29.56% is higher than the cost of capital (12%) then the project proposal is acceptable.

The IRR of the Low Dyke Hotel's acquisition of the Floating Oyster Restaurant has been established in a situation in which the yearly cash flows were different. In investment situations of annuities, where the cash flows will be the same for all the years, the internal rate of return is determined in the following manner.

Assume that the Low Dyke Hotels can purchase new kitchen equipment at a cost of €72,000.03 that will save €19,974.53 per year in operating costs. This kitchen equipment has a life of 7 years. The calculation of the internal rate of return will be done in two steps.

Step 1 Determine the annuity discount factor

Step 2 Look in the factor tables (exhibit 15.19) at the row of 7 periods under what rate of discount the established discount factor is positioned. That rate is then considered as internal rate of return.

As such, the IRR of the Low Dyke Hotels' purchase of new kitchen equipment will be established in the following manner:

Step 1: Determine the annuity discount factor.
This is done by dividing the initial investment cost by the annuity.

$$\frac{€72,000.03}{€19,974.53} = 3.604592$$

Step 2: check in the present value factor of an annuity table (exhibit 15.19) and try to locate in the row of 7 periods under what rate of discount the factor 3.604592 is to be found. This factor is located under rate of discount 20%. This 20% will then be considered as the internal rate of return for the new kitchen equipment.

4 Comparing the NPV and IRR methods

The decision to accept or reject an investment proposal can be made using either the NPV method or the IRR method. The different approaches used in the methods are summarized as follows:

Net present value method

- Compute the investment proposal's net present value, using the organization's hurdle rate as the discount rate

- Accept the investment proposal if its net present value is equal to or greater than zero; otherwise reject it.

Internal rate of return method

- Compute the investment proposals, internal rate of return, which is the discount rate that yields a zero net present value for the project.

- Accept the investment proposal if its internal rate of return is equal to or greater than the organization's hurdle rate; otherwise reject it.

Notice that the hurdle rate is mentioned in each of the two methods.

The NPV method exhibits two potential advantages over the IRR method. First, if the investment analysis is carried out by hand, it is easier to compute a project's NPV than its IRR. For example, if the cash flows are uneven across time, trial and error must be used to find the IRR. This advantage of the NPV approach is not as important, however, when a computer is used.

A second potential advantage of the NPV method is that the analyst can adjust for risk considerations. For some investment proposals, the further into the future that a cash flow occurs, the less certain the analyst can be about the amount of the cash flow. Thus, the later a projected cash flow occurs, the riskier it may be. It is possible to adjust NPV analysis for such risk factors by using a higher discount rate for later cash flows than earlier cash flows. It is not possible to include such a risk adjustment in the IRR method, because the analysis solves for only a single discount rate, the project's IRR.

5 Assumptions underlying DCF analysis

Four main assumptions underlie the NPV and IRR methods of investment analysis.

- In the present value calculations used in the NPV and IRR methods, all cash flows are treated as though they occur at the end of the year. The additional computational complexity that would be required to reflect the exact timing of all cash flows would complicate an investment analysis considerably. The error introduced by the year-end cash flow assumption generally is not large enough to cause any concern.

- DCF analyses treat the cash flow associated with an investment project as though they were known with certainty. Although methods of capital budgeting under uncertainty have been developed, they are not widely used in practice. Most decision makers do not feel that the additional benefits in improved decisions are worth the additional complexity involved. As mentioned above, risk adjustment can be made in a NPV analysis to partially account for uncertainty about the cash flow.

- Both the NPV and IRR methods assume that each cash inflow is immediately reinvested in another project that earns a return for the organization. In the NPV method, each cash inflow is assumed to be reinvested at the same rate used to compute the project's NPV, the organization's hurdle rate. In the IRR method, each cash inflow is assumed to be reinvested at the same rate as the project's internal rate of return.

- A DCF analysis assumes a perfect capital market. This implies that money can be borrowed or lent at an interest rate equal to the hurdle rate used in the analysis.

In practice, these four assumptions are rarely satisfied. Nevertheless, DCF models provide an effective and widely used method of investment analysis. The improved decision making that would result from using more complicated models is seldom worth the additional cost of information and analysis.

15.7   Incidence of taxes on DCF analysis

Generally when taxes affect a decision, an expert inside or outside the organization should be consulted because tax laws are complex and they change regularly. After tax cash flows should be used in DCF calculations because tax payments constitute an outflow of cash, and competing projects may have different tax allowances and charges which might influence the investment decisions. The following procedure is used for converting pre-tax cash flows to post-cash cash flows.

- Determine the investment incentives available for the equipment
- The allowance are deducted from the pre-tax cash flow (net income + depreciation) leaving a figure of taxable income.
- When the equipment is disposed of, any residual revenue is shown as cash inflow.
- Business tax is chargeable on each year's taxable income and on the average is expected to be paid 12 months later.
- After tax cash flow which comes in for discounting consists of pre-tax cash flows less tax paid.
- It is usually assumed that there is income being generated elsewhere in the company against which capital allowances may be offset. Therefore a cash inflow of tax may be recorded in respect of a project where insufficient profit is made on it to absorb tax allowance.
- If no profits are available in the company to use up capital allowances they may be carried forward until such time as there are profits available against which to set the allowances.

When a business makes a profit, it usually must pay income taxes, just as individuals do. Since many of the cash flows associated with an investment proposal affect the company's profit, they also affect the company's income tax liability. The following equation shows the items that appear on an income statement.

$$\text{Income} = \text{revenue} - \text{expenses} + \text{gains} - \text{losses}$$

Any aspect of an investment project that affects any of the items in this equation generally will affect the company's income tax payments. These income tax payments are cash flows, and they must be considered in any DCF analysis. In some cases, tax considerations are so crucial in a capital investment decision that they dominate all other aspects of the analysis.

After-tax cash flows
The first step in a discount cash flow analysis for a profit seeking enterprise is to determine the after-tax cash flows associated with the investment projects under consideration. An after-tax cash flow is the cash flow expected after all tax implications have been taken into account. Each financial aspect of a project must be examined carefully to determine its potential tax impact.

A hotel will be used to illustrate the tax implications of various types of financial items, The Lemon Tree Hotel is quite profitable, and the management is considering several capital projects that will enhance the company's future profit potential. Before analyzing these projects, consider the tax issues the company faces. For this analysis assume that The Lemon Tree Hotel's income tax rate is 40.00%. Thus, if the company's income before tax is €1,000,000.00, its income tax payment will be €400,000.00 (€1,000,000.00 × 40.00%).

Cash revenue

Suppose The Lemon Tree Hotel's management is considering the purchase of new restaurant equipment. The sales manager estimates that new restaurant equipment will allow the company to increase annual revenues by €100,000.00. Further, suppose that this incremental revenue will be received in cash during the year (meaning that all credit sales will be paid in cash within a short time period). The Lemon Tree Hotel's additional annual revenue results in an increase of €70,000.00 per year in cost of goods sold. Moreover, the additional merchandise sold will be paid for in cash during the same year as the related sales. Thus, the net incremental cash inflow resulting from the sales increase is €30,000.00 per year (€100,000.00 − €70,000.00).

What is The Lemon Tree Hotel's after-tax cash flow from the incremental sales revenue, net of cost of goods sold? As the following calculation shows, the company's incremental cash inflow from the additional sales is only €18,000.00.

Incremental sales revenue, net of cost of goods sold (cash inflow)	€ 30,000.00
Incremental income tax (cash outflow) €30,000.00 × 40%	(€ 12,000.00)
After-tax cash flow (net inflow after taxes)	€ 18,000.00

Although the incremental sales amounted to an additional net cash inflow of €30,000.00, the cash outflow for income taxes also increased by €12,000.00. Thus, after-tax cash inflow from the incremental sales, net of cost of goods sold, is €18,000.00.

A quick method for computing the after-tax cash inflow from the incremental sales is the following:

Incremental sales revenue, net of cost of goods sold × (1 − Tax rate)
= After-tax cash inflow
€30,000.00 × (1 − 40%) = €18,000.00

Cash expenses

What are the tax implications of cash expenses? Suppose the addition of the restaurant equipment under consideration by The Lemon Tree Hotel's management will involve hiring an additional employee, whose annual compensation and fringe benefits will amount to €20,000.00. As the following computation shows, the company's incremental cash outflow is only €12,000.00.

Incremental expense (cash outflow)	€ 20,000.00
Reduction in income tax (reduced cash outflow) €20,000.00 × 40%	(€ 8,000.00)
After-tax cash flow (net outflow after taxes)	€ 12,000.00

Although the incremental employee compensation is €20,000.00, this expense is tax deductible. Thus, the company's income tax payment will be reduced by €8,000.00. As a result, the after-tax cash out flow from the additional compensation is €12,000.00.

A quick method for computing the after-tax cash outflow from the incremental expense is shown below:

Incremental cash expense × (1 – tax rate) = After-tax cash outflow
€20,000.00 × (1 – 40%) = €12,000.00

Non-cash expenses

Not all expenses represent cash outflows. The most common example of a non-cash expense is depreciation expense. Suppose The Lemon Tree Hotel management is considering the purchase of the restaurant equipment that costs €30,000.00. The equipment has no salvage value and will be depreciated as follows:

Exhibit 15.27 **Depreciation plan restaurant equipment**

The only cash flow shown in exhibit 15.27 is the restaurant equipment's acquisition cost of €30,000.00 at time zero. The depreciation expense in each of the next five years is not a cash flow. However, depreciation is an expense on the income statement, and it reduces the company's income. For example, €3,750.00 depreciation expense in year 1 will reduce The Lemon Tree Hotel's taxable income by €3,750.00. As a result, the company's year 1 income tax payment will decline by €1,500.00 (40% × €3,750.00).

The annual depreciation expense associated with the equipment provides a reduction in income-tax expense equal to the firm's tax rate times the depreciated deduction. This reduction in income taxes is called a depreciation tax shield. To summarize, depreciation is a non cash expense. Although depreciation is not a cash flow, it does cause a reduced cash outflow through the depreciation tax shield.

Depreciation or any other non cash expense × tax rate = Reduced cash outflow for income taxes

Year 1 Depreciation of €3,750.00 × 40% = €1,500.00

Is not a cash flow   Is a cash flow

Exhibit 15.28 shows The Lemon Tree Hotel depreciation tax shield over the depreciable life of the proposed restaurant equipment.

Exhibit 15.28 **The Lemon Tree Hotel depreciation tax shield**

Year	Depreciation Expense	Tax Rate	Cash flow reduced Tax Payment
1	€ 3,750.00	40%	€ 1,500.00
2	€ 7,500.00	40%	€ 3,000.00
3	€ 7,500.00	40%	€ 3,000.00
4	€ 7,500.00	40%	€ 3,000.00
5	€ 3,750.00	40%	€ 1,500.00

The cash flows constituting the depreciation tax shield occur in five different years, the last column of exhibit 15.28. Thus, in a discounted cash flow analysis, we still must discount these cash flows to find their present value.

Cash flows not in the income statement
Some cash flows do not appear on the income statement. They are not revenues, expenses, gains, or losses. A common example of such a cash flow is the purchase of an asset. If The Lemon Tree Hotel purchases the restaurant equipment of €30,000.00, the acquisition cost is a cash outflow but not an expense. A purchase is merely the exchange of one asset (cash) for another. The expense associated with the equipment's purchase is recognized through depreciation expense recorded throughout the asset's depreciable life. Thus, the cash flow resulting from the purchase of an asset does not affect income and has no direct tax consequences.

Exhibit 15.29 **Proposed purchase of restaurant equipment for the Lemon Tree Hotel**

	Time 0	Time 1	Time 2	Time 3	Time 4	Time 5
		The Lemon Tree Hotel Purchase of Restaurant Equipment (r = 12%, n = 5)				
Acquisition cost	€ 30,000.00					
After tax cash flow from incremental sales revenue net of cost of goods sold...		€ 18,000.00	€ 18,000.00	€ 18,000.00	€ 18,000.00	€ 18,000.00
After tax cash flow from incremental compensation expense...		€ 8,000.00	€ 8,000.00	€ 8,000.00	€ 8,000.00	€ 8,000.00
After tax cash flow from depreciation tax shield, depreciation expense...		€ 1,500.00	€ 3,000.00	€ 3,000.00	€ 3,000.00	€ 1,500.00
Total cash flow	€ 30,000.00	€ 11,500.00	€ 13,000.00	€ 13,000.00	€ 13,000.00	€ 11,500.00
Discount factor	1	0.892857	0.797194	0.711780	0.635518	0.567427
Present value	€ 30,000.00	€ 10,267.86	€ 10,363.52	€ 9,253.14	€ 8,261.73	€ 6,525.41
	NPV	€ 14,671.66				

Completing the analysis by preparing a NPV analysis of the proposed restaurant's equipment acquisition results in the situation depicted in exhibit 15.29 under conditions of an after-tax hurdle rate of 12%. Since the NPV is positive, the restaurant equipment should be purchased.

Timing of tax deductions

It has been assumed in the analysis of The Lemon Tree Hotel restaurant equipment purchase that the cash flows resulting from income taxes occur during the same year as the related before tax cash flows. This assumption is realistic, as most businesses must make estimated tax payments throughout the tax year. They generally cannot wait until the following year and pay their prior year's taxes in one lump sum.

15.8 Choosing between projects

Mutually exclusive projects (two or more project alternatives where acceptance of one alternative automatically excludes acceptance of any of the remaining) have been assumed to have the same useful life. In reality, many mutually exclusive projects do not have equal lives. In such situations, the three approaches to decision making are as follows:

- Assume that the shorter lived project is followed with another project and that the combined lives of the two projects equal the life of the mutually exclusive longer lived project.
- Assume that the longer lived project is disposed of at the end of the shorter lived project's life.
- Ignore the difference in the lives of the two mutually exclusive projects.

The third approach is reasonable, only if the lives are both long and the difference is inconsequential. For example, a difference of one year for proposed projects with 14- and 15-year lives may be immaterial.

The first approach is illustrated in exhibit 15.30. In this example, a hotel is considering whether to replace its laundry washer with Machine A, which has a ten-year life and no salvage, or with Machine B, which has a five-year life and no salvage value. At the end of Machine B's life, Machine C, which will have a five-year life and no salvage, will be acquired. Thus, the life of Machine A (ten years) equals the combined lives of Machines B and C. The capital budgeting model and discount rate used are the NPV and 12%, respectively. The results suggest that Machine B should be purchased now followed by Machine C at the end of year five.

The second approach that of assuming the longer lived project is disposed of at the end of the short-lived project's life is illustrated in figure 15.31. The same situation is assumed as in exhibit 15.30 except the comparison is only for five years as Machine B is totally used at the end of year five. In addition, at the end of year five, Machine A is assumed to have a salvage value of €35,000.00. The NPV of Machines A and B are €1,463.00 and €4,057.00, respectively. Therefore, based on the available information, Machine B would be purchased.

- Machine A costs €75,000.00 and provides a project cash flow of €15,000.00 per year for its ten-year life.
- Machine B costs €30,000.00 and provides a project cash flow of €15,000.00 per year for its five-year life of years 1 through 5.

Exhibit 15.30 **Comparison of machine acquisition with different lives – first approach**

Years	Cash Flows		
	Alternative A **Machine A**	**Alternative B** **Machine B**	**Machine C**
0	€ 75,000.00	€ 30,000.00	
1	€ 15,000.00	€ 15,000.00	
2	€ 15,000.00	€ 15,000.00	
3	€ 15,000.00	€ 15,000.00	
4	€ 15,000.00	€ 15,000.00	
5	€ 15,000.00	€ 15,000.00	€ 55,000.00
6	€ 15,000.00		€ 15,000.00
7	€ 15,000.00		€ 15.000.00
8	€ 15,000.00		€ 15,000.00
9	€ 15,000.00		€ 15,000.00
10	€ 15,000.00		€ 15,000.00
	Alternative A		**Alternative B**
	€ 84,753.35		€ 84,753.35
	€ 75,000.00		€ 61,208.48
NPV	**€ 9,753.35**	**NPV**	**€ 23,544.87**

- Machine C (purchased to replace Machine B) costs €55,000.00 at the end of year five and provides project cash flow of €15,000.00 per year for its five-year life of years 6 through 10.

Exhibit 15.31 **Comparison of machine acquisitions with different lives-second approach**

Years	Cash Flows	
	Machine A	**Machine B**
0	€ 75,000.00	€ 30,000.00
1	€ 15,000.00	€ 15,000.00
2	€ 15,000.00	€ 15,000.00
3	€ 15,000.00	€ 15,000.00
4	€ 15,000.00	€ 15,000.00
5	€ 50,000.00	€ 15,000.00
	NPV – Machine A	**NPV – Machine B**
	€ 45,560.24	€ 54,071.64
	€ 28,371.34	
	€ 75,000.00	€ 30,000.00
NPV	**– € 1,068.42**	**€ 24,071.64**

In exhibit 15.31 Machine A costs €75,000.00 and provides cash flow of €15,000.00 per year for five years and then may be sold for €35,000.00. Machine B costs €30,000.00 and provides project cash flow of €15,000.00. It has no salvage value.

Glossary

Acceptance-or-rejection decisions – these are decisions in which managers already have or can easily have the funds and must make the decision whether to accept or reject the project.

Accounting rate of return (ARR) – this is an approach to evaluating projects based on the average annual project income divided by the initial investment.

Annuity – this is a stream of equal payments that are made at regular intervals over a fixed period of time.

Average rate of return (ARR) – this is an approach to evaluating projects based on the average annual project income divided by the average investment.

Capital-rationing decisions – these are decisions whereby managers must decide which of the several acceptable projects would be the best one to invest in.

Compound interest – this is an interest payment computed on the amount of the principal plus any previously accumulated interest that affected the original principal.

Cost of capital – is the rate of return that a business could make when executing a project if it so chose and when compared with other investments with equivalent risks. This can also be stated as the opportunity cost of the funds used in the project.

Discount rate – this is the term attributed to the rate of interest used in the discounting process when finding a present value.

Discounted cash flow (DCF) methods – these are investment analysis methods in which an assessment of the present values of future net cash flows are taken into consideration in the investment decision making process.

Hurdle rate – this is the minimum acceptable rate of return, comparable to the project's cost of capital, that must be met or exceeded for a project to be accepted.

Internal rate of return (IRR) method – this is a common DCF method in which a project is evaluated based on comparing its rate of return to the established hurdle rate.

Net present value (NPV) method – this is a common DCF method in which the present values of a project's future cash flows are calculated and compared to the initial project costs.

Payback method – this is a method that tries to determine how long it will take for the expected net cash inflows to payback the investment outflows.

Simple interest – this is an interest payment computed on only the amount of the principal for one or more periods.

Time value of money – this is the notion that the value of a currency is worth more today than in the future due to its possibility of earning interest if invested.

Multiple choice questions

15.1   In which of the following type of capital budgeting decision must the manager decide amongst alternative worthwhile projects?
   a   capital rationing
   b   acceptance
   c   rejection
   d   capital discounting

15.2   The following factor is excluded in the payback method of making capital investment decisions?
   a   the net cash inflows
   b   the net investment cash outflows
   c   the project cost
   d   the time value of money

15.3   In assessing the accounting rate of return, the incremental accounting income is divided by:
   a   average investment
   b   incremental investment
   c   initial investment
   d   marginal investment

15.4   The capital investment decision method in which the decision is made based on its comparison to the true economic return earned by the asset over its life is:
   a   the average rate of return method
   b   the internal rate of return method
   c   the net present value method
   d   the payback method

15.5   In a proposed investment project, what will be the course of action if the internal rate of return is 16% and the hurdle rate is 17.5%?
   a   the project should be accepted
   b   the project should be reassessed using the accounting rate of return
   c   the project should be reassessed using the average rate of return
   d   the project should be rejected

Exercises

15.1   As accountant of the motel, your manager wishes to know the outcomes of four possible investments 8 years from now, and you are asked to determine the future values of each one.

	Principal	Interest rate	Remarks
First investment	€ 850,000.00	14.00%	compounded annually
Second investment	€ 750,000.00	12.00%	simple interest
Third investment	€ 70,000.00	12.00%	8 yearly investments and to be compounded annually
Fourth investment	€ 900,000.00	13.00%	half now and half after four years and to be compounded twice a year

15.2 The table below present expected future net cash flows for the Mata Hari Restaurant. Use the anticipated discount rates to determine the present values of each of the expected cash flow.

Year	Expected cash flow	Anticipated discount rate
1	€ 1,250,000.00	11.00%
2	€ 1,320,000.00	11.00%
3	€ 1,450,000.00	12.00%
4	€ 1,510,000.00	12.00%
5	€ 1,654,000.00	13.00%
6	€ 1,760,000.00	12.00%
7	€ 1,985,000.00	12.00%
8	€ 2,135,000.00	11.00%
9	€ 2,456,000.00	11.00%
10	€ 3,125,000.00	10.00%

15.3 Martin and Mirabel are about to put their life savings of €50,000,000.00 into a new project that is expected to generate the following net income streams.

The project is expected to have no salvage value at the end of the 10 years and you are asked to advise Martin and Mirabel on how to proceed using the accounting rate of return method of capital investment analysis. Martin and Mirabel also inform you that they need a return on their investment of at least 30%. Should they proceed with the project?

Projected net incomes	
Year 1	(€ 1,834,250.00)
Year 2	€ 197,340.00
Year 3	€ 258,060.00
Year 4	€ 3,495,448.00
Year 5	€ 7,020,750.00
Year 6	€ 23,613,755.00
Year 7	€ 23,402,500.00
Year 8	€ 17,321,645.00
Year 9	€ 15,758,105.00
Year 10	€ 14,226,822.50

15.4 The management of the Bull's Run are considering expanding their activities by building and running a 3-D entertainment hall. The estimated investment information is as follows:

The management has asked you to provide them with answers to the following questions:
a what will be the payback period?
b what is the accounting rate of return?
c what is the net present value?
d what is the internal rate of return?

Investment	€ 1,000,000.00
Incremental annual revenues	€ 1,050,000.00
Incremental annual expenses	€ 850,000.00
Depreciation	linear
Discount rate	14.00%
Salvage value	null
Investment horizon	10 years

References for further reading

Books:
AHMA-FMC, (1997), Hotel Internal Control Guide, Educational Institute – American Hotel and Motel Association, Lansing, Michigan

Andrew, W, P, Damitio, J. W. & Schmidgall, R. S. (2007), Financial Management for the Hospitality Industry, Pearson – Prentice Hall, Upper Saddle River, New Jersey

Berry, A. & Jarvis, R., (2006), Accounting in a Business Context, 4th edition, Thomson, Bedford Row, London

Cote, R. (2001) Accounting for Hospitality Managers, Educational Institute, 4th edition, – American Hotel and Lodging Association, Lansing, Michigan

Cote, R. (2006), Basic Hotel and Restaurant Accounting, 6th edition, Educational Institute – American Hotel and Lodging Association, Lansing, Michigan

Davies, T. & Boczko, T., (2005), Business Accounting and Finance, 2nd edition, McGraw-Hill Education, Maidenhead, Berkshire

Glautier, M. W. E. & Underwood, B (2001), Accounting Theory and Practice, 7th edition, Pearson Education Limited, Harlow, Essex

Gowthorpe, C., (2005), Business Accounting and Finance for non specialists, 2nd edition, Thomson, Bedford Row, London

Guilding, C., (2002), Financial Management for Hospitality Decision Makers, Butterworth-Heinemann, Jordan Hill, Oxford

HACNY/AH & LEI/HF & TP, (2006) Uniform System of Accounts for the Lodging Industry, 10th revised edition

Hales, J. A., (2005), Accounting and Financial Analysis in the Hospitality Industry, Elsevier Butterworth-Heinemann, Jordan Hill, Oxford

Harris, P. J. & Hazzard, P. A., (1987) Managerial Accounting in the Hotel and Catering Industry – volume 2, 4th edition, Hutchinson Education, London

Hilton, R. W., (2008), Managerial Accounting: Creating Value in a Dynamic Business Environment, 7th edition, McGraw-Hill Irwin, Boston

Jagels, M. G., (2007), Hospitality Management Accounting, 9th edition, John Wiley & Sons, Hoboken, New Jersey

Schmidgall, R. S., (2006), Hospitality Industry Management Accounting, 6th edition, Educational Institute – American Hotel and Lodging Association, Lansing, Michigan

Stice, E. K., & Stice J. D., (2006), Financial Accounting: Reporting and Analysis, 7th edition, Thomson South Western, Mason, Ohio

Internet:
Bureau of Labour Statistics, U.S. Department of Labour, *Career Guide to Industries, 2008-09 Edition*, Hotels and Other Accommodations, on the Internet at http://www.bls.gov/oco/cg/cgs036.htm (visited *October 18, 2009*)

Answers to end of chapter multiple choice questions

Answers chapter 1

1.1 c   1.2 d   1.3 b   1.4 c   1.5 a

Answers chapter 2

2.1 c   2.2 d   2.3 d   2.4 a   2.5 d

Answers chapter 3

3.1 b   3.2 c   3.3 b   3.4 b   3.5 d

Answers chapter 4

4.1 a   4.2 c   4.3 c   4.4 a   4.5 a

Answers chapter 5

5.1 d   5.2 c   5.3 c   5.4 c   5.5 d

Answers chapter 6

6.1 d   6.2 b   6.3 a   6.4 b   6.5 d

Answers chapter 7

7.1 b   7.2 d   7.3 c   7.4 c   7.5 d

Answers chapter 8

8.1 a   8.2 b   8.3 b   8.4 d   8.5 c

Answers chapter 9

9.1 d   9.2 a   9.3 a   9.4 c   9.5 b

Answers chapter 10

10.1 b   10.2 c   10.3 a   10.4 c   10.5 b

Answers chapter 11

11.1 c   11.2 c   11.3 a   11.4 b   11.5 c

Answers chapter 12

12.1 b   12.2 d   12.3 c   12.4 d   12.5 c

Answers chapter 13

13.1 d   13.2 c   13.3 b   13.4 c   13.5 b

Answers chapter 14

14.1 d   14.2 c   14.3 c   14.4 d   14.5 c

Answers chapter 15

15.1 a   15.2 d   15.3 c   15.4 b   15.5 d

Appendix

Factor tables

					Future value interest factor of €1 per period at i% for n peridods, FVIF (i,n).						
Period	**1%**	**2%**	**3%**	**4%**	**5%**	**6%**	**7%**	**8%**	**9%**	**10%**	**Period**
1	1.010000	1.020000	1.030000	1.040000	1.050000	1.060000	1.070000	1.080000	1.090000	1.100000	1
2	1.020100	1.040400	1.060900	1.081600	1.102500	1.123600	1.144900	1.166400	1.188100	1.210000	2
3	1.030301	1.061208	1.092727	1.124864	1.157625	1.191016	1.225043	1.259712	1.295029	1.331000	3
4	1.040604	1.082432	1.125509	1.169859	1.215506	1.262477	1.310796	1.360489	1.411582	1.464100	4
5	1.051010	1.104081	1.159274	1.216653	1.276282	1.338226	1.402552	1.469328	1.538624	1.610510	5
6	1.061520	1.126162	1.194052	1.265319	1.340096	1.418519	1.500730	1.586874	1.677100	1.771561	6
7	1.072135	1.148686	1.229874	1.315932	1.407100	1.503630	1.605781	1.713824	1.828039	1.948717	7
8	1.082857	1.171659	1.266770	1.368569	1.477455	1.593848	1.718186	1.850930	1.992563	2.143589	8
9	1.093685	1.195093	1.304773	1.423312	1.551328	1.689479	1.838459	1.999005	2.171893	2.357948	9
10	1.104622	1.218994	1.343916	1.480244	1.628895	1.790848	1.967151	2.158925	2.367364	2.593742	10
11	1.115668	1.243374	1.384234	1.539454	1.710339	1.898299	2.104852	2.331639	2.580426	2.853117	11
12	1.126825	1.268242	1.425761	1.601032	1.795856	2.012196	2.252192	2.518170	2.812665	3.138428	12
13	1.138093	1.293607	1.468534	1.665074	1.885649	2.132928	2.409845	2.719624	3.065805	3.452271	13
14	1.149474	1.319479	1.512590	1.731676	1.979932	2.260904	2.578534	2.937194	3.341727	3.797498	14
15	1.160969	1.345868	1.557967	1.800944	2.078928	2.396558	2.759032	3.172169	3.642482	4.177248	15
16	1.172579	1.372786	1.604706	1.872981	2.182875	2.540352	2.952164	3.425943	3.970306	4.594973	16
17	1.184304	1.400241	1.652848	1.947900	2.292018	2.692773	3.158815	3.700018	4.327633	5.054470	17
18	1.196147	1.428246	1.702433	2.025817	2.406619	2.854339	3.379932	3.996019	4.717120	5.559917	18
19	1.208109	1.456811	1.753506	2.106849	2.526950	3.025600	3.616528	4.315701	5.141661	6.115909	19
20	1.220190	1.485947	1.806111	2.191123	2.653298	3.207135	3.869684	4.660957	5.604411	6.727500	20
25	1.282432	1.640606	2.093778	2.665836	3.386355	4.291871	5.427433	6.848475	8.623081	10.834706	25
30	1.347849	1.811362	2.427262	3.243398	4.321942	5.743491	7.612255	10.062657	13.267678	17.449402	30
35	1.416603	1.999890	2.813862	3.946089	5.516015	7.686087	10.676581	14.785344	20.413968	28.102437	35
40	1.488864	2.208040	3.262038	4.801021	7.039989	10.285718	14.974458	21.724521	31.409420	45.259256	40
50	1.644632	2.691588	4.383906	7.106683	11.467400	18.420154	29.457025	46.901613	74.357520	117.390853	50

Future value interest factor of €1 per period at i% for n periods, FVIF (i,n).

Period	11%	12%	13%	14%	15%	16%	17%
1	1.110000	1.120000	1.130000	1.140000	1.150000	1.160000	1.170000
2	1.232100	1.254400	1.276900	1.299600	1.322500	1.345600	1.368900
3	1.367631	1.404928	1.442897	1.481544	1.520875	1.560896	1.601613
4	1.518070	1.573519	1.630474	1.688960	1.749006	1.810639	1.873887
5	1.685058	1.762342	1.842435	1.925415	2.011357	2.100342	2.192448
6	1.870415	1.973823	2.081952	2.194973	2.313061	2.436396	2.565164
7	2.076160	2.210681	2.352605	2.502269	2.660020	2.826220	3.001242
8	2.304538	2.475963	2.658444	2.852586	3.059023	3.278415	3.511453
9	2.558037	2.773079	3.004042	3.251949	3.517876	3.802961	4.108400
10	2.839421	3.105848	3.394567	3.707221	4.045558	4.411435	4.806828
11	3.151757	3.478550	3.835861	4.226232	4.652391	5.117265	5.623989
12	3.498451	3.895976	4.334523	4.817905	5.350250	5.936027	6.580067
13	3.883280	4.363493	4.898011	5.492411	6.152788	6.885791	7.698679
14	4.310441	4.887112	5.534753	6.261349	7.075706	7.987518	9.007454
15	4.784589	5.473566	6.254270	7.137938	8.137062	9.265521	10.538721
16	5.310894	6.130394	7.067326	8.137249	9.357621	10.748004	12.330304
17	5.895093	6.866041	7.986078	9.276464	10.761264	12.467685	14.426456
18	6.543553	7.689966	9.024268	10.575169	12.375454	14.462514	16.878953
19	7.263344	8.612762	10.197423	12.055693	14.231772	16.776517	19.748375
20	8.062312	9.646293	11.523088	13.743490	16.366537	19.460759	23.105599
25	13.585464	17.000064	21.230542	26.461916	32.918953	40.874244	50.657826
30	22.892297	29.959922	39.115898	50.950159	66.211772	85.849877	1ĭ1.064650
35	38.574851	52.799620	72.068506	98.100178	133.175523	180.314073	243.503474
40	65.000867	93.050970	132.781552	188.883514	267.863546	378.721158	533.868713
50	184.564827	289.002190	450.735925	700.232988	1,083.657442	1,670.703804	2,566.215284

Future value interest factor of €1 per period at i% for n periods, FVIF (i,n).

Period	21%	22%	23%	24%	25%	30%	35%
1	1.2100	1.2200	1.2300	1.2400	1.2500	1.3000	1.3500
2	1.4641	1.4884	1.5129	1.5376	1.5625	1.6900	1.8225
3	1.7716	1.8158	1.8609	1.9066	1.9531	2.1970	2.4604
4	2.1436	2.2153	2.2889	2.3642	2.4414	2.8561	3.3215
5	2.5937	2.7027	2.8153	2.9316	3.0518	3.7129	4.4840
6	3.1384	3.2973	3.4628	3.6352	3.8147	4.8268	6.0534
7	3.7975	4.0227	4.2593	4.5077	4.7684	6.2749	8.1722
8	4.5950	4.9077	5.2389	5.5895	5.9605	8.1573	11.0324
9	5.5599	5.9874	6.4439	6.9310	7.4506	10.6045	14.8937
10	6.7275	7.3046	7.9259	8.5944	9.3132	13.7858	20.1066
11	8.1403	8.9117	9.7489	10.6571	11.6415	17.9216	27.1439
12	9.8497	10.8722	11.9912	13.2148	Ĭ4.5519	23.2981	36.6442
13	11.9182	13.2641	14.7491	16.3863	18.1899	30.2875	49.4697
14	14.4210	16.1822	18.1414	20.3191	22.7374	39.3738	66.7841
15	17.4494	19.7423	22.3140	25.1956	28.4217	51.1859	90.1585
16	21.1138	24.0856	27.4462	31.2426	35.5271	66.5417	121.7139
17	25.5477	29.3844	33.7588	38.7408	44.4089	86.5042	164.3138
18	30.9127	35.8490	41.5233	48.0386	55.5112	112.4554	221.8236
19	37.4043	43.7358	51.0737	59.5679	69.3889	146.1920	299.4619
20	45.2593	53.3576	62.8206	73.8641	86.7362	190.0496	404.2736
25	117.3909	144.2101	176.8593	216.5420	264.6978	705.6410	1,812.7763
30	304.4816	389.7579	497.9129	634.8199	807.7936	2,619.9956	8,128.5495
35	789.7470	1,053.4018	1,401.7769	1,861.0540	2,465.1903	9,727.8604	36,448.6878
40	2,048.4002	2,847.0378	3,946.4305	5,455.9126	7,523.1638	36,118.8648	163,437.1347
50	13,780.6123	20,796.5615	31,279.1953	46,890.4346	70,064.9232	497,929.2230	3,286,157.8795

18%	19%	20%	Period
1.180000	1.190000	1.200000	1
1.392400	1.416100	1.440000	2
1.643032	1.685159	1.728000	3
1.938778	2.005339	2.073600	4
2.287758	2.386354	2.488320	5
2.699554	2.839761	2.985984	6
3.185474	3.379315	3.583181	7
3.758859	4.021385	4.299817	8
4.435454	4.785449	5.159780	9
5.233836	5.694684	6.191736	10
6.175926	6.776674	7.430084	11
7.287593	8.064242	8.916100	12
8.599359	9.596448	10.699321	13
10.147244	11.419773	12.839185	14
11.973748	13.589530	15.407022	15
14.129023	16.171540	18.488426	16
16.672247	19.244133	22.186111	17
19.673251	22.900518	26.623333	18
23.214436	27.251616	31.948000	19
27.393035	32.429423	38.337600	20
62.668627	77.388073	95.396217	25
143.370638	184.675312	237.376314	30
327.997290	440.700607	590.668229	35
750.378345	1,051.667507	1,469.771568	40
3,927.356860	5,988.913902	9,100.438150	50

40%	45%	50%	Period
1.4000	1.4500	1.5000	1
1.9600	2.1025	2.2500	2
2.7440	3.0486	3.3750	3
3.8416	4.4205	5.0625	4
5.3782	6.4097	7.5938	5
7.5295	9.2941	11.3906	6
10.5414	13.4765	17.0859	7
14.7579	19.5409	25.6289	8
20.6610	28.3343	38.4434	9
28.9255	41.0847	57.6650	10
40.4957	59.5728	86.4976	11
56.6939	86.3806	129.7463	12
79.3715	125.2518	194.6195	13
111.1201	181.6151	291.9293	14
155.5681	263.3419	437.8939	15
217.7953	381.8458	656.8408	16
304.9135	553.6764	985.2613	17
426.8789	802.8308	1,477.8919	18
597.6304	1,164.1047	2,216.8378	19
836.6826	1,687.9518	3,325.2567	20
4,499.8796	10,819.3222	25,251.1683	25
24,201.4324	69,348.9783	191,751.0592	30
130,161.1116	444,508.5083	1,456,109.6060	35
700,037.6966	2,849,181.3270	11,057,332.3209	40
20,248,916.2398	117,057,733.7166	637,621,500.2141	50

Future value interest factor of an ordinary annuity of €1 per period at i% for n periods, FVIFA (i,n).

Period	1%	2%	3%	4%	5%	6%	7%
1	1.000000	1.000000	1.000000	1.000000	1.000000	1.000000	1.000000
2	2.010000	2.020000	2.030000	2.040000	2.050000	2.060000	2.070000
3	3.030100	3.060400	3.090900	3.121600	3.152500	3.183600	3.214900
4	4.060401	4.121608	4.183627	4.246464	4.310125	4.374616	4.439943
5	5.101005	5.204040	5.309136	5.416323	5.525631	5.637093	5.750739
6	6.152015	6.308121	6.468410	6.632975	6.801913	6.975319	7.153291
7	7.213535	7.434283	7.662462	7.898294	8.142008	8393838	8.654021
8	8.285671	8.582969	8.892336	9.214226	9.549109	9.897468	10.259803
9	9.368527	9.754628	10.159106	10.582795	11.026564	11.491316	11.977989
10	10.462213	10.949721	11.463879	12.006107	12.577893	13.180795	13.816448
11	11.566835	12.168715	12.807796	13.486351	14.206787	14.971643	15.783599
12	12.682503	13.412090	14.192030	15.025805	15.917127	16.869941	17.888451
13	13.809328	14.680332	15617790	16.626838	17.712983	18.882138	20.140643
14	14.947421	15.973938	17.086324	18.291911	19.598632	21.015066	22.550488
15	16.096896	17.293417	18.598914	20.023588	21.578564	23.275970	25.129022
16	17.257864	18.639285	20.156881	21.824531	23.657492	25.672528	27.888054
17	18.430443	20.012071	21.761588	23.697512	25.840366	28.212880	30.840217
18	19.614748	21.412312	23.414435	25.645413	28.132385	30.905653	33.999033
19	20.810895	22.840559	25.116868	27.671229	30.539004	33.759992	37.378965
20	22.019004	24.297370	26.870374	29.778079	33.065954	36.785591	40.995492
25	28.243200	32.030300	36.459264	41.645908	47.727099	54.864512	63.249038
30	34.784892	40.568079	47.575416	56.084938	66.438848	79.058186	94.460786
35	41.660276	49.994478	60.462082	73652225	90.320307	111.434780	138.236878
40	48.886373	60.401983	75.401260	95.025516	120.799774	154.761966	199.635112
50	64.463182	84.579401	112.796867	152.667084	209.347996	290.335905	406.528929

Future value interest factor of an ordinary annuity of €1 per period at i% for n periods, FVIFA(i,n).

Period	11%	12%	13%	14%	15%	16%	17%
1	1.000000	1.000000	1.000000	1.000000	1.000000	1.000000	1.000000
2	2.110000	2.120000	2.130000	2.140000	2.150000	2.160000	2.170000
3	3.342100	3.374400	3.406900	3.439600	3.472500	3.505600	3.538900
4	4.709731	4.779328	4.849797	4.921144	4.993375	5.066496	5.140513
5	6.227801	6.352847	6.480271	6.610104	6.742381	6.877135	7.014400
6	7.912860	8.115189	8.322706	8.535519	8.753738	8.977477	9.206848
7	9.783274	10.089012	10.404658	10.730491	11.066799	11.413873	11.772012
8	11.859434	12.299693	12.757263	13.232760	13.726819	14.240093	14.773255
9	14.163972	14.775656	15.415707	16.085347	16.785842	17.518508	18.284708
10	16.722009	17.548735	18.419749	19.337295	20.303718	21.321469	22.393108
11	19.561430	20.654583	21.814317	23.044516	24.349276	25.732904	27.199937
12	22.713187	24.133133	25.650178	27.270749	29.001667	30.850169	32.823926
13	26.211638	28.029109	29.984701	32.088654	34.351917	36.786196	39.403993
14	30.094918	32.392602	34.882712	37.581065	40.504705	43.671987	47.102672
15	34.405359	37.279715	40.417464	43.842414	47.580411	51.659505	56.110126
16	39.189948	42.753280	46.671735	50.980352	55.717472	60.925026	66.648848
17	44.500843	48.883674	53.739060	59.117601	65.075093	71.673030	78.979152
18	50.395936	55.749715	61.725138	68.394066	75.836357	84.140715	93.405608
19	56.939488	63.439681	70.749406	78.969235	88.211811	98.603230	110.284561
20	64.202832	72.052442	80.946829	91.024928	102.443583	115.379747	130.032936
25	114.413307	133.333870	155.619556	181.870827	212.793017	249.214024	292.104856
30	199.020878	241.332684	293.199215	356.786847	434.745146	530.311731	647.439118
35	341.589555	431.663496	546.680819	693.572702	881.170156	1,120.712955	1,426.491022
40	581.826066	767.091420	1,013.704243	1,342.025099	1,779.090308	2,360.757241	3,134.521839
50	1,668.771152	2,400.018249	3,459.507117	4,994.521346	7,217.716277	10,435.648773	15,089.501673

8%	9%	10%	Period
1.000000	1.000000	1.000000	1
2.080000	2.090000	2.100000	2
3.246400	3.278100	3.310000	3
4.506112	4.573129	4.641000	4
5.866601	5.984711	6.105100	5
7.335929	7.523335	7.715610	6
8.922803	9.200435	9.487171	7
10636628	11.028474	11.435888	8
12.487558	13.021036	13.579477	9
14.486562	15.192930	15.937425	10
16.645487	17.560293	18.531167	11
18.977126	20.140720	21.384284	12
21.495297	22.953385	24.522712	13
24.214920	26.019189	27.974983	14
27.152114	29.360916	31.772482	15
30.324283	33.003399	35.949730	16
33.750226	36.973705	40.544703	17
37.450244	41.301338	45.599173	18
41.446263	46.018458	51.159090	19
45.761964	51.160120	57.274999	20
73.105940	84.700896	98.347059	25
113.283211	136.307539	164.494023	30
172.316804	215.710755	271.024368	35
259.056519	337.882445	442.592556	40
573.770156	815.083556	1163.908529	50

18%	19%	20%	Period
1.000000	1.000000	1.000000	1
2.180000	2.190000	2.200000	2
3.572400	3.606100	3.640000	3
5.215432	5.291259	5.368000	4
7.154210	7.296598	7.441600	5
9.441968	9.682952	9.929920	6
12.141522	12.522713	12.915904	7
15.326996	15.902028	16.499085	8
19.085855	19.923413	20.798902	9
23.521309	24.708862	25.958682	10
28.755144	30.403546	32.150419	11
34.931070	37.180220	39.580502	12
42.218663	45.244461	48.496603	13
50.818022	54.840909	59.195923	14
60.965266	66.260682	72.035108	15
72.939014	79.850211	87.442129	16
87.068036	96.021751	105.930555	17
103.740283	115.265884	128.116666	18
123.413534	138.166402	154.740000	19
146.627970	165.418018	186688000	20
342.603486	402.042491	471.981083	25
790.947991	966.712169	1,181.881569	30
1,816.651612	2,314.213721	2,948.341146	35
4,163.213027	5,529.828982	7,343.857840	40
21,813.093666	31,515.336327	45,497.190750	50

Future value interest factor of an ordinary annuity of €1 per period at i% for n periods, FVIFA (i,n).

Period	21%	22%	23%	24%	25%	30%	35%
1	1.0000	1.0000	1.0000	1.0000	1.0000	1.0000	1.0000
2	2.2100	22200	2.2300	2.2400	2.2500	2.3000	2.3500
3	3.6741	3.7084	3.7429	3.7776	3.8125	3.9900	4.1725
4	5.4457	5.5242	5.6038	5.6842	5.7656	6.1870	6.6329
5	7.5892	7.7396	7.8926	8.0484	8.2070	9.0431	9.9544
6	10,1830	10.4423	10.7079	10.9801	11.2588	12.7560	14.4384
7	13.3214	13.7396	14.1708	14.6153	15.0735	17.5828	20.4919
8	17.1189	17.7623	18.4300	19.1229	19.8419	23.8577	28.6640
9	21.7139	22.6700	23.6690	24.7125	25.8023	32.0150	39.6964
10	27.2738	28.6574	30,1128	31.6434	33,2529	42.6195	54.5902
11	34.0013	35.9620	38.0388	40.2379	42.5661	56.4053	74.6967
12	42.1416	44.8737	47.7877	50.8950	54.2077	74.3270	101.8406
13	51.9913	55.7459	59.7788	64.1097	68.7596	97.6250	138.4848
14	63.9095	69.0100	74.5280	80.4961	86.9495	127.9125	187.9544
15	78.3305	85.1922	92.6694	100.8151	109.6868	167.2863	254,7385
16	95.7799	104.9345	114.9834	126.0108	138.1085	218.4722	344.8970
17	116.8937	129.0201	142.4295	157.2534	173.6357	285.0139	466.6109
18	142.4413	158.4045	176.1883	195.9942	218.0446	371.5180	630.9247
19	173.3540	194.2535	217.7116	244.0328	273.5558	483.9734	852.7483
20	210.7584	237.9893	268.7853	303.6006	342.9447	630.1655	1,152.2103
25	554.2422	650.9551	764.6054	898.0916	1,054.7912	2,348.8033	5.176.5037
30	1,445.1507	1,767.0813	2,160.4907	2,640.9164	3,227.1743	8,729.9855	23,221.5700
35	3,755.9379	4,783.6447	6,090.3344	7,750.2251	9,856.7613	32,422.8681	104,136.2508
40	9,749.5248	12,936.5353	17,154.0456	22,728.8026	30,088.6554	120,392.8827	466,960.3848
50	65.617.2016	94,525.2793	135,992.1536	195,372.6442	280,255.6929	1,659,760.7433	9,389.019.6556

Present value interest factor of €1 per period at i%for n periods, PVIF (i,n).

Period	1%	2%	3%	4%	5%	6%	7%	8%
1	0.990099	0.980392	0.970874	0.961538	0.952381	0.943396	0.934579	0.925926
2	0.980296	0.961169	0.942596	0.924556	0.907029	0.889996	0.873439	0.857339
3	0.970590	0.942322	0.915142	0.888996	0.863838	0.839619	0.816298	0.793832
4	0.960980	0.923845	0.888487	0.854804	0.822702	0.792094	0.762895	0.735030
5	0.951466	0.905731	0.862609	0.821927	0.783526	0.747258	0.712986	0.680583
6	0.942045	0.887971	0.837484	0.790315	0.746215	0.704961	0.666342	0.630170
7	0.932718	0.870560	0.813092	0.759918	0.710681	0.665057	0.622750	0.583490
8	0.923483	0.853490	0.789409	0.730690	0.676839	0.627412	0.582009	0.540269
9	0.914340	0.836755	0.766417	0.702587	0.644609	0.591898	0.543934	0.500249
10	0.905287	0.820348	0.744094	0.675564	0.613913	0.558395	0.508349	0.463193
11	0.896324	0.804263	0.722421	0.649581	0.584679	0.526788	0.475093	0.428883
12	0.887449	0.788493	0701380	0.624597	0.556837	0.496969	0.444012	0.397114
13	0.878663	0.773033	0.680951	0.600574	0.530321	0.468839	0.414964	0.367698
14	0.869963	0.757875	0.661118	0.577475	0.505068	0.442301	0.387817	0.340461
15	0.861349	0.743015	0.641862	0.555265	0.481017	0.417265	0.362446	0.315242
16	0.852821	0.728446	0.623167	0.533908	0.458112	0.393646	0.338735	0.291890
17	0.844377	0.714163	0.605016	0.513373	0.436297	0.371364	0.316574	0.270269
18	0.836017	0.700159	0.587395	0.493628	0.415521	0.350344	0.295864	0.250249
19	0.827740	0.686431	0.570286	0.474642	0.395734	0.330513	0.276508	0.231712
20	0.819544	0.672971	0.553676	0.456387	0.376889	0.311805	0.258419	0.214548
25	0.779768	0.609531	0.477606	0.375117	0.295303	0.232999	0.184249	0.146018
30	0.741923	0.552071	0.411987	0.308319	0.231377	0.174110	0.131367	0.099377
35	0.705914	0.500028	0.355383	0.253415	0.181290	0.130105	0.093663	0.067635
40	0.671653	0.452890	0.306557	0.208289	0.142046	0.097222	0.066780	0.046031
50	0.608039	0.371528	0.228107	0.140713	0.087204	0.054288	0.033948	0.021321

40%	45%	50%	Period
1.0000	1.0000	1.0000	1
2.4000	2.4500	2.5000	2
4.3600	4.5525	4.7500	3
7.1040	7.6011	8.1250	4
10.9456	12.0216	13.1875	5
16.3238	18.4314	20.7813	6
23.8534	27.7255	32.1719	7
34.3947	41.2019	492578	8
49.1526	60.7428	74.8867	9
69.8137	89.0771	113.3301	10
98.7391	130.1618	170.9951	11
139.2348	189.7346	257.4927	12
195.9287	276.1151	387.2390	13
275.3002	401.3670	581.8585	14
386.4202	582.9821	873.7878	15
541.9883	846.3240	1,311.6817	16
759.7837	1,228.1699	1,968.5225	17
1,064.6971	1,781.8463	2,953.7838	18
1,491.5760	2,584.6771	4,431.6756	19
2,089.2064	3,748.7818	6,648.5135	20
11,247.1990	24,040.7161	50,500.3366	25
60,501.0809	154,106.6184	383,500.1185	30
325,400.2789	987.794.4630	2,912,217.2121	35
1,750,091.7415	6,331,511.8378	22,114,662.6419	40
50.622,288.0994	260,128,294.9257	1.275.242,998.4281	50

9%	10%	Period
0.917431	0.909091	1
0.841680	0.826446	2
0.772183	0.751315	3
0.708425	0.683013	4
0.649931	0.620921	5
0.596267	0.564474	6
0.547034	0.513158	7
0.501866	0.466507	8
0.460428	0.424098	9
0.422411	0.385543	10
0.387533	0.350494	11
0.355535	0.318631	12
0.326179	0.289664	13
0.299246	0.263331	14
0.274538	0.239392	15
0.251870	0.217629	16
0.231073	0.197845	17
0.211994	0.179859	18
0.194490	0.163508	19
0.178431	0.148644	20
0.115968	0.092296	25
0.075371	0.057309	30
0.048986	0.035584	35
0.031838	0.022095	40
0.013449	0.008519	50

Present value interest factor of €1 per period at i% for n periods, PVIF (i,n).

Period	11%	12%	13%	14%	15%	16%	17%	18%
1	0.900901	0.892857	0.884956	0.877193	0.869565	0.862069	0.854701	0.847458
2	0.811622	0.797194	0.783147	0.769468	0.756144	0.743163	0.730514	0.718184
3	0.731191	0.711780	0.693050	0.674972	0.657516	0.640658	0.624371	0.608631
4	0.658731	0.635518	0.613319	0.592080	0.571753	0.552291	0.533650	0.515789
5	0.593451	0.567427	0.542760	0.519369	0.497177	0.476113	0456111	0.437109
6	0.534641	0.506631	0.480319	0.455587	0.432328	0.410442	0.389839	0.370432
7	0.481658	0.452349	0.425061	0.399637	0.375937	0.353830	0.333195	0.313925
8	0.433926	0.403883	0.376160	0.350559	0.326902	0.305025	0.284782	0.266038
9	0.390925	0.360610	0.332885	0.307508	0.284262	0.262953	0.243404	0.225456
10	0.352184	0.321973	0.294588	0.269744	0.247185	0.226684	0.208037	0.191064
11	0.317283	0.287476	0.260698	0.236617	0.214943	0.195417	0.177810	0.161919
12	0.285841	0.256675	0.230706	0.207559	0.186907	0.168463	0.151974	0.137220
13	0.257514	0.229174	0.204165	0.182069	0.162528	0.145227	0.129892	0.116288
14	0.231995	0.204620	0.180677	0.159710	0.141329	0.125195	0.111019	0.098549
15	0.209004	0.182696	0.159891	0.140096	0.122894	0.107927	0.094888	0.083516
16	0.188292	0.163122	0.141496	0.122892	0.106865	0.093041	0.081101	0.070776
17	0.169633	0.145644	0.125218	0.107800	0.092926	0.080207	0.069317	0.059980
18	0.152822	0.130040	0.110812	0.094561	0.080805	0.069144	0.059245	0.050830
19	0.137678	0.116107	0.098064	0.082948	0.070265	0.059607	0.050637	0.043077
20	0.124034	0.103667	0.086782	0.072762	0.061100	0.051385	0.043280	0.036506
25	0.073608	0.058823	0.047102	0.037790	0.030378	0.024465	0.019740	0.015957
30	0.043683	0.033378	0.025565	0.019627	0.015103	0.011648	0.009004	0.006975
35	0.025924	0.018940	0.013876	0.010194	0.007509	0.005546	0.004107	0.003049
40	0.015384	0.010747	0.007531	0.005294	0.003733	0.002640	0.001873	0.001333
50	0.005418	0.003460	0.002219	0.001428	0.000923	0.000599	0.000390	0.000255

Present value interest factor of €1 per period at i% tor n periods, PVIF (i,n).

Period	21%	22%	23%	24%	25%	30%	35%	40%
1	0.826446	0.819672	0.813008	0.806452	0.800000	0.769231	0.740741	0.714286
2	0.683013	0.671862	0.660982	0.650364	0.640000	0.591716	0.548697	0.510204
3	0.564474	0.550707	0.537384	0.524637	0.512000	0.455166	0.406442	0.364431
4	0.466507	0.451399	0.436897	0.422974	0.409600	0.350128	0.301068	0.260308
5	0.385543	0.369999	0.355201	0.341108	0.327680	0.269329	0.223014	0.185934
6	0.318631	0.303278	0.288781	0.275087	0.262144	0.207176	0.165195	0.132810
7	0.263331	0.248589	0.234782	0.221844	0.209715	0.159366	0.122367	0.094865
8	0.217629	0.203761	0.190879	0.178907	0.167772	0.122589	0.090642	0.067760
9	0.179859	0.167017	0.155187	0.144280	0.134218	0.094300	0.067142	0.048400
10	0.148644	0.136899	0.126168	0.116354	0.107374	0.072538	0.049735	0.034572
11	0.122846	0.112213	0.102576	0.093834	0.085899	0.055799	0.036841	0.024694
12	0.101526	0.091978	0.083395	0.075673	0.068719	0.042922	0.027289	0.017639
13	0.083905	0.075391	0.067801	0.061026	0.054976	0.033017	0.020214	0.012599
14	0.069343	0.061796	0.055122	0.049215	0.043980	0.025398	0.014974	0.008999
15	0.057309	0.050653	0.044815	0.039689	0.035184	0.019537	0.011092	0.006428
16	0.047362	0.041519	0.036435	0.032008	0.028147	0.015028	0.008216	0.004591
17	0.039143	0.034032	0.029622	0.025813	0.022518	0.011560	0.006086	0.003280
18	0.032349	0.027895	0.024083	0.020817	0.018014	0.008892	0.004508	0.002343
19	0.026735	0.022865	0.019580	0.016788	0.014412	0.006840	0.003339	0.001673
20	0.022095	0.018741	0.015918	0.013538	0.011529	0.005262	0.002474	0.001195
25	0.008519	0.006934	0.005654	0.004618	0.003778	0.001417	0.000552	0.000222
30	0.003284	0.002566	0.002008	0.001575	0.001238	0.000382	0.000123	0.000041
35	0.001266	0.000949	0.000713	0.000537	0.000406	0.000103	0.000027	0.000008
40	0.000488	0.000351	0.000253	0.000183	0.000133	0.000028	0.000006	0.000001
50	0.000073	0.000048	0.000032	0.000021	0.000014	0.000002	0.000000	0.000000

19%	20%	Period
0.840336	0.833333	1
0.706165	0.694444	2
0.593416	0.578704	3
0.498669	0.482253	4
0.419049	0.401878	5
0.352142	0.334898	6
0.295918	0.279082	7
0.248671	0.232568	8
0.208967	0.193807	9
0.175602	0.161506	10
0.147565	0.134588	11
0.124004	0.112157	12
0.104205	0.093464	13
0.087567	0.077887	14
0.073586	0.064905	15
0.061837	0.054088	16
0.051964	0.045073	17
0.043667	0.037561	18
0.036695	0.031301	19
0.030836	0.026084	20
0.012922	0.010483	25
0.005415	0.004213	30
0.002269	0.001693	35
0.000951	0.000680	40
0.000167	0.000110	50

45%	50%	Period
0.689655	0.666667	1
0.475624	0.444444	2
0.328017	0.296296	3
0.226218	0.197531	4
0.156013	0.131687	5
0.107595	0.087791	6
0.074203	0.058528	7
0.051175	0.039018	8
0.035293	0.026012	9
0.024340	0.017342	10
0.016786	0.011561	11
0.011577	0.007707	12
0.007984	0.005138	13
0.005506	0.003425	14
0.003797	0.002284	15
0.002619	0.001522	16
0.001806	0.001015	17
0.001246	0.000677	18
0.000859	0.000451	19
0.000592	0.000301	20
0.000092	0.000040	25
0.000014	0.000005	30
0.000002	0.000001	35
0.000000	0.000000	40
0.000000	0.000000	50

Present value interest factor of €1 per period at i% tor n periods, PVIF (i,n).

Period	21%	22%	23%	24%	25%	30%	35%	40%
1	0.826446	0.819672	0.813008	0.806452	0.800000	0.769231	0.740741	0.714286
2	0.683013	0.671862	0.660982	0.650364	0.640000	0.591716	0.548697	0.510204
3	0.564474	0.550707	0.537384	0.524487	0.512000	0.455166	0.406442	0.364431
4	0.466507	0.451399	0.436897	0.422974	0.409600	0.350128	0.301068	0.260308
5	0.385543	0.369999	0.355201	0.341108	0.327680	0.269329	0.223014	0.185934
6	0.318631	0.303278	0.288781	0.275087	0.262144	0.207176	0.165195	0.132810
7	0.263331	0.248589	0.234782	0.221844	0.209715	0.159366	0.122367	0.094865
8	0.217629	0.203761	0.190879	0.178907	0.167772	0.122589	0.090642	0.067760
9	0.179859	0.167017	0.155187	0.144280	0.134218	0.094300	0.067142	0.048400
10	0.148644	0.136899	0.126168	0.116354	0.107374	0.072538	0.049735	0.034572
11	0.122846	0.112213	0.102576	0.093834	0.085899	0.055799	0.036841	0.024694
12	0.101526	0.091978	0.083395	0.075673	0.068719	0.042922	0.027289	0.017639
13	0.083905	0.075391	0.067801	0.061026	0.054976	0.033017	0.020214	0.012599
14	0.069343	0.061796	0.055122	0.049215	0.043980	0.025398	0.014974	0.008999
15	0.057309	0.050653	0.044815	0.039689	0.035184	0.019537	0.011092	0.006428
16	0.047362	0.041519	0.036435	0.032008	0.028147	0.015028	0.008216	0.004591
17	0.039143	0.034032	0.029622	0.025813	0.022518	0.011560	0.006086	0.003280
18	0.032349	0.027895	0.024083	0.020817	0.018014	0.008892	0.004508	0.002343
19	0.026735	0.022865	0.019580	0.016788	0.014412	0.006840	0.003339	0.001673
20	0.022095	0.018741	0.015918	0.013538	0.011529	0.005262	0.002474	0.001195
25	0.008519	0.006934	0.005654	0.004618	0.003778	0.001417	0.000552	0.000222
30	0.003284	0.002566	0.002008	0.001575	0.001238	0.000382	0.000123	0.000041
35	0.001266	0.000949	0.000713	0.000537	0.000406	0.000103	0.000027	0.000008
40	0.000488	0.000351	0.000253	0.000183	0.000133	0.000028	0.000006	0.000001
50	0.000073	0.000048	0.000032	0.000021	0.000014	0.000002	0.000000	0.000000

Present value interest factor of an (ordinary) annuity of €1 per period at i% forn periods, PVIFA (i.n).

Period	1%	2%	3%	4%	5%	6%	7%	8%
1	0.990099	0.980392	0.970874	0.961538	0.952381	0.943396	0.934579	0.925926
2	1.970395	1.941561	1.913470	1.886095	1.859410	1.833393	1.808018	1.783265
3	2.940985	2.883883	2.828611	2.775091	2.723248	2.673012	2.624316	2.577097
4	3.901966	3.807729	3.717098	3.629895	3.545951	3.465106	3.387211	3.312127
5	4.853431	4.713460	4.579707	4.451822	4.329477	4.212364	4.100197	3.992710
6	5.795476	5.601431	5.417191	5.242137	5.075692	4.917324	4.766540	4.622880
7	6.728195	6.471991	6.230283	6.002055	5.786373	5.582381	5.389289	5.206370
8	7.651678	7.325481	7.019692	6.732745	6.463213	6.209794	5.971299	5.746639
9	8.566018	8.162237	7.786109	7.435332	7.107822	6.801692	6.515232	6.246888
10	9.471305	8.982585	8.530203	8.110896	7.721735	7.360087	7.023582	6.710081
11	10.367628	9.786848	9.252624	8.760477	8.306414	7.886875	7.498674	7.138964
12	11.255077	10.575341	9.954004	9.385074	8.863252	8.383844	7.942686	7.536078
13	12.133740	11.348374	10.634955	9.985648	9.393573	8.852683	8.357651	7.903776
14	13.003703	12.106249	11.296073	10.563123	9.898641	9.294984	8.745468	8.244237
15	13.865053	12.849264	11.937935	11.118387	10.379658	9.712249	9.107914	8.559479
16	14.717874	13.577709	12.561102	11.652296	10.837770	10.105895	9.446649	8.851369
17	15.562251	14.291872	13.166118	12.165669	11.274066	10.477260	9.763223	9.121638
18	16.398269	14.992031	13.753513	12.659297	11.689587	10.827603	10.059087	9.371887
19	17.226008	15.678462	14.323799	13.133939	12.085321	11.158116	10.335595	9.603599
20	18.045553	16.351433	14.877475	13.590326	12.462210	11.469921	10.594014	9.818147
25	22.023156	19.523456	17.413148	15.622080	14.093945	12.783356	11.653583	10.674776
30	25.807708	22.396456	19.600441	17.292033	15.372451	13.764831	12.409041	11.257783
35	29.408580	24.998619	21.487220	18.664613	16.374194	14.498246	12.947672	11.654568
40	32.834686	27.355479	23.114772	19.792774	17.159086	15.046297	13.331709	11.924613
50	39.196118	31.423606	25.729764	21.482185	18.255925	15.761861	13.800746	12.233485

45%	50%	Period
0.689655	0.666667	1
0.475624	0.444444	2
0.328017	0.296296	3
0.226218	0.197531	4
0.156013	0.131687	5
0.107595	0.087791	6
0.074203	0.058528	7
0.051175	0.039018	8
0.035293	0.026012	9
0.024340	0.017342	10
0.016786	0.011561	11
0.011577	0.007707	12
0.007984	0.005138	13
0.005506	0.003425	14
0.003797	0.002284	15
0.002619	0.001522	16
0.001806	0.001015	17
0.001246	0.000677	18
0.000859	0.000451	19
0.000592	0.000301	20
0.000092	0.000040	25
0.000014	0.000005	30
0.000002	0.000001	35
0.000000	0.000000	40
0.000000	0.000000	50

9%	10%	Period
0.917431	0.909091	1
1.759111	1.735537	2
2.531295	2.486852	3
3.239720	3.169865	4
3.889651	3.790787	5
4.485919	4.355261	6
5.032953	4.868419	7
5.534819	5.334926	8
5.995247	5.759024	9
6.417658	6.144567	10
6.805191	6.495061	11
7.160725	6.813692	12
7.486904	7.103356	13
7.786150	7.366687	14
8.060688	7.606080	15
8.312558	7.823709	16
8.543631	8.021553	17
8.755625	8.201412	18
8.950115	8.364920	19
9.128546	8.513564	20
9.822580	9.077040	25
10.273654	9.426914	30
10.566821	9.644159	35
10.757360	9.779051	40
10.961683	9.914814	50

Present value interest factor of an (ordinary) annuity of €1 per period at i% for n periods, PVIFA (i,n).

Period	11%	12%	13%	14%	15%	16%	17%	18%
1	0.900901	0.892857	0.884956	0.877193	0.869565	0.862069	0.854701	0.847458
2	1.712523	1.690051	1.668102	1.646661	1.625709	1.605232	1.585214	1.565642
3	2.443715	2.401831	2.361153	2.321632	2.283225	2.245890	2.209585	2.174273
4	3.102446	3.037349	2.974471	2.913712	2.854978	2.798181	2.743235	2.690062
5	3.695897	3.604776	3.517231	3.433081	3.352155	3.274294	3.199346	3.127171
6	4.230538	4.111407	3.997550	3.888668	3.784483	3.684736	3.589185	3.497603
7	4.712196	4.563757	4.422610	4.288305	4.160420	4.038565	3.922380	3.811528
8	5.146123	4.967640	4.798770	4.638864	4.487322	4.343591	4.207163	4.077566
9	5.537048	5.328250	5.131655	4.946372	4.771584	4.606544	4.450566	4.303022
10	5.889232	5.650223	5.426243	5.216116	5.018769	4.833227	4.658604	4.494086
11	6.206515	5.937699	5.686941	5.452733	5.233712	5.028644	4.836413	4.656005
12	6.492356	6.194374	5.917647	5.660292	5.420619	5.197107	4.988387	4.793225
13	6.749870	6.423548	6.121812	5.842362	5.583147	5.342334	5.118280	4.909513
14	6.981865	6.628168	6.302488	6.002072	5.724476	5.467529	5.229299	5.008062
15	7.190870	6.810864	6.462379	6.142168	5.847370	5.575456	5.324187	5.091578
16	7.379162	6.973986	6.603875	6.265060	5.954235	5.668497	5.405288	5.162354
17	7.548794	7.119630	6.729093	6.372859	6.047161	5.748704	5.474605	5.222334
18	7.701617	7.249670	6.839905	6.467420	6.127966	5.817848	5.533851	5.273164
19	7.839294	7.365777	6.937969	6.550369	6.198231	5.877455	5.584488	5.316241
20	7.963328	7.469444	7.024752	6.623131	6.259331	5.928841	5.627767	5.352746
25	8.421745	7.843139	7.329985	6.872927	6.464149	6.097092	5.766234	5.466906
30	8.693793	8.055184	7.495653	7.002664	6.565980	6.177198	5.829390	5.516806
35	8.855240	8.175504	7.585572	7.070045	6.616607	6.215338	5.858196	5.538618
40	8.951051	8.243777	7.634376	7.105041	6.641778	6.233497	5.871335	5.548152
50	9.041653	8.304498	7.675242	7.132656	6.660515	6.246259	5.880061	5.554141

Present value interest factor of an (ordinary) annuity of €1 per period at i% for n periods, PVIFA (i,n).

Period	21%	22%	23%	24%	25%	30%	35%	40%
1	0.826446	0.819672	0.813008	0.806452	0.800000	0.769231	0.740741	0.714286
2	1.509460	1.491535	1.473990	1.456816	1.440000	1.360947	1.289438	1.224490
3	2.073934	2.042241	2.011374	1.981303	1.952000	1.816113	1.695880	1.588921
4	2.540441	2.493641	2.448272	2.404277	2.361600	2.166241	1.996948	1.849229
5	2.925984	2.863640	2.803473	2.745384	2.689280	2.435570	2.219961	2.035164
6	3.244615	3.166918	3.092254	3.020471	2.951424	2.642746	2.385157	2.167974
7	3.507946	3.415506	3.327036	3.242316	3.161139	2.802112	2.507523	2.262839
8	3.725576	3.619268	3.517916	3.421222	3.328911	2.924702	2.598165	2.330599
9	3.905434	3.786285	3.673102	3.565502	3.463129	3.019001	2.665308	2.378999
10	4.054078	3.923184	3.799270	3.681856	3.570503	3.091539	2.715043	2.413571
11	4.176924	4.035397	3.901846	3.775691	3.656403	3.147338	2.751884	2.438265
12	4.278450	4.127375	3.985240	3.851363	3.725122	3.190260	2.779173	2.455904
13	4.362355	4.202766	4.053041	3.912390	3.780098	3.223277	2.799387	2.468503
14	4.431698	4.264562	4.108163	3.961605	3.824078	3.248675	2.814361	2.477502
15	4.489007	4.315215	4.152978	4.001294	3.859263	3.268211	2.825453	2.483930
16	4.536369	4.356734	4.189413	4.033302	3.887410	3.283239	2.833669	2.488521
17	4.575512	4.390765	4.219035	4.059114	3.909928	3.294800	2.839755	2.491801
18	4.607861	4.418660	4.243118	4.079931	3.927942	3.303692	2.844263	2.494144
19	4.634596	4.441525	4.262698	4.096718	3.942354	3.310532	2.847602	2.495817
20	4.656691	4.460266	4.278616	4.110257	3.953883	3.315794	2.850076	2.497012
25	4.721340	4.513935	4.323243	4.147425	3.984888	3.328609	2.855567	2.499444
30	4.746265	4.533792	4.339094	4.160103	3.995048	3.332061	2.856791	2.499897
35	4.755875	4.541140	4.344724	4.164428	3.998377	3.332991	2.857064	2.499981
40	4.759580	4.543858	4.346724	4.165903	3.999468	3.333241	2.857125	2.499996
50	4.761559	4.545236	4.347687	4.166578	3.999943	3.333327	2.857142	2.500000

19%	20%	Period
0.840336	0.833333	1
1.546501	1.527778	2
2.139917	2.106481	3
2.638586	2.588735	4
3.057635	2.990612	5
3.409777	3.325510	6
3.705695	3.604592	7
3.954366	3.837160	8
4.163332	4.030967	9
4.338935	4.192472	10
4.486500	4.327060	11
4.610504	4.439217	12
4.714709	4.532681	13
4.802277	4.610567	14
4.875863	4.675473	15
4.937700	4.729561	16
4.989664	4.774634	17
5.033331	4.812195	18
5.070026	4.843496	19
5.100862	4.869580	20
5.195148	4.947587	25
5.234658	4.978936	30
5.251215	4.991535	35
5.258153	4.996598	40
5.262279	4.999451	50

45%	50%	Period
0.689655	0.666667	1
1.165279	1.111111	2
1.493296	1.407407	3
1.719515	1.604938	4
1.875527	1.736626	5
1.983122	1.824417	6
2.057326	1.882945	7
2.108500	1.921963	8
2.143793	1.947975	9
2.168133	1.965317	10
2.184920	1.976878	11
2.196496	1.984585	12
2.204480	1.989724	13
2.209986	1.993149	14
2.213784	1.995433	15
2.216403	1.996955	16
2.218209	1.997970	17
2.219454	1.998647	18
2.220313	1.999098	19
2.220906	1.999399	20
2.222017	1.999921	25
2.222190	1.999990	30
2.222217	1.999999	35
2.222221	2.000000	40
2.222222	2.000000	50

About the author

Michael N. Chibili is a Hospitality Management Accounting lecturer in the Institute of International Hospitality Management at Stenden University of Applied Sciences. He holds a BSc and an MSc in Economics from the University of Yaoundé and also an MA in International Service Management from CHN-London Metropolitan University.

Index

ABC process *159*
absolute difference *99*
acceptance-or-rejection decisions *296*
account format *42*
accounting *14*
accounting controls *235*
accounting conventions *66*
accounting information *14*
accounting principles *16*
accounting rate of return *300*
accounting standard *42*
accounting statements *32*
accounts payable *37*
accounts payable ageing schedule *147*
accounts receivable *68*
accounts receivable ageing schedule *144*
accounts receivable management *144*
accounts receivable turnover *115*
accruals convention *66*
accrued expenses *37*
accumulated other comprehensive income (loss) *42*
acid test ratio *114*
activity ratios *122*
activity-based budgeting approach *279*
activity-based costing *157*
additional paid-in capital *41*
administrative and general expenses *58*
administrative controls *235*
advance deposits *38*
after-tax cash flows *322*
airport hotels *23*
allocation base *161*
Allowance for Bad Debts *68*
Allowance for Doubtful Accounts *68*
annuity *307*
approaches to pricing *185*
asset *32*
asset turnover *124*
asset use efficiency *129*
authority *233*
average beverage inventory *123*
average collection period *115*

average daily rate (ADR) *125*
average food inventory *122*
average food service cheque *127*
average occupancy per room *124*
average rate of return *301*
average rate ratio *214*
average total asset *124*
average total fixed assets *123*
average working capital *115*

BAD CQ *288*
BAD PQ *284*
bank reconciliation *249*
base selling price *198, 206*
base-year analysis *101*
bed-and-breakfast inns *24*
benchmark *127*
beverage cost percentage *126*
beverage inventory turnover ratio *123*
blacklisting might *147*
bottom up approach *187*
boutique hotels *24*
breakeven analysis *221*
breakeven point *221*
budget *274*
budget committee *281*
business entity principle *16*

calculating single and double rates *190*
capital budgets *280*
capital investment *296*
capital stock *41*
capital-rationing decisions *296*
cash *32, 76*
cash budgets *280*
cash cows *211*
cash cycle *142*
cash equivalents *76*
cash flow statement *77*
cash flows *76*
cash inflows *76*
cash management *143*
cash on cash return *122*
cash outflows *76*
cash surrender value of life insurance *35*
casino hotels *23*
category A items *204*
category B items *204*

causal forecasting methods *263*
commitments and contingencies *39*
common size analysis *102*
comparative analysis *99*
competitive intangibles *35*
competitive method *186*
complimentary occupancy percentage *124*
compound interest *302*
compounding *303*
conference hotels *23*
conservatism principle *18*
consistency principle *17*
contribution margin *200, 208, 211, 220*
contribution margin pricing method *200*
contribution margin ratio *221*
controllable and non-controllable costs *156*
corporations *41*
cost allocation *160*
cost centre *160*
cost of capital *314*
cost of goods sold *57*
cost principle *16*
cost-volume-profit analysis *219*
costs *154*
current assets *32*
current liabilities *36*
current liabilities management *146*
current maturities of long-term debt *38*
current ratio *114*
CVP analysis *220*
cyclical pattern *257*

debt service coverage ratio *118*
debt to equity ratio *117*
declining balance method of depreciation *70*
deferred charges *35*
deferred income taxes *33*
deferred income taxes (current) *38*
deferred income taxes (non-current) *35, 39*
delivery charges *71*
Delphi method *259*
department budgets *280*

departmental income 58
depreciation 34, 69, 324
destination hotel 19
detective controls 235
differential room pricing 190
direct cost 155
direct method 80, 162
direct method of cost allocation 164
discount grid 193
discount rate 304, 314
discounted cash flow 314
discounting 193, 304
discounts 71, 193
discretionary cost 156
dogs 211
due to/from owner, management company, or related party 33, 37
DuPont analysis 129

earnings before fixed charges (EBFC) 58
earnings before interests and taxes 59
earnings per share 120
econometric models 263
economic order quantity (EOQ) 146
effective interest rate 148
equation of the straight line 174
equity multiplier 130
equivalent occupancy 193
expense variance 287
expenses 52
expert judgment 259
exponential smoothing 262
extended-stay hotels 23
external users 15

factor tables 305
financial accounting 15
financial discounts 71
financial leverage 130
financial statement 52
financial statement analysis 94
financial statements 94
financing activities 79
fixed assets 34
fixed asset turnover 123
fixed charge coverage ratio 118
fixed charges 59
fixed cost 155
fixed or static budgeting approach 276
flexible budgeting approach 276
food cost percentage 126
food inventory turnover ratio 122

food pricing approaches 195
food service seat turnover 125
forecasting 255
forecasts 255
format 54
formats of balance sheets 42
full disclosure principle 17
full-service properties 22
fundamental accounting equation 32
future value factors 306
future values 305

gains 52
generally accepted accounting principles (GAAP) 16
goals 14
going concern principle 17
goodwill 35
gross operating profit 58
gross operating profit per available room (GOPPAR) 121
gross return on assets 119

highest price method 196
high price method 185
high/low two-point method 170
historical data patterns 257
horizontal analysis 99
hospitality industry 19
Hubbart formula 187

income before fixed charges (IBFC) 58
income before fixed charges margin 121
income before fixed charges per available room 121
income statement 52
income taxes payable 38
incremental budgeting approach 277
incremental expense 323
incremental revenue 323
index approach 101
indirect cost 155
indirect method 81
information 14
ingredients mark-up pricing method 197
intangible assets 35
internal control 234
internal control proposals 241
internal rate of return 318
internal users 15
interpolation 318
intuitive method 185
intuitive price methode 196
inventory 33, 57, 66

inventory holding period 123
inventory management 145
investing activities 79
investment centre 161
investments 34

joint cost 155

kaizen budgeting approach 277

labour cost percentage 126
labour-intensive 204
legal intangibles 35
liability 36
limited liability companies 40
limited-service hotels 22
linear method of depreciation 69
liquidity ratio 114
long term debt to total capitalization ratio 117
long term liabilities 38
long-range planning 274
loss 52, 58
loss leader method 196

MABA 161
management accounting 15
management accounting process 18
mark-up method 186
mark-up multiple 197
mark-up with accompaniment costs 199
market research 259
market segmentation 212-213
marketable securities 32
master budgets 281
matching convention 66
matching principle 18
materiality principle 18
menu engineering 208
menu engineering worksheet 209
menu mix 211
menu mix percentage 212
mix of sales 127
monetary unit principle 17
mortgage notes, other notes, and similar liabilities 38
multiple occupancy percentage 125
multiplier 200, 206

naïve method 260
nature of the hospitality industry 19
net income 52
net income or loss 59
net loss 59

net operating income margin ratio *122*
net operating income per available room *121*
net present value *315*
net profit or loss *59*
net realizable value *67*
net return on assets *119*
non cash activities *79*
non-current receivables *34*
non-labour-intensive *204*
notes payable *37*
number of times interest earned ratio *117*

objective pricing methods *196*
objectives *14*
objectivity principle *17*
obligations under capital leases *38*
operating activities *79*
operating budget *273*
operating cash flow ratio *114*
operating cash flows to total liabilities ratio *118*
operating cycle *142, 255*
operating efficiency *129*
operating efficiency ratio *120*
operating equipment *33, 35*
operating income *59*
operating ratios *125*
operational planning *274*
operations budgets *280*
opportunity cost *156, 315*
organizational chart *233*
other departmental expenses *58*
owners' equity *39*

paid occupancy percentage *124*
partnerships *40*
payback method *298*
payroll and related expenses *57*
percentage approach *101*
perfect elasticity *185*
perfect inelasticity *184*
performance review *127*
periodic inventory system *67*
perpetual inventory system *67*
planning *274*
plough horses *211*
post-income tax analysis *228*
potential average double rate *214*
potential average rate *214*
potential average single rate *214*
pre-income tax analysis *228*
prepaid expenses *33*
present value *304*
present value factors *309*

preventive controls *235*
price cutting method *185*
price discrimination *212*
price elasticity *184*
price elasticity of demand *184*
price-to-earnings valuation ratio *120*
pricing *184*
pricing rooms *186*
prime-ingredient mark-up method *198*
product life-cycle analogy *259*
profit *77*
profit and loss statement *52*
profit centre *161*
profit factor *212*
profit margin *119*
profitability ratios *119*
project planning *274*
property and operations maintenance expenses *58*
property, plant and equipment – PP & E *34*
puzzles *211*

qualitative forecasting methods *259*
quantitative forecasting methods *259*

rack rate *193*
random variations *257*
rate spread *214*
ratio *112*
ratio analysis *112*
ratio pricing method *201*
realization convention *66*
realization principle *18*
reasonable price method *196*
receivables *33*
recognition convention *66*
regression analysis *174, 263*
relative difference *99*
relative elasticity *185*
relative inelasticity *185*
relative room size approach *188*
relevant and non-relevant costs *156*
report format *42*
resort hotels *23*
responsibility *233*
responsibility accounting *160*
restricted cash *32, 36*
retained earnings *41*
return on owners' equity *120*
returns of goods *70*
revenue management *212*
revenue variance *285*

revenues *52, 55*
room rate achievement factor *214*
room rate discounting *193*
rule of a thousand approach *186*
rule of thumb method *185*
RV parks and campgrounds *24*

SABA *161*
safety margin *224*
sales and marketing expenses *58*
sales revenue centre *160*
sales revenue per available customer (REVPAC) *126*
sales revenue per available room (REVPAR) *125*
salvage value *69*
scatter diagram *173*
seasonal pattern *257*
segregation of duties *238*
semi-fixed and semi-variable costs *155*
separating mixed-costs *169*
short term investments *32*
simple interest *302*
simple linear regression model *174*
simple mark-up by a multiplier *197*
simple moving averages *260*
simple prime costs method *202*
simulation modelling *263*
single service analysis *222*
smoothing constant *262*
sole proprietorships *39*
solvency ratio *116*
solvency ratios *116*
specific prime costs method *204*
standard cost *154*
standard recipes *196*
standards *112*
stars *209*
step method *162*
step method of cost allocation *166*
strategic planning *274*
subjective pricing methods *196*
sunk cost *156*

time period principle *17*
time series forecasting methods *260*
time value of money *297*
total REVPAR *126*
trade discounts *71*
treasury stock *41*
trend pattern *257*
trial and error method *185*

trial and error technique *318*
turnover *55*

undistributed operating expenses *58*
Uniform System of Accounts for the Lodging Industry (USALI) *43, 54*
unit elasticity *185*
utility expenses *58*

variable budgeting approach *276*
variable cost *155*
variance *282*
variance analysis *282*
vertical analysis *102*

weighted moving averages *261*
working capital *142*
working capital cycle *142*
working capital management *76*

working capital turnover ratio *115*

yield *214*
yield management *212*
yield statistic *214*

zero-base budgeting approach *278*